HANK GREENBERG

The Story of My Life

◆

Edited and with an Introduction by Ira Berkow

◆

IVAN R. DEE
Chicago

www.ivanrdee.com

Library of Congress Control Number: 2009934552

ISBN: 978-1-56663-837-1 (pbk : alk. paper)

CONTENTS

PERMISSIONS
ACKNOWLEDGMENTS

Grateful acknowledgment is made to the following for permission to reprint previously published material:

Associated Press: Excerpt from an article by Whitney Martin dated June 22, 1945. Reprinted with permission of the Associated Press.

Contemporary Books, Inc.: "Speaking of Greenberg" from *Collected Verse* by Edgar A. Guest. Copyright 1934 by Contemporary Books, Inc. Reprinted by permission of Contemporary Books, Inc.

The *Detroit News*: Excerpts from the *Detroit News*: article by Joe Falls, Copyright 1933; article by Harry Salsinger, Copyright 1934; article by Bud Shaver, Copyright 1934; letter by Lorna Dodd, Copyright © 1986; two articles by Bud Shaver from the *Detroit Times* dated September 13, 1934, and March 15, 1935. Reprinted with permission of the *Detroit News*, a Gannett Newspaper.

Hearst Corporation: Excerpt from an article by Bill Slocum from the *New York American*, September 24, 1940. Copyright Hearst Corporation. Reprinted by permission of Hearst Corporation.

International Herald Tribune Corporation: Excerpt from article by Arthur E. Patterson from the *New York Herald Tribune*, February 28, 1941. Reprinted by permission of I.H.T. Corp.

New York News, Inc.: Excerpts from article by Jack Smith from the *New York Daily News*, 1938, and additional article dated February 19, 1946. Copyright 1938, 1946 by New York News, Inc. Reprinted with permission.

The New York Times Company: Excerpt from "Trosky Is Future Gehrig of Loop." Copyright 1935 by The New York Times Company. Reprinted by permission. All Rights Reserved.

The Sporting News: Excerpts from article by Fred Lieb, 1935, and Bob Considine, 1947. Reprinted by permission of *The Sporting News*.

ACKNOWLEDGMENTS

Because Hank Greenberg died before he could finish this book, there were gaps in the manuscript that I attempted to fill.

Many people contributed to the completion of this book but none more than Mary Jo Greenberg, Hank's wife, and Hank's three children, Glenn Greenberg, Stephen Greenberg, and Alva Greenberg Gahagan.

Also providing indispensable assistance were Hank's sister and brothers, Lillian Golson and Ben and Joe Greenberg.

Other family members who were generous with their time and information were Marilyn Greenberg, Myrna Greenberg, and Donald Golson.

I also want to offer my appreciation to Caral Gimbel Lebworth for her contribution.

I want to thank Jon Segal and Ruth Fecych of Times Books for their care with this book—and with its editor.

I offer gratitude to Larry Klein for his characteristic diligence in researching newspaper and library files, and for his suggestions in regard to the manuscript.

I am appreciative of Arthur Pincus and Murray Olderman for their reading of the manuscript, and for their editorial insights into it.

Numerous others were helpful in a variety of ways, and I wish to thank:

Harold Allen, Joe Altobelli, Luke Appling, Elden Auker, Dick Bartell, Jim Benagh, Bob Berman, Stu Black, Phil Cavarretta, Ben Chapman, Herman "Flea" Clifton, Andy Cohen, Sid Cohen, Rocky Colavito, Jimmy Connors, Bill Dickey, Joe DiMaggio, Nate Dolin, Leo Durocher, Harry Eisenstat, Joe Falls, Bob Feller, Rick Ferrell, Anne Taylor Fleming, Karl Fleming, Charlie Gehringer, Harold Goldstein, Izzy Goldstein, Lefty Gomez, Mel Harder, Ray Hayworth, Billy Herman, Elon "Chief" Hogsett, Steve Jacobson, Billy Jurges, Dr. Rex Kennamer, Ralph Kiner, Sandy Koufax, Hal Lebovitz, Bob Lemon, Ed Levy, Al Lopez.

And Bill Madlock, Walter Matthau, Barney McCoskey, Don McNeely, Dutch Meyer, Morris Moorawnick, Dr. Norman Nemoy, Hal Newhouser, Richard M. Nixon, Marv Owen, Shirley Povich, Bobby Riggs, Billy Rogell, Charlie Rose, Al Rosen, Bill Rosen, Bus Saidt, Mrs. Heinie Schuble, Truett "Rip" Sewell, Eric Show, Sam Smith, George "Tuck" Stainback, Bob Steinberg, Billy Sullivan, George "Birdie" Tebbetts, Mary Frances Veeck, Charlie Wagner, and Ted Williams.

I also wish to thank Bill Dean, Bill Guilfoile, Tom Heitz, and Pat Kelly of the Baseball Hall of Fame; Don Ewald of the Detroit Tigers; Bob Rosen and Seymour Siwoff of the Elias Sports Bureau; and Steve Gietschier of *The Sporting News*.

Numerous books were also of significant help, including: 1947—*When All Hell Broke Loose in Baseball*, by Red Barber (Doubleday, 1982); *On Equal Terms*, by Lucy S. Dawidowicz (Holt Rinehart & Winston, 1982); *Baseball When the Grass Was Real*, by Donald Honig (Coward, McCann & Geoghegan, 1975); *The World of Our Fathers*, by Irving Howe (Harcourt Brace Jovanovich, 1975); *The Jewish Baseball Hall of Fame*, by Erwin Lynn (Shapolsky Books, 1986); *The Baseball Encyclopedia* 7th ed., edited by Joseph L. Reichler (Macmillan, 1988); *The Glory of Their Times*, by Lawrence Ritter (Morrow, 1984); *Baseball's Great Experiment*, by Jules Tygiel (Oxford, 1983); and *Baseball Goes to War*, by William B. Mead (Farragut, 1985).

INTRODUCTION

To a small boy, the name alone—Hank Greenberg—was magical, larger than life, like that of some storybook character. And yet he was a historical figure who seemed rather out of date when I was growing up in Chicago in the late 1940s; his was a name more suited to a past time, a past America. The paradox, though, was that Greenberg's having been a baseball player gave him a contemporary status. After all, there is nothing more current than the records, anecdotes, and memories of yesterday's baseball heroes. Unless it is those of today's. It is a strange thing about baseball: The stories are handed down the way that Homer's stories of legendary figures in battles with a one-eyed monster or a Trojan horse once were passed down.

I remember my Uncle Julius talking about Hank Greenberg, not just as a baseball player, not just as a prominent or highly visible Jew, but as a symbol, a beacon. And more: Greenberg, one of the all-time great home-run hitters, carried with him the burden of the historical Jews, facing great odds against injustice and hatred, and withstanding it all not only to survive, but to prevail.

My Uncle Julius told me how, in 1938, Greenberg had hit 58 home runs with about a week to go in the season. He needed only two more to tie and three to break Babe Ruth's record for most home runs in a single season—even then, probably the most revered record in sports. And "they" didn't pitch to him, because Greenberg was a Jew, said Uncle Julius, fostering the legend.

These were the stories I heard when I began following baseball in 1948.

It happened that Greenberg retired as a baseball player in 1947, the year before my cultural awakening, so I had no personal sense of him as a ballplayer. I never even collected a baseball card with his picture on it.

My Uncle Julius was born in Russia around the turn of the century, came to America with my grandparents as a boy, had lived in Chicago, and became a baseball fan. Not a rabid fan—I doubt he ever went to a ball game—but he knew the names and followed, somewhat, the pennant races. And, beyond that, he had an eye—an experienced eye, to be sure—for anti-Semitism in sports, as he had found anti-Semitism on the streets of Chicago, particularly in fights with "the goyim" on the other side of Roosevelt Road, on the West Side of Chicago.

He hated the Cubs, even though I was growing up a Cub fan, as were most of my friends. Uncle Julius said the Cubs were anti-Semites. There were no Jews on the Cubs, were there? Frankly, I didn't know. (Later I'd find out that there were very few Jews in baseball, period. The Cubs had, for the most part, no more or fewer Jews than any other teams.) He also considered them Jew-baiters, and may have got that right. In the 1935 World Series, the Cubs hurled such vicious racial remarks at Greenberg that the plate umpire had to stop the action, go to the Cub dugout, and warn some players that he'd throw them out of the game if they didn't stop. I also learned later that bench jockeying, the most personal kind of bench jockeying, was a standard part of baseball, and epithets were hurled whenever one side thought it might find a weakness in the possibly thin skin of an opposing player.

The White Sox, in Chicago, had had a few obscure Jewish players when my Uncle Julius had become a fan. Moe Berg was one. Berg was an extraordinary man who had earned a bachelor's degree from Princeton and a law degree from Columbia and was a spy during World War II for the American forces. It was said that Berg knew ten languages but couldn't hit in any of them. In later years, when I visited the Baseball Hall of Fame in Cooperstown, New York, I saw a photograph of a Major League All-Star team that had made a trip to Japan in the 1930s. Each player had autographed the picture; Berg had written his name in Japanese.

When it came to having a favorite team in the big leagues, Uncle Julius was not swayed by hometown loyalties. He was a Detroit Tiger fan. The Tigers, of course, had been Hank Greenberg's team.

But big-league baseball, generally, and his views of Jews who played the game were, for Uncle Julius, and for many like him, a test of acculturation. It resembled how the Italians rooted for "Poosh-'em Up" Tony Lazzeri and Joe DiMaggio of the New York Yankees, or the Polish rooted for Al Simmons of the Philadelphia A's, and, some years later, the way the blacks cheered in the stands and in their hearts for Jackie Robinson of the Brooklyn Dodgers.

To be able to talk knowledgeably about the pennant race, about the nuances of managerial strategy, the worth of various players was, and still is, a common thread—maybe *the* common thread—running through the boyhood and manhood of many, if not most, Americans.

Baseball has been *the* American game. Jacques Barzun, the writer and educator who was born in France but came to live in America, once wrote something that has been quoted so often it's nearly a cliché, yet it remains pertinent. "To know the heart and mind of America," Barzun wrote, "one must learn baseball."

Uncle Julius did. He learned about how the individual must perform sometimes nearly in isolation yet remain part of the bigger picture of teamwork, of the opportunity to rise democratically on sheer ability alone, and he learned it was as tough to succeed in that game as it was to succeed in the country at large, on the frontiers or in the great urban sprawls.

It was a great country and a miserable country at the same time. There was hope and disappointment. The streets weren't paved with gold, as the poor Europeans who dreamed of coming to America believed, and the ghettos, they'd soon find out, were overcrowded, dank, ridden with disease, and often filled with despair. But still, with one's sweat and brains and imagination, a little gold—and sometimes a lot of gold—could be earned.

Baseball reflected all this. You struck out, but there was always another time at bat. You made an error in the field, but on the next ball you might make a dazzling catch to save the game.

In America, anything was possible. In baseball, anything was possible. Baseball was a wholly American game. Baseball *was* America.

Uncle Julius himself never rose very far up the economic scale in America. Nonetheless, like Jews as well as non-Jews, others in unfortunate situations as well as those who managed to grab their piece of the American pie, Uncle Julius was elevated by heroes.

In America in the 1930s, only a few Jews enjoyed high national visibility: entertainers such as Al Jolson, the Marx Brothers, and Edward G. Robinson; Bernard Baruch, the great financier; Supreme Court Justices Benjamin Cardozo, Louis Brandeis, and Felix Frankfurter; Secretary of the Treasury Henry Morgenthau, Jr. And there were some who headed Hollywood studios and there were a handful of other highly placed businesspeople.

In the 1930s, there was more need for heroes, for dreams and hopes, than perhaps at any other time in this nation's history. It was the Great Depression, when even brain surgeons, it was said, had to sell apples on street corners to earn a living. And sports were a visible and prominent forum for heroes, much as it is today. Athletes do not perform behind closed doors, but succeed or fail, sweating and straining, in front of huge crowds.

Some Jews, like the Irish before them, and like some blacks and Hispanics later, used sports to rise from the ghetto. In the first third of this century, the most prominent sports were boxing and baseball. There was a scattering of Jews in other sports, such as football and tennis, but boxing was the sport of the ghetto since physical space was so limited. Baseball was for wide-open territory. Baseball was for grassy fields, not cement squares or small gymnasiums in narrow buildings. And the champions came from the Jewish ghettos: Barney Ross and Benny Leonard and Jackie Fields and Slapsie Maxie Rosenbloom.

Years afterward, a fight trainer named Whitey Bimstein spoke about the disappearance of Jewish fighters: "When the kids didn't have what to eat, they were glad to fight. Now that any kid can get a job, they got no ambition."

What he meant, of course, was that they no longer had either the ambition or the necessity to regularly take a punch in the nose.

When Greenberg broke into Major League baseball—his first full year in the big leagues was 1933, the same year Adolf Hitler became chancellor of Germany—Jews were continuing their struggle as a people to make it in America. The life in Europe, for many immigrants, was something to put behind them. But, as in Europe, obstacles persisted. Most colleges in this country imposed quotas on Jews. Restrictions in most big businesses kept Jews from rising to levels of significance, and anti-Semitism continued to grow in many areas in America.

From Detroit, ironically enough, Father Charles E. Coughlin, a reactionary Catholic priest, delivered messages of hatred against Jews, primarily in newsletters and on his national radio shows. German Bund rallies held in cities across the country cheered the views of Father Coughlin and of Hitler and the Nazi regime. Meanwhile, Hank Greenberg was hitting home runs and leading the Tigers to pennants in 1934, 1935, 1940, and 1945—twice being named the American League's most valuable player.

In America, a younger generation of Jews was trying to assimilate. Jews, like other minorities, were often shortening or changing their last names. "For business reasons," they said. To pass, perhaps, or at least not to be too obvious, so that barriers might be lowered.

In the early twentieth century, several Jews played Major League baseball. They included one named Ewing and one named Cooney and another named

Kane and one known as Bohne. Each was born Cohn or Cohen. Each had changed his name for, presumably, "business reasons."

One Jew who kept his name was Andy Cohen, who entered the Major Leagues in 1926 and played 226 games as an infielder with the New York Giants.

In preparing this book, I spoke to Cohen. He recalled an incident when he was with Minneapolis in the minor leagues and was playing in Louisville, Kentucky.

"A guy in the stands, a big guy who turned out to be an iceman, kept hollering at me the whole game, 'Christ killer,'" said Cohen. "He hollered, 'Christ killer this' and 'Christ killer that.' I got sick of it. I took a bat and went to the stands and looked up at him and said, 'Yeah, come down here and I'll kill you, too.'"

He recalled another incident when he joined Waco in the Texas League. "On one of my first plays," he said, "I ran to catch a fly ball out in short left field. I made a good catch and the fans gave me a pretty big hand. Then I heard one guy yell out, 'Just like the rest of the Jews. Take everything they can get their hands on.' It was a left-handed compliment. That one didn't bother me."

Other Jews in baseball, and certainly Greenberg, would have incidents in baseball sparked by their Jewishness that would remain indelibly etched in their memories. But not only did other Jews take notice.

A woman named Rosemary LeBoeuf, in a letter to *The New York Times*, wrote, after Greenberg's death: "He was a beacon to goyim, too. I . . . grew up in Catholic Detroit. To my classmates' recital of Jewish faults, I had always the last word: 'Yeah? What about Hank Greenberg?' And they could never say he wasn't a 'real Jew.' The world knew he didn't play on the Holy Days. Later, his Air Force record was a highly visible reproach to those who insisted that Jews were under-represented in the military."

Greenberg didn't change his name. And though he didn't flaunt his Jewishness, he didn't hide it either. In this regard, one of the most significant things he ever did was something he did not do: In 1934, during the heat of the pennant drive in the American League, Greenberg didn't play on Yom Kippur, the holiest day of the year for Jews.

It was a difficult decision for Greenberg, who was a symbol not only of the historic Jew but also of the assimilated Jew. His decision to sit out an important game created great interest and controversy in America. For, Orthodox Jew and assimilationist Jew alike, most felt an undeniable sense of pride in Greenberg's having taken this very visible position at a time of pennant-shaking and world-shaking events. It may have been the first time in American history that a Jew in public life, by dint of the circumstantial news focus, had such attention called to his religion.

"He was the perfect standard-bearer for Jews," recalled Shirley Povich, the longtime sports editor and sports columnist for the *Washington Post,* and a Jew himself. "Hank was smart, he was proud, and he was big."

Greenberg would also become one of only two Jewish ballplayers elected into the Baseball Hall of Fame. He was the first, in 1956; Sandy Koufax followed in 1971.

Greenberg was smart enough—and devoted enough—to discover how to make himself, a player with somewhat limited skills, into one of baseball's great players. Teammates and opponents as well as writers and historians generally agree that no one had a more scientific approach to baseball, and practiced longer and more diligently than Greenberg. As a young man he was smart enough to handle effectively contract negotiations with experienced heads of ball teams. Owners had nearly complete control of the players in those days—players couldn't change teams by free agency as they can now; the players had only their arguing skills and threats of a holdout to sway the stubborn owners. Ty Cobb would hold out, and Walter Johnson, and Joe DiMaggio—and Hank Greenberg. Greenberg would become the first $100,000 player in baseball history. He was one of the few players to rise to become a general manager and an owner of a Major League team. And he was astute enough, after that, to become a millionaire stock market investor.

He was proud enough to fight, when anti-Semitic remarks were made to him. Proud enough, too, to have a deep sense of humanity, not just Jewishness. There were times, however, when he wished for nothing more than to be just a ballplayer, and not always the "Jewish ballplayer." It was generally enough of a burden to carry the bat to home plate—the bat that he held straight up in his powerful stance—and to use it so effectively against the dazzling fastballs and curveballs of Bob Feller and Lefty Grove, and Dizzy Dean.

There is a famous picture taken before the 1937 All-Star game in Griffith Stadium in Washington, D.C. Seven of the most prominent sluggers of the time are lined up: Lou Gehrig, Joe Cronin, Bill Dickey, Joe DiMaggio, Charlie Gehringer, Jimmie Foxx, and Greenberg. Each is leaning on a bat. The remarkable thing is how much bigger Greenberg looks than the others. At six foot four and a half inches, Greenberg was at least two or three inches taller than the next tallest, Dickey or Gehrig. (Babe Ruth had retired two seasons before, but Greenberg was nearly three inches taller than Babe Ruth, too.)

Meeting Greenberg for the first time, in 1973, when I was a sports columnist for Newspaper Enterprise Association, a newspaper syndicate, I was struck by just how big, how imposing he really was. His dark hair was carefully combed straight back and he wore a well-tailored suit. He looked exceedingly fit, though he walked with a slight stoop. He was sixty-two years old and had been having back problems, but he had walked slightly stooped since childhood, when he was ashamed at how much taller he was than most of his schoolmates. Despite his great successes in later years, he never stood quite as straight as he might have.

Over lunch at the Men's Bar of the Roosevelt Hotel, he was confident, bright, curious about the world around him, quick to laugh, quick to banter, and quick to argue, too. Like many intelligent men I've known, he delighted in a battle of wits, sometimes a ferocious one.

He was also, I had come to learn, an iconoclast of sorts. He and his friend Bill Veeck were alone among baseball team owners or former owners who had testified on behalf of Curt Flood in his suit against baseball's reserve clause, which bound a man to a team as long as the team wanted to keep him.

Greenberg was also an iconoclast about some of the legends that had risen around him in the last forty years, or since he had become a Major League ballplayer. He gave me none of the expected answers about his thoughts on Jews, on being a Jew, on how they pitched to him when he was going for Babe Ruth's season home-run record in 1938, or about home-run hitting in general. (He maintained it was runs batted in, and not home runs, that was the most important criterion for a power hitter, and it was his runs-batted-in records of which he was most proud.) We talked about the stock market, the Nixon administration, the war in Vietnam, and the Broadway theater, as well as the merits of the spitball.

We talked for about four hours. This was a man who was considerably more than a former star ballplayer. This was a man who read widely, listened to opinions about the world around him, and formulated his own viewpoint.

I saw him now and then through the years. We'd talk on the phone occasionally if I was writing about something that I wanted to run by him.

I remember sitting poolside with him at a Las Vegas hotel. He was entered in a celebrity tennis tournament, and I was there doing a story. He had just come from hitting tennis balls with someone and stopped to chat. He began telling a story about the 1947 Pirates, with whom he had played his last season. It was a terrible team, but, in retrospect, a very funny one.

"I wasn't used to this kind of team—this losing, and a lot of guys drinking and carousing," said Greenberg. "I had been with the Tigers for nine seasons, and we had won four pennants and two World Series and everything was serious and bent on winning.

"Not the Pirates. Billy Herman was in his first year as a manager. He was a nice guy, maybe too nice, and he just locked the door of his office and didn't want to know what the players were doing.

"Well, one afternoon, one of the players got married and a bunch of the guys attended and got looped. We had a game that night. I think Kirby Higbe was pitching for us, and the guys were making errors all over the place."

Now Greenberg stood, laughing, to demonstrate.

"And Kirby—" Suddenly, Greenberg grabbed one leg and began to hop around. "A cramp!" Greenberg groaned. "I have a cramp!"

He wasn't kidding. He grimaced, and yet still laughed—he was determined, despite his intense pain, to finish his story.

"Herman comes out to the mound to get Higbe out of there," moaned Greenberg. "Oh! Oh! My leg—! And Higbe—Higbe—Oh!" Greenberg grabbed his leg but kept laughing. "Higbe says, 'I can't pitch when they're drunk out there.'"

Greenberg was hopping around. "And Herman says, 'Who's drunk?'

"And Higbe—Higbe—Higbe says, 'Everyone!'"

With that, Greenberg collapsed into a chair, laughing and moaning, as he ended the story.

Everyone there laughed at Greenberg's story, and the way Greenberg was telling it. Right through the pain. Later I thought that it was this kind of perseverance, this drive, this kind of view of the goal that was surely a great part of the inner Greenberg, the ballplayer, the man.

I liked Hank Greenberg, liked being around him. So did most people. It went beyond his being a former star player, a former symbol of a people. He had about him both grandeur and an earthy quality—a compelling combination.

Yet when he asked me to help him write his autobiography I said no.

Actually, it was his son Stephen who asked on behalf of his father. Stephen called from Los Angeles sometime in the summer of 1986. He said that his father had, for the last year or so, been dictating into a tape recorder his life story and thoughts on baseball, about his playing days and about the current scene, and that he had had most of it transcribed. For years, publishers had been after him to write his autobiography, but he kept refusing. He felt he wasn't quite ready. Sometime around 1975 he wrote a long, three-part reminiscence with his current views of the game for *Sports Illustrated*, with the aid of a staff writer. But Greenberg didn't care for the presentation, and refused to allow it to be printed. As for a book, he told Stephen that he'd just as soon wait, because one day he hoped to do something "really important," and he'd want to get that in the book. "And I never found out what that really important thing was," said Stephen.

Now, for reasons he'd later explain, Hank Greenberg had decided to tell his story.

I said that I had just finished writing a biography that had taken four years, and I was wrung out. I just couldn't think of working on another book right now.

He said that if I wanted to reconsider, he would wait.

I put the Greenberg book out of my mind. It really wasn't anything I wanted to do, as much as I liked Hank.

Then I began to think about it, and the more I thought about it, the more I thought it was something I did want to do. If not for me, if not for Hank Greenberg, then maybe for Uncle Julius, and for all the other Uncle Juliuses, regardless of religion, race, or nationality.

I called back about a week later and asked Stephen if the offer still held. He said it did.

About a month later I flew out to Los Angeles. A dinner had been arranged so I could meet with Hank and Stephen, and Hank's wife, Mary Jo, and Stephen's wife, Myrna.

We were to meet in a restaurant near the Beverly Hills Tennis Club, where Greenberg was a member and played regularly, against amateurs like himself, and even against a pro on occasion, like his pal Jimmy Connors. Greenberg, in fact, was proud of the fact that he once beat Connors. "Of course," admitted Greenberg, "I made Jimmy play right-handed."

I was the first to arrive at the restaurant and was shown to a table. Soon Stephen and Myrna arrived. I sensed there was something odd going on, but I wasn't sure what it was.

It turned out that Hank wasn't coming to dinner.

"I'm sorry," said Stephen, "but I don't think you'll be able to see him."

I didn't understand.

"I'll have to swear you to secrecy," said Stephen.

I agreed to be sworn.

"Dad's in the hospital," he said. "It's cancer of the kidney. He's been sick with it for a year, and he just doesn't want anyone outside of the immediate family to know. There's been an elaborate charade. He has simply dodged most people, and he's had us and Mary Jo making excuses why he can't see them."

"Why the secrecy?" I asked.

"I'm not sure," said Stephen, "other than that Dad doesn't want a lot of sympathy, doesn't want calls and letters from people."

"Even friends?"

"Even friends. Even his best friends. He thinks he can beat it, and, when he does, he figures then he can tell people. He's beaten most other things; he thinks he can do the same with this."

Greenberg was then seventy-five years old. It would not be an easy fight.

Stephen gave me Hank's manuscript, which came to about 800 pages. It was not in any kind of book order, just random thoughts that had occurred to him. I found them fascinating but not enough to make a book. It would take work, and how could we accomplish it?

There would be a time, Stephen hoped, when his father was feeling better, and I could sit with him and do what a writer is supposed to do: dig into the mind of the subject for broader concepts and more telling details of his experiences.

In the meantime, I went through the manuscript and made notes and constructed about a hundred questions. I sent them to Stephen, who told me he'd sit with his father, asking the questions and getting the responses.

His father tried, but he tired easily.

A few weeks after I had been to Los Angeles, I was scheduled to return and spend time with Hank. On the morning I was supposed to leave, Stephen called and said his father was not up to it. It wasn't looking good for him. About a week later, on September 4, 1986, Hank Greenberg died.

These were understandably sad times, but the family asked me to continue work on the book, and I said I would.

Now the story had to be fleshed out by others besides Hank. So I interviewed many people in Greenberg's long and full life and was fortunate to receive the assistance of Larry Klein in researching newspaper and magazine files concerning the life and times of Hank Greenberg.

In the end, I didn't want to turn the book from an autobiography into a biography. I hoped that Hank's words would be enough, and there would be enough of them, to carry the book, splicing in, when appropriate and at the necessary length, interviews with others and material from research clips.

I'd like to think that portrayed here are the many sides of Greenberg, the many sides of a man, a big man, an important man, but a man nonetheless, with flaws. He rankled some, even in his own family; he had a few fistfights during his career, and even after; he made some enemies. But even those with whom he contended, I learned, respected him. None of us is loved by everyone; it can't be so. And Hank, because he had strong beliefs and stood up for them, wouldn't have wanted it to be so.

At the memorial for Hank a few months after his death, Stephen said:

"He taught me lessons that I will carry forever. But most of all he taught me that you don't have to break every record to achieve greatness. You don't have to be invincible to be strong, and you don't have to be perfect to be loved."

For the most part, except for transitions, I stayed out of the written text itself. I edited, I compiled, I orchestrated. I wanted the result to be, as much as possible, the story of Hank Greenberg's life as told by Hank Greenberg.

This is that book.

—Ira Berkow
New York City
July 1988

C H A P T E R   1

When I was a kid the neighbors used to say, "Mrs. Greenberg has such nice children. Too bad one of them has to be a bum." I was the bum. Every day I'd play ball in Crotona Park, across the street from our house in the Bronx. Anytime there was less than a foot of snow, I was playing baseball. The neighbors shook their heads and warned my mother.

Baseball wasn't looked upon as a business, and most of the guys in the game were pretty rowdy. So my parents didn't think much of me pursuing it. They thought I ought to be studying instead of playing baseball. I grew up with typical Jewish parents whose objective was to send their children to college to become doctors or dentists or lawyers or schoolteachers. As a matter of fact, my two brothers, Ben and Joe, and my sister, Lillian, all graduated from college and all went into professional work. But I loved baseball and stuck with it.

In my early days, I was completely engrossed and captivated by baseball. I'd play baseball hours on end. On weekdays after school, I'd rush to the park with my glove, bat, and ball and come home only after it got dark. Weekends were completely devoted to the old field, and instead of coming home for lunch, I'd fill my pockets with fruit and candy and stay down at the ballpark all day. We would break for lunch and sit up in the stands and have a little water with our food and that was good enough. We were just in love with playing baseball and the days weren't long enough.

To improve my fielding, I'd have guys play "pepper" with me, hit or bunt the ball and I'd catch it. I'd count how many balls I fielded without an error, and after I missed one I'd start counting all over again.

To improve my hitting, I'd get friends and kids hanging around the park to pitch to me and to shag balls. Usually one would pitch and two or three would shag in the outfield. Sometimes I'd have a couple of infielders, too. There was no backstop in Crotona Park, which meant I had to hit the ball, because if it got past me I was the one who had to chase it.

The idea was to hit fly balls to the guys shagging and get one to each of them often enough so that they wouldn't get bored and quit. But you couldn't hit the ball too far away from them because they'd get tired. You had to be careful not to hit the ball hard straight back at the pitcher, because if he got hit he'd quit and go home, too.

I got so I was able to hit fly balls within ten or fifteen feet of where I wanted them in the outfield, or hit ground balls within a few feet of where I was aiming in the infield. And whenever a bad pitch came in, I could throw my bat at it and stop it from getting by me. I wasn't a natural ballplayer like Babe Ruth or Willie Mays, but if you practice the way I did—all day long, day after day—you're bound to get pretty good.

I wasn't the only one who was so nuts about baseball. Many of us played until we dropped. We played other sports, including basketball, which I also loved. One winter day we had been playing three-on-three basketball outdoors in the park for hours when I got a little tired and said, "I'm groggy, I'm groggy." Somehow the word got turned around to "bruggy," and Bruggy became my boyhood nickname. It's such a ridiculous name, and yet all through high school that was what I was called. Years later, when I was in the Major Leagues, I was riding on the subway in New York and I heard two guys talking. "Oh, sure," one of them said, "I know Bruggy well. We're great friends. We used to play at Crotona Park."

I turned and looked at a guy I'd never laid eyes on. He was going on and on about his close friendship with Bruggy and finally I couldn't stand it. "Excuse me," I said, "but you're not old enough to have played with Hank Greenberg." I decided to give the guy an out, so I added, "You must have played with his younger brother Joe."

Instead of taking the out, the guy got annoyed. "I did, too, play with Hank," he said, his voice getting louder. "Don't you tell me who *I* played with, buddy!"

So I got mad, too, and I jutted my face into his face and I said, "You know something? You're full of crap! *I'm* your old pal Bruggy, and I never saw you before."

His face dropped, and the minute I said it I felt ashamed. I had embarrassed him in front of his pal. I had acted bush, and from then on I always went along with it when I met a guy like that. I'm always running into those shaggers from

Crotona Park, all 10,000 of them. I smile and give them a big handshake and tell them I remember them well, even when they're total strangers.

When I couldn't get to the ball field, I used to practice at home. My father, David Greenberg, owned the Acme Textile Shrinking Works in Manhattan (he shrunk material before it was made into suits) and we led a fairly middle-class life. We lived in a three-story building, 663 Crotona Park North, which was sandwiched in between two apartment buildings each about five stories high. We had a little space, one little runway between our house and one of the other apartment buildings, and we usually used this if we had to come through the back way or if there was a delivery. I persuaded my dad to let me use the backyard for a sliding pit. I told him that in the wintertime the grass wouldn't grow anyway, and that it would come back in the spring, and I'd get rid of the sawdust if he would just let me use it for a short period so I could perfect my sliding.

He said yes and I made the pit in the backyard. I would start from the front of the house and run down the alleyway about twenty-five yards, turn left and swing right into the sliding pit, working on my different techniques. This is how, for a big lumbering man, I became fairly adept at sliding. The neighbors used to look down from their apartments and see me come running down the alleyway and then, for some stupid reason, slide into the backyard. They all thought I was nuts.

My mother would say to me, "Why are you wasting your time playing baseball? It's a bum's game."

My father used to holler at me that I would never make anything of myself, but when the next day came, I was back playing baseball.

I know I spent so much time at baseball because I wanted to make myself a better ballplayer, yet I suspect it was more complicated than that. I'm no psychologist, but I think one reason I spent so much time at it was related to the fact that I was six foot three when I was only thirteen. I was awkward and had a bad case of adolescent acne and felt out of place. At school, I'd squeeze behind one of those tiny desks, and if I had to go to the blackboard it would be the event of the day: All the kids would titter because I'd tower way above the teacher. Everybody always teased me. "How's the air up there?" I heard that a dozen times a day. At home, if we had guests they'd be astounded: "My God, look how much he's grown! He's grown two feet in a week."

I began to think I was a freak. I felt everybody was laughing at me and I was embarrassed. I was always slouching around, more or less hiding, never standing up straight.

Sports was my escape from all that. Many of the very things that were social liabilities were assets in sports. I felt comfortable with athletics, and I think that had a lot to do with why I spent most of my time in Crotona Park, or sliding into the pit in my backyard.

At first, at the park, I stood around the edges as they were choosing up sides, and often as not I'd be left out and I'd walk over to the sidelines to snivel for a while. But before long I was getting into every game. Most of the time we'd play with an old taped ball, heavy and waterlogged, and you felt like you were putting the shot out there. We liked to tape the balls with Johnson & Johnson adhesive tape, but that stuff was expensive, and we wound up using electrical tape that weighed a ton. We'd play till dark, till you could hardly see the ball (that's why we preferred white adhesive tape), and by the time I'd get home, my mother and father and brothers and sister would be sitting around the table waiting for me. My father would bawl me out, which didn't make the slightest difference when it came time for the next day's game.

When I was born, exactly forty-five minutes after the new year, at 12:45 A.M. on January 1, 1911, my family lived in Greenwich Village, in New York City, in a second-floor apartment of a tenement house at 16 Barrow Street. When I was about a year old we moved a few blocks to a sixth-floor walkup on Perry Street.

A small group of Jewish families lived in this same apartment building. We all spoke the same language, and as a result we lived close to each other. That was common among the immigrants who came from Europe.

My father was born in Roman, Romania, and my mother, Sarah, was born in Falticeni, about seventy-five miles away. Her maiden name was Schwartz. My parents didn't know each other from Romania, but met in New York.

Baseball didn't exist in Greenwich Village. The neighborhood kids played one-o-cat, or stickball, or some other game that could be played on a city street. There was no place to play baseball, and nobody thought about the game, or missed it. Kids down in the Village thought the national pastime was beating up kids of other nationalities. On one of the nearby blocks was a group of Irish families. When their kids weren't fighting each other, they were fighting us Jewish kids.

Halloween was a holiday for schoolchildren. It wasn't an official holiday, but we learned to stay home on that day because in order to get to school we had to pass from one end of the block to the other, and in those days the kids used to take the long black stockings they wore, fill them with what was supposed to be chalk, and whack you with it, leaving a white stain on you. The Irish kids and the Italian kids who fought each other constantly would call an armistice on Halloween and gang up on the Jews. And instead of filling their stockings with chalk, they frequently used ashes and sometimes even a rock or a solid piece of coal. If you tried to go to school, you'd get hit on the side of the head. So over the years we learned that Halloween was a day we should stay home from school.

"Look out," my mother would say when I was leaving the house, "don't get the sock!"

I can also remember that on Perry Street our primary bill of fare was a pail of milk and plenty of fruit. My dad always thought that if he fed his kids well they would be healthy and grow up to be strong, so he kept the house well supplied with the basic foods. If you were hungry for a snack you'd get milk and bread, and for dessert it would be fruit.

By the time I was six or seven years old, the neighborhood had become very rowdy and tough. Since we were a minority and greatly outnumbered, most of the Jewish families decided that they'd better go to the outlying districts, and we moved to the Bronx. In those days, going from lower Manhattan to the upper Bronx was a big move. It was also a turning point in my life because of Crotona Park, its large athletic field, and school sports.

In Public School 44 we had a baseball team and a basketball team. I played on both. A big, tall kid was almost required to be an athlete in those days, particularly in public school.

In my early days in public school, athletics occupied about 85 percent of my mind and time. The rest of the time was devoted to studies. I wouldn't call myself a good student. I passed, because your parents wouldn't allow you not to pass in school. It wasn't that difficult. I had a better than average mind, and I managed to get passing grades without too much effort, but I was never really a student in the sense that my sons are. I didn't have the same training and background, and I didn't have the same urging from my parents. My parents kept an Orthodox Jewish home, and both Yiddish and English were spoken, and I would be bar mitzvahed.

My dad was a hard worker. He had to go down to lower Manhattan every day. The long ride must have taken at least an hour each way. By the time he returned home, he was pretty tired, so he didn't supervise our studies in any way. And my mother was preoccupied with taking care of the household chores and four children. Ben was four years older than me, Lillian was exactly two years older (she was also born on January first), and Joe was five and a half years younger than me. We had a big house, with ten rooms, and it seems like all my mother did was clean and sew and wash and bake. She did all her own baking on Friday. We went through the religious services, which most Jewish families did Friday night and Saturday, and I recall that my mother was so busy that we kids were more or less free to do what we chose. As long as we stayed out of serious trouble and managed to get passing grades in school, we had no problems at home.

But I vividly remember my father disciplining me. In wintertime I'd go down to the recreation center and play basketball until closing time, 9:00 P.M. I frequently got in trouble with my dad because I would come back with my shirt wringing wet and I'd sneak into the house, and sometimes my homework wasn't done. On rare occasions he'd be waiting for me, and the strap would come out and I'd get belted a few times.

In later years I often thought that all the preaching and talking is great, but the times you remember most are when the rod isn't spared. I've often used this same philosophy on my children. That occasional whipping or spanking sticks in one's memory, and it's what I think discipline is all about.

My closest buddies in those years were my teammates. Most of the fellows I grew up with were athletes. There wasn't much social life at that time. We were afraid of girls or didn't have time to even look at them. It was all athletics, but it's funny that while the Giants and Yankees were playing ball not too far away, it was like another world. Travel was restricted to subway rides, and no one had a nickel to get on the subway, let alone the money to buy a ticket to a ball game.

I wasn't even aware of Major League Baseball until I was in high school. And then the Giants became my favorite team because they were winning. I saw my first game when I was fourteen years old. My dad took me to see the Giants at the Polo Grounds. Frankie Frisch got seven hits to beat the Philadelphia Phillies in a doubleheader. I never forgot it.

By then I was following baseball. I remember all the Giants and the Yankees in the World Series in the early twenties, and the great rivalry of the subway series. One store had an electric scoreboard in the window, and the lights would flash when a man would get on base, and they would have two lineups printed on the side and a little bulb to indicate who was at bat. We'd stand out on the street for hours watching the game with hundreds of other people. That was the only way we could follow the World Series because going to the game was out of the question. No one I knew from the Bronx ever went to a World Series game. That luxury seemed to be reserved for people who came from Manhattan.

The Bronx in those days was actually the country. There were horses and wagons in the streets. The streetcars were few and far between. Most travel was done on foot. When I graduated from grammar school, I went to Morris High School Annex, which was about a fifteen-minute walk through the park. When the new high school, James Monroe, was built in 1925, all the kids in my neighborhood were assigned there, which was probably five miles away. You could get there by streetcar, but it was a long ride. You had to go down Tremont Avenue and then transfer, which took well over an hour. We kids learned to take the shortcut past all the railroad tracks, the New York Central Railroad, and we walked to school every day.

It was a good forty-minute walk, but it was something you just accepted. That's how we got to school, that's how we got to the movie house, that's how we got to a lot of places to play ball. Nobody drove in those days. There were no cars around. We'd play stickball in the streets, and every once in a while, on a Sunday, there'd be a few cars and it added to the enjoyment and excitement of the game to catch a ball and avoid being run down by an irate motorist. They'd blow their horns and jam on the brakes, but the kids didn't pay much attention. The game was more important.

When I got older I discovered the pool hall. Hanging around the pool hall became a status symbol. It indicated that you were getting to be a man and you could afford to be with the big boys and listen to their jargon and conversation and it made you feel a little more important, a little more grown up. The kids in my neighborhood went to Lefty's Pool Hall. Lefty was a congenial gentleman and a marvelous pool player with a great sense of humor. He used to give us kids lessons, then give us a handicap and play us for five or ten cents, but he was so good that he always managed to win in the end. It was frustrating, but we all still kind of looked up to Lefty. A guy who could shoot pool the way he could was somebody special. Pool was one of the few forms of recreation kids had in those days. Books were rare because you couldn't afford them, and there weren't many sports books. We did read paperbacks like Horatio Alger and Zane Grey, and I read Jack London and *Call of the Wild* and cowboy stories by William McCloud Raines.

It wasn't until I was well along in high school that I even became conscious of girls. I didn't have any particular interest in them, but some of my friends did and they dragged me along and we'd talk to girls, but that's as far as it went.

I also had no interest in football, yet I had a football career at James Monroe High School. It consisted of just one season, my senior year. At six foot three I was bigger than most of the other kids and had played all the other sports and was well known in school. To prove that I wasn't a coward, I went out for football. I didn't enjoy it at all. I was an end, and most of the plays went through the middle where you had to do a little blocking. Defensively you had to protect for the end run, but it wasn't my type of game. It didn't seem to be skillful enough. It was all brute strength and a lot of bruises, and the practices were long and boring and the weather was foul.

But I was a regular and had the good fortune to catch a touchdown pass in the last game of the season against our archrival, George Washington High School. I was sort of a semihero for making that catch and scoring, so the season was a success.

I played on the soccer and basketball teams and was also on the track team briefly. I was never a fast man, nor was I any good at high jump or hurdles or broad jump. My role on the track team at James Monroe was as a shot putter. I don't recall distinguishing myself at any of the meets, although I did earn my letter.

But, of course, all of this paled next to baseball.

I suppose it's hard for the present generation to understand, but in my childhood baseball was everything, the only sport that really mattered, and a star ballplayer was a hero on a par with Sergeant York or Charles Lindbergh. Baseball was just about the only game you could find on the sports pages. The reporters used a couple of columns to cover a game and described every key play. Even the semipro games were written up in detail in the important papers like *The New York Times*. In the dead of winter the newspapers concentrated on what had happened during the previous baseball season and what was going to happen in the next. If Tris Speaker developed a case of the sniffles, the paper sent a man to interview his doctor, and when Babe Ruth had a bellyache it was news.

Every penny arcade had sample baseball cards in the window, and you'd run inside and feed your pennies into a machine in the hope of getting a picture of Rogers Hornsby, Christy Mathewson, or some other great star. My brother Joe and I used to save up till we each had ten pennies, and then we'd walk fifty blocks to the penny arcade to spend them on the cards. It seemed like we never got the cards we wanted: Ruth and Cobb and Speaker and players like that. We always wound up with Red Kress or Earl Smith or Heinie Groh, and we'd cuss and complain all the way home.

Baseball took on another dimension for me at James Monroe. The coach was Tom Elliffe, who I guess had read all of the Frank Merriwell books and was a frustrated ballplayer. He fancied himself a master strategist, and he was so eager to win that he went out and recruited players who didn't go to school. Some were three or four years older than we were. In 1928 we knew we had a good team, but we needed a pitcher, so somebody recruited Izzy Goldstein (who later went all the way to the Tigers before developing arm trouble). Izzy was twenty years old; he'd been out of school, playing semipro ball, for several years, but we reenrolled him in the eleventh grade at James Monroe long enough for him to take us to the city finals. We did his homework for him and took his tests for him, and in the finals at the Polo Grounds against James Madison High, Izzy pitched a good game. But I had a bad day; I didn't get a hit and I let a ball go through my legs for a triple, and we lost 4–1.

I wasn't all that great a ballplayer in high school. My old basketball coach, Irwin Dickstein, wasn't far off when he said later, "Hank never played games, he worked at them. He wasn't the natural athlete. His reactions were slow and he had trouble coordinating his big body. He couldn't run a lick because of his flat feet. . . . I believe his size made him self-conscious. He was a great competitor because he hated to lose to smaller boys." Dick left something out. I hated to lose to larger boys, or medium-sized boys, or anybody. Maybe that was because a lot of our childhood ball games were for cash. We used to play in the Bronx Quarter League, so named because each player would put up a quarter and the winner would take all. For a meager $2.25, split nine ways, you should see how we played! Unfortunately most of the games never finished because the losing team would always find fault with some decision by the umpire along about the sixth or seventh inning and then they'd have a big fight and everyone would get their money back. Only rarely did you manage to win or lose anything.

Playing those games was fun, particularly when you were playing with fellows much older than you. Some claimed they had played in the minor leagues; some said they had played semipro ball. Semipro ball was very big in the twenties. All the neighborhoods had teams, and the games were made up where you'd put a sum of money together and go down and challenge another team. You'd collect $100, and during the game some kid would pass the hat and spectators would put a nickel or a dime in and maybe you'd collect another $5 that way. When you'd go to other neighborhoods to play, you had to be sure that the plate umpire was on the level, because many of the games were decided by ball-and-strike calls he made. If you didn't have an impartial umpire, you'd get the worst of it. Unless you really thought you were much better than the opposing team, you didn't challenge them, because there was no way to win.

During the years I practiced at Crotona Park, they had a groundskeeper named Mr. O'Connor, a genial old gentleman who was very kind to us kids. When I got out of school I used to rush to the field and start batting out those long flies. At that time there were two famous policemen in the neighborhood, Matt McGrath and Pat McDonald, Olympic heroes in the twenties. They had won gold medals in the 1912 Olympics (McDonald in the shot put, McGrath in the hammer throw). They'd practice their tosses, but always far enough away so they didn't get in our way on the ball field. They evidently got off duty around 3:00 P.M. and by the time they came up to Crotona Park and changed into athletic clothes, it was around 4:00 P.M. McDonald would fling the hammer about a hundred yards. He'd have a little circle and whirl like a dervish. Both of them were built extraordinarily well. They were each about six foot five and weighed about 275 pounds, so you can imagine what they looked like to us kids. They were giants. They were both police captains, which was a position of great authority in those days. I'd have trouble with McDonald because while he was getting ready to fling that shot, I'd be batting those flies out. These kids were so intent on catching the fly balls that sometimes they'd run into the path where he was throwing, and, of course, he felt responsible for where it landed. Many times he'd wind up with great fury and get ready to release the shot when, boom, he'd see a kid out of the corner of his eye and then he'd have to put the brakes on. When this happened he was like a mad bull. He was so furious that he'd chase us from time to time. We'd always claim that possession was nine tenths of the law, and since we got there first, we were entitled to the field. He felt otherwise.

Mr. O'Connor would try to keep the peace, but I was really McDonald's mortal enemy because I was the guy responsible for hitting those flies. Looking back, I guess I was pretty selfish about it, but I was too young and too dumb to realize it. I recall vividly one opening day of the American League baseball season, and McDonald and McGrath attended the game. They came to practice and I was already on the field. By this time I had graduated from high school, and McDonald and I hadn't had much to say to each other over the years except for him to bellow at me and for me to take off whenever he got close. I didn't want to get in his clutches. So when he called me over I approached reluctantly. In his strong Irish brogue he said, "Young man, I just came from watching the Yankees play and, by God, you hit a ball better than Lou Gehrig."

Well, that was the greatest compliment I ever had, and I was thrilled for days that Mr. McDonald, who I'm sure didn't feel too kindly toward me, had the courtesy to pay me such a high compliment. I think that was the first time there was any indication that I might be on my way to becoming a professional baseball player.

In those years people didn't have the mobility they have now, so though I lived only a few miles from Yankee Stadium, I had never even seen the Yankees play. It hadn't entered my head that I had anything in common with Major Leaguers. And now Pat McDonald was telling me I hit the ball as hard as one of the great stars of the game.

When I was in high school, nobody ever dreamed of becoming a professional baseball player. Only a few professional players came out of New York City at that time. Lou Gehrig, of course, was one of the few. I played baseball because I loved the game and planned to play college baseball—that is, until Paul Krichell of the New York Yankees appeared.

Krichell was the scout who signed Gehrig, and he had come to one of our high school games in 1928 to see one of our pitchers. He didn't care much for the pitcher, but I had had a good day at bat and at first base, and he got interested in me.

I graduated from James Monroe in February 1929, and because my folks wanted me to, I enrolled at New York University for the fall semester. My parents were eager for their kids to have the college education they'd never had.

Meanwhile, I kept on with my routines at Crotona Park and played on a few sandlot and semipro teams while waiting to start college. Wherever I played, there was Mr. Krichell, watching me and taking notes.

I had volunteered my services to the Red Bank Towners, a semipro team in nearby New Jersey. They looked at my size and my swing and put me in right field and promised me $7 a game, even though I was just out of high school. In the first two games I didn't get anything resembling a hit, and in one stretch I fanned four straight times. Playing the outfield for the first time in my life, with a first baseman's mitt on my hand, I was lost. Once I ran back for a line drive and it conked me on the back of the head. I averaged about four errors a game, which may be a record for right fielders, and the Red Bank Towners were thoroughly disgusted with me. But the next weekend they came up a player short and they said they would play me, but no $7. I said they should at least pay my carfare, and they did: $3.03. In return I hit three towering home runs into the woods. That's how I was. Totally erratic and inconsistent.

I had been all-scholastic basketball center in my senior year, and I had no trouble getting an athletic scholarship to NYU. In basketball, I was much taller than the rest of the players, and I was a pretty physical player. I weighed about 215 or 220 pounds at that time. I was all skin and bones, but I was pretty strong. I guess I was agile for my size, a little awkward I'm sure, but anyway I was acclaimed the best center in the City of New York, a great honor in those days. We won the city championship one year, and we were always the Bronx champions. For a while after I got out of high school I thought I'd become a professional basketball player.

In my time, the players didn't shoot as much as they do today, and the games were much slower. I played in the days when you had a jump ball after every field goal, and I even played in the days when they had the two-handed dribble. I was never a good shooter and had no touch at all; as big as I was, I scored very few points. But I was a good defensive man and a good rebounder.

Basketball was somewhat like semipro baseball. There were no professional basketball teams per se; most teams represented some community center or YMHA or some social club. Honey Russell, one of the all-time great players, used to organize teams and would call me to play sometimes. I could get between $5 and $25 a game. Even the best players would get no more than $50 or $100 per game. I'm talking about the greatest players in the game at that time. So I realized then that there wasn't enough money in the game for me to pursue it; so baseball turned out to be the only sport that one could consider seriously as a profession. Still, I enjoyed basketball. I loved the physical contact. I didn't like it in football, but I did in basketball. And if today's salaries existed then, and I had the choice between basketball and baseball, I probably would have been a basketball player.

But in those days baseball was still uppermost in my mind.

I knew that New York kids sometimes went to the Polo Grounds to shag flies when the Giant irregulars hit in the morning, and I asked for permission to join them. Back came the word, from John McGraw, manager of the Giants, to Max Schneider, a director of the Giants and a friend of my father: Henry Greenberg had already been scouted by the Giants; he would never be a ballplayer. McGraw didn't even want him shagging flies at the Polo Grounds. What a blow!

That's when I really went to work on my hitting. I would get to Crotona Park at seven or eight in the morning and hang around until some kid would arrive and shag for me. I'd throw the ball up myself and crack it out there. Then somebody else would arrive and I'd get him to pitch, and pretty soon there'd be eight or ten kids shagging and throwing to me. I did this for days at a time.

One day an older man saw me playing in a game and asked me if I'd be interested in playing for a semipro team called the Bay Parkways, named after their ballpark on Bay Parkway in Brooklyn. The Bay Parkways played other teams on the regular semipro circuit, teams like the Detroit Clowns and the Bushwicks, and there were always a few former professionals in their lineup. The nice thing about it was you got paid—or you were supposed to. I didn't do much in the first game, and nobody paid me anything. The next Sunday I hit three home runs in a doubleheader, and still nobody paid me. So I went to George Lippe, the manager, and said, "Mr. Lippe, I'm not coming back anymore."

He said, "Why not?"

"I didn't get paid," I said.

"I thought you were an amateur," Lippe said.

"I am an amateur," I said, "but, look, Mr. Lippe, it took me two hours to get out here and it's gonna take me that long to get home. I won't be home until about eleven tonight, and I left home at eight in the morning. Besides, I had a pretty good day. I expect to get paid, or I'm not coming back."

"Listen, kid," Lippe said, "we thought you were playing as an amateur. Here." He fumbled around in his pocket and brought forth a $5 bill. "You come back next Sunday for the doubleheader and I'll pay you ten dollars."

Ten dollars for a kid just out of high school was pretty good. To give you an idea, when I started at NYU I got a $3-a-week allowance, and that paid for the five-cent carfare going and the five cents coming back, plus lunch, and I still had $1.25 free to spend as I pleased.

So that week after my first game in Brooklyn I practiced all day every day, which gave me a terrific advantage over the other semipro players. They had to work, and they could only practice when time permitted. The next Sunday we played the House of David, the bearded ones, a fine semipro team. I was rapping the ball all over the place, and in *The New York Times* it said, "Hyman Greenberg, youthful first baseman for the Parkways, was largely responsible for

his team's victory in the opener, six runs being scored on his two circuit clouts."
That wasn't the first or the last time the press misnamed me; at other times I
was called Buggy, Hy, Herman, Harry, and Buggsy, but I got used to it.

I practiced all week and hit well the next Sunday, and after twenty-one games
with the Bay Parkways, I was hitting .454. That brought a few scouts in, and
pretty soon I was on my way to the Blackstone Valley League in Massachusetts,
a semipro circuit. A Detroit scout named Jean Dubuc had landed me on the
East Douglas team; I think he found me the job because he wanted to hide me
away from the other scouts in the New York area, but he needn't have bothered. The Giants had already studied me and found me wanting, and Paul
Krichell, the Yankee scout, had looked me over in high school and I thought
he had lost interest.

If you could visualize East Douglas, Massachusetts, and the East Douglas ball
club and the Blackstone Valley League, you would understand much of the
United States in the 1920s. The town revolved around the Schuster Woolen Mills
and its owner, Walter Schuster. I don't think there was a square inch of East
Douglas that Mr. Schuster didn't own, and I'm including the churches and the
school. The town was a fiefdom, and Mr. Schuster was the king, but a benev-
olent one. Baseball was his only outside interest. He once promised Lefty Grove
$1,000 in advance and $100 a strikeout to pitch against the East Douglas team
in an exhibition game. Grove struck out seventeen and collected $2,700, the
most, as far as I know, that anyone at that time had ever been paid to pitch
an exhibition game.

Mr. Schuster developed ballplayers like Gene Desautels and Bump Hadley
and Wes Ferrell, and when I first went up there, the lineup was so tough that
I couldn't even break in.

The arrangement was that I would stay in a hotel owned by Mr. Schuster and
eat in a restaurant owned by Mr. Schuster and it would all be on him. But, of
course, nobody was offering a schoolkid a salary in those days, not even Mr.
Schuster. I wouldn't have cared if I'd been playing ball, but I was strictly a bench-
warmer. And my whole social life in East Douglas consisted of sitting around
the hotel, walking two blocks to the pool hall and running a rack, and returning to the hotel to play cribbage. My companions were Gene Herbert, a star
player for Holy Cross, and a beat-up old pitcher from North Carolina whose
name I can't even remember. When I announced to the manager that I was going
home, he put me in a game and I hit a home run. The wind caught it and it

looked twice as good as it really was, and Mr. Schuster got so excited that he almost swallowed his chewing tobacco. He jumped off the bench, where he customarily sat surrounded by his three managers, and when I finished rounding the bases he pounded me on the back. After the game, he took me aside and said, "I understand you're going home."

"Yes sir," I said.

"Now listen to me," he said, gripping my arm tightly. "You've got to promise to come back for next week's game. Promise!"

I started to stutter and stammer, but he wouldn't let me speak. "We need you," he said. "We've got to have you!" He pulled out his wallet and started peeling off these brand-new bills, fives and tens, and pressed them on me. Then he instructed one of his drivers to take me to Worcester to catch the train to New York, and the driver saw to it that I had a Pullman berth for the overnight ride home.

I'd never been in a sleeper before, and I pulled the curtains and took the money out and began to count: $175! That was two months' wages for an average workingman in those days. I had never seen so much money in one place before, and I didn't know what to do. I put the money under the pillow and sat up all night watching it. I was convinced that if I fell asleep somebody would come in and rob me.

Naturally, I continued to play for Mr. Schuster, and one week a Washington Senators scout came over from Boston, where the Senators were playing, and asked me if I'd like to take batting practice with the club. I showed up when and where he told me, got dressed in the Washington clubhouse, and came out to the bench. It was a thrill for me to gawk around at all the stars I had read about in the newspaper. I was an awkward kid with acne, and very self-conscious. I sat on the bench in a strange uniform, and none of the Washington players would even look at me. Then a heavy-set guy came up and said, "How about having a catch, kid?" It was Fred Marberry, a great pitcher and a great human being. He understood the situation, and he wanted to give me a break.

A few minutes later batting practice began, and who was pitching but Walter Johnson, "The Big Train," retired as a player and managing the team. He signaled me to step into the batter's box, and I walked in with a bad case of the jitters. Johnson was then forty-two years old, but he still had something that I had never seen before: a fastball with a hop. Whoever heard of that in the Quarter League? I kept missing his pitches altogether or popping them foul. The other guys were crowding around the batting cage and growling. "Okay," they'd say after each pitch, "that's it. That's it! Get him out of there!" I was dying. By the time Mr. Johnson waved me away, I'd taken about twenty cuts and hadn't hit a fair ball.

So now I figured I was dead with two Major League clubs—the Giants and the Senators. Imagine my surprise, then, when Paul Krichell came up to scout me again, and when I went back home after the East Douglas season was over, he took me down to meet the famous Yankee general manager, Ed Barrow, in the team's office on 42nd Street and Sixth Avenue. "How'd you like to play for the Yankees?" Mr. Barrow said.

"I'd like to very much," I blurted out.

"Here," he said, "take these." He ripped off four passes, good for general admission, and told me to go out and watch the Yankees play. On the last day of the season Mr. Krichell joined me at the ballpark.

We sat in a first-row box right next to the Yankee dugout. When Lou Gehrig came out and took his place in the on-deck circle in the bottom half of the first inning, Krichell leaned over and whispered to me, "He's all washed up. In a few years you'll be the Yankees' first baseman."

I heard what Krichell was saying, but it made no impression on me because I was so awed by the sight of Gehrig kneeling in the on-deck circle only a few feet away. His shoulders were a yard wide and his legs looked like mighty oak trees. I'd never seen such sheer brute strength. "No way I'm going to sign with this team," I said to myself, "not with *him* playing first base."

I said, "That Lou Gehrig looks like he's got a lot of years left."

Mr. Krichell continued to try to pooh-pooh the idea. "Look at how his batting average has slipped," he said.

And as we sat there talking, a very peculiar thing happened right in front of our eyes. In his last game of 1929, Gehrig needed at least two hits to reach .300, and in his last two times at bat he laid down bunts and the Philadelphia third baseman, Jimmy Dykes, didn't even try to throw him out. When a power hitter like Gehrig bunts twice in a row, it's a dead giveaway that something is up, and when a great third baseman like Jimmy Dykes doesn't try to throw him out either time, you know that somebody is doing somebody else a big favor. But the A's had already clinched the pennant, and the game meant nothing, and everybody liked Lou Gehrig. Thanks to Dykes, Gehrig wound up hitting an even .300. But that was supposed to be a bad year for him. And, of course, he went on to have many more successful seasons.

Somehow the Yankees had not gotten around to making me a firm offer. The Senators, despite my awful day against Walter Johnson, offered me $10,000 to sign, but by now I had developed an affection for Jean Dubuc and his Detroit organization. The Tiger offer was $3,000 cash and another $6,000 when I reported after finishing my freshman year at college. I went home to discuss the matter.

Many people didn't look upon baseball as a business. Most of the guys were pretty rowdy. And my parents hadn't thought much of me pursuing it. They thought I ought to be studying instead of playing baseball.

"Pop," I said, "are you against baseball as a career?"

He nodded.

"The Tigers offered $9,000," I said.

My father whistled softly. "$9,000?" he said. "You mean they want to give you that kind of money just to go out and play with the baseball?"

"That's right," I said.

"And they'll let you finish college first?"

"Yes."

My father sat down to collect himself. "I thought baseball was a game," he said finally, "but it's a business—apparently a very good business. Take the money."

I had told Dubuc I was planning to go to college, that I had a scholarship to NYU and that my dad and my mother were insistent that I attend college, so I didn't feel that I could sign.

But he amended the offer. I would sign the contract and get paid $6,000 on the front end when I signed, and $3,000 when I reported to Detroit four years later.

It seemed that Krichell got wind of the fact that Detroit was trying to sign me, so he made an effort to get me to sign and the Yankees offered me $10,000—a thousand more than the Tigers—but I had had a look at Lou Gehrig, and said no thank you.

That was the prime reason I signed with Detroit. It certainly was not the glamour of playing with Detroit, since I knew nothing about the town, nothing about the ballpark; all I knew was that Detroit was the team made famous by Ty Cobb, Harry Heilmann, Sam Crawford, Hughie Jennings, Donie Bush, and all the other great Tigers.

It was my good fortune to sign with the Tigers because the Detroit ballpark turned out to be perfect for a right-handed hitter and Detroit was a great baseball town. I've never had any regrets that I didn't play for the Yankees. I think Yankee Stadium would have been a tough ballpark for me; it was for all right-handed hitters. And who knows what would have happened had I played in the shadow of Gehrig. I might never have made the grade. So going with Detroit was a good decision, one that I based solely on my own intuition, and it turned out to be the best thing that could have happened to me.

In September 1929 we accepted the first installment of $6,000 from Jean Dubuc, and I asked my father to put it into the stock market for me. He bought me $6,000 worth of American Tobacco B. The very next day my stock climbed to $6,800, but a month later the money was wiped out in the crash. My father thought it was a tragedy, but to me it was nothing. I was all wrapped up in baseball. Money didn't mean a thing.

I enrolled in New York University and at the end of the fall term, along about January, I got the urge to play baseball. For a few weeks I worked in my father's plant, but when spring came and the papers were full of stories about the ball clubs going into spring training, I got very eager. "Pop," I said, "I've got to go down there. I've got to play."

"What about college?"

"College can come later," I said. "Right now I want to play ball."

I wrote Frank Navin, the owner of the Tigers, and asked permission to join the club. He sent me a railroad ticket to Tampa, Florida. I never returned to school. I was the only one of David and Sarah Greenberg's four children who didn't graduate from college.

CHAPTER 2

My contract with Detroit provided that I wouldn't be optioned out at lower than Triple A ball, which is one step below the Major Leagues. Of course, I was supposed to be going to college for four years, and they figured that when I was twenty-two or twenty-three years old I should be ready for Triple A ball. But the Tigers permitted me to join them at training camp. Because I was signed to a Major League contract, they had no choice.

The thought of getting on a sleeper, an overnight sleeper, and traveling to Florida was thrilling. It would be the first time I had been so far from home, and I would be away for at least six weeks. The training camp opened late in February or on the first day of March 1930, and if I was lucky enough to stay with the Tigers I wouldn't be back up north until April.

I reported to Tampa, a raw rookie, just nineteen years old. I was in the same clubhouse and on the same field with some of the outstanding ballplayers whom I had read about: Dale Alexander, Harry Rice, Roy Johnson, Marty McManus, Bob "Fat" Fothergill, Waite Hoyt, Charlie Gehringer. I sat around the clubhouse with my eyes wide open and my mouth shut and just listened to them and watched them. They were all grown men, well groomed and well dressed, who had been in the Major Leagues for some time. I guess most of them didn't understand why I was there. I was an eager beaver and chased a lot of balls and did a lot of shagging, and they occasionally let me go to bat. I could hit a long ball, even though these weren't game conditions.

We trained at a racetrack about half a mile from the hotel. It was the old Tampa Bay Hotel, which was later turned into the University of Tampa. It was one of those tremendous hotels in Spanish-mosque type of architecture with all the domes and spires; it's a museum piece now. Only the very wealthy could afford to stay there, and they were surprised that ballplayers were also guests.

It was very unusual. As a matter of fact, this was about the time when ballplayers were finally accepted in first-rate hotels. The hotel served breakfast from seven to nine, lunch from noon to two, and dinner from seven to nine. Of course, we were never there for lunch. We'd have our lunch at the ballpark—a sandwich and a glass of milk. After working out for long hours, we were hungry for dinner. My room was a long way from the dining room, and I used to count the minutes until seven and try to be first on line to get into the dining room. So did most of the ballplayers.

After dinner we'd sit out on the lawn near the bandstand and listen to the band play.

The ballplayers didn't want to mingle. I had no real conversations with any of them. The only person I really talked to was a clubhouse boy, Alex Okray, who subsequently became the clubhouse boy for Detroit when I became a regular many years later. It was his first year away from home, too.

He told me not to worry about the snubs; it was just part of the game. I was seen as a threat to the other guys' jobs, and naturally they weren't going to take kindly to me.

One day in batting practice I hit a ball back to the mound and sent lefty Phil Page to the doctor. A few minutes later I decked another pitcher, Staples, with a line shot just over his head, and a few of the regulars grumbled about it as though I was trying to destroy the pitching staff out of spite.

Our manager, Bucky Harris, started me in the first exhibition game, against the Boston Braves and Johnny Cooney. Before the game started Cooney took me aside and said, "Kid, I'm gonna give you one you can hit." I don't know why, maybe he heard about my troubles. He was just as good as his promise, and I hit that fat pitch over the fence.

The next morning, one of the Detroit papers reported: "Henry Greenberg, the prize rookie, stole the show. He made a couple of sensational plays at first base. His first chance was right in the dirt and he dug it up, and his trip to the plate resulted in a home run and Babe Ruth never hit a ball harder." The article called me "the greatest prospect in years," and said I was "a joke on Col. Jake Ruppert, owner of the Yankees. Greenberg lives only two blocks from Yankee Stadium."

But there are only so many kindly pitchers like Johnny Cooney, and soon I was getting my share of strikeouts and pop-ups. When the season started I was farmed to Hartford in the Class A Eastern League. As a result, spring training was a lonesome period in many ways, and yet it opened up new vistas for me. I knew I wouldn't have been able to enjoy myself had I remained in school.

The owner of the Tigers, Frank Navin, decided that I would be unprepared to play Triple A baseball without some minor league experience, and he convinced me that the best place to go would be to an A league in which the competition wouldn't be as keen. I took his advice, realizing that he had my interest at heart. He wanted me to make good as badly as I wanted to make good, and so I waived the clause in my contract requiring him to send me to Triple A ball.

At Hartford I ran into a problem. Hartford was the first team that Lou Gehrig played for in his debut as a professional baseball player. Lou, of course, had graduated from Columbia University and so was four years older than I was when he had reported to Hartford. Because I was a first baseman from New York, the fans there anticipated that I would play as well as Lou did. Unfortunately, I was very green and inexperienced. I was eager, but still that inexperience was terribly important, particularly when you had to play every day. And I felt all the pressure.

Playing semipro ball three times a week was quite different from playing every day against professional ballplayers. I tried hard but I was a big, awkward giraffe at first base. I missed pop flies over my head. I would get my feet tangled on ground balls. At bat, I struck out thirteen straight times.

I lasted twelve games in Hartford, and batted .214—a total bust. I hit a home run and a triple in my last game, but by that time the Hartford management had decided that I couldn't hold my own. I think they cut me back so quickly because I was drawing $500 a month, which was more than any of the other players on the team, and I wasn't earning it. So Hartford returned me to Detroit, and Detroit reassigned me to Raleigh, North Carolina, in the Piedmont League, a class C league. Of course, that was quite a drop in caliber of play from Hartford, but it was a Detroit farm club. When I reported they knew I was there to stay, because the club had $9,000 invested in me and they were certainly going to take a long look for $9,000.

Well, the next thing I knew I was playing badly for Raleigh. I was in a slump and if it hadn't been for an elderly pitcher named Dusty somebody, I might never have broken out of it. One day he hollered the full length of the bus, "Look at you, you big bum! What a slugger you are! I'm hitting .155 and you're slugging along at a terrific pace of .151!" That really made me sore, and that day I got four for four, and pretty soon I was hitting around .300. I finished at .314, and with 19 homers, one of the leading home-run hitters on the team.

The year in Raleigh was an experience. At first I didn't fit in. My teammates were a bunch of farm boys and I was a big, ungainly kid from the city. One day I was standing on the field when I became aware of a teammate walking slowly around me, staring.

"What're you looking at?" I asked.

"Nothing," he said. "I've never seen a Jew before. I'm just looking." The way he said it, he might as well have said, "I've never seen a giraffe before." I let him keep looking for a while, and then I said, "See anything interesting?"

"I don't understand it," he said. "You look just like anybody else."

"Thanks," I said. Maybe he was expecting somebody in a yarmulke and a long beard, or someone with horns. I encountered some hostility, but I'd say much more curiosity than hostility.

I recall another significant incident. After being in Raleigh for a couple of months, I was approached by a gentleman who was a baseball fan. He was Jewish, and he asked me if I would come to his home for Friday night supper. I accepted eagerly. When I got there, the man and his wife introduced me to their daughter. After dinner the parents left us and there I was, stuck with the daughter. I invited her to a movie. After the movie I took her for a soda and then home. I mention this because it was my *first date with a girl,* and it was my last date with that girl.

In the minor leagues I did what I had always done. I got to the ballpark early, whether it was a game day or an off day, and practiced hitting and fielding. It wasn't hard to talk some of the other guys into doing the same thing. What else was there to do in most of those minor league towns besides play ball? We were young, in our teens or early twenties, hardly any of us married, so we'd hustle out to the ballpark at ten in the morning and have fun while waiting for the game to start.

We traveled from one end of North Carolina to the other in a bus that was so old and decrepit we sometimes had to "will" it over the crests of hills. We'd get up speed on the downhills and then head up the ups, and many a time we'd reach the top at about two miles per hour with all the ballplayers shouting and screaming, "C'mon! Giddyap! Giddyap, you son of a bitch!"

At the time, the Raleigh players seemed so skilled, so polished, but now that I look back, I realize that only one other teammate made the majors. They all lived on dreams and schemes—what they'd become, how much they'd make, how they'd hold out for more money, how they'd wow the women—and they grabbed at gimmicks. Flea Clifton, the only other teammate to get to the majors, showed up one day with a bat made of Cuban wood, a gray model with wide grains and a bottle shape. Each night he soaked his bat in water, and that was supposed to keep it from cracking or chipping. Flea guarded that bat with his life; he'd fight anybody who came near it. He was a tough little guy, even though he weighed only about 150 pounds. On the road, he used to eat nothing but doughnuts and bananas. He said they were cheap and filling and they stretched his meal money. Flea was the only ballplayer who could show a profit on $1-a-day meal money.

After the Raleigh season ended the Tigers brought me up to travel with the big club for the last three weeks of the season.

I reported to Navin Field. This was the first time I had ever been to Detroit. The Tigers were in fifth place and going nowhere, and I figured they'd give me a lot of work at first base. Instead, I sat on the bench.

I took batting practice with the irregulars and did a little infield practice after the regulars got off the field. But our star pitcher, Earl Whitehill, fancied himself a great first baseman, and he'd always run over and work out at first base when it was my turn to play there. What could I say to Earl Whitehill, winner of seventeen games? So I'd just fume and go out to center field with a ball and throw it against the wall by myself, with my back turned to the rest of the club.

My locker was next to Waite Hoyt, who had been a superstar pitcher with the Yankees. In the three weeks that I dressed and undressed next to him, I don't ever recall him saying a single word to me. As far as Bucky Harris was concerned, my only conversation with him was when the clubhouse door was locked one day and I was inside. Someone pounded on the door. I rushed over and opened it, and there was Bucky. He just nodded and walked right by me. That was the way they treated rookie ballplayers in those days; if anything, they made you feel as self-conscious and conspicuous as they possibly could because you posed a threat to their jobs.

I got in one game, as a pinch hitter against the Yankees in a game that was hopelessly lost. The pitcher was Red Ruffing, and I was as good as out before

I ever reached the plate. It was my first official at bat in the Major Leagues and I was scared to death. I knelt in the on-deck circle and looked out at Yankees like Babe Ruth and Lou Gehrig and Ben Chapman and Bill Dickey and Lyn Lary, and said to myself, "What am I doing here?"

I don't know how I got to the plate, or what I swung at, or how I even connected with the ball. I popped up to Tony Lazzeri, and I figured that everybody in the stands must have thought I was a gawky freak. It was over—that first at bat. The next time up, I'd be more self-assured, and I'd get a chance to show what I could do.

As the season drew to a close, I stayed on the bench. I couldn't understand why they didn't give me a chance to play in a game or two. The excuse was they were trying to finish .500 or get in the first division, or something like that. In any case, Dale Alexander, the regular first baseman, who was hitting something like .340 or .350, was playing every day, and rightfully so. I was eager and I thought, well, there could be no harm done if I played a little. It couldn't make any difference in the standings one way or another.

I kept asking Jean Dubuc, the scout who had recommended me to Detroit and who was then a coach for the Tigers. He said not to worry, that I would get in. So I bided my time and finally it got down to the last day of the season. I packed my Model A Ford in the morning (I had bought it in Raleigh for $375 and spent a lot of my time polishing it) and drove to Navin Field and suited up in a fairly good mood, everything considered. I thought surely they would put me in the last game, which was an unimportant one, just going through the motions, and most clubs play their minor league ballplayers in the last game, just to give them a taste of Major League competition.

The lineup was posted on the bulletin board, and my name wasn't on it. I thought Dale Alexander would take one turn at bat and then I'd go in. After the first turn at bat, and the second turn at bat, and the third turn at bat, I still wasn't in the lineup. We got down to the eighth inning, and now there was very little chance that I was even going to get to bat because the team was winning. I sat on the bench really fuming and very unhappy. At the start of the top half of the eighth inning, Bucky Harris said, "Greenberg, get in there and play first base." By this time I'd worked myself into such a state that I could hardly see. I stood up, bumped my head on the dugout roof, and said to Harris, "I ain't gonna play for this team." I stamped past all the ballplayers and went down the runway into the clubhouse. I was changed inside ten minutes and on my way back to New York. And that's how I left the Detroit club in my first year of professional baseball. I guess that was pretty fresh for a rookie, but that's how I felt and that's what I did, and I never had any regrets.

Funny thing was, I never got a letter, never heard a word about it from the front office. They didn't give a damn. I was on option and they knew I wasn't going back to Detroit the next year. They were too insensitive and dumb to worry about the feelings of a nineteen-year-old rookie.

When I got back to New York I ran a red light and a big blustering Irish cop stopped me. He came up to me and looked the car over and asked for my license. I had my North Carolina license plates. He asked me what I did for a living. I said, "I'm a professional ballplayer."

He looked at my driver's license again and burst out laughing. "And who in the hell ever heard of a professional ballplayer named Greenberg?" he said. I've often wondered if that policeman ever remembered that remark when I became a regular with Detroit. I suppose it was unusual for a Jewish fellow with the name Greenberg to be a professional baseball player. That incident was the fitting end to my first professional season.

I was sort of a semicelebrity around my neighborhood that fall. Everybody in my group knew where I had been and what I had been doing, and even being a minor league player, in those Depression years, was quite an accomplishment. I slept late and spent my time just working out until the weather got bad. Then I went down to the YMHA on 92nd Street in Manhattan and played handball. I began to drive down to Times Square and go to the movies or to the theater and to some of the restaurants. It was really the beginning of a change in my life. For a boy who was raised in the Bronx and never left his neighborhood suddenly to become a man of the world was quite a change. (It might seem a little premature to say that, but at the time I felt I was becoming a man of the world.)

That winter slipped by, and I was all set to start my second year in professional baseball. I was ordered to Beaumont in the Texas League.

◆

During that winter, Greenberg wrote a letter to Frank Navin, the owner of the Tigers. The content of Greenberg's letter is clear from Navin's response:

Dear Mr. Greenberg:

Replying to yours of the ninth, I sent you to Beaumont [an A league team] because I figured you would get much more training with that club than with Evansville [a class B team]. Evansville does not start training until April 1 whereas the Beaumont Club starts about March 1.

Mr. Zeller [Jack Zeller, the Tigers' general manager] explained to me he sent you a contract calling for $300 a month, stating that was all the Evansville Club could pay, but if you remained with the Beaumont Club they will pay you $400, which is all you could get from any Double A club with your record. If you can make the grade at Beaumont you can consider you are progressing very rapidly. I think it is foolish for you to talk about Double A baseball. You would not have been retained at Raleigh last year were it not for the fact we are interested in that club and insisted that they keep you. After the fourth of July however you started to improve in your playing and were of some use to Raleigh the latter part of the season.

You must understand you received a big salary last year for playing Class C baseball. The average salary at Raleigh last year was $225 a month.

I am sorry you were not satisfied with the treatment. You were given a $9,000 bonus to sign with the understanding you were to go to college for four years and play baseball in college, also play baseball during the summer. . . . Instead you cut out the four years entirely. . . . When you first went to camp last year it looked like you would make Double A but as soon as the pitcher began to get something on the ball you showed very plainly your lack of experience. . . .

Don't say to any baseball man that you did not get a chance at Hartford and in the same breath say you were in twelve games—because anyone who knows anything about the game will tell you twelve games will give any player plenty of opportunity to demonstrate whether he will make the grade in any league. Baseball is not run for the youngster. . . .

Relative to the bad treatment you received in Detroit, we took you to Detroit so you could get acquainted with Major League surroundings and not to play ball, thinking it might help you. If it had come about that Manager Harris could have used you in a game he would undoubtedly have done so. It seems to me it comes with rather poor grace from a boy who has just made good in Class C to criticize a Manager of Harris' well-known ability. . . .

Of course, it may be possible that a younger and brighter school of ball players is developing, who know more than the manager and coaches of a Major League club, but at this time I will have to string along with the players who have demonstrated their ability on the field.

So far as I am concerned, if you do not see fit to accept the contract tendered you by the Beaumont Club that is a matter entirely up to you.

Very truly yours,

Frank J. Navin

◆

I was ready to report to Beaumont, in the Texas League. It was supposed to be a really tough league, and I was eager to play for the team. In the spring of 1931 I loaded up my Model A Ford and four and a half days later I drove into Orange, Texas, about thirty miles from Beaumont, where the team was training. It wasn't uncommon to see men walking around with guns and holsters. We stayed in a boardinghouse for $7 a week with three gigantic meals. The closet was the shower.

Beaumont had a first baseman named Ray Fritz, who had played with Evansville the previous season. He was older than I was, and a little ahead of me. I soon learned that Beaumont had no intention of keeping me. I was assigned to Evansville, in the 3-I League. That was a big disappointment, but I went to Evansville. I was twenty years old, and I figured this was my last chance. So I dug in and hit .318 with 15 home runs. I still made a lot of mistakes, but I gradually improved. All my hard work and all the time I spent working on my fielding and taking batting practice started to pay off. I think before the close of the 1931 season I was pretty well accepted in the Tiger organization as one of their promising prospects.

Some of us Evansville players stayed in a boarding house that the Tonnemacher family owned. The players who preceded you would tell you which boarding houses fed you the best and had the best accommodations. The Tonnemachers were famous because they had two daughters and two sons, and they were all avid baseball fans and loved to have the players living with them. The family charged $12 a week for room and board. Whenever we came back from a road trip to the Tonnemacher house, it was a real homecoming. In later years, when I was playing for Detroit, I always tried to get the Tonnemachers tickets for games in Chicago and St. Louis.

In Evansville I learned how to drink beer. Prohibition was still in effect in those days and most of the beer was what was called "near beer." It was manufactured by whoever was peddling the beer. It was a hot summer, and after the games we'd all go down to a friend's basement and drink beer and talk about the game.

In that league, some of the cities were seven or eight hours away by bus. Oftentimes I would sit on top of the bus along with the baggage; there were always a couple of fellows up there. We'd sleep or talk. When we traveled inside the bus, most of the time was spent singing the old-time songs, like "Let Me Call You Sweetheart" and "Sidewalks of New York." Looking back on it now, it was a great period of my life.

Our team finished first in one half of the season, so we played for the division championship. There was one particular incident during the playoffs that I'll never forget. We were playing in Quincy, Illinois, and I had challenged their third baseman, Cap Crosley, who was much smaller than I. I slid into third base, and he did something or other, and we had a kind of jawing session. All of the fans got on me, and after the game I was rushed into the dugout, and the fans were all out on the field and around the dugout, snarling and yelling at me and calling me names. It was scary. The Evansville players finally had to form a cordon around me to escort me back to the bus. There was no police protection in those ballparks. What shocked me was the next day's headlines in the Quincy paper: FANS CHARGE FIGHTING BALLPLAYER—GREENBERG IS BARELY SAVED BY OFFICERS. Well, you can imagine how that headline incited the fans for the next day's game.

Fortunately, the Quincy ball club beat us, and I got out of there alive. So the 1931 season came to a close, and that winter I prepared myself, because I knew full well I'd have a permanent job with the Beaumont Exporters. Ray Fritz had not been very successful at Beaumont, and they had a bad team. So I knew the job was mine; at least that's what they wrote in my contract.

Strangely enough, I had difficulty with my contract even in the minor leagues. I was always getting paid a little less than I wanted. I went from $500 a month with Hartford to $300 when I played for Evansville and then to $400 when I played for Beaumont. Every league had its own salary limits and there wasn't much you could do about it. Everybody was so eager to play, and in those Depression days $400 a month seemed like a lot of money.

◆

On March 7, 1932, Frank Navin responded to a letter from Greenberg:

Dear Sir:

I have yours of the 5th. I will take the matter up with the Beaumont Club and see if some satisfactory arrangements can be made. Of course you understand conditions are not nearly as good this year as they were in 1931. Members of our club have taken big cuts in their salaries and were perfectly satisfied because they knew the conditions. . . . It would seem that $350 a month this year is as much as $400 last year because the dollar keeps on increasing in value right along.

Now, I am going to tell you something for your own good. If you want to get out of baseball, do so and it will be all right with everyone concerned, but don't write to any club owner telling him you are going to quit unless you are satisfied because not one ball player in a thousand quits, no matter what their salary is, at least until they have reached the Major Leagues. The less said about quitting the game the better it will be for you unless you have actually made up your mind to quit.

Your work last year at Evansville was fair and it is a very grave question in my mind whether you would make good with any Double A club. If you join Beaumont and have a good season there it will be very satisfactory to me.

Very truly yours,
Frank J. Navin

CHAPTER 3

Beaumont was hot as blazes, and we only played day games there. To make matters worse, someone came up with the idea of having red uniforms. So we sweated in these heavy, coarse horse blankets for uniforms while playing in temperatures of a hundred degrees.

But the joy of playing and feeling that we were getting a little closer to the Major Leagues was uppermost in our minds. We were a young group—we had only one or two older fellows to give us a little balance—and most of us were prospects and players assigned by the Detroit organization and were looking forward to climbing up the ladder and making the Major League club.

The Texas League had eight teams: Dallas, Fort Worth, Houston, Tyler, Longview, Shreveport, Galveston, and Beaumont. Dallas was the only one you could really call a city. Houston wasn't much and Fort Worth was just a cow town. But some of the smaller towns struck it rich with oil, and at times the big money literally flowed onto the field. Fans would throw out silver dollars if you made a good play or good effort—even if you were with the visiting team. Now $4 or $5 was a lot of money at the time. You could eat for five days with $5. The players would really scramble around for the money. It was funny to see.

The Texas League was an outstanding minor league. If you were good enough in that league you could step right into the majors. Many players had done it. Dizzy Dean was one, and Paul Dean, Paul Derringer, and Ducky Medwick played against me there.

It was renowned as "The Pitcher's League," and I soon found out why. Any pitcher who could stand up under the heat of cities like Beaumont and Dallas could stand up anywhere. We'd play night games at Galveston and Houston, and you could see the heat coming off the field in shimmering waves. Saltwater mosquitoes would arrive and we'd sit and swat them all through the games. In those days the visiting ball club had no showers; we had to go back to our hotel to change after the game. If we were in, say, Houston, we'd go back to the Rice Hotel, peel off our red-flannel uniforms, and hang them on the tips of those slow-swirling ceiling fans. Those cramped little rooms soon smelled like the locker room of a gym. We didn't know any better, I guess. We were on our way to the majors. That's all we knew, all we cared about.

One of the restaurants in Beaumont—there were only two—was a Greek restaurant and the owners would give away prizes for outstanding achievements. This restaurant gave an award for the first three-base hit. We played in a small ballpark named Stuart Stadium where, if you hit one, it would either be out of the park or off the fence and you'd be lucky to get a double. I remember being very annoyed at this very unfair prize, because it was very unlikely that I would ever get a three-base hit with my speed. I thought I was being discriminated against. However, the first time at bat, I squiggled the ball over the first base-man's head, and it trickled down into the right-field corner. That was the only way I could possibly get a three-base hit, and I did get that $25 meal ticket. That probably lasted me a month. Remember, you could have a full meal for fifty cents in those days, and that was eating an awful lot of food.

For the first time in my professional baseball career we traveled by train to certain cities, like Dallas, because it was too far by bus. Those trains were cattle cars with one or two passenger cars attached to them. They didn't have any air-conditioning in those days, so to keep from being smothered to death you had to open the windows. When you did the cinders would blow in, covering you with soot and dirt. So you closed the windows. One player would yell, "Open those windows!" and then another player would yell, "Close those windows!" But it was plush for us players traveling by train. It was one step closer to the dream of playing Major League ball where all the teams traveled by train.

Schoolboy Rowe showed up that year, 1932, and what a phenomenon he was. He never played in another minor league, and there he was starting out in Class AA. He was twenty-two years old, almost six foot five, over 200 pounds, and one of the proudest human beings who ever came out of Waco, Texas, or his other hometown, El Dorado, Arkansas. I wouldn't say that Schoolboy retained his terrific pride all through his career in baseball, but in that first year with Beaumont he was nothing but pride and arm. He wasn't satisfied when he won six in a row for us, and when his streak got up to around ten or twelve, he was telling everybody that he might never stop, might win every start for the rest of the year.

We came into Houston with Schoolboy's streak intact, and when the last half of the ninth inning came around the game was tied. Houston got a man to third base with one out, and our infield moved in. I made a mental note to cut off the man at the plate, but when a ground ball was hit hard to me I decided to get the batter first and by the time I threw home the winning run had scored. What? Well, *of course* it was a bonehead play. And after I'd made it—and ended Schoolboy's win streak—my only interest was in getting the hell off the field as quickly as possible. As I started across the mound I saw that Rowe was still standing there.

"C'mon, Schoolboy," I said, "the ball game's over."

He was muttering, "I ain't leavin'! I ain't agonna go! They can't beat Schoolboy Rowe on a play like that. Schoolboy don't lose games like that."

"C'mon, Schoolboy!" I said, grabbing him by the arm, but he just stood there, and then I could see the tears beginning to slide down his face.

"This game ain't over," he blubbered. "It can't be over!"

I was dying of embarrassment. I felt bad enough, blowing the game, and here's our pitcher refusing to leave the mound and crying his head off while these hometown fans from Houston are starting to walk around us and stare at Schoolboy. I finally dragged him off the field. (Funny thing was, a year later, in Washington, I hit the longest home run of my career to help Schoolboy win his sixteenth straight game and tie an American League record, so I figure we're even for what I did to him in Houston.)

Near the end of the season we played Dallas, our big rival, in a series, and we had to beat them to win the league championship. It was quite a series, and at one point I had a run-in with Zeke Bonura, who was playing first base for Dallas. I hit a ball deep to shortstop. The shortstop's throw to first came on one bounce, Zeke backed up to field it, and he was right in the base path. There was no place for me to go except to run into him and knock him down, which I did. All the ballplayers charged onto the field. There was a lot of jawing and talking, not much swinging.

The newspapers made a big thing of the fight.* When we arrived at the ballpark the following day the place was jammed. After infield practice, I was advised not to go into the Dallas clubhouse to change my shirt, which was the common practice in those days. They suggested that I go under the stands to the umpires' quarters. I saw this unfamiliar man sitting inside, a big, powerful-looking man shining his revolver. I couldn't understand it, and when I came back, I told

---

* A newspaper reporter in New York recounted the incident: "The baseball free-for-all started between a New York Jewish boy, Henry Greenberg . . . and Zeke Bonura, a former college football player. . . . Dallas reports have it that Bonura won the fight, but Del Baker, who manages the Exporters, said that Greenberg can beat the big Italian lad any day of the week. Greenberg . . . had run full force into Bonura on the basepath, sending him sprawling. Bonura got to his feet and socked

all the players about it. One of them said, "Why, sure, that's John King. He's umpiring behind the plate today to be sure there's no riot at the ballpark."

John King was a legendary character who had been a left-handed hitter in the Texas League for many years. He was a .380 hitter but never went up to the Major Leagues because he couldn't hit left-handed pitching. They've often told stories about his distaste for left-handed pitchers. One of the stories they tell was that King had come out of a restaurant and had seen a beggar on the street with his tin cup, and his arm extended, begging for a little handout. King slipped a quarter in the cup. As he turned around, he saw the beggar pull the quarter out of the cup with his left hand and John went back and grabbed the coin out of his hand, and said, "No left-handed son of a bitch is going to get any of my money."

Some years later, after King had retired from baseball, he found oil on his property and became a millionaire. He took a position as an honorary umpire in the Texas League. He didn't do too much umpiring, but he liked being associated with the game. And the league had appointed him to umpire this day to keep order. Just before the game, King sauntered around the baselines with his six-shooter in plain sight, and there was very little noise out of anyone that day.

My 1932 season at Beaumont was by far my best in the minors. I hit 39 home runs and drove in 131 runs and was picked as the most valuable player in the league. But the Dallas sportswriters never forgave me for banging into Bonura and starting the fight. When I was voted most valuable player, they refused to accept it. They held a vote of their own, and a Dallas player, the second baseman Bryne James, won.

That year we won the Texas League championship and played in the Dixie World Series against Chattanooga. They came to Beaumont for the first game, and I hit a home run that won the game and made a backhand stop on a throw in the ninth inning with the tying run crossing the plate. I was kind of a mini-hero for the first game. From then on, though, it was all downhill. As I remember, we lost the next four games, and that closed out the Texas League season for me.

the New York boy, sending him back several paces. Then Schoolboy Rowe, a big pitcher who was coaching on third, took a hand and grabbed Bonura, sending him to the ground. Within two seconds players on both clubs . . . sailed into the battle royal. The crowd swarmed on the field. . . . The milling lasted for five minutes. Greenberg would not discuss the fight, but his manager said that Greenberg was last man to stop fighting."

♦

On January 4, 1933, Frank Navin wrote this letter:

Dear Mr. Greenberg:

I herewith enclose contract for the season of 1933 calling for $500 a month. On receipt of signed contract at this office, duplicate will be sent to you.

Baseball, like everything else, has suffered badly from business conditions and unless things improve there is not much to look forward to. Baseball owners are going along the best they can with the hope things will change. As far as you personally are concerned I am quite anxious that you remain with us this year and I will make a sort of probationary contract up to May 15. If you remain with us after that date we will make an increase in the contract, depending on just how valuable you are to us.

Manager Harris has an idea he can make a third baseman out of you as we have a young first baseman who went over well last year and will not fit in any other place because he throws left-handed. I feel it would make considerable difference on our club if you can make third base, providing you can hit Major League pitching the same as Minor League pitching.

The battery men will leave for San Antonio about the first of March, and the other members of the club about a week later.

I trust you are having a good winter and with kind regards, I am,
Very truly yours,
Frank J. Navin

The twenty-two-year-old Greenberg swiftly began to compose a reply:

Dear Mr. Navin:

Enclosed you will find my contract unsigned. I don't know just how you feel about it but I know that your letter was an unpleasant surprise to me.

Greenberg then scratched out the second sentence, and wrote:

I was surprised when I learned that the figures called for $500 a month but on top of that my surprise turned to amazement when I read the contents of the letter.

On January 20, Navin replied:

> *I have yours of the 17th and wish to advise that a contract calling for the same amount you received last year is a considerable increase over one for the same amount last year, for the reason commodities of all kinds have decreased 30 per cent; consequently the buying power of the dollar has increased that much.*
>
> *As far as I am concerned I am very much pleased with your spirit and I hope you will succeed in remaining with us. I only pointed out to you the conditions as they exist at the present time on the club. I will state frankly that Jack Zeller thinks you will make the club, but from my experience of about thirty years, it is a very hard matter to tell just what a youngster will do.*
>
> *In the three years you have been out you have shown an improvement every year and there is no reason why you should not keep on improving for three or four years to come.*
>
> *You know we could not put you out another year on option without losing title to you, therefore your work will be considered very carefully before taking any action in your case.*
>
> *You have created a very good impression on the Minor League clubs we are associated with and naturally I am gratified with your efforts to become a Major Leaguer and want to do everything I can to encourage you; therefore I will give you a regular contract for the season calling for $600 a month.*
>
> *Hoping this will be satisfactory, I am,*
> *Very truly yours,*
> *Frank J. Navin*

◆

The next year I went to spring training with the big club, along with several of my Beaumont teammates: Schoolboy Rowe, Flea Clifton, Pete Fox, Frank Rieber, and a few others. It was the first time in three years that I saw players who had watched me in my great moment of shame when I had bawled and announced that I would never play for the Tigers, and I was happy that none of them brought it up.

On Bucky Harris's recommendation, the Tigers had shelled out $75,000—big money in those days—for Harry Davis, a classy-fielding first baseman with no power. But he'd had a pretty fair year in 1932, hit around .270, and the Tigers felt they needed a third baseman more than a first baseman, and Harris was determined for his man to make good.

So Harris greeted me in spring training with, "Kid, I'm glad to see you. You're gonna be my third baseman."

Third baseman! Imagine, I had never played or *dreamed* of playing third base.

"I don't know how to play third base," I told Harris. "I haven't played third base since I was in grade school."

"Oh, there's nothing to it," Harris said. "You get out there and practice and you'll do a great job."

I put on a fielder's glove and worked like a dog. But I was awkward. I had never used anything but a first baseman's mitt, and I didn't even know how to work the fingers on a regular glove. The coaches hit ground balls to me by the hour, and I missed quite a few. I also had trouble throwing. My arm was too strong, and I had a tendency to drill holes into Charlie Gehringer at second base on double-play balls. One day we were playing an exhibition game against the University of Texas at Austin, and I ripped off a cannon shot about six feet wide of Charlie and into right field, and then I booted another one by cutting in front of Billy Rogell at shortstop when he had the play practically made. I really made a mess of it.

The next day I wasn't in the lineup. No one said a word to me. The following day I wasn't in the lineup again, and furthermore, I'm not listed to take batting practice with the regulars. Still, nobody's said a thing to me. However, I was starting to get the message.

On top of that little problem, a Detroit sportswriter reviewed the ball club's spring training and described me as "a big sweaty kid who looked pretty grotesque. . . ." He said I was too big, I couldn't stand a Major League pace, I would get fat and slow down, and I would suffer fallen arches: "Big fellows like that always get fallen arches."

The writer said I would never be much of a fielder, that I was clumsy and slow. As a hitter, he said, I was good only in spring training; the pitchers would murder me when they bore down. Anyway, I was too much of a swinger, except on days when I took too many pitches.

As if that review wasn't bad enough, the only person I could talk to was Del Baker, my old Beaumont manager, who was now a Tiger coach. "The hell with it," I said to him one day. "I don't know how to play third base, I'll admit it. If they don't expect me to make errors there, they're crazy." And without asking anybody's permission, I junked the fielder's glove and put on my first baseman's mitt and began working out at first base again, Harry Davis or no Harry Davis. One day a newspaperman noticed that I was fielding fungoes at first base until late in the afternoon, and he said, "How long are you gonna keep that coach out there hitting fungoes?"

"Till I can field first base as well as Harry Davis," I said.

"That'll be a long time," the writer said, and walked away.

Just before the 1933 season opened, Bucky Harris went to Washington to spend a weekend with his family, and Del Baker let me play first base in an exhibition game at Norfolk. I fielded well and hit a single, double, and triple. A few days later we were in the Polo Grounds for two exhibition games, and every Greenberg for a hundred miles around was there to see me in action. [But Greenberg didn't get into either game.]

When the season opened in Detroit, Harry Davis was still on first. I was going crazy with inactivity because I was used to playing every day in the minor leagues. Detroit had a place called Belle Isle, like Central Park in New York, where they'd play choose-up games on Saturdays and Sundays. So I'd go out there at 8:30 or 9:00 in the morning and get in a game.

Harry Davis played first base for Detroit for the first several weeks of the season, even though he was hitting about .200. Finally I got disgusted and couldn't contain myself any longer. After the game ended one day, I showered, dressed, and marched straight up to the front office and asked the switchboard operator if I could see Mr. Navin. She didn't know who I was. I told her: "I'm Hank Greenberg. I'm on the team."

Mr. Navin said to come into his office, and as I walked in I was trembling.

"Mr. Navin," I blurted out, "I can't play ball sitting on the bench. I'm gonna get fat. If you people don't want me to play, then let me go someplace where I can."

"We can't do that, Hank," Navin said. "We've already optioned you three times, and if we do it again we lose you."

"Well, lose me, then," I said.

"No," he said. "We don't intend to lose you. You go sit on the bench and study what's going on and learn something. You're not wasting time, and you'll get your chance to play. I promise you that."

Two weeks later, after Bucky posted the lineup with Harry Davis at first base, the telephone rang in his office in the clubhouse. Bucky talked for a few minutes and then walked to the bulletin board, scratched out Davis's name and put in mine. I'm certain that Mr. Navin had called and insisted that I be given a chance against the St. Louis pitcher, who happened to be a lefty named Lloyd Brown. I went none for three, and sat down for another three weeks. Then I got my second chance, against the same Lloyd Brown. This time I got hold of a few, got some hits, and soon I was in the lineup against all lefties. I hit my first Major League home run on May 6, 1933, off Earl Whitehill, then with the Senators, and I figured that paid him back for not letting me work out at first base three years before. My second home run came twenty days later, off Rube Walberg of the A's.

Once the Tigers had put me in the lineup, then everybody at Belle Isle knew me, so I couldn't play there anymore. Besides, the Tigers had gotten wind of it and put a stop to it. But I continued to work hard. In those days they didn't have weights and Nautilus equipment. I decided that the smart thing to do was to develop my muscles by hitting. I would hit and hit and hit and hit. After a while I could damn near control the bat against the ball and hit it where I wanted to. I hit a lot of singles and doubles when I wanted to, but most of the time I was swinging for the fence.

This was the middle of the Depression, 1933. Almost everyone was broke. Frequently in that first year everybody would have the same routine after breakfast: We'd go to the lobby and sit and wait until they felt it was time to go to the park, around 11:30 or 12:00 for a 3:00 game. Naturally we'd want to read the newspapers to pass the time. We would wait until someone finished the newspaper and as soon as they laid it down on a chair, indicating they were through with it, there would be a mad dash to get the paper. It was funny. I think the price of a newspaper was two cents, but nobody wanted to spend that money when they didn't have much of it.

◆

"When I first came to Detroit," Greenberg once told Detroit sportswriter Joe Falls, "I remember staying at the Wolverine for $8 a week. They gave you a room and a bed but no closets. It was no problem. We did what other players did. We hung our clothes on the rod in the bathroom. It wasn't so bad because we took most of our showers at the ballpark. . . . The big deal was the Detroit Leland. They served a complete dinner and they had a full orchestra. You had to decide whether it was worth a dollar and a quarter. Plus you also had to leave a twenty-five-cent tip. I thought about it all the time and finally said, 'Aw, let's give it a try.' The truth is, they had a good-looking waitress there and I was hoping I could impress her with a twenty-five-cent tip.

"As for tipping—in those days a nickel was considered a pretty good tip for breakfast, and ten cents for lunch, and maybe fifteen cents for dinner. We'd hardly ever tip more than that. We used to tease Schoolboy Rowe for once leaving a two-cent tip at dinner. A two-cent tip! We never let him forget it."

◆

Schoolboy arrived in Detroit at the start of the 1933 season with a sweater and a pair of pants. He had no jacket, no tie, and that's what life was like for him, coming from Arkansas and playing in the Texas League. He had just graduated from high school and didn't know anything about dressing up. That was the style of a lot of ballplayers in those days.

Going out to the ballpark, four or five players would crowd into one taxi, and we'd split the fare. Very few people, maybe Charlie Gehringer, a star, and Chief Hogsett, a veteran pitcher, would share a cab with only one other player.

Detroit was always considered a great baseball town, starting from the days of Ty Cobb and Hughie Jennings and Harry Heilmann and Sam Crawford and Bob Fothergill. Throughout the state, the Tigers were the team. Fans would listen on the radio, with Ty Tyson announcing. Navin Field was considered a good place to watch the game. The stands were up close to the infield and when it was jammed, you felt like you were in one of those chicken fights. Everyone was hovering over the field, and the atmosphere was very intimate, making it a good park to play ball in.

I was kicked out of a game in that first year. We were playing in Chicago, and George Moriarty was the umpire behind the plate. I was at bat with the bases loaded. Moriarty called me out on a very wide pitch and I got upset. Bucky Harris came running out of the dugout to home plate. He was arguing with Moriarty. I didn't know at that time that Bucky and George weren't exactly friends. George had been the manager of the Tigers. When they let him go, they appointed Bucky. Anyway, Bucky was giving George the devil, calling him all kinds of things, and George was standing there paying no attention to me and jawing back at Bucky. Finally, Bucky got tired and started back to the dugout. I had been standing there listening to this exchange, and I yelled at Moriarty, "That goes for me, too." Moriarty turned to me and said, "Get out of here, you fresh busher. You're out of the game." I didn't realize that a veteran like Harris could say all kinds of things to him, but a first-year man in the Major Leagues couldn't get away with anything.

◆

When Greenberg arrived in Detroit, in 1933, America was deep in the Depression. And, of course, Detroit wasn't spared. Joe Falls would later describe it in the *Detroit News*: "Men watched their factories close up and stood by the front gates in small groups and wondered what was happening and when they could get back to work again. They used fires in iron barrels to keep warm and looked up at the dust-covered windows and tried to figure out how to get enough money together to buy supper for their families. Soup lines were forming in the streets and some people did sell apples on the corners. But there was one place in town that was insulated from the grim realities of the Depression—the ballpark. The banks could close, but never the ballpark. . . . There was normalcy there. . . . Besides, it cost only a buck to get in. Detroit, a hardworking town, needed a lift in the 1930s. There was excitement in the air at the corner of Michigan and Trumble. The Tigers were stirring things up so much that no one there seemed to notice the hard times."

Greenberg would later say: "I was young and trying to make my own way. I knew things were rough on the outside. I knew what was going on. We didn't see those things or feel those things inside the ballpark. We were involved in our own jobs. Everybody was behind us, everybody was cheering for us. . . ."

"Greenberg," Falls wrote, "was a little different from anybody else on the team. In a sense he was different from anybody else in the league. He was the only Jewish ballplayer around and presented no particular problem away from the field. [Actually, there were a handful of Jewish players in the Major Leagues, such as Moe Berg, Harry Danning, Milton Galatzer, Phil Weintraub, and Buddy Myer of Washington, who was half Jewish, but none were as prominent in the Major Leagues in his time as Greenberg.] At the ballpark, it was different. They would shout their slurs at him, particularly the Yankees.

"'They always had a couple of guys in the dugout just doing that to you. Some of the things they yelled were pretty nasty but I could always handle it pretty well. That's because everybody got it. Italians were wops, Germans were krauts, and the Polish players were dumb polacks. Me, I was a kike or a sheeny or a mockey. I was big so I made a good target. The only thing that bothered me was there were a lot of Italians, Germans, and Poles, but I was the only Jewish player who was making a name for himself and so they reserved a little extra for me.'"

The Jewish community in Detroit, though, not unexpectedly, embraced him.

◆

My first year in Detroit, I had hardly made the team when the Jewish fans there wanted to give me a dinner and a Cadillac. I immediately turned it down. I knew that if I accepted an automobile, I would be obligated to every one of those fans who chipped in $10 or $20, and I didn't want anyone to feel that they owned me. I've never wanted to be pushed around, and that was the tendency of the Jewish baseball fans in those days. Nobody was rushing to give other rookies a dinner because of their religion. I just felt funny about it, and I always have. I've tried to live within the proper boundaries of my religion and have never done anything to bring discredit on Jews.

◆

On May 6, 1933, Hank Greenberg started for the Tigers for the first time. They were playing the Washington Senators in what began as an ordinary ball game. "It was no spring day. The sky was overcast and there was much chill in the wet breeze," wrote John Keller in the *Washington Evening Star*. "The unfavorable weather had much to do with holding the crowd down to 3,500."

In the bottom of the eighth, Greenberg hit his first big-league home run. It cleared the scoreboard in left center and landed in the street beyond. The blow came off Whitehill, the former Tiger, and was Greenberg's second Major League hit in 14 at bats. The other was a single.

"Greenberg, graceful as a shoemaker," wrote Shirley Povich in the *Washington Post*, turned "razzberries" into "a deafening and prolonged cheer as he crossed the plate."

A few weeks later, in Washington, Heinie Manush, the Senators' outfielder, and "Hank Goldberg," as the *Washington Post* referred to Greenberg, "had words and threatened each other." There appeared to be bad blood between the two ball clubs and, the *Post* wrote, "The Nats are sore. They've long felt that Tiger pitchers throw at heads. . . . [The fight between] Manush [and Marberry] might have been related to earlier beanballs."

By August, Greenberg had firmly established himself as the Tigers' regular first baseman, and after a game in Detroit against the Senators, Shirley Povich wrote: "When this Greenberg hits a ball on the nose, it stays hit. That home run he socked today [on the twenty-second] in the sixth to break a 4–4 tie with a man on base was no bunt. It was a towering fly that was labeled home run from the time it left the bat and cleared the street behind left field by yards, ending up in a woodshed 50 yards beyond the fence."

When the Yankees, the defending World Series champions, came to Detroit on June 25, *The New York Times* reported: "The largest crowd at Navin Field this season . . . a throng of 28,000, occupying every available vantage point in the park, cheered as the Tigers won (6–5) with a 12th-inning rally." Greenberg drove in Gehringer from second with a single for the winning run.

Babe Ruth, near the end of his career, "was a bench warmer . . . [for] the first time unless forced out by injury." Ruth was in a slump, having gone 2 for 17 since his sixteenth of the season in St. Louis nearly a week earlier. "The heat is terrific," said Yankee manager Joe McCarthy, "and Babe just asked for a little respite." A few days later, Ruth, "still on a voluntary vacation," said *The New York Times*, "got into the game as a pinch-hitter in the seventh with a Yankee rally under way and the bases loaded. His effort was a weak foul fly to Greenberg."

But on the last day of the series in Detroit, Ruth returned to action and hit a 3-run homer in the eighth inning to help the Yankees win 10–7. The drive, about 455 feet, was one of the longest ever hit in Navin Field.

◆

Babe Ruth was by far the greatest ballplayer who ever lived. He had more talent, ability, and charisma than any player ever. The only player who was comparable, and I can't put him in the same class as the Babe, was Willie Mays.

Babe was unique. He ate and drank as he pleased. He was the fans' favorite, and he always came through in the clutch. Everybody admired him. When we went to Yankee Stadium, Babe would come out last, and everybody on the field would stop what they were doing and watch him take batting practice. I never saw anything like it in my whole life. They never did that for any other ballplayer—DiMaggio or anybody else. It was Babe. He was a *star*. In street clothes he looked like Santa Claus, but when he put on that baseball uniform he was all business. There's no doubt that he revolutionized the game. When the Babe hit 54 home runs in 1920, he had hit more home runs than fourteen of the fifteen other teams in the Major Leagues.

What many people don't realize about the Babe is that he was a fantastic all-around athlete, with natural talent and natural instincts. When I broke in with the Tigers in 1933, Babe was playing left field. One day a guy hit a long fly to left with a man on second base. Babe went back to the wall, stopped, turned around, and looked, as if the ball was going out of the park. At the last second, Babe turned and caught the ball. Then he threw to second and caught the runner for a double play. What timing! I never saw anything like that before, but Babe had been playing for twenty years. In his prime he could do anything. He could pitch, he could steal bases, he could throw, he could run, he could hit, and he could win.

One story about Babe particularly amused me. He was a ladies' man, as was well known, and sometimes when the train would stop in the early morning hours, he'd get off and have some girl waiting for him. He was always chasing women and drinking booze. Anyway, on this particular day the Yankees were playing the White Sox in Chicago and Mark Roth, the Yankees' traveling secretary, said to Miller Huggins, the manager, "Why don't you get rid of that bum, Ruth? All he does is disrupt the team. He's always late, has no discipline. Why don't you get rid of him?" So Huggins said, "Okay, if that SOB comes in late today I'm going to fine him." Sure enough, Babe came in late. Everybody was on the field. Babe went out on the field and the whole place was in turmoil. Babe just tipped his hat and spit his tobacco.

The game went eight innings and Babe tied it up with a home run. It was getaway day, and the Yankees had to catch a train for St. Louis. It looked like they were going to be late and miss the train. In the dugout after the tenth inning, Babe announced, "Don't worry about it. I'll finish it for you." He walked up in the top of the eleventh and hit one practically over the right-field roof in Comiskey Park and won the game. Babe went down the ramp to the clubhouse to take his shower. An hour later the Yankees are at the train station boarding their coach to St. Louis. Mark Roth, still eager to have Huggins fine the Babe for showing up late for the game, nudged Huggins on the arm and said, "There he is." As they approached Ruth on the platform, Huggins smiled and said. "Hiya, Babe." Then he walked on, leaving Roth mumbling to himself.

I continued my habit of getting to the ballpark early for extra batting practice and often for some extra fielding practice. I did it in Detroit and everywhere on the road except in New York. The Yankees wouldn't let me in early. In Fenway Park in Boston I climbed on the top of the left-field wall to retrieve baseballs I'd hit up there.

For a short while I had a problem in Shibe Park in Philadelphia. After about half an hour of batting practice one day, the groundskeeper came over and said we had to leave. As usual, I had a whole crew with me—a pitcher and several guys to shag balls in the outfield. We were getting our gear together, preparing to leave, when an elderly gentleman none of us had noticed, sitting about twenty rows up in the grandstand, called to me. I went up to see what he wanted and he said, "I very much admire what you are doing, young man. You tell that groundskeeper to assist you in every way possible. Tell him that those are John Shibe's instructions. And if he doesn't like it, send him right up here to see me." Needless to say, I never had any trouble in Shibe Park afterward.

By the time the 1933 season was over I was feeling pretty good. I wound up the season with the regular first baseman's job, against lefties *and* righties, and I hit .301, with 12 homers and 87 runs batted in, in 117 games. I was making $600 a month as a Major Leaguer and it looked like I had found steady work at first base. There was a big family celebration when I got home, and then a big neighborhood celebration. All my pals were elated; my mother and father were overnight big-shots; even the neighbors were asked to pose by photographers. What a feeling of euphoria came over me! "Look at you," my mother said. "The Napoleon of the Bronx!"

"Mom," I said, "what's wrong with that?" Personally, I was enjoying every second of it. I was getting paid for fulfilling the wildest dreams of my childhood.

"They didn't have to pay me. I'd have paid *them* to play. Listen, the truth was it was more than fun. It was heaven." That was my old teammate, Goose Goslin, quoted in an interesting book, *The Glory of Their Times,* by Lawrence Ritter. Ritter quoted several players as saying that baseball was "heaven" in those days, and a lot of people said, "Yeah, sure, everything seems wonderful when you're reminiscing about it." But baseball was fun. Baseball was the most pleasant way to make a living that's ever been invented.

I was fascinated by the people I met in baseball. Most of the players came from rural areas—about half of my Detroit teammates were from the South—and they knew all kinds of things that I had never learned. Their whole life experience was with animals, and they knew how animals lived—how they copulated, what they ate, how they behaved. They saw the whole pattern of life in terms of animals and crops and soil, and there wasn't any situation that they couldn't describe in agricultural terms. When I first came up, I was dismayed by this, but I soon learned that the other players had their lexicon and I had mine, and one was as expressive and descriptive as the other. When they got hold of a pitch and drilled it over the fence, they'd come back to the bench and say, "Boy, I really cowtailed that one!" A fly ball became a can of corn. They seemed to have a homespun knack for describing people, too. When Pete Fox and I got our first look at six-foot-eight pitcher Mike Wayant, Pete whistled and said, "Man! He's big enough to have two belly buttons." Only belly buttons wasn't the precise word he used. When some particularly oversexed rookie came along, they'd say he was "horny as a hound dog in heat," and this sort of remark would puzzle a Bronx boy who had never heard the word "horny" and had never seen a "hound dog," and didn't know what "heat" meant. But after a while I caught on.

That kind of talk began to come naturally, and it didn't even sound vulgar anymore. Most of our intimate nicknames for one another had to do with fornication or defecation (they persist today). The better we liked each other, the worse the names.

My first roommate was Joyner "Jo-Jo" White from Georgia. He was called Jo-Jo because of the way he pronounced his native state. And no two people could be more different than me, coming from the Bronx, and Jo-Jo White, claiming he came from Atlanta. Well, when we pinned him down, it was twenty-five miles out of Atlanta, a little town, Red Oak, Georgia, that didn't even show up on the map. Anyway, our relationship was terrific. We used to fight the Civil War every night. Jo-Jo would say, "Why my granddaddy would chase your granddaddy right up the goddamn hill and run his ass off." I hated to tell him that this would have been impossible, as my granddaddy had been in Romania at the time, but that didn't keep Jo-Jo from carrying on. He couldn't conceive of anybody coming from any place except Georgia, or being brought up on anything but a dirt farm, and he still could not assimilate the idea that the South had lost the Civil War.

Jo-Jo was a center fielder and leadoff hitter. He had great speed and really knew how to slide. I used to urge him to get on base, because I would try to drive in runs and lead the league in RBIs. One time he was on third and I faced a fellow by the name of Mickey Haefner, a short left-hander who didn't have much on the ball. The game wasn't close and there was no need for Jo-Jo to try to steal home, but he did. He was thrown out. As he was lying there on the ground, I said, "The next time you do that, I'm going to hit you right on the head with the bat." He deprived me of a good chance at an RBI, and he did it deliberately because he knew it would burn me up.

That winter I got to thinking about my contract, and I was convinced that I ought to get a Major League contract. Prior to that time I had always been paid a monthly salary, which meant that if management sent you down, the minor league club could then reduce your salary. I figured that I was entitled to $1,000 per month, and since it was a five-and-a-half-month season I asked the club for $5,500—a $2,200 raise. I guess as far as Mr. Navin was concerned, that was totally unreasonable.

◆

Navin wrote to Greenberg on January 17, 1934:

Dear Mr. Greenberg:

You had a good year for a youngster and there is no reason why you cannot go on, although it will be more difficult for you this year because the pitchers will pay more attention to you and work on your weaknesses more than last year. This has been demonstrated to me twenty-five or thirty times in my baseball career and it was also a lesson to you last year shown by the reverses to one of our outfielders who hit very well in 1932 but fell down quite badly last year for the simple reason the pitchers started paying more attention to him. [Navin apparently was referring to outfielder Gerald Walker, who had hit .323 in his rookie year in 1932 and dropped to .280 in 1933.] Once a hitter perks up over the .300 mark for a season the pitchers start working on him the next year and a great many times the effect is very deadly on the player.

There is a great deal of room for improvement in your work but you have the aggressiveness and the willingness to learn, which will be of great benefit to you. I feel the club will be benefitted by Mickey Cochrane's catching and hitting, and he should be a good manager because he has the necessary requirement.

Hoping you are enjoying a pleasant winter and wishing you the best of luck for the 1934 season, I am,

Very truly yours,

Frank J. Navin

◆

Mickey Cochrane had come over from Philadelphia as the player/manager, replacing Bucky Harris. My becoming a regular for the Tigers had been a hard pill for Bucky to swallow because he had so strongly recommended purchasing Harry Davis from the Toronto club for $75,000. [Greenberg doesn't imply that this was the reason for replacing Harris, but it may have been a factor, along with the Tigers having finished fifth in the American League for the second straight year under Harris. And in Cochrane the Tigers were also getting a standout catcher, a position at which they had been weak.]

◆

On February 1, Navin wrote Greenberg at the Biscayne-Collins Hotel in Miami Beach, Florida, where he was on vacation, in response to a letter from Greenberg turning down Navin's contract offer.

Dear Mr. Greenberg:

Replying to your letter of January 24 . . . I did not expect to have any trouble with you because I haven't had any trouble of any consequence with any ball players since Ty Cobb held out until April 25, 1913 [about three weeks late], and then decided to come in. That was my last serious trouble and I don't want to have any more, but of course if conditions come up that make it impossible for me to do business with a ball player we have to go on just the same. However, I try to treat all players as I should like to be treated if I were a player and by following that policy I have gotten along pretty well with the majority of my ball players. . . .

I enclose contract for the season of 1934 calling for $4,500. This is more than a 25 per cent increase over your contract of last year and I trust you will be well satisfied with it.

Very truly yours,
Frank J. Navin

On February 8, Navin wrote to Greenberg again:

Dear Sir:

I have yours of February 6. Your letter was somewhat arrogant, especially the last part of it, which is clearly intended as a "bluff." Now I have always made it a practice to "call all bluffs" and I am going to "call" yours. According to baseball rules, I have to send you a contract before the 15th of February, consequently I am enclosing a contract calling for $4,500 a year. The next step is up to you.

Very truly yours,
Frank J. Navin

◆

I was scared but I didn't budge.

Mickey Cochrane came down to Miami Beach and called me up. He knew I was holding out and he was very eager to get the team to Lakeland, Florida, on March 1, the reporting date. Mickey was a highly charged ballplayer, excitable and dynamic. As a catcher and, for that matter, as a hitter, he was unsurpassed, in my opinion. We talked about my contract. He said he hoped that I would get together with Mr. Navin and report, because he had planned on me as his regular first baseman. He was looking forward to the new season with enthusiasm, especially because we had made some changes over the winter. We had acquired Goose Goslin, Fred Marberry, and Alvin Crowder, and we had all these young guys like Pete Fox and Schoolboy Rowe and myself, who were now second-year veterans. Mickey thought we had a pretty good ball team. He urged me to get in touch with Mr. Navin.

Well, in late February I got a message at my hotel to please call the long-distance operator in Detroit because Mr. Navin was trying to contact me. I returned the call. He got on the phone. His first words were, "What do you want?" I said that I had a message to call him, and I was doing just that.

He said, "Well, listen, young man, don't you be threatening to retire or quit; I've handled ballplayers like Ty Cobb and nobody has ever quit on me and no one is ever going to, and if you want to retire from baseball, just do it and stop threatening."

I said, "I have no intention of retiring or quitting. I just want to get what I think I'm entitled to."

He said, "We've given you a good raise. We've offered you $5,000, and that's a good salary. Furthermore, we're making a Major League contract for $5,000."

I said, "Mr. Navin, I don't care whether it's a Major League contract or not. I want $1,000 per month, which adds up to $5,500. If you don't want to give me a Major League contract and don't think I'm going to stick for the balance of the season, then send me a contract for $1,000 per month, and I'll sign it."

He said, "We're not going to do that. I'll tell you what we'll do with you. I'll give you a $5,000 Major League contract, and if the team finishes 1–2–3, I'll give you a $500 bonus."

By this time, with only a week to go before camp opened, I was very eager to get signed. I was as anxious to get there as Cochrane was to have me there. So I grasped at this face-saving device and told Mr. Navin that I would be very happy to sign with the understanding that if the team finished 1–2–3 I'd be entitled to a $500 bonus.

What a joke! The team hadn't finished higher than fourth in nine years, so Mr. Navin wasn't taking any great chances.

But I said, "Thank you very much, Mr. Navin. I really appreciate that. I'll be there for spring training on March first, sir."

CHAPTER 4

Over the winter I always tried to stay in shape, mostly by playing squash and handball indoors. When I reported to camp it didn't take me more than a week of batting practice and I'd be ready to go.

In 1934, the first year we trained in Lakeland, the first thing Cochrane told us was, "Listen, we're going to win. We're not going to lose." He also showed us how to get a man on first, move him over to third, and then get him in. And we would use what he told us during the entire season. We needed somebody to take charge and show us how to win and that's what Mickey did. We didn't always drive a runner in with hits; there was the strategy of winning ball games with sacrifice flies and ground balls. Cochrane was the one who taught us how to do it. He was an inspirational leader.

He'd been on three pennant winners with Philadelphia—in 1929, 1930, and 1931—and winning was a way of life with him, a winning spirit that was really infectious. He was the greatest fighting spirit on the ball field, a little Irishman with a red face. He would go through a brick wall to catch a ball. On a close play at the plate, when the throw was going to be late, he used to knock the runner on his seat before he caught the ball. He couldn't stand to see a guy scoring a run for the opposition. He could run; he could throw; he could steal bases; and he could talk to those umpires about getting his pitcher the strikes on the close calls. That's all we needed, one man like that.

Rip Sewell was a rookie pitcher for the Tigers that spring. We were playing an exhibition game against the Cardinals and he started to get on my ass because I hadn't got a hit in the game. I told him to cut it out, but the more I told him to lay off, the more he needled me.

When we got on the bus after the game, I sat down and Sewell sat behind me. He started to throw things at me, little pieces of paper and other little things, and made remarks and laughed.

I said, "Please cut it out, Rip."

He said, "I'm not doing anything."

I said, "Yes, you are. Please leave me alone."

He said, "What the hell's the matter with you?"

I said, "Listen, Rip, when this bus reaches Lakeland, and we get off this bus, I'm going to beat the shit out of you. I just want you to think about it from here until we get back to Lakeland." Everybody laughed.

◆

Sewell remembered what happened this way:

"My relationship with Hank had been very wonderful, until we got into a fight. We started together down in Beaumont. That's where I first met Hank. Anyway, Hank sat down on the bus and he raised the window. I was sitting in the back. We all just had a shower and Denny Carroll, our trainer, asked Hank to pull that window down. He didn't say nothing, because he was mad before we started because Gerald Walker had put his hands over Greenberg's face and said, 'Get that sour look off your face, Hank.'

"I tapped Hank on the shoulder and said, 'Hank, would you pull the window down?'

"He said, 'Who you talking to, you Southern son of a bitch.' That's the way it started. He called me a rookie fresh Southern son of a bitch. So I said, 'Well, you big Jew bastard.'

"He said, 'I'm gonna whip your ass when we get to Lakeland.'

"I said, 'You could whip my ass now if you want to stop this bus.'

"He said, 'All right with me.'

"There wasn't another word until we got to Lakeland."

◆

We got to the hotel, and there were a number of people in front of it. As we got off the bus, I grabbed Sewell and started pummeling him. He couldn't fight, so he grabbed me around the knees. The only thing I could do was pound him on the head. I was embarrassed for him.

◆

"I stepped off the bus and he popped me upside the head. We fought and fought," Sewell said.

Billy Rogell, the Tiger shortstop, was on the bus with Sewell and remembers: "It always starts with that Jew thing again. Sewell said, 'You Jew bastard,' or something like that and that's the way the damn thing started. There really wasn't much of a fight because we broke it up too fast."

Sewell: "Cochrane asked me what happened. I told him. Cochrane said, 'Okay, Rip, you're going to the minor leagues.'"

◆

Sewell always held it against me that he was sent to the minor leagues and lost out on the World Championship. Playing ball, he didn't bother me and I didn't bother him. We just stayed away from each other. I just let bygones be bygones.

I never thought about anti-Semitism then. All I thought about was being a ballplayer. None of the people I was involved with were bankers or business-men, so I was never aware of the business and social barriers to Jews that existed in this country in the 1920s and 1930s. There was never any talk of anti-Semitism in my neighborhood. Everybody kept his place, so we were never aware of it. If you lived in a Jewish neighborhood and everybody was Jewish, all you knew was that there were goyim—the Gentiles—out in the world, but you didn't know about anti-Semitism. But I would learn.

One day I heard a story from Malcolm Bingay, the editor-in-chief of the Detroit Free Press. He covered the Detroit team in 1908 and 1909 when they won the pennant. He was a great friend of Ty Cobb. He told me that Cobb once said, "The reason I know I can hit is that when I get up to the plate and the bases are full, I grab the bat and say to myself, 'Look at that unfortunate bastard out there hav-ing to face the great Ty Cobb with the bases full.' I convinced myself that if the bases were full, the pitcher would be scared of me, not the other way around."

I adopted that philosophy later in my career and in life and tried to convince myself that, with men on base and everybody calling me names, they were really afraid of me and I had the edge. I was the only player who would swing *three* bats in the on-deck circle. Others swung only two. As I strode to the plate, I would discard two of the bats, walk into the box, dig in, and glare at the pitcher, as if to say, "Come on and throw it. I'll knock it downtown." It was a psycho-logical ploy. I just wanted them to have respect for me. It worked a lot of the time, and it was good for my ego.

It also helped that I kept a mental book on the pitchers, as well as statistics on all the players. I was what was known as a guess-hitter and I looked for certain pitches in certain situations, and therefore had to know who I was bat-ting against. I had pretty good success in knowing what was coming. And, of course, if you know what's coming up, you have a big advantage.

We had an outstanding team. The infield—with Charlie Gehringer at second, Billy Rogell at short, and Marv Owen at third—was superb both defensively and offensively. In 1934 our infield batted in a record 462 runs: 139 for me, 127 for Gehringer, 100 for Rogell, and 96 for Owen. The next year we batted in 400 runs again—including 170 for me and 108 for Gehringer.

In the outfield, Goose Goslin batted in about 100 runs each year, and Jo-Jo White, Pete Fox, and Gee Walker did their share, too. With Schoolboy Rowe, Tommy Bridges, Elden Auker, Firpo Marberry, and General Crowder pitching, and Cochrane catching, I think we had one of the all-time great teams.

We had four future Hall of Famers on that team—Gehringer, Goose, Cochrane, and me. Gehringer was possibly the best second baseman who ever lived, a marvelous player, and Mickey Cochrane was maybe the best all-around catcher.

Nineteen thirty-four went into the record books as the making of a ballplayer as far as I was concerned. Early in the season I was batting sixth in the lineup. Goose Goslin was hitting in the cleanup spot. It was the only time in my Major League career that I was down that low in the lineup. I had always batted cleanup. I was always the leading home-run hitter on my team. After about the first thirty or forty games I started to raise my average and drive in runs, and finally Cochrane put me in the cleanup position. From then on I really went to town and so did the team. We started to win ball games and, the first thing we knew, we were in first place, battling the Yankees for the American League championship.

◆

The Yankees led the American League for much of the early season, while the Tigers stayed in second place. After the All-Star game break the Yankees came into Detroit for a four-game series with a three-and-a-half-game lead over the Tigers. The Tigers won two of the first three games.

Of the fourth game, on July 15, *The New York Times* said:

"Henry Greenberg dealt the Yankees a crushing blow at Navin Field before 26,000 highly excited fans.

"With the score tied at 2-all in the sixth inning of the last game in this crucial series, [Greenberg] blasted a double that cleared the bases of two occupants. The encouragement this hit provided sent the Tigers on to greater heights and they won the ball game, 8–3.

"Tonight, the Yankees trail league-leading Detroit by 1½ games."

At the end of July, Harry Salsinger of the *Detroit News* wrote:

"The development of Greenberg is one of the most amazing features of an amazing baseball season. He was a good hitter last year and a long one, but today he is one of the most powerful sluggers who has come along in years. All at once he gained the confidence. . . . The unusual feature of Greenberg's development is that Greenberg's fielding has improved with his hitting. He was probably the weakest fielder among the first basemen of the American League last season but today his defensive work is as good as you will see. . . .

"He is, on top of his mechanical skill, an ideal kind of player. He is of the winning type, the ultra-aggressive competitor with loads of courage and at his best in the tight spots.

"The boy Greenberg has grown into quite a baseball player."

Bud Shaver, of the *Detroit Times*, wrote that Greenberg is "the most energetic researcher in baseball . . . [and is] tireless in his quest for perfection, wants to know all the answers and isn't backward about asking.

"He argues continually with anybody at any time, probing calmly into other people's minds for information, knowledge, and ideas. He has a mind of his own, too, a good one, which he exercises as religiously as he does his muscles.

"He parrots no opinions, but challenges any statement which is not in line with his own experience. He does it not to be contentious or contrary, but to find the answers.

"Greenberg will listen with attentive respect to anyone whose baseball experience entitles [him to] it, but he is not content with trite answers. He inquires also the whys and wherefores.

"This active, inquiring turn of mind is a large factor in Greenberg's improvement. . . ."

An example of Greenberg's inquiring mind, wrote Shaver, was the following exchange with Jimmie Foxx, the great first baseman and slugger:

"After hours, Greenberg cultivated Foxx's acquaintance and frankly asked for information and advice.

"Foxx . . . wasn't stingy with advice.

"'He told me some things which have helped me,' said Greenberg. 'I've put them into practice and already I can see the difference.'"

"One thing which bothered Hank was the proper manner in which to grip the bat. So he asked Foxx.

"'You worry too much about how you hold the bat and your position at the plate,' said Foxx. 'Don't think about how you hold your hands. Just grip your bat in a comfortable way so that it feels natural. Concentrate on watching the ball and then swing into it and hit it.

"'If you are worrying about the position of your hands on the bat, how far you carry the bat back and other details of your swing, you can't possibly concentrate your attention upon the most important thing of all—hitting the baseball.

"'You crouch over too much,' continued Professor Foxx. 'Don't do that. Don't bend your knee. Stand firmly upon both feet in a comfortable position with your head up so you can watch the ball.

"'If you lean over or crouch, your vision is not proper. You are watching the ball from a strained and difficult angle.

"'Stand up closer to the plate. It's a more comfortable position and you get more power into your swing.'

"Greenberg did not accept Foxx's advice as gospel, until he had tested its reasonableness as regards himself in actual practice.

"'You see,' Greenberg explained, 'Foxx is one person and I am another. What might be right for him might be all wrong for Greenberg. But some of the things he has told me and shown me are sound and fit in all right with me. . . . That advice about my hands, my stance and my swing I have found helpful. I do feel more comfortable up at the plate and I have more confidence, because I am free to concentrate on the business of hitting the ball.' . . .

"Baseball is no two-hour job for Greenberg. He works at it 24 hours a day, because when he dreams he dreams about the day when he will be a great ballplayer.

"When Greenberg finishes his baseball career he will be able to write the best textbook ever written upon hitting and playing first base, because he is the most tireless student since Cobb."

There were also discussions of Greenberg the Jewish ballplayer. Paul Gallico wrote in the *New York Daily News* that "New York ball clubs for years have been searching for a sort of talisman, or philosopher's stone, in the shape of a Jewish ballplayer. The last seen around town was when the Giants had a schlemiel named Andy Cohen who was always falling down on his way to first base or getting his legs crossed during the course of a play. His name was OK but his batting average was terrible and so he vanished from the scene."

In an Indianapolis Jewish periodical, under the headline THE JEWISH BABE RUTH, Bertram Jones wrote: "In this long quest [for a Jewish star], the Giants tried out scores of players, among them Phil Weintraub from Chicago, Andy Cohen from El Paso, Jake Levy from Charlotte, Harry Rosenberg from San Francisco and Moe Solomon from Indianapolis, while the Yankees looked over Jimmy Reese from Oakland."

And in the *American Hebrew* and *Jewish Tribune*, Greenberg was described as "that elusive Hebrew star."

◆

A truly exciting moment in my Major League career took place on September 10, 1934—Rosh Hashanah, the Jewish New Year. The team was fighting for first place, and I was probably the only batter in the lineup who was not in a slump. But in the Jewish religion, it is traditional that one observe the holiday solemnly, with prayer. One should not engage in work or play. And I wasn't sure what to do. It became a national issue. There was a big question in the press about whether I would play first base for the Tigers that day.

On the front page of that morning's *Detroit Free Press* was a headline in Yiddish, and then over it the English translation, "Happy New Year, Hank." To this day, I am very proud of that.

◆

Beneath the headline was a large picture of Hank Greenberg, number 5, swinging at a pitch, his Tiger cap pulled low on his head, his pants baggy and ballooning at the knees in the style of the day.

Before the game, wrote Charles P. Ward in the *Detroit Free Press*, "Hank sat on the Tiger bench and looked gloomily down the line at Rogell, Gehringer, and Owen. He eyed Goose Goslin and Jo-Jo White and Auker, who was going to pitch.

"Greenberg said to a reporter, 'We're only four games ahead of the Yankees now. Suppose I stay out of the game and we lost the pennant by one game? That will keep the boys out of the World Series after they have worked so hard all season to get into the Series. Would that be justice? What'll they think? And what will Detroit think?'

"Hank had no way of telling, for down the bench the boys were grimly spitting tobacco juice upon the floor and waiting for the game to get going. Out in the stands the fans didn't know what Hank was going through."

And Elden Auker, the Detroit submarine pitcher, recalled years later:

"I didn't know what Rosh Hashanah was. The papers said Hank wasn't going to play because it was a Jewish holiday. That's when I found out what Rosh Hashanah was. He didn't take batting practice. I was a little upset because I thought I'm going to pitch a ball game without Hank. He was pretty important to us.

"I came from Kansas and I never knew what a Jew was. Never gave it a thought. I would say Hank was the first Jewish person I ever met. The Jewish people in those days weren't in Kansas. And I never looked at Hank any other way except just like a guy looks at the rest of the guys. And so all I knew was, I hoped Hank would play."

Marv Owen, the Detroit third baseman, recalled:

"Hank and I were next-door locker mates for six years. Here comes Rosh Hashanah and I get to the clubhouse and Hank is sitting on top of his stool with no uniform on. I walked over to him and said, 'What the hell is the matter with you, you sick?' He said, 'No.'

"I said, 'Is something bothering you?'

"He said, 'I don't know what to do.'

"'You gotta play ball, that's what you gotta do.'

"'No, it's one of my church holidays.'

"I said, 'Hank, I got an idea. In twenty minutes we're all going to be out there for batting practice. The first thing that comes to your mind, do it. If it says, play—play. If it says don't play—don't play.' We got through batting practice and we come in, there's Hank in his uniform. He says, 'I'm going to play.'"

◆

The newspapers had gone to the top rabbi in Detroit and asked him if it would be socially acceptable for me to play on that day. The rabbi was supposed to have looked in the Talmud and he came up with the theory that since it was the start of a new year, and it was supposed to be a happy day, he found that Jews in history had played games on that day, and he felt that it would be perfectly all right for me to play baseball. That momentous decision made it possible for me to stay in the lineup on Rosh Hashanah, and lo and behold I hit two home runs—the second in the ninth inning—and we beat Boston 2–1.

◆

Bud Shaver wrote: "Greenberg probably never before hit a ball as hard as he hit that second pitch that Gordon Rhodes tossed up to him in the ninth. He smashed a slow ball over the scoreboard in the seventh, a towering drive that cleared the barrier with some to spare, and Rhodes made the fatal mistake of trying to throw a fast one past the big fellow in the ninth with the count one ball and no strikes.

"Hank met the pitch perfectly. The ball sailed on a line, cleared the wall beyond the scoreboard and Henry trotted around the bases as the crowd swarmed on the field. At the plate, Hank was met by a milling throng and it was with difficulty that he made his way to the clubhouse. . . .

"The traditional tenacity of the world's oldest and most beleaguered people today had played its part in a pennant race—winning a ball game. . . . There was more than the mighty bone and sinew of Hank Greenberg behind those two home runs which went whistling out of Navin Field. . . . They were propelled by a force born of the desperation and pride of a young Jew who turned his back on the ancient ways of his race and creed to help his teammates. Greenberg said, 'The good Lord did not let me down. . . .'"

Marv Owen later recalled: "The next day I get to the park, he's in uniform, and he's down in the dumps. I said, 'Goddamnit, Hank, you won the ball game with two home runs, what's wrong?'

"He said, 'When I got back to my hotel my phone rang half the night. I caught hell from my fellow parishioners, I caught hell from some rabbis, and I don't know what to do, it's ten days until the next holiday—Yom Kippur.'

"I said, 'Don't worry, when it comes you'll make the right decision like you did yesterday.'"

In an article the day after Rosh Hashanah, Dan Daniel of the *New York World-Telegram* mentioned that American League bench jockeys "ragged" Greenberg with "pants presser," a racial reference, and a common one, referring to the many tailors among Jews and Jewish immigrants. Such slurs increasingly troubled and angered Greenberg, but he tried to ignore them, not always successfully.

Yom Kippur, ten days after Rosh Hashanah, was, as Owen recalled, another important decision for Greenberg. Yom Kippur is the day of atonement, the most sacred holiday of the year for Jews.

On Yom Kippur, September 18, *The New York Times* wrote that the Tigers had the American League pennant all but "signed, sealed and delivered." And that Greenberg, who was batting .338 with 25 home runs, "was the most important cog" on the team. But this time, Greenberg chose not to play.

The *New York Evening Post* went to Greenberg's parents in the Bronx for another angle on the story.

"We are an Orthodox family," Mr. Greenberg was quoted as saying. "He promised us when we saw him in Philadelphia on Detroit's last trip to the East that he would not play on Rosh Hashanah or Yom Kippur. He wrote us later that he was sorry he had played on Rosh Hashanah, but Mickey Cochrane said he was needed and Henry could not refuse very well."

"It's not so terrible, either," Mrs. Greenberg cut in. "I see young men go to the temple in the morning and then maybe do worse things than Henry did."

"Yom Kippur was different," Mr. Greenberg said. "I put my foot down and Henry obeyed."

◆

It was big news. I even received attention from Edgar Guest, the nationally syndicated popular newspaper poet. He wrote a poem about me concerning the Jewish holidays.

This is how it went:

SPEAKING OF GREENBERG
by Edgar A. Guest

The Irish didn't like it when they heard of Greenberg's fame
For they thought a good first baseman should possess an Irish name;
And the Murphys and Mulrooneys said they never dreamed they'd see
A Jewish boy from Bronxville out where Casey used to be.
In the early days of April not a Dugan tipped his hat
Or prayed to see a "double" when Hank Greenberg came to bat.
In July the Irish wondered where he'd ever learned to play.
"He makes me think of Casey!" Old Man Murphy dared to say;
And with fifty-seven doubles and a score of homers made
The respect they had for Greenberg was being openly displayed.
But on the Jewish New Year when Hank Greenberg came to bat
And made two home runs off Pitcher Rhodes—they cheered like mad
    for that.

Came Yom Kippur—holy fast day world wide over to the Jew—
And Hank Greenberg to his teaching and the old tradition true
Spent the day among his people and he didn't come to play.
Said Murphy to Mulrooney, "We shall lose the game today!
We shall miss him on the infield and shall miss him at the bat,
But he's true to his religion—and I honor him for that!"

I was a hero around town, particularly among the Jewish people, and I was very proud of it.

On Yom Kippur, my friends, a family named Allen, took me to shul [synagogue]. We walked in about 10:30 in the morning and the place was jammed. The rabbi was davening [praying]. Right in the middle of everything, everything seemed to stop. The rabbi looked up; he didn't know what was going on. And suddenly everybody was applauding. I was embarrassed; I didn't know what to do. It was a tremendous ovation for a kid who was only twenty-three years old, and in a synagogue, no less!

People remember that I didn't play on Yom Kippur. They remember it as every year, but in fact the situation arose only once, in 1934.

It's a strange thing. When I was playing I used to resent being singled out as a Jewish ballplayer, period. I'm not sure why or when I changed, because I'm still not a particularly religious person. Lately, though, I find myself wanting to be remembered not only as a great ballplayer, but even more as a great *Jewish* ballplayer.

I realize now, more than I used to, how important a part I played in the lives of a generation of Jewish kids who grew up in the thirties.

I guess I was a kind of role model, and strangely enough, I think this may have begun in sports with Babe Ruth, though, of course, much of the interest in me had the special nature of my religion. When Babe emerged as the great home-run hitter, the baseball fans took him to heart and made a hero out of him. While Babe wasn't exemplary off the field, they overlooked it and only talked about his prowess on the field. He was a hero and despite his sexual appetite and drinking too much and eating too much, he also used to go to a lot of hospitals and visit kids who were sick, and the photographers would go with him. He did a lot of good in that respect. From then on, ballplayers were elevated from being just more or less outcasts in society; they were becoming accepted. Even the best hotels were accepting them. The players started to dress a little better and act a little differently and they curbed their manner of speech somewhat.

In a nutshell, the Major League ballplayer became a respectable citizen. And so the ballplayer learned that he had to set an example for young America, for the kids, and do all sorts of things like autographing and making appearances at different places, trying to be a role model. That was expected of ballplayers, since they were getting all this publicity and adulation from the fans.

It was also a somewhat optimistic time economically, and this also helped focus people's attention on baseball. Detroit was just starting to come out of the Depression in 1934. The newspapers used to comment frequently on the emergence of the Detroit Tigers as a pennant-winning team, since it was the first time they had won a pennant in twenty-five years. They claimed that the spirit of Detroit, the enthusiasm of the fans, plus the brightening economic picture all came together to create a very exciting, charged atmosphere in Detroit.

CHAPTER 5

Malcolm Bingay, who later became editor-in-chief of the *Detroit Free Press,* made an eastern trip with us in 1934 because he covered the Tigers in 1909, when they had won their last pennant. He had written under the name of "Iffy the Dopester," and it was very popular. Malcolm and I sat on the train and discussed baseball and he extolled the virtues of the old-timers. He told me about how Ty Cobb used to score from first base on a single. That's almost impossible, but he said Cobb did it frequently. Naturally I challenged that statement and we argued about it. Well, we were in Boston one day and I was on first base with two out. Goose Goslin, a left-handed hitter, was up and the count was 3 and 2. I'm off with the pitch, and Goose hits a ground ball to the left of the second baseman who knocks it down and pushes it out into short right field. I round second and I see the second baseman picking up the ball and trying to throw Goslin out at first base. I figured that the first baseman would never dream that I'd try to score on that play, so I kept going and slid home in a cloud of dust—safe! With that, I rose, looked up at Malcolm in the press box behind home plate, and said, "That's your old Ty Cobb, Malcolm!"

You can be sure that was the first and last time I ever scored from first base on a single.

Jo-Jo White and Mickey Cochrane had a play which you would never see today. When Jo-Jo was on second base with none out, Mickey would fake a bunt on the first pitch but deliberately miss the ball. That would draw the infield in. Then, on the second pitch, Mickey again would square away to bunt, the third baseman would come charging in, and Jo-Jo would steal third because nobody was covering. Mickey, of course, would miss the pitch or take it. And we'd have a man on third with nobody out, instead of wasting a sacrifice.

That's the kind of plays the ballplayers worked on in those days. They had the time, they had the inclination, and they had the competition for their jobs. If you didn't perform, if you weren't a .300 hitter, you might wind up in the minor leagues. There was so much competition that every club had a couple of ballplayers in the minors who were ready to come up and take your place, whereas today you frequently see an outfielder playing first base or a third baseman playing first base or a third baseman playing outfield. They switch around their jobs; none of them really learn how to play their positions as perfectly as we did. When a ballplayer came up and he was a shortstop, he remained a shortstop for his career.

In 1934 the Detroit infield played every game, 154 of them, with the exception of me, and I played 153 games, having stayed out of that one game because of Yom Kippur. The important thing was that, combined, we drove in those 463 runs, which is by far the largest number of runs for any infield in the history of the game. Yet that little tidbit hardly got out to the public. Even today, besides Gehringer, Rogell, Owen, and me, only a few fans know about it. But that's the way they kept secrets in Detroit. They didn't believe in publicizing the ballplayers because they were afraid they might have to pay them a little more money if they did. Meanwhile, we clinched the pennant, then went on to play the St. Louis Cardinals in the World Series.

◆

Tom Meany, on September 17, noted: "Detroit has gone mad about the Tigers. One local paper has nine writers for each game." Dan Daniel wrote that Hank Greenberg was "the chief reason for the Tigers' success," and Sam Murphy in the *New York Sun* wrote: "Hank Greenberg, the young Jewish player . . . [is] one of the best players who ever wore that famous Bengal livery."

◆

Two unusual items are worth noting. One was that the 1934 season was the first time in the history of the Detroit club, which stretched back some sixty years, that it drew a million fans in home attendance.

Also, this was the introduction of radio broadcasting of the World Series. The Ford Motor Company of Detroit had put up $100,000 for the broadcasting rights. Judge Landis, the baseball commissioner, not certain what to do, assigned the money to the players' pool. Little did he know at the time that subsequently millions of dollars would go into the players' pool through television and radio revenues. It set the precedent and almost twenty years later, when I represented the owners on the pension committee, it was an established fact that the television money belonged to the players.

The Cardinals had been a hot ball club in September, winning twenty of their last twenty-five games. Our natural opponents, at least we thought they were going to be our opponents, were the New York Giants, our old traveling mates in spring training. They had been leading the league most of the year and looked like they were on their way to a pennant when the Cardinals made the charge in September, coming from seven games back. The Dean boys continued pitching well—Dizzy won thirty games and Paul nineteen—and so, to our surprise, we were to face the Cardinals rather than the Giants.

◆

While the World Series was about to begin, another sporting event was also just getting started, from both an organizational and political standpoint. That was the 1936 Olympics, which would come to be known as the Nazi Olympics and were to be staged in Berlin, Germany. The United States Olympic Committee had, upon assurance from Germany that German Jews would not be discriminated against in selection of the German Olympic team, voted unanimously to accept Germany's invitation to participate in the games. In 1934, Avery Brundage, the chairman of the USOC, went to Germany, according to the acerbic columnist Westbrook Pegler, "to look into certain vague rumors regarding the treatment to which the Jew is subjected under Adolf Hitler, and, happily, was able to assure his colleagues that the Germans would be fair and sportsmanlike to all Jewish athletes for the duration of the games. . . .

"[The Germans] might even require Jewish swimmers to race their heats with an anvil under each arm and Jewish high jumpers to wear the standard Oregon boot as part of their equipment. But there is only a limited amount of fair play in Germany at this writing, and, on the basis of the census figures, the Jews ought not to complain if the Aryans give themselves 95 percent of the available supply and the other 5 percent to the Jews."

On another continent another Jew, Hank Greenberg, was now involved in a sporting event that had also captured the attention and imagination of millions.

◆

Much has been written about the 1934 World Series over the years because it was a classic series, going seven games. There were two very exciting teams. The Cardinals had Frank Frisch as manager and second baseman; Leo Durocher at shortstop; and the Dean boys, Dizzy and Paul, pitching. Including Rip Collins at first base and Pepper Martin at third, they had a solid ballplayer at every position, as did we.

◆

In the *New York Sun* on October 2, the day before the 1934 World Series began, an article noted:

"The first controversy of the 1934 Series may be waged around Hank Greenberg's glove . . . the elaborate bicycle-taped webbing Hank has rigged up in the opening between the big thumb and the squat body of the first baseman's mitt. He has it protruding over the rim of his mitt about three inches, looking for all the world like a miniature lacrosse stick. . . .

"There is nothing in the rule book to bar it. It [the problem] is the sticky surfacing which Hank applies to his mitt in the course of a ball game. He gets it from the licorice which he chews and squirts onto the glove. It makes the glove sticky, it makes the ball stick, and it makes Hank a surer first baseman.

"Having battled his way through the regular season defending himself against the charge of unfair practice, Hank is prepared to combat any Cardinal protests. He is going right on with his licorice chewing, but only on one side of his mouth. On the other he has a wad of gum. Umpires have come up to Hank before and asked him what he was chewing.

"'Gum,' he has answered, truthfully enough, and produced it.

"He is ready to do it again—with the licorice shifted out of bounds in favor of gum whenever it becomes necessary."

Frisch, entering his eighth World Series, said, "I'll never forget my first World Series. That was 1921. I didn't know where I was or what was going on. . . . I didn't know whether I was coming or going. All I remember was that I was so nervous I couldn't talk. . . . That's why I get a kick out of watching young players in their first World Series. It's bound to get your nerves. You're not human if it doesn't—the crowds and the excitement and the big stakes. . . . That is one thing Dizzy Dean does. He boasts and then goes out and makes good."

Dean won the first game, 8–3, though his fastball and breaking balls weren't "sharp," according to Dean himself. Greenberg singled in the sixth inning and homered into the newly constructed bleachers in Navin Field in the eighth.

Dean later explained the home run this way: "I got a kick out of pitching to Greenberg. He couldn't see my fastball so I tells Frankie Frisch that I wanted to see this feller hit one. I'd heard tell he was some shakes as a batter so I gave him one where he liked it. He cow tailed it, too. . . . [But] anybody could have hit that ball for a home run. Our clubhouse boy could have done it."

Durocher also gave little credit to Greenberg:

"Greenberg got that homer off a curve that didn't break. He [Dean] was just tired after a big season. . . ."

In the next two games Greenberg managed only one hit (a triple) in eight at bats and struck out three times.

In the bottom of the third inning of the second game with St. Louis leading 2–0 and two outs for Detroit, wrote Joe Williams in the *New York World-Telegram*, "Cochrane was loudly cheered when he came to bat and walked. Then Gehringer singled Mike over to third and brought up Hank Greenberg, putting him on the spot again, with a chance to tie up the game. Up to now this entire series seems to consist of putting Hank on the spot.

"The first two pitches were balls and then [Bill] Hallahan south-pawed two strikes over, both called. Hank struck out on a fastball inside and the threat was over. Greenberg muffed the same chance yesterday against Dizzy Dean, fanning on the same sort of pitch."

"In the third inning [of the third game in St. Louis] . . . ," wrote Roy Stockton in the *St. Louis Post Dispatch*, the "Tigers were on second and third with only one out and the stands rumbling with alarm. Again Paul [Dean] turned to his pet and his fastball was good enough to strike out the powerful Greenberg, who helped by swinging at a bad pitch on the third strike."

". . . In the ninth, with White on first and two out and the score 4–0, in favor of St. Louis, Greenberg tripled to the wall, scoring White. But Detroit could get nothing else, and lost 4–1. In the dressing room afterward," wrote Tom Meany in the *New York World-Telegram*, "Diz beckoned the newspapermen to him in a mock gesture of confidence and said, 'Now, boys, don't let this get out, but you know that ball Greenberg hit in the ninth—well, Paul just laid it in there for him. Felt sorry for the poor guy, striking out all the time!'"

By now, in fact, Greenberg had struck out four times in the Series with men in scoring position. Until that triple, Greenberg had been up eight times with men on, but had failed to advance a single runner.

And Schoolboy Rowe commented: "I am hoping that the long triple by Hank . . . is the break in [his] hitting slump. He hasn't been hitting in his usual form, even though he did pole a powerful homer in the opening game. . . . He just is pressing too much, I think. Once he starts to hit we will be a different-looking team. . . ."

By Game 4, Stockton was writing: "Hank Greenberg, the wild-swinging first baseman, who batted fourth during most of the league season, will drop to sixth position in the hitting order, with Goose Goslin moving up to . . . cleanup."

Greenberg later admitted that "before the Series I was so nervous I couldn't eat." And he had been playing that way, but in Game 4, Greenberg broke out of his slump, going 4-for-5. It was only a momentary bright spot, however, and one of his few in the Series. In the next game, facing Dizzy Dean, he was 0-for-3, and struck out once.

The Tigers won Game 5, 3–1. Greenberg was 0–3 with a strikeout.

◆

In Game 6, we had Schoolboy Rowe on the mound against Paul Dean. We came back to Detroit leading three games to two, and it looked like we were going to clinch the World Series with Schoolboy, our ace pitcher—who had won twenty-four games and lost only eight during the season—on the mound at home before the home fans.

Unfortunately that was not the case, as Paul Dean and the Cardinals beat us by a score of 4–3. I went 1-for-4, an RBI single. It was now three games apiece, and we were to face Dizzy Dean in the seventh game.

◆

Dean, who enjoyed needling the opposition in his Ozark fashion, came onto the field before pitching the seventh and deciding game of the Series in Detroit, and, wrote Roy Stockton in the *Saturday Evening Post*, "he paused a moment at the Detroit dugout, where he spied Hank Greenberg.

"'Hello, Mose,' said Dizzy. 'What makes you so white? Boy, you're a-shakin' like a leaf. I get it; you done hear that Old Diz was goin' to pitch. Well, you're right. It'll all be over in a few minutes. Old Diz is goin' to pitch, and he's goin' to pin your ears back.'"

Leo Durocher recalled years later that Dean would do this kind of thing regularly. "Once," said Durocher, "Dizzy went into the Brooklyn clubhouse and began going down the batting order and telling hitters how he was going to pitch to them. 'You, nuthin' but fastballs.' 'You, I'm gonna start with a curve.' 'And you, the first pitch is gonna be behind you.'"

Durocher later recalled Dean hollering to Greenberg after he made an error, "Hey, Moe"—"Moe" or "Mose," for "Moses," was a common name applied jocularly to Jewish players—"c'mon in the clubhouse and get your meal money. You're the best player we got."

More than simply making fun of Greenberg off the field, Dizzy Dean was criticized by some for his on-field activities while pitching to Greenberg. Joe Williams of the *World-Telegram* wrote that Dean's "behaviorism" to Greenberg "of the Bronx was both vulgar and unsporting," and "strikes me as being ridiculous. Mr. Dizzy would throw his curve at our Hankus and start laughing even before the ball got to the plate. Our Hankus would make a motion with his bat as if he were painting a fence, and he would be out. In this manner our Hankus fanned three times, and Mr. Dean had a very large and jovial afternoon.

"From the standpoint of baseball there was nothing wrong about the performance that our Hankus couldn't have corrected by driving the ball down Mr. Dizzy's throat. It just happened that he wasn't good enough to do this. . . . "

◆

Before the seventh and final game, it had been nip and tuck between the teams. We split the first two games in Detroit, and we won two out of three in St. Louis. We beat Dizzy in one game, and lost to Paul Dean twice. That was our real stumbling block. We had more trouble with Paul Dean than we did with Dizzy, although Dizzy did win two out of the three games that he appeared in.

We had to start a rookie pitcher in the final game—Elden Auker, who had only the third best record on our staff. Cochrane had to rely on him because we had failed to clinch the Series in the sixth game.

Well, Dizzy shut us out 11–0 in the seventh game after the Cardinals scored seven runs off Auker in the third inning. The game became famous because it was the first time in a World Series that a player was asked to leave the game. When Ducky Medwick, who had tripled, slid into third base, and had kind of a tiff with Marv Owen, our third baseman, the fans had to vent their spleen and threw debris on the field. We were losing by a big score, and it looked like the World Series was going down the drain. Judge Landis had to call time and ask Medwick to leave the field to avoid a riot. There was no telling what might have happened if Medwick had continued in the game.

◆

In the last inning of the final game, with Detroit losing 11–0, and two on and one out, Greenberg struck out against Dean for the third time in the game, and the ninth in the series. Owen batted next and hit into a force play and the Series was over.

Greenberg would admit that "Dean made me look like a monkey. . . . They tell me I swung at the ball two feet over my head. I don't doubt it." But it wasn't just the pitching that was troublesome. The bench jockeying was vicious, and months later Frank Frisch acknowledged this: "We had a hot ball club last year. I'm not bragging— I'm just telling you we were hot, hot and colorful. . . . I'm talking about the Deans and [Pepper] Martin and Durocher and Medwick and the rest of them. They didn't care about anything and weren't afraid of anybody. They came out the first day [of the Series] and almost the first fellow they saw in the Detroit dugout was Rowe, so they started on him and, believe me, they gave him plenty of that 'How'm I doin', Edna?' and stuff like that, and then they started on Greenberg, and the things they said to him were something awful. All during the series there were four fellows on our bench that you wouldn't think would ever say a word to anybody, but they kept after Greenberg until the poor guy was nearly crazy. . . . "

Near the end of the Series, Hugh Bradley of the *New York Post* wrote that "indeed, although [Greenberg] has been rather dismal upon several occasions when runners looked pleadingly at him from third base, the Tigers have not done so badly with him during the present affair. . . . [He continues to be] a dangerous hitter. . . ." He believed, from observing him "closely in the dugout and on the field [that], . . . young Hank is one of the Detroit players who definitely is not cracking under the strain and who is not giving up."

◆

The Cardinals gave me hell in the 1934 Series. I didn't have a great Series, but I didn't have a bad one either. But the press was looking for a scapegoat. The Cardinals called me everything under the sun. Anyway, I struck out nine times in seven games, but I also drove in seven runs, one short of the record for RBIs in the World Series at the time, and hit .321 in my first World Series, not terrible. And I did better than Goslin and Gehringer and the rest.

◆

Back in New York, Greenberg, wrote the *Jewish Daily Bulletin*, received "a hero's welcome." At one banquet an old friend told the audience, "Hank was always a big fellow . . . [and] until a few years ago was the gangliest guy you ever saw. Undoubtedly the Tiger scout remarked to Bruggy about this matter and told him he'd go places if this awkwardness were removed. And what do you think Hank did? That guy, weighing 215 pounds and standing six foot four, took dancing lessons to develop himself into a Major League ballplayer."

Greenberg also attended a dinner at the Town Hall Club in support of the second Maccabean Games, or "International Jewish Olympics," to be held the following April in Tel Aviv, Palestine. Besides Greenberg, some of the other "outstanding Jewish sports personalities" at the function, according to the *New York Herald Tribune*, were Harry Newman, quarterback of the football Giants; Benny Leonard, former world middleweight boxing champion; Nat Holman, CCNY basketball coach; Irving Jaffee, former Olympic skating champion; Abel Kiviat and Pinkie Sober, former national track champions; and Miss Millicent Hirsch, tennis player.

Over the winter, as usual, Greenberg stayed in shape by playing mostly handball and squash. According to an old friend, Bill Rosen, he once had taken boxing lessons, to be "ready if necessary to handle himself." A newspaper photo showed Greenberg with boxing gloves punching a speed bag. But a subsequent newspaper item during that time said that Greenberg had decided not to take boxing lessons because, he thought, they "might hurt my hands."

◆

Early in my career I sometimes played in basketball games during the off-season. My last basketball game was played, though, after the '34 World Series. A semi-pro basketball team called the Brooklyn Jewels, comprised of graduates of the great St. John's College basketball team, hired me to play one game with them in Brooklyn. They advertised that I was being paid $100 a minute, an outlandish, fabulous sum of money for basketball players. What they didn't say was that they only played me for three minutes, so my total take was $300. That publicity stunt naturally made the newspapers, and Mr. Navin caught wind of it and wrote me this letter:

Dear Mr. Greenberg:

I notice in the papers that you are going to engage in basket-ball [sic]. I wish you would look at your contract, under Section 4, and see where you agreed when you signed same that while you were under contract or reservation that you would not engage in any exhibition of football, basketball, hockey or other athletic sport. The worst possible thing a person of your build and who is bothered with his feet could do is to play basket-ball—in addition to the fact that it slows you up. Bucky Harris told me that he figured that playing basket-ball cost him five years of professional baseball. He meant that it slowed him up so that he was not of any use five years before he was through playing baseball.

Notwithstanding this, you agreed not to play the game, and I would like to call your attention to this fact because I figure that you should live up to your contract.

I will not go any further into the matter until I hear from you.

Very truly yours,

Frank J. Navin

◆

Greenberg decided to give up basketball.

Navin also wrote about the $500 bonus Greenberg would get if the Tigers finished in first, second, or third place, plus Greenberg's monthly salary of $500. Instead of receiving $1,000, Greenberg only got $868.74. As Navin explained:

Friend Greenberg:

I am enclosing herewith check No. 17774, on the National Bank of Detroit, payable to your order in the amount of $868.74. This check, plus the following charges as turned in by Arthur Sheahan, totaling $48.00 and itemized as follows:

Your brother's room at Kingsway Hotel, St. Louis—$1.50.

Suit Roll, Uniform, and Jacket—$46.50.

Total the amount of the last check that you should receive from Detroit; namely $416.74—plus $500 bonus.

You will be given a check covering the charge of $46.50 when the uniform, jacket, and suit roll are returned to Detroit.

With kind regards and best wishes for a pleasant winter, I remain

Very truly yours,

Frank J. Navin

On January 15, 1935, Navin sent another letter to Greenberg, who was vacationing in Miami Beach.

Friend Greenberg:

Enclosed find contract for the season of 1935 calling for $10,000. I also enclose duplicate of same for your records.

The enclosed clipping was out of The Times. *I hope at the end of the season Mr. Barrow will revise his opinion.*

With kind regards, I am,

Very truly yours,

Frank J. Navin

The clipping read:

TROSKY IS FUTURE GEHRIG OF LOOP

"Ed Barrow [general manager] of the Yankees says Hal Trosky, Cleveland's first sacker, is the future Lou Gehrig of the league.

"'He is a much greater ballplayer than Hank Greenberg,' said Barrow. 'He will develop much faster than Greenberg and someday will rank as the greatest hitting first baseman in his league.'

"All that remains to be seen. But it is not getting around the fact that Mr. Trosky is doing right by himself."

In fact, Trosky had had a terrific season in 1934, his rookie year, batting .330 (9 points fewer than Greenberg), hitting 35 home runs (9 more than Greenberg), and driving in 142 runs (3 more than Greenberg).

◆

That winter there was a lot of discussion in the Greenberg household regarding how much money I would get paid for 1935. Mr. Navin attended a Major League meeting in New York in January 1935. He was at the Commodore Hotel and invited me to visit him to discuss my contract. He had said the previous winter that I hadn't proven myself as a Major Leaguer and I had to show that I could perform for two years, rather than one, before I could indicate that I had made good in the Major Leagues. Well, I had done just that, even beyond my expectations, and certainly beyond his, since we had won the pennant. I was looking forward eagerly to seeing him and presenting him with my ideas for my salary.

I met him at the Commodore Hotel. Since I had received only $5,000 for my performance in 1934, I did not hesitate when he asked me what I wanted for 1935. I said, "I think I'm worth $15,000." Of course, that was tripling my salary. I expected some argument from him, but he surprised me.

He said, "Young man, you've proven that you are going to have a good year, and I'm going to give you $15,000. However, I'm going to give you a $10,000 contract and a $5,000 bonus."

I said, "I don't care how you give it to me, as long as you and I understand that my salary is $15,000. That's the starting point for the following year, and I don't intend to have you tell me that it was $10,000."

He said, "That's all right; we understand each other. I'm going to send you a contract for $10,000 and I'm going to write you out a check right now for $5,000." And he did. I took this check for $5,000 and, as I remember, I was afraid to take the subway back to the Bronx, so I walked across the street and went to the Bowery Savings Bank and opened up an account for $5,000 right then and there.

Of course, when I got back to the house, everybody in the family was waiting to learn how I had come out. I gave them all a chance to guess at how much I would get and none of them guessed as high as $15,000. In 1935, that $15,000 was an awful lot of money, particularly for a twenty-four-year-old man. The economy hadn't blossomed that much, many people were still out of work, and very few salaries in the American League were higher than that. And here I had only finished my second year in the Major Leagues.

CHAPTER 6

A strange thing happened to me at spring training in 1935.

Before an exhibition game against the Brooklyn Dodgers, I was comparing myself to their players. It suddenly dawned on me that no one on the Brooklyn team had my talent. It was the first time it really occurred to me that I was no longer trying to make good. From that point on I believed I was really an established, key player in the American League.

It is so important to have confidence in yourself. You can't just tell yourself that you can do the job, but after you've proven you can do the job and convinced yourself that you're capable of carrying out a certain level of performance, then you've really got it made.

◆

Greenberg always sought ways to improve his game, a quest that included his equipment. "Hank Greenberg, the Tigers' giant first baseman, is determined to stop all line drives which come his way, if he has to use all the cowhide in Texas," wrote Bud Shaver in the *Detroit Times* on March 13, 1935.

"Last year Hank had a glove made which looked like a mattress for a Singer midget. This year he has a bigger one. It is a half-inch larger in diameter and it looks somewhat like a lobster trap. . . .

"It has a thumb as long as Jimmy Durante's schnozzle. . . . Between the thumb and the rest of the mitt, Hank has something which looks like a fishnet.

"It is his own idea and three glove designers have quit at the place where Hank has his mitts manufactured because Hank insists on having them made that way.

"Hank is that way. He has ideas of his own, which is one of the reasons he is going to be a whale of a ballplayer. He never discards his own notions until completely convinced that someone else's are better.

"Hank approaches life from what might be called a skeptical and scientific attitude. He takes nothing for granted and he'll argue far into the night, if anyone is tough enough to hold out that long.

"Mr. Greenberg is something of a debunker, too. Anyone foolish enough to go around parroting common fallacies in Hank's hearing is leading with his chin."

On March 23, a *Detroit Times* eight-column headline read: GREENBERG LOOMS AS OUTSTANDING PLAYER FOR 1935, with the subhead: Tiger Slugger Training Self to Win Honor. And below that, the story by Shaver noted that "When the ballots are counted in the election of the No. 1 man of baseball at the end of the 1935 season, don't be surprised if the name of Henry Greenberg leads all the rest.

". . . Hank is not satisfied with mere greatness. He wants to be the best."

◆

Well, we got off to a rousing start that spring of 1935. The team got into first place early in the race and stayed there. I had an exceptionally fine first half. I led the league in home runs and believe I set a record with 110 runs batted in by the All-Star game. I came down to the closing week of the season with a chance to win the triple crown. I think I was leading the league at about .338 or .339—and I can recall the day when my average began to drop.

I was playing in Boston, batting against Wes Ferrell. I was 1-for-4 with a home run, and the last time at bat I hit a drive on one hop to Ferrell. It bounced off his glove; he went to retrieve it, and his throw pulled the first baseman off the bag. I thought I had a base hit on that, but the next day when I looked in the newspaper, it was 1-for-5 instead of 2-for-5—the official scorer had called it an error instead of a hit—and my average dropped a point or so. That was very discouraging to me. We went on to Chicago to close out the season. I had 36 home runs, and we had four games to play in two days—doubleheaders on Saturday and Sunday. I think it was the first time that I hit a real slump. I went 0-for-16 in those four ball games. I didn't get any hits, home runs, or runs batted in. To my chagrin, Jimmie Foxx hit 2 home runs in the last game of the Philadelphia team season in Shibe Park, and his home runs tied my record for the season.

In 1984, forty-nine years later, I got a letter from a friend who was a substitute player on the Washington Senators in 1937, and he told me that the Washington catcher was telling Foxx what pitches were coming up. After the game, the catcher was bragging about how he managed to keep me from leading the league in home runs. The pitcher hadn't been aware during the game that his own catcher was giving signs away to the enemy, and when he heard about it, he walked up and punched the catcher in the nose.

I did lead in RBIs, though, with 170. [The next closest was Gehrig, with 119 runs batted in, followed by Foxx with 115, and Trosky 113, all, curiously enough, first basemen. Greenberg's league-leading margin of 51 runs batted in was startling. No other batter in Major League history had ever won the RBI title by a margin of over 40.]

◆

In July, Greenberg, while at the Hotel New Yorker with the Tigers, received a letter and a newspaper clipping from Navin. It seemed simply a friendly gesture, maybe one to give an added psychological boost to Greenberg in his pursuit of the home-run record. And an inspired Greenberg certainly couldn't hurt the gate for the Tigers. It was also in the middle of the season, and so Greenberg couldn't possibly use it against Navin for contract negotiations.

> *Dear Henry:*
> *Someone sent me the enclosed from the* Christian Science Monitor.
> *Thought you would be interested in reading same.*

The headline on the story read: GREENBERG IS ONLY ONE HOMER BEHIND BABE RUTH'S PACE.

The story related how Greenberg "could be earning a very comfortable living outside of baseball and probably with much less effort. But 'Hank' wouldn't get nearly as much fun out of working with his father in the textile industry as he does in driving in runs. . . .

"For some reason he always had trouble hitting in Yankee Stadium, with many of his friends in the grandstand and bleachers. Perhaps he was pressing too hard, trying to make an impression for his friends. However, recently he found the range of Yankee pitching, smashing out 2 long home runs, a double and single in five trips to the plate."

The article also stated that Greenberg had 25 home runs (as of July 5) and Babe Ruth had 26 that date in 1927, the year he set the single-season record of 60.

About a week before that, Greenberg learned that Gehrig had been named to first base on the American League All-Star team. In a doubleheader on that day with the Browns, Greenberg hit 3 homers and boosted his RBI total to 85.

After the game, wrote Charles Ward in the *Detroit Free Press*, "Hank sat in a secluded corner of the lobby of the Tiger hotel and thoughtfully puffed on a cigar.

"'How many RBIs have I got?' he asked an acquaintance.

"'Eighty-four,' he was told.

"'You're wrong,' he replied. 'The number is eighty-five.'

"'How many does Gehrig have?' he asked after a few puffs of his cigar.

"'You don't know, eh? Well, he'll be batting for quite a while before he gets up to eighty-five.'"

The Tigers traveled to Philadelphia and one morning Greenberg was opening his mail at the breakfast table, which he was sharing with Bud Shaver of the *Detroit Times*. "Greenberg passed across a letter, scrawled in a childish hand with pencil on cheap, blue-ruled tablet paper," wrote Shaver. "It was from a 13-year-old Jewish girl. There were a few misspelled words.

"Hank is no cad. He wouldn't give out a letter for publication even from a 13-year-old, but there are one or two things in the letter we are privileged to reveal.

"To that little 13-year-old girl, Hank is a Jew in shining armor. She had been bitterly disappointed in Max Baer [the Jewish boxer who had lost the heavyweight championship to Jimmy Braddock in June of 1935] and was banking all on Hank. She begged him not to fail her or his people. There are thousands of little boys and girls like her.

"'You have an immense responsibility,' we remarked, passing it back.

"Hank's face was grave as he tucked the soiled little letter away in his pocket.

"'Yes, I have,' he said soberly."

◆

In my early years with the Tigers, there was a Detroit restaurant by the name of Joe Muir's Fish House. It was a family affair, and the best-known seafood house at the time. Joe Muir was a big amiable German. I loved to go there three or four times a week. He was always very hospitable and he'd put me off in a corner and wouldn't let people interrupt my meal and ask for autographs. Sometimes, when I hit a home run that put the Tigers ahead or won a game, before I got to the restaurant after the game the headlines in the late afternoon paper would say, HANK HIT ONE. Many times I'd go into Joe Muir's place and all the patrons would get up and give me a standing ovation. It was embarrassing and very heady stuff for a kid who was only twenty-three or twenty-four years old. I hope I didn't let it go to my head. I tried not to, but it was still very gratifying to have people acknowledge you, not only at the ballpark but around town.

◆

The question of the Jewish athlete, the Jewish ballplayer, continued to be raised periodically. In fact, as Greenberg would note, rarely was his name mentioned in print without "Jewish" or "Hebrew ballplayer" accompanying it. In the summer of 1935,

Fred Lieb, in *The Sporting News*, wrote, "As for the New York Jewish fans, they no longer are asking why there are no good Jewish ballplayers. When they took pen in hand in late June or early July, it was to express their indignation that Lou Gehrig, rather than their own Hank Greenberg, was picked as the American League's All-Star first baseman in the big July 8 game with the All Nationals in Cleveland, and who now appears to have an excellent chance to be named the league's MVP for 1935. . . .

"Next to Greenberg among the Jewish ballplayers of all time, we must rank Charles Solomon (Buddy) Myer, clever second baseman of the Washington Senators. . . . Myer has been a splendid ballplayer ever since coming into the American League in 1925. He has always been a hard and aggressive player and good hitter. . . .

"There have been some good Jewish players, but the best of them unquestionably was Erskine Mayer. . . . [1915, with the Philadelphia Phillies] was Mayer's one outstanding season (with a 21–15 won-lost record) but he had at least a half dozen years in the majors. . . .

"Johnny Kling . . . was of part Jewish blood and for many years was placed at the top of the list by Hebrew fans. Were Johnny of full Jewish blood, I would rank him next to Greenberg among the foremost Jewish players of all time. . . . He was a . . . great catcher. . . .

"The Giants have two Jewish lads on their 1935 roster, Phil Weintraub, baseball's best-dressed pinch hitter, and Hank Danning, a pretty lively catching prospect from Los Angeles. . . . Last season National League pitchers couldn't get [Weintraub] out. He hit .351 [in thirty-five games]. This year Phil is hitting just half of that. . . .

"While McGraw and [Bill] Terry, his successor, have tried out a whole raft of Jewish players [he mentioned Moe Solomon, Jack Levy, Harry Rosenberg, and Andy Cohen], the Yankees have experimented with only two, Dolly Stark and Jimmy Reese."

One New York Jewish periodical, in the midst of the interest in Greenberg, recalled "the hysteria that was raised when the Giants brought Andy Cohen here to replace Hornsby [in 1926]. Andy was thoroughly Jewish, too, and when he hit a home run in the opening game of the season, he became the king of the Bronx. At one time his life story was appearing in three different metropolitan gazettes simultaneously.

"But the largest Jewish community in the country demands something more than racial kinship in its ballplayers. Mr. Cohen proved to be just another second baseman, and in due course he went the way of all mediocrity. There was no display of grief, no dolorous protests."

Greenberg's fame, meanwhile, was spreading, and this young man from the Bronx was beginning to meet intriguing people beyond baseball.

◆

We were playing in Washington one time in 1935 and I was invited to FBI head-quarters with Cochrane, Gehringer, and Goslin. It was a thrill to go there and meet J. Edgar Hoover. It was during the early stages of the FBI, and Hoover was a great hero. He was then playing a very romantic role in American history. We spent the afternoon visiting Hoover's office. He took us down to the shooting range and all the papers published a picture of the five of us shooting. I later knew Hoover very well because he used to come to New York, and my good friend Louis Marx [the highly successful toy manufacturer] was a pal of his. We used to sit in the Club Room night after night, just talking. [In later years, Greenberg was invited to the White House to meet two presidents, Harry Truman and Richard Nixon.]

We won the pennant again, coming in three games ahead of the second-place Yankees. The Cubs had won the National League pennant with a twenty-one-game winning streak in September, sweeping past the Cardinals. It was considered the most spectacular unbroken winning streak to capture a pennant that had been recorded through the closing weeks of a Major League race.

Now we began the World Series of 1935 against the Chicago Cubs, and it was pretty evenly matched. They had a lot of old veterans and a solid pitching staff, with guys like Lon Warneke, Guy Bush, and Larry French. Pat Malone was still pitching for them, and so was Charlie Root. We were rolling high; we had won two pennants in a row, and I was really looking forward to this World Series.

◆

In a World Series preview that appeared in the *New York Evening Post*, Stanley Frank wrote that Greenberg "can be out-foxed, since he's always trying to outguess the pitcher. Can be made to pop up on a good fastball inside or on a high curve with a lot of stuff on it. . . . Not too sure on low throws at first or on fast grounders which skid close to the dirt."

But in an Associated Press story the emphasis was somewhat different: ". . . Greenberg's slugging has overshadowed the fact he also has developed into one of the best defensive first basemen in the game.

"The big Jewish boy, with a mark of .993 for the season, has a remarkable defensive record. . . ."

"[Greenberg] admitted he's nervous," said a United Press dispatch, which went on to describe Greenberg as "the most honest—and the only honest—ballplayer in the world."

For the opening game in Detroit the weather, noted a writer in the Chicago *Daily News*, couldn't have been more perfect. . . . [Commissioner Kenesaw] Landis must have ordered [it] himself. That rain that was here yesterday was gone, and it was clear and sunny. The frost which blanketed the park at dawn had dissipated in the face of a warm autumn sun. . . .

"Outside the park the scalpers did a brisk business. They were asking (and getting) $25 for a $6.60 ticket."

The largest crowd ever to witness a ball game in Detroit, 47,391, was on hand for the game.

Greenberg put on a show in batting practice as "the entire Cub cast stopped their warmup drill to watch Greenberg at the plate. Hank obliged by driving the next pitch into the stands, his fifth of the practice."

◆

We lost the first game. [Greenberg went hitless in three times at bat—grounding to third twice and popping to third—as the Tigers were shut out 3–0, Lon Warneke over Schoolboy Rowe.] And I learned that the Cubs were a bunch of tough SOBs. Charlie Root, Larry French, four or five other guys, they started riding me, calling me Jew this and Jew that. Behind the plate was Umpire George Moriarty; he walked over to the Cubs' bench and told them to stop riding me. They said it was none of his goddamned business and that they would ride me if they pleased. Moriarty got into a beef with one of the ballplayers. And later Landis fined him, as well as some of the Cub players.

◆

"Moriarty stopped the game in the second inning while he walked to the Cub dugout to warn Manager [Charlie] Grimm he would clear the bench if they didn't stop razzing Greenberg," the Associated Press reported.

"The Cub bench continually shouted at the Tigers from start to finish of the game, with Greenberg, whose station was nearest to the bench, taking most of the verbal sallies. . . . Billy Herman, Frank Demaree, and Bill Jurges were the Cub players who were singled out for oral potshots by the Tigers. . . ."

A story in the *New York Sun* quoted Moriarty: "No ballplayer can call me the names they did and get away with it. I told Grimm at Detroit if I heard any more such profanity as they yelled at Greenberg that I'd chase five of them off the bench with Grimm leading the procession."

One of the players on the Cubs, a rookie outfielder named Tuck Stainback, who would later be a teammate of Greenberg's in Detroit, recalled years later that some of his Cub teammates "got on Hank's back. . . . I remember Jurges hollering, 'Throw him a pork chop, he'll never hit it!'"

Jurges years later recalled the 1935 Series: "It's ribbing each other. What the hell."
Did he remember the pork chop line?

"Oh, no," he said, "I don't remember anything like that. But we'd kid back and forth.
The thing is, years ago the benches used to ride different ballplayers. It was a common thing. That's the way it was. In regard to Hank, I don't remember anything serious. He was a helluva guy. He could swing a bat, there's no question about it."

Phil Cavarretta, the Cubs' first baseman then, remembered that "the language was kind of rough. Detroit was on some of our players. We tried to retaliate. We figured if we got on them a little heavy this would disturb them and they would lose some of their concentration when they were at bat. . . . Like I say, some of the words were sort of foul. This is what Hank didn't like. Naturally, the umpire, Moriarty, said knock this stuff off. If you're going to get on somebody, clean the words up. But they kept on. I was only a nineteen-year-old kid at the time. I'd get up there and I'd hear it—'you dirty dago' and 'wop' and things like that. With an Italian, if they call you a dirty dago that's pretty heavy. This upsets you. But getting back to Hank, some of the words shouldn't be printed."

Like calling him a Jewish son of a bitch, or something along those lines?

"Yeah, they were kind of fighting words."

After the first game, wrote Tom Meany in the *New York World-Telegram*, Greenberg "had nothing to say about the bench jockeying."

"'It's all in the game,' said Hank. 'Why squawk about it now? I was a sucker to let them get my goat.'"

After the season, though, Greenberg did talk about it.

◆

I told the papers that I thought the Cubs should have been fined and that Moriarty [who apparently retorted to the Cubs with profanity of his own] should have been exonerated instead of being fined. Landis got mad and wrote me a long, formal letter. "How dare you say this, what did you hear? Tell me what you heard," etc.

◆

Part of the commissioner's letter to Greenberg, on October 30, read: ". . . you are requested to forward to me, in affidavit form, your testimony respecting the subject matter, and specifically, the language used between players Herman, Jurges and English and umpire Moriarty. That language was the occasion of the fines. . . ."

Greenberg wrote back: "I wish to state that I did not overhear any part of the argument between Moriarty and players. Therefore I could not be more explicit in my last letter."

◆

Landis got on me like a district attorney. I said that I didn't hear anything, but I just assumed. He told me not to assume anything. If I had anything to say, back it up, or keep my mouth shut. But that's the way he ran baseball, with an iron fist, and that's the reason baseball prospered at that time.

Much later in my career George Moriarty and I became very good friends. Back in the early 1900s he played third base for Detroit, and he used to steal home. Somebody wrote a poem about him, and the title was "Never Die on Third Moriarty." All through the rest of his life George felt he knew something about stealing home. When he was umpiring on third base, and on occasion when I'd get on third, he coached me on how to take a lead so I could steal home. I never had the guts enough to try, because I didn't think I could make it. I'd run down the line, and he'd keep insisting that I take a bigger lead. I was always afraid that I was going to get picked off. But it was interesting to see Moriarty, who was umpiring at third base, coaching me on how to steal home for the Tigers. It became a joke among the players, but I never got up the nerve to try it.

◆

The weather for Game 2 of the Series was cold and windy, 48 degrees at noon. In the stands the customers turned up their overcoat collars and some wrapped themselves in blankets they had brought. "Old-timers," wrote Dan Daniel in the *WorldTelegram*, "said that this was the coldest day for a World Series since 1907, when the Tigers and Cubs played in a snowstorm." It was also during Game 2 that Joe Jacobs, the fight manager, in a box seat, made his famous observation: "Gee, it's cold. I should of stood in bed."

◆

In the second game we started off with a four-run first inning. My home run with Charlie Gehringer on base scored the last two runs. In the seventh inning I was on first base after being hit by a pitch, and Fox singled to right field. I rounded third on the hit, and when the ball was thrown to second base I decided to try to score. I slid into home plate. Gabby Hartnett had the plate blocked, and as he fell on me, my left wrist curled up against my body, and when I fell I snapped it back. I finished the ball game but afterward I had excruciating pain in my wrist. That evening I spent the whole train ride to Chicago soaking my hand in extremely hot water and then in an ice bucket. I repeated this for hours, but the next day my wrist had swollen to twice its size. I had X rays taken and it was determined that I had sprained it. It was impossible for me to play; I could barely put my glove on. That finished me for the 1935 World Series, a keen blow to my aspirations to help the Tigers win the world championship after our loss in the Series the year before.

◆

Yom Kippur in 1935 fell on October 7, the day of the scheduled sixth game of the Series. Greenberg's father told the press before the Series began that Hank's worry over whether he'd play that game was the cause of his recent batting slump.

"We are Orthodox Jews," said David Greenberg, "and while not fanatical, or going to the synagogue every day, we always observe the two great holy days, the two days of New Year's and Yom Kippur.

"The boy has been to everybody including Mr. Navin and while they tell him they can't make him play they explain they have no substitute for him. After all, he belongs to the public and not just to himself."

Mrs. Greenberg added, "We've raised all our children to be Orthodox and I don't want him to play, but he will, anyway.

"That is for him to decide."

Dan Daniels reported that ". . . [yesterday] was Yom Kippur, the holiest day of the year for Jews. Greenberg, an Orthodox and devout believer, was eager to play, but his left wrist was so swollen he could not grip a bat."

◆

The team went on to win the World Series in six games. Naturally, I was disappointed that I couldn't play. I was in uniform, but I felt like a stranger on the ball team that I helped lead to the pennant. The Series was clinched in Detroit, and the whole city went wild. The demonstrations in the streets were the greatest celebration in the history of Detroit.

◆

Late in October of 1935 the balloting for the most valuable player in the league was announced. Greenberg was the winner in the American League by a unanimous vote of the eight representatives (one for each of the teams in the league) of the Baseball Writers Association of America. Wes Ferrell, who had won twenty-five games for the Red Sox, was second. Myer of the Senators, who had led the league in hitting, was fourth.

CHAPTER 7

After the close of the season some friends invited me to stay around Detroit for a week or so. My wrist continued to throb. One of my friends suggested that I get another X ray. I did, and the doctor told me that I had a fractured wrist. I reported this to Mr. Navin, and he was very gruff about it, he almost acted as though I was lying. The season was over, so there was no reason to tell him I had a broken wrist when I didn't have one. However, he reluctantly sent me out to the Ford Hospital, where the team doctor was, to take another X ray. They verified that I had a broken wrist and told me to go back to the ballpark. They said they would communicate their findings to Mr. Navin, and he would discuss it with me.

Well, I went back to the ballpark and Mr. Navin was very cavalier about the injury. He said, "Young man, you do have a broken wrist. They'll put it in a cast for you, but don't leave the cast on too long, because you don't want your wrist to become immobile. Just don't worry about it; it'll be all right." His attitude annoyed me. When I left his office I made up my mind that he would pay the price in spring training when he wanted me on the ball field. I was going to remember the way he belittled my broken wrist and, when it came time to talk contract, things would be different.

Unfortunately, Mr. Navin died suddenly that winter, so I never had a chance to bring up the subject of my broken wrist. Out of the blue we learned that Walter O. Briggs was a silent partner in the club. Mr. Navin was president and owner, his brother Charles was secretary, and nephew Art Sheahan was the road secretary. There was a girl at the switchboard and a secretary, and that was the staff. I always dealt with Mr. Navin and I assumed he owned the club. It turned out that he and Mr. Briggs had a deal that the surviving partner could buy out the dead partner's half. Of course, that's what Walter Briggs did when Mr. Navin died. He became full owner in 1936. He was still the owner when I left in 1946. Mr. Briggs was not a baseball man. He was head of Briggs Manufacturing. I think one division made bathtubs and toilet facilities and the other made some parts for automobiles. It was a big organization and Mr. Briggs was well thought of in the community. He had four or five children and they all married into the prominent social circles of Detroit.

Mr. Briggs was a paraplegic—apparently he had had polio when he was about thirty years old—and they had to wheel him around. He loved to come to the games on Sundays. Of the thousands of games I played in and watched during my years in baseball, few stand out in my memory. But one that does was a Sunday game that Mr. Briggs came to.

The game that day had no significance in the standings, but it was unique. We were playing the Philadelphia Athletics and that morning it had been drizzling and the skies were ominous. It looked like we might be rained out. You knew that if there was any chance of getting the ball game in, the umpires would do it; the club didn't want to lose the Sunday crowd. The home team has the right to either cancel the game or start the game. Once they announce that they're starting the game, then the responsibility of continuing or canceling passes to the umpires.

Mr. Briggs had his own box right near the Detroit dugout. On this particular day, we waited around to see what would happen even though it was raining fairly hard and the umpires had the infield covered. Mr. Briggs was wheeled to his box, and he had a big umbrella over him. We knew that if there were any chance of playing, this game was going to proceed.

They took the canvas off the infield. The rain had subsided but it was still coming down and there was a lot of water in the outfield near the drains, particularly in left field. The ballplayers wanted the game canceled. Everybody was afraid of going 0-for-4 and having a bad day, and I was no different. But we were forced to play. The game proceeded, and when it rained harder, Bill Summers, who was the chief umpire behind the plate, said, "Well, Mr. Briggs wants to see a ball game and, by God, we'll give him one."

So we played through the game even though it was raining pretty hard. I got a triple and a home run. I would play in a blizzard if I could get two hits in a game! I had been bitching earlier, but I was getting the hits because the pitchers couldn't control the curveball. All they could do was throw fastballs up there. It was almost like batting practice. You knew what was coming up, and the pitchers were slipping on the mound and the ball was getting wet between pitches and they had to throw them out. We got 9 runs. Along about the seventh inning, Bill Dietrich, who was pitching for Philadelphia, unwound two wild pitches. The first one hit in the middle of the screen way over the catcher's head. The umpire threw another ball to him, and he fired another one up the screen. With that, Bill Summers screamed, "Game canceled," and everybody dashed off the field.

◆

And while occasionally strange things occurred on the ball field, there were also unusual goings-on in the front office, as far as Greenberg was concerned.

◆

Mr. Briggs was now the sole owner of the ball club, and without having met him or even having heard of him, he started to dicker with me when I told him what I wanted, and that was a salary of $35,000. The club was offering me $25,000, a $10,000 raise. I had read that Al Simmons had signed for $33,000 per year when he went from Philadelphia to Chicago after the 1932 season, and I was determined to make more money than Simmons. Mr. Briggs got very annoyed with my demands.

So for the first and only time in my baseball career, I became an official hold-out. When spring training started, I was among the missing.

◆

Charles F. Navin, Frank Navin's brother, began handling the salary negotiations for Briggs. On March 9, 1936, Navin wrote to Greenberg:

> *Dear Hank:*
>
> *Well yesterday was the 8th of the month and the day on which you were supposed to report at Lakeland provided you had signed your contract. I received your letter of February 21st in which you returned the last contract that I sent you.*
>
> *Nothing has changed the club's position in the way of salary offered to you. . . .*
>
> *I am going to make one last effort and am returning to you the last contract that I sent. Possibly you will want to change your mind and send it into the office so that you can report to the training camp. You know*

84

you are not doing yourself any good by staying away from the camp this Spring. I can positively state that if you do not sign the contract that I am enclosing by Wednesday, March 11th, the decision will be made to make the offer—when you finally do sign—at least $2,500.00 less than the contract that am sending to you now.

I have always given you credit for being a sensible young man and one who would use reason and good judgment in all of your dealings, and if you are that type of an individual, it is up to you to sign the contract, send it in to our office and get down to the training camp just as soon as you can.

◆

After holding out for the first two weeks of March, I got a call from the ball club to come down to Lakeland to discuss my salary. Mr. Briggs was at his winter home in Miami and was coming to Lakeland, and he wanted to sit down and talk to me. Being eager to play and not being a holdout at heart—I held out more out of chagrin at the way they had handled it—I went to Lakeland. Some Detroit sportswriters were saying that I was demanding too much and some said that the Tigers couldn't do without me. It was a big discussion in Detroit, baseball being the most important thing in the lives of Detroit fans. There were some who resented my holdout, and other people who were for me.

When I reported to Mr. Briggs, Mickey Cochrane was also in the room. Mickey, by this time, had been elevated to the position of general manager as well as player/manager. During the discussions Mickey was very annoyed. He had played eleven years and in five World Series and was now a player/manager, and he claimed that I was asking for more money than he was getting.

My response was that if he wasn't getting $35,000, then he wasn't getting paid enough, that I didn't care what he was getting, but I felt that I was worth $35,000.

The discussions got rather heated, and finally Mr. Briggs indicated that they would compromise with me. I said, "Thirty-five thousand is the salary that I am entitled to. I didn't hold out to negotiate. I wasn't trying to get a little more money. If you feel strongly that I am not entitled to $35,000, I'll accept your $25,000 contract." This bowled them over. They readily got me to sign a $25,000 contract. All I was trying to do was establish my point, that when I made a salary demand, that was what I wanted. I wasn't going to be like most ballplayers who asked for more than they really wanted because they knew the ball club would then compromise and they would wind up with a few thousand more than the club originally offered. My feeling was, once the club knows you're going to negotiate in that manner, they'll always lower their initial offer so you'll end up with less than you would have if the club felt you were negotiating from a realistic position.

They rushed to give me a $25,000 contract. But I had established a point with Mr. Briggs, with whom I felt I was going to have a long and, I hoped, friendly relationship. If I could play ball and have good seasons, I knew that eventually I'd make up that extra $5,000 that I might have gotten in a compromise. I know that he would have resented it because no one likes to be pushed into a position where he has no choice and feels like he's being held up.

Over the winter we had acquired Al Simmons in a trade with Chicago. With Al's experience we looked like the odds-on favorite to win the American League pennant again. The club was full of confidence. We still had a young ball club, along with enough veterans. With Cochrane behind the plate to keep us on our toes, it looked like we were well on our way to a third straight pennant.

But a lot of injuries changed our plans.

I got off to a flying start, hitting around .350 and leading the league in runs batted in. In Washington in early May, in the twelfth game of the season, Marvin Owen fielded a ground ball at third base. He flipped it over to me at first base and I stretched to get the throw, which was fading into the baseline. The batter was Jake Powell, and he ran into me coming down the line. I always felt he could have avoided the collision, but I guess he felt he was entitled to the base path and if he could knock the ball out of my hand, which he did, he would be safe.

Unfortunately, I cracked the same bone in my left wrist as I had in the 1935 World Series. As a result, I was out for the rest of the season.

◆

A year later, in the July 15, 1937, *New York World-Telegram*, Dan Daniel, writing from Detroit, observed that the crowd of 22,500 in Navin Field "booed Powell all afternoon. A local paper had run a story questioning whether, after all, Jake's having put Greenberg out for the season last year could have been accidental."

◆

I was encouraged into thinking I would play again in 1936. I kept working out with the team and then, as the season progressed, the doctors decided that it would be safer and wiser for me not to attempt to come back during the season since the team wasn't going anyplace. Mickey Cochrane had been hit by a pitched ball in Yankee Stadium about a month later, so he was also out for the season. The whole team collapsed. Our aspirations for winning three pennants in a row went up in smoke. I went home around August and decided that the best thing to do would be to stay in shape and wait for the next season. The Tigers finished a distant second to the Yankees. It had been a bleak year for the club, and for me.

Being out of baseball in the summertime was a new experience for me, not having had a vacation from baseball from the time I left high school. I went back to New Jersey the latter part of that summer [his parents had a summer residence in Long Branch] and played handball with one hand and swam in the ocean. It was like a vacation, but of course I did miss the game and I missed the team.

I looked forward to regaining the use of my left hand. I worked constantly to stay in shape, to be thoroughly prepared to start the 1937 season.

◆

Nineteen thirty-six was the first year since 1914 that Babe Ruth was not in the Major Leagues. He had retired early in the 1935 season.

◆

When I think of poor Babe, I think of how management got him out of the American League. The Yankees hustled up a deal in which he would go to the Boston Braves after the 1934 season. Judge Fuchs, the president of the Boston Braves, gave him some stock and told him that he was a club owner now. They had him over there to play for a little while, but he was all washed up. He was forty years old and his legs were shot. As far as I know his health might have been bad. But in any case he went over there. Before many weeks passed he realized he couldn't play every day. He also realized that his Braves stock meant nothing because the club was bankrupt. So was Judge Fuchs.

The Babe had been so excited about going over to the National League, thinking baseball was repaying him for all his years of great service to the game. At least he had the good sense to go out in a blaze of glory, after hitting 3 home runs in one of his last games in Pittsburgh—one on top of the roof—which had never been done before.

There's no denying that Babe was hard to handle during his career, but he was just head and shoulders above anybody in the game. He loved life and he wasn't a stickler for the rules. I don't suppose he stayed in the best of condition but he did produce, and he was the most popular ballplayer in the history of the game. Somebody should have had a little more compassion when they maneuvered him out of the American League.

Jake Ruppert, the Yankees' owner, said, "Well, Ruth, you can't manage yourself, so how are you going to manage the ball team?" This was his answer when the Babe asked for a chance to manage the Yankees. Everybody else passed him over, too.

I understand that Frank Navin wanted to give him a chance at Detroit, but Babe had some golfing arrangement in Honolulu and never even showed up in Detroit. Undependability in such areas was one of his big faults. So Navin got discouraged and brought Mickey Cochrane from the Athletics, which was a real break for all of us because I don't think Ruth could have done the job. First of all, Ruth couldn't play and Cochrane was still one of the great catchers when he came over to us. And he was an inspiration as a manager, so I think we got a lucky break. Still, I felt bad for the Babe; still felt that, despite his faults, baseball didn't do right by him.

◆

While Greenberg was sitting out most of 1936, a rookie named Joe DiMaggio was making his first appearance for the Yankees.

◆

Two players in particular have always impressed me. They were just natural hitters, never had to work hard at it, or so it seemed. They were just born to hit. They had the perfect stride, perfect swing, and made it seem easy. I know looks can be deceiving, but neither one would show any emotion, and therefore you never knew if they were really straining or really worrying. They were also terrific fielders; they had the same easy, graceful motion in the field as at bat. They were Joe DiMaggio and Charlie Gehringer.

Charlie, of course, I played alongside for many years. I used to see Joe at Toots Shor's restaurant in New York. I'd meet him there and we'd have lunch and sit around all afternoon talking about baseball, even though he wasn't a big conversationalist. Joe never went to the gym in the winter, he never worked out, he just kept his weight down and when spring training started, he was ready to hit. And that was the case with Charlie Gehringer. As Lyn Lary, who was short-stop for the Yankees, said about Gehringer, "They'd wind him up to hit .350 when the season opened." Of course, that's a slight exaggeration, but it was almost true. Many times they said if you gave Charlie Gehringer a time at bat in the middle of the winter, he'd probably hit the first pitch for a single. That was the type of ballplayers they were. Both were very quiet, not outspoken. You couldn't get much out of them, but on the ball field their playing looked effortless. Because I had to struggle all the way to improve my fielding and improve my hitting, I was always envious of them.

An interesting thing arose in my contract negotiations for 1937, it was unlike anything that happens today. The club signed me to a one-dollar-a-year con-tract, and we agreed that if I could play I'd get my $25,000 a year, but I'd have to prove in spring training that I was capable of playing. That shows you the difference in the way ballplayers were handled in those days compared to the way they are treated today. No ballplayer today would think of signing a con-tract and having to prove himself, particularly after winning the Most Valuable Player award and leading the team to two championship seasons in the previ-ous two years. But I was full of confidence and feeling that I would have no difficulty regaining my batting eye, and I went down to spring training with the contract and proved that I could play. When the season opened, I was paid at the rate of $25,000.

Nineteen thirty-seven was, personally, my best year. I say this because ballplay-ers appreciate that runs batted in are all that's important to a ball team. It isn't how many doubles you get or what your batting average is or how many home runs you hit. Those are important, but the bottom line is who drives in the runs. And in 1937 I drove in 183 runs.

Charlie Gehringer used to bat ahead of me, and if we had a man on first base and Charlie was up, I'd yell, "Get him to third, Charlie, just get him to third. I'll get him in." That was my goal, to get that man in. It got to be a standing joke. Once Charlie said to me, "I suppose if I hit a double with a man on first, you'd probably trip him if he tried to go past third base."

I thought it was my best year in the Major Leagues even though in 1940 I was again voted Most Valuable Player. Of course, they select the MVPs based primarily on whether you play for a championship team. I guess the writers just generally assume that you can't be the most valuable player in the league if you're not able to help your team to a pennant. In many ways that's the proper perspective. On the other hand, if a fellow is playing with a weak team, no matter what he does, it won't make any difference. It takes more than one man to win a championship. In 1937, driving in 183 runs was quite an accomplishment. It was one RBI short of the American League record held by Lou Gehrig, who did it in 1931, the year after Hack Wilson of the Cubs set the Major League record of 190, which still stands.

I was primarily concerned with and concentrated on driving in runs. I had always had my eyes set on beating out Gehrig's American League record. With this in mind, I was just concentrating with men on base even more than I normally did because I was within reach of breaking the record, and this was one record that I wanted to establish, as it looked like it was going to stand a long time.

It came down to the final series of the season with a chance for me to break the record. We were playing Cleveland in Detroit. In Game 153 of the season—the next to last—I came to bat with three men on base. I had at that point 181 runs batted in for the year. Mel Harder was pitching, the entire outfield had shifted around to left field, and right field was wide open. With the bases loaded, I had kind of a checked swing and the ball looped down the right-field line. As I trotted to first I had visions of all three men scoring, which would have tied the American League record for runs batted in. But the ball landed foul by a few inches, and I was called back to the plate. I then hit a long fly ball which scored one runner, and that gave me 182 runs batted in with one more game left to play.

We were in second place in the league standings, well behind the Yankees, and the Indians were in fourth place. In most instances the last game of the season with two teams that are not contenders in the pennant race is usually left for the rookies to play. It's often a high-scoring game, and neither team cares very much. The players are loose; they're all ready to check out and go on home and forget about the season, unless they had a good one. But since I was going for the record, I played and a very unusual thing happened. The pitcher was a guy named Johnny Allen, who had been stricken with appendicitis earlier in the year and had not started a game for Cleveland until July 1. He came back and had a remarkable record of 15 and 0; he was going for the American League record, which was sixteen wins in a row in one season.

It was unusual for the best pitcher on a team to be pitching in the last game of the season. We had, on the other hand, a pitcher by the name of Jake Wade going for us. He had only recently been called up from the minor leagues. He was a nervous, skinny, tall, left-handed pitcher. Whistlin' Jake Wade was his nickname because he used to whistle whenever he was nervous, and that particular day he did plenty of whistling.

In the first inning I came to bat with a man on second base and one out and singled to left field, which made 183 runs batted in. I assumed that Jake Wade would be knocked out of the box early and Johnny Allen would have his victory; Allen would leave the game in the fifth or sixth inning, once Cleveland was ahead and it looked like he had the game and his record sewed up. I had visions of breaking the record, because I could either hit a home run or drive in a couple of runs with men on base, and I had certainly planned to play the whole ball game. None of that happened.

Jake Wade pitched a one-hit, no-run game, and beat Johnny Allen, 1–0. So Allen lost his chance to tie the American League record for sixteen consecutive victories, and I lost out to Lou Gehrig by one run batted in. To this day I'm second in the league with 183 runs batted in.

Thus ended the 1937 season.

◆

At one point in the 1937 season Greenberg received help, but of another kind. Having Rudy York, the rookie slugger, follow him in the order was important to his batting. "With him behind me," said Greenberg, "I get more good balls to hit, pitchers are not so ready to walk me, knowing that the next batter they have to face is likely to hit the ball out of the park." In 1937, York batted .307, hit 35 homers, and drove in 103 runs.

◆

Besides just missing Gehrig's RBI record, there was one other disappointment for me in the 1937 season. It had to do with the All-Star game. Thinking of the All-Star games doesn't bring back fond memories for me. The games started in 1933, the year I broke into the Major Leagues, and naturally I didn't have the kind of year then even to be considered an All-Star. But in 1934, the year we won our first pennant in Detroit, I had a pretty good year. I drove in 139 runs and hit .339. I wasn't selected, but I could understand that, because Gehrig and Foxx were stars, and their performances were as good as or better than mine. I wasn't disappointed. The disappointment started in 1935, the year I drove in over 100 runs by the All-Star game and wound up with 170 for the year, and I didn't get selected for the All-Star team. That annoyed me because I had established myself with two good seasons in a row, and we had won the pennant for two years straight.

I thought to myself, What do you have to do to be selected to the American League All-Star team? In any case, I broke my wrist and was out for the 1936 season. When 1937 came along I came up with a spectacular year. Sure enough, I was picked for the All-Star team and went to Washington for the game, but I spent it sitting on the bench. All I did was sign autographs for a day and a half. I took the hot train ride from Detroit to Washington and back again. That was the year that Joe McCarthy, the Yankee manager, decided to start all his Yankee players and kept them in there. McCarthy used only one pinch hitter, Jimmie Foxx. I didn't even get a chance to take a turn at bat. I was really annoyed.

When the 1938 All-Star game came up and I was selected—even though I was having kind of a slow season—I refused to go and used those three days of All-Star break to work on my batting.

◆

During the 1938 All-Star break Greenberg spent the three days working on his hitting with semipro pitchers. "I paid them ten, twenty bucks to pitch to me all day."

The Associated Press reported on July 3, 1938: "Detroit today requested the release of first baseman Hank Greenberg from participating in the All-Star game Wednesday in Cincinnati. . . . [The club] wished to have Greenberg's injured right wrist X-rayed and examined. . . ."

At the time it seemed that there was little wrong with Greenberg's wrist. Even though he was hitting only .285 with "a measly 45 runs batted in," not his best season in these departments, he had hit 22 homers in 69 games and was keeping pace with Ruth's record season.

"I know I took a panning because some folks thought I tried to duck the All-Star game," Greenberg was quoted in the New York Evening Post a few days after the game. "Here are the facts. I really had a sore wrist and so I stayed home and doctored it. I was glad of the three-day rest I could give it.

"After getting all keyed up about playing in the All-Star match they would have left me sitting on the bench again."

◆

When play resumed right after the All-Star break, we played Washington in Detroit in a doubleheader, and I hit four consecutive home runs—two in my last two times at bat in the first game. That put me well up on Babe Ruth's record, and from then on, why, I was shooting for home runs, chasing the record.

The Detroit ballpark was the best park for hitting home runs for me. It was a good environment, good background, and the fences were just the right distance for pulling the ball—340 feet down the left-field line, and then it cut across rather sharply so that left-center was 365. The fence in left was pretty tall, and it was a good poke, but not like center field where it became very difficult to hit a home run. The center-field fence was some 440 or 450 feet from home plate.

Other parks were also suitable for me. Sportsmen's Park in St. Louis had distances similar to Navin Field. The big difference was that the weather in St. Louis was hot and it made hitting the ball for distance so much easier because the extreme heat caused the ball to carry well.

Philadelphia was a great ballpark to play in—it had a good background to see the ball—but even when the A's were on top they didn't have the fan patronage.

Boston was another ballpark that was relatively easy for me. It had a short left-field fence with a high wall, some 290 feet to the wall and a tall fence. If you got the ball in the air, you could carry to that fence without difficulty. The center-field bleachers were no more than 380 or 390; it was still a good drive, but it was possible to hit one to the center-field bleachers. I was a pull hitter by this time and there was no sense in trying to hit outside pitches out of the ballpark. In most parks that always resulted in a long, long fly, 400 feet out.

The center fielder would park under it, then you'd come back to the bench and all the fans would be oohing and aahing and saying, "Oh, my God, if he had only pulled that one." Little did they realize that the pitcher was trying to get you to hit the ball out there. He was more than happy to let you hit the ball to deep center field, because he knew his center fielder would pull it in; I tried to wait until the ball came in over the part of the strike zone that I found suitable so I could pull it over the left-field fence.

So there were four ballparks that were good to hit in for a right-handed hitter who was trying to hit for distance. One of the parks that was difficult was Yankee Stadium, where you had to hit the ball right down the line, 301 feet, because then the box seats curved away drastically. You had to hit a ball 380 or 390 to hit a home run in New York, unless you were lucky.

93

When I first came to the Major Leagues, Cleveland played at League Park. This was an old park, wooden stands, built in an oblong shape, 290 feet to the right-field fence and 385 feet to left field. They had to build the right-field fence up, with an extra screen very high, because the distance was so short from home plate. They didn't even do a good job. They left the girders exposed; so if the ball hit the girders, which it sometimes did, instead of dropping where it was supposed to it squirted out to center field. It made a guessing game out of playing outfield in Cleveland. (Today, of course, the new stadiums are all symmetrical and everything is modernized. I don't really like it; there is no individuality at all in today's ballparks. They're almost plastic and not very attractive.) Well, finally, in 1932, in the midst of the Depression, the federal government decided to build a stadium for Cleveland on a WPA project. They built it down by Lake Erie, where they had plenty of room, and they put people to work. Municipal Stadium seated 80,000 people. You can just imagine on days when they didn't have a popular event or the weather wasn't good—with one of those fogs that would often roll in—it was a very uninspiring place to play. There weren't any spectators—or at least there didn't seem to be. There was a big track on the infield so the fans were very far away from it. If you were sitting in the bleachers, you were more than 500 feet from home plate. (That also applied to Fenway Park in Boston, which was an odd-shaped ball field, but the infield was right there where you could almost reach out and touch the players.) It was almost impossible to hit a home run in Municipal Stadium. The distances from home plate were so great that if you didn't just drop one down the line, you'd never hit a home run there.

Griffith Stadium in Washington was also a tough ballpark for any hitter to hit a home run; you'd have to hit it about 380 down the line.

Chicago was also a tough ballpark because the wind always seemed to be blowing in. It was a windy city, and getting the ball up in the air with the wind blowing made it very difficult to hit one out of the park, but also the fences were about 345 down the line and curved rapidly, so you had to hit a long ball. Center field was 440 feet to the wall.

In Detroit the wind, on rare occasions, would blow a long fly ball back onto the playing field. Because we had a double-decker in left field, frequently even with the wind blowing, if you hit a ball low enough, it would cut through the wind or be shielded by the double-deck stands, so you still could get your home run.

Even though I was hitting homers in 1938, I was in and out of slumps. One of the pitchers who could help put a batter in a slump was Wes Ferrell. A game

I remember best with Ferrell was one in which he got hit hard. He was with Washington at the time and one of their leading pitchers. (He was also a marvelous hitter for a pitcher, a good athlete. He should be in the Hall of Fame. Why his name has been overlooked I'll never understand, but his record measures up to anybody's.) He was a great competitor, and got so angry when he lost that he just wouldn't speak to anyone. In fact, he was only angry with himself—he never got on his teammates—just annoyed with the results of his own pitching. One particular day against us he had a nice 5- or 6-run lead, and it was the bottom of the fourth inning when suddenly the rains came down. Naturally we were pulling for the rains to continue so the game would get washed out and, of course, Wes Ferrell and the Senators were pulling for the rain to stop and so were the fans, because they wanted to get in at least four and a half innings, which would make it a complete game.

So we sat around for about an hour with the rain coming down and jeered at Ferrell, who was pacing in the dugout. He couldn't wait to get back in action. Finally the rain let up a little bit, though it was still drizzling. At that point the ground crew came out. It was comprised of three black men who came to home plate and stamped the area down with their feet. (That was the kind of ground crew that Clark Griffith, the owner of the Senators, employed. He was always trying to save money rather than trying to improve things at the ballpark. He claimed that he couldn't afford to do it.) After the game resumed, we scored 7 runs and Ferrell got yanked from the game.

Farrell went into the dugout; we were all yelling at him from across the field. I noticed that he sat down in the corner of the dugout where none of the other players were even close to him. Pretty soon he started picking at his glove. He was tearing his glove apart, just ripping it away. He couldn't tear it fast enough. It was difficult to do, but he was so annoyed and so unhappy and the more he ripped his glove, the more his teammates moved away from him, and the more we gave him hell: "Go get 'em, Wes." "You can do it, Wes." They told me that he went into the clubhouse before the game was over and tore his uniform to shreds. He took his watch out of his pocket and jumped on it and smashed it to smithereens. That's the kind of competitor Wes Ferrell was.

The end of this story is that Mr. Walter O. Briggs, the owner of the Tigers, was having a shave at the Detroit Athletic Club that afternoon and listening to the game on the radio. During the course of that game, when we were down 6 or 7 runs, he said to the barber, "If we win today, I'm going to buy every one of the ballplayers a suit of clothes." Sure enough, after we won and got back to Detroit, we got a note from the management that Mr. Briggs was ordering us each a suit of clothes from his private tailor.

In those days, to be sent up to get a suit of clothes made to order, which few of the players had ever had, was a big deal. Most bought their clothes whole-sale [off the rack]. We each got a custom-made suit of clothes. The price of the suits then was about $125 each, a fortune. The most amusing thing was that when I went to get my suit fitted, the tailor, Sam Grenadier, told me that Rudy York had ordered three suits. One Mr. Briggs was paying for and two Rudy was going to pay for himself. Well, when you think of Rudy York, who came from Cartersville, Georgia, with a population of maybe 5,000 people, what he was going to do with three $125 suits God only knows.

◆

In July 1938, Jack Smith wrote in the *New York Daily News*: "Hank lazed back on the Tiger bench the other day when I queried him. 'Yes,' he laughed. 'Funny thing. I've been asked two questions all season. For the first two months everybody wanted to know when I would snap out of my slump. Now all I hear is, "Hank, do you think you can break Ruth's record?"

"'Well, the answer to both questions is the same: I don't know. I'm not counting on breaking the record and I'm not letting it bother me. The Babe was the greatest home-run hitter we ever had, but the best he could do was 60. Only two others, Foxx and Hack Wilson, hit over 50 [Foxx had 58 in 1932 and Wilson had 56 in 1930], so it's pretty tough for anybody, including myself, to do better than the best.

"'Seriously, though, if I can keep pace with the record until September 7, I think I can do it. Babe hit 6 homers that first week in September, then he tapered off. His season ended a week earlier than mine. With breaks I think I can do it.'

"Hank isn't one of those hit-'em-a-mile-or-miss sluggers. He is one of the tough-est men in the league to fool. Lou Gehrig paid him a great compliment the other day. 'We didn't think Hank would be the hitter he is now,' Lou said. 'But I'll tell you this. There's many a time I'd rather see Gehringer at the plate than Hank, especially when a long hit means the ball game.'

"Hank justly gives himself the most credit for his development. 'I think this busi-ness of saying so-and-so made me a great hitter is the bunk in most cases. Certainly I took tips from a few players [he cited Jimmie Foxx, whom he said he modeled him-self after when he first came up, and Tony Lazzeri, who had advised him to move up on the plate in order to follow the ball better and hit the outside pitches], but I'm the one who worked on my hitting. I'm the one who practiced until my hands were so blistered I couldn't lift the bat. I remember once an old catcher was telling me I'd have to change my stride or I'd never hit .200 in any league. The manager came over and said, "Leave the kid alone. I don't care if he strides downtown as long as he wallops that ball." . . .'

"Hank rose, took a bat from the rack and hustled to the batting cage for practice swings."

Shortly before the All-Star game, when the Tigers were playing the White Sox, an incident occurred involving Greenberg.

◆

The White Sox bench had been getting on me. They were located along the first-base line, and they had been razzing me throughout the game. When Joe Kuhel got on first base, they all yelled to him to take a big lead and then slide back into first base and spike me. Sure enough, Kuhel deliberately took a long lead and drew the throw over from the pitcher and as he came sliding into me, he just tore my shoes from under me. I thought it was unnecessary and deliberately provoked, and so I reached down and slapped Kuhel, but before anything could happen we were parted. That created an incident but nothing really developed, just a lot of words with very few punches thrown, but we were both put out of the game.

◆

Associated Press from Chicago: "William Harridge, President of the American League, announced today that Hank Greenberg had been fined $50 for his part in a disturbance with Joe Kuhel. . . .

"Harridge criticized 'certain' White Sox players for what he termed 'unsportsmanlike conduct and use of insulting and abusive language to members of the opposing team.'

"He said he had warned manager Jimmie Dykes of the Sox that 'Any players found guilty of a repetition of these tactics will be ejected from the game, with suspension following.'

"Greenberg charged that Kuhel deliberately spiked him sliding into first base. Greenberg swung at Kuhel and members of both teams rushed to them to prevent a fight."

Years later Elden Auker, the Detroit pitcher, recalled: "During the ball game somebody from the White Sox dugout yelled out that Hank was a yellow Jew son of a bitch. When the ball game was over Hank took off his spikes and everything and he walked across the way and opened the door. He walked right into the White Sox clubhouse, which was just across the aisle from our clubhouse, and said, 'The guy that called me a yellow son of a bitch get on his feet and come up here and call it to my face.' Not a guy moved. He was damn lucky, because Hank would have killed him. Hank was a tough guy."

Birdie Tebbetts, then a young reserve catcher on the Tigers and a Detroit team- mate of Greenberg's for seven seasons, also remembered that incident.

"Hank walked into the White Sox locker room and said, 'I don't know who called me a yellow Jew bastard, but whoever it was, stand up and say it to my face.' Ted Lyons, the pitcher, and a nice guy and a friend of Hank's, decided to walk toward Hank and Hank said, 'Hey, Ted, I don't have any argument with you.' Hank knew who it was. And he made his statements directly to that guy instead of the whole club. But the guy never said another word."

Of the Kuhel spiking incident, Charles Ward wrote in the *Detroit Free Press*, ". . . the brawl was almost renewed in the Chicago clubhouse after the game when Greenberg . . . marched in and hurled challenges at both Kuhel and Dykes. Neither challenge was accepted. . . ."

Tebbetts recalled years later: "There was nobody in the history of the game who took more abuse than Greenberg, unless it was Jackie Robinson. . . . I was there with Hank when it was happening and I heard it. However, Hank was not only equal to it, he was superior to most of the people who were yelling at him. And in the case of Jackie Robinson, Jackie had no place to go after a ball game and Greenberg could go anyplace in the world. Greenberg had to bear that terrible burden on the field, Jackie had to bear it all his life. I wasn't in the National League with Jackie, but I was with Hank and Hank consistently took more abuse than anybody I had ever known.

"In those days there was an awful lot of what we called jockeying. There's no room for it now because the organists have taken over. It was between innings. We got our feelings across to everybody. Umpires, hitters, pitchers. It was a continuous thing. There were bench jockeys who'd get on the edge of the bench and yell obscenities or jokes or something about a guy's personal life.

"And you'd hear it out in the stands. To Greenberg you'd hear 'Jew bastard' or 'kike son of a bitch.' Nobody else could have ever withstood the foul invectives that were directed toward Greenberg, and he had to eat them. Or else he would be out of every game he played."

Tebbetts recalled another time when the Yankees were riding Greenberg from the bench during a game. "Hank walked over to the Yankee bench," said Tebbetts, "and challenged everybody on the team."

Harry Eisenstat, a twenty-two-year-old left-handed pitcher, and a Jew, had been purchased by the Tigers after pitching briefly for three seasons for Brooklyn. He would, as he said years later, follow Greenberg around "by the coattails" and listen to his advice. One piece of advice he received concerned card playing in the clubhouse.

Eisenstat: "Hank just said, 'Harry, I would suggest that you don't play cards, because you're liable to have some redneck who may have a comment when he loses.' And that's all. We dropped it. I understood what he meant.

"Hank introduced me to a lot of the Jewish people in the Detroit community, and he showed me how to dress. He used to wear quality clothes, and I remember he used to wear Sulka ties, which cost about $35 or $40 even in those days.

"I still recall a lot of times people would say, 'Well, isn't it tougher playing ball because you're Jewish?' And we'd say, 'No.' People used that as a cop-out in life. Too many times you hear people saying, 'Well, because he's Jewish,' or whatever. That's not the case. Hank told me, 'Don't ever use the term, "because you're Jewish," if you don't do well. You do well in playing ball, you'll never hear it come up. But if you don't do well, other people will use that as an excuse.' Hank said, 'It should be more of an incentive to be successful.'

"I relieved most of the time and there was a doubleheader, either in 1938 or 1939, and I pitched five innings in the first game and four innings in the second game as a reliever. Hank hit three home runs in the two games and I pitched a total of nine shutout innings. We won both games and everybody was happy. And I still remember Mickey Cochrane saying, 'Fellas, lock yourselves in your rooms tonight because the Jews in Detroit are going crazy.'"

Eisenstat recalled how Greenberg reacted when in a slump:

"It would be nothing for Hank to say, 'Harry, you're not pitching today, how about coming out, I'm not hitting too well. I'll meet you in the ballpark at nine tomorrow morning.' He would work on the way a certain pitcher would pitch to him, like Red Ruffing used to pitch him tight all the time. Hank used to say, 'Keep throwing the ball in on my fists.'

"So there would just be him and me and a couple of the ground crew shagging in the ballpark. They would do anything for Hank because he had a lot of empathy for people. He always said hello to the ticket takers, how's your family, are the kids all right, if he knew the kids were ill, he'd always be there to help.

"I saw him once after a game with some ballplayer, I forgot who it was, and a kid went over to the player and asked for an autograph. The player had lost the game the day before and he was nasty to the kid and refused to sign his autograph. The kid felt shunned. And Hank, I still recall—it was at Briggs Stadium— Hank went over to the kid, the kid was in tears, sent for a ball, signed it, and gave it to him."

◆

I really had very few altercations throughout my baseball career. In fact, I had one scrap in Decatur, Illinois, when I played in the 3-I League, and one in Dallas when we were in the playoffs in the Texas League in 1932. And the incident with Joe Kuhel of the White Sox, and the one with the Yankees.

The Yankees had us beaten something like 8–2. I had hit a home run earlier in the game, but I came up in the eighth inning with nobody on base, and we were some 6 runs behind. The count went to 1 ball and 2 strikes. For some reason I was looking for a curveball and the pitcher just wound up and fired one behind my head. Well, I did duck, but not far enough out of the way of the ball, and it hit the button on top of my cap. I don't mind telling you I turned white; I realized then that my career could very well have been ended right there and how lucky I was that I hadn't been beaned. It was the only time I ever came close to being beaned in all the years that I played. For some reason or other, this time I was frozen at the plate. It was a totally unnecessary brushback pitch, I went out to fight, and I very nearly was put out of the game.

Another time Cal Hubbard kicked me out of a game when I was sitting on the bench minding my own business. He was upset with the Detroit ball club. There was a disputed play down the right-field line and the whole bench was getting on him. He turned to me and said, "Greenberg, you're out of here." Mr. Harridge fined me $50, but after I gave him my explanation, he returned the $50. That incident, the Kuhel incident, and the time when I was a rookie and Bucky Harris was arguing with George Moriarty, and I said, "That goes for me, too," those were the only times that I was asked to leave the team during a game.

I never got in trouble with the umpires. I told them what I thought. I built a reputation and I got the best of most calls from the plate umpires. The other decisions on the base paths were few and far between. I never got any umpire mad at me, and nobody was ever out to get me.

All of the umpires stayed at the Leland Hotel in Detroit, which is where I stayed. So when we were playing at home, I got acquainted with a lot of the American League umpires, and we had a different relationship than most ballplayers and umpires have. Once they get to know you and you get to know them, there's no chip on their shoulder when you get out to the ballpark. It's that attitude of trying to show me up, that's what the umpires always say. I never had that problem, and I tried to develop a friendly relationship with all the umpires. I think I got my share of calls at home plate. At least I certainly didn't get the reputation of being "Five-Strike Greenberg" without getting some pretty good calls.

◆

As Greenberg continued to keep pace with Babe Ruth's single-season home-run record (he had 29 by the third week in July), his relationship with opponents, as well as umpires, would grow in importance.

Ben Chapman, who played for several Major League teams, was considered one of the toughest bench jockeys in baseball, and he was tough on Greenberg. He was also rough on Jackie Robinson after Robinson broke the color barrier in the National League in 1947. Chapman was then the manager of the Philadelphia Phillies. It was Chapman who was supposed to have thrown a black cat on the field to try to shame Robinson. And Robinson's most difficult moment, he would say later, was when he swallowed his pride in his rookie year and "buried the hatchet" with Chapman and posed with him for a photograph.

◆

Ben Chapman played for the Yankees. He was a genuine Jew-baiter. Whenever he would have a bad day in the outfield, the Jews at Yankee Stadium would get after him because he made remarks about Jews. In 1983 I saw Ben Chapman at the All-Star game in Chicago and he gave me a big hello, "Good to see you, partner. Remember the good old days down in Daytona Beach when I was working for you?" I had forgotten. [Chapman had demonstrated base-running techniques to the Cleveland Indians one spring in the 1950s when Greenberg was the general manager of that team.] "Boy, those were the days, I loved them. You're a great guy, Hank, everybody in baseball thinks so." But no matter what the words said, I knew and still know that men like Ben Chapman, and there were a lot of men like him in baseball, hated my guts and resented my success all the more because I am a Jew.

◆

Years later Ben Chapman, living in Birmingham, Alabama, recalled Greenberg: "He could do it all except run. He could hit, he could field, and he was a helluva nice fella. As a matter of fact, after I got fired from Philadelphia he helped me go down to Florida with the Indians and help with the base runners. He was a real good guy. . . .

"I was a bench jockey. So was everybody else. If you could just affect the fellow, get him a little agitated, you were that much ahead. The best bench jockey I ever knew was Leo Durocher. Jimmie Dykes was good, too. And they let me have it, too—'Southern son of a bitch.' Most of what was said was stuff like, we'd call to our pitcher, 'See how he looks sitting down.' You know what I mean by that. 'Throw one at him.' 'Stick one in his ear.' 'Did you pay alimony last month?' All that kind of thing. Anything that would come to mind. They call a Polish guy a Polack so-and-so, they'd call me a Southern so-and-so, they'd call Greenberg a Jewish so-and-so. It was accepted practice. It only changed after Jackie Robinson. They rode everybody. They didn't play any favorites. When Jackie came in we rode him. What the heck. That was my job. It's always been vicious."

On July 25, 1938, the *New York Evening Post* reported: "American League pitchers claim that Gene Desautels of the Red Sox has discovered how to stop Hank Greenberg from hitting. The catcher conducts a hot and heavy argument with him when Hank is at bat. . . ."

On July 26, Greenberg hit his thirtieth and thirty-first home runs of the season. This left Greenberg two homers off the pace set by Babe Ruth in 1927, eleven years earlier.

On July 27, Greenberg hit his thirty-second and thirty-third homers of the season. In *The New York Times* it was reported:

"Greenberg's present pace is ahead of Babe Ruth's. . . . Ruth drove his 33rd of the year in the Yankee's 95th game . . . Greenberg's 33rd came in Detroit's 88th game."

On July 29, Greenberg hit two more in one game for numbers 34 and 35.

Greenberg told the *New York Evening Post* that he would know more about breaking Ruth's record at the end of August.

"Why, three years ago I had 30 homers at the end of July," he recalls ruefully, "and ended up with exactly 36. Six homers the last two months of the year! Those 17 the Babe smacked in September are going to be the hurdle. You have to look at a lot of kid pitchers at the end of the season because the Tigers are out of the race. And the kids are wild and apt to walk you."

Gehrig noted that, with 37 home runs on August 1, "Greenberg can beat the Babe's mark. . . . Greenberg has great wrist leverage on account of his height and long arms.

He can power that ball to any field. . . . [But] September is the tough month, never forget it. Rudy York's great showing last year during that month [when he hit 17 home runs] was amazing for a first-year man. Just the same, if York was that good Greenberg has a chance to equal the pace."

Joe McCarthy said: "I hope he does it. Greenberg is a fine ballplayer."

Red Ruffing, the Yankee pitcher, also thought Greenberg had a good chance at the record: "I never feel safe when I look up and see that big guy at the plate. . . . Greenberg's size impresses the pitcher, and he has such strong arms and wrists that when he hits the ball solidly it starts going places. He doesn't have to take a full cut at a ball to knock it over the roof or into the grandstand."

Greenberg was more cautious about his chances at the record than the Yankees appeared to be. He told a newspaperman: "I'll begin to give it serious thought if I finish August with 50 homers. If I don't, I'm cooked. . . . I've got to hit like hell this month to make up for Ruth's great September. That's the tough month. Shadows fall earlier on the field, the wind is stronger, and every club brings up a lot of wild rookie pitchers. They haven't walked me yet, but I'm afraid they will. . . . I may go six weeks before I get another. . . . All of a sudden I started to time the ball better and regulate my stride. I feel great, that's all. Harry Heilmann may have the right dope. He says I'm a lousy hitter having a good season. Maybe he's right."

On August 4 the *Herald Tribune* reported: "Greenberg has slowed up in his quest for Babe Ruth's home-run record. He has not been able to make any homers so far this series [with the Yankees]." Greenberg then had 37 home runs.

On August 6 the Tigers—in fifth place in the American League, seventeen games out of first—dismissed their manager, Mickey Cochrane, and replaced him with Del Baker, the third-base coach. Walter Briggs said he did it "for the good of the club and in justice to the supporting fans." "Cochrane," wrote the *Herald Tribune*, "was close to tears as he shook hands with Detroit players." Al Simmons would note that Briggs had got into the habit of calling Cochrane to task for the way he was handling his pitching (including calling from his yacht after listening to a game on the radio).

In his first game under the new manager, Greenberg belted his thirty-eighth homer of the season, and his first in a week, since July 30. He then went into a batting slump and emerged from it on August 18 with two hits, both singles, but no home runs. On the following day, though, he hit three homers in a doubleheader against the Browns, to bring his total to 41. Greenberg was still ahead of Ruth's record pace. Ruth did not hit his forty-first until August 27.

Greenberg said, "What if I do break it? It will be just like those guys who flew the Atlantic after Lindbergh. The Babe was the first to do it."

At the end of August, Ruth, then forty-three years old and a Brooklyn coach, asked to become an active player again. He had made the statement in Pittsburgh to John McDonald, the traveling secretary of the Dodgers. Perhaps Ruth, seeing the attention Greenberg was getting, and the attention his own record was getting, was roused to return to the playing field.

"I telephoned Larry MacPhail [the Dodger president] about the Babe's desire to play," said McDonald. "MacPhail was unable to state whether the request would be granted or not, but he did say that it was under consideration." The following day Burleigh Grimes, the manager of the Dodgers, gave the response for the team: "I like Babe Ruth. I care for the Dodgers. For the welfare of both I am turning down his request to be reinstated as an active player this year."

On the last day of August, Greenberg, replying to whether he could break Ruth's record, said: "I've heard that question so much . . . that I even hear it now in my sleep. . . . Maybe I oughta get some cards printed with 'Who knows?' on them. . . . Somebody'll break it some day for sure. . . .

Greenberg added that "Detroit's no bargain for a right-handed hitter no matter what people say. . . ." He also displayed a few assorted bruises on his arm, side, and hip. "I was hit by pitched balls. How do I know what for? They don't send letters along with each ball. . . ."

On that day, August 31, Greenberg hit his forty-sixth homer, in Yankee Stadium, and now, going into September, he needed 14 homers in thirty-two games in this, the last month of the season, to tie the record, and 15 to break it. Greenberg was six days and six games ahead of Ruth's pace.

In the *New York Sun* there was a large ad for "a Hank Greenberg color photo coming in the following Sunday's *New York Daily News*—5 cents." The headline read: CAN HANK ECLIPSE BABE? Also advertised as coming in that Sunday's paper were two full-color pages of pictures of Fred Astaire and Ginger Rogers doing their latest dance, "The Yam," in their new movie, *Carefree*.

And in the *Daily News* there was another, more social question concerning Greenberg: "Tall, dark, handsome and prosperous, Hank is baseball's most eligible bachelor. His name has been linked with fair ladies from New York to Miami, but Hank merely grins at the mention of marriage."

The matter of Greenberg and Jewishness also continued to be a topic of discussion. From a Jewish periodical published in Boston: "We have had pogroms before;

we have had wars before; we have had trouble with Arabs before. But never before have we had a Jewish home-run king.

"At the present writing Greenberg has smashed 46 home runs. A home run for those who don't know is the name given to the hitting of a baseball which travels so far that the hitter can run around a big diamond before the ball is thrown back. . . .

"A genuine baseball fan just can't be an anti-Semite. The name of Greenberg was shouted out in Fenway Park last week in eight different languages and in 21 different English dialects. [Greenberg had played in Boston on August 28 and 29.]

"Greenberg is another form of good-will emissary for the Jewish people. . . ."

◆

In the latter half of the season, most of the publicity that Detroit got and, for that matter, most of the league publicity, centered on whether I could break Babe Ruth's record. Those were the days before television and without the newspaper coverage that they have today, but there was still quite a to-do about it. In each town we went to the story was my record and how many games I was ahead of the Babe, and so it went down into September with me leading Babe. But what people forget is that Babe had hit three home runs in the last two days of the season. If you were close to the record, you had to be way ahead of Babe if you were going to break it.

◆

By the end of the first week in September, Greenberg still had 46 home runs. Babe Ruth, commenting on Greenberg, said, "The strain is too great. The boys are forever reminded about that record and it is bound to tell on them. It's telling on Greenberg now. I don't think he'll be able to make it now."

Greenberg hit his forty-seventh on September 9. At this point, not only was he looking ahead at the record, but behind him, too, since Jimmie Foxx, now with Boston, hit two home runs on September 10 and had a total of 44.

On the following day, September 11, against the White Sox in Detroit, Greenberg hit two homers off Ted Lyons. He now had 49. Ruth had 50 on that date in 1927, though he had played three more games.

The next day Greenberg belted his fiftieth of the season into the upper deck in left field. This put him four games ahead of Ruth. It was Greenberg's 134th game; he had twenty remaining. "But," noted the Associated Press, "Greenberg must hit more than one homer in every two games to better the mark." It was reported that the odds were ten to one against Greenberg breaking the record.

Ruth, who was then suffering with a broken toe, "scowled with momentary pain," wrote Jimmy Powers in the *New York Daily News*, "and then his moon face broke into a friendly grin.

"'Greenberg? A great kid, Hank,' Ruth said. 'Sure, I wish him luck. And late September is not as tough as you think to hit 60. Doubleheaders pile up and scores are high. Pitchers are worn out from a long summer's campaign. Hank'll be all right if they don't walk him too much. You can't hit a home run on pitchouts.'"

An unnamed Tiger player told Jerry Mitchell of the *New York Evening Post*: "He walks up and down the dugout during batting practice telling everybody that he isn't worrying about it, isn't even thinking about it. . . . But he's thinking about it all the time and probably pressing too hard out there. . . ."

Charlie Gehringer years later recalled Greenberg during his pursuit of Ruth's home-run record. "I knew he was under a lot of pressure and he was nervous about it," Gehringer said. "I rode with him on the train one time and we were talking about it. You could see that it was in him. I assume it even kept him awake nights, but he never really said that.

"He seemed to think he was going to make it. Stay cool and just pick out a good pitch and do what you have been doing all season, you didn't put any more pressure on yourself. I think he'd be the last guy to say 'I can't do it' or 'This is too tough on me.'"

It also seemed that Greenberg's chances were brighter than might be thought, since sixteen of the Tigers' remaining games were scheduled in Detroit, where Greenberg had hit 31 homers in sixty-two games, an average of one every other game.

On September 16, Greenberg's long high fly "squeezed over the fence with the bases empty," wrote Jimmy Powers in the *New York Daily News*. It was number 51.

The following day he hit two more homers, numbers 52 and 53, off Monte Pearson of the Yankees. Sam Murphy in the *New York Sun* reported that "Pearson was under orders to pitch to Greenberg today." Apparently, the orders were from the manager, Joe McCarthy. The Yankees, with fifteen games to play, were just one game away from clinching the American League pennant.

Greenberg was two games ahead of Ruth's pace. He needed 8 homers to break the record, and had fifteen games in which to try.

In the two-game series that followed, against the Senators in Detroit, Greenberg was 1-for-5 with a single in the first game, and 1-for-3 with a single in the second. He hit one long fly in the second game that was caught. "I remember Hank standing at the plate and just swinging for the fences," said Rick Ferrell, then a Senator catcher. "He hardly left the plate."

On September 21, in the first game of a doubleheader, Greenberg hit his fifty-fourth in Philadelphia. The second game was called after five innings because of darkness. This was Detroit's 142nd game—with twelve games left in the season. Ruth had hit his fifty-fourth in his 145th game.

"Next summer," Greenberg was quoted, "I'm going to hit more naturally. Manager Baker agrees with me that trying for home runs exclusively isn't worth it. I'd be more valuable to the club if I was loosened up more at bat." But since the Yankees had run away with the pennant, and the Tigers were in fourth place, it didn't seem harmful to the ball club, and certainly not for Greenberg, at this point, to attempt to break the home-run record.

On September 23, in a doubleheader against the Indians, Greenberg hit two more home runs, his fifty-fifth and fifty-sixth. The second game was called after the seventh inning because of darkness. Both of Greenberg's homers were off his former teammate, Earl Whitehill. Greenberg did break one record that afternoon. He set the Major League mark for hitting 2 homers in one game most often during a single season. He had done it ten times so far in 1938.

On September 24, against the Indians, Greenberg was 0-for-2, with two walks.

He was now three games ahead of Ruth's pace. Greenberg had 56 in 145 games, Ruth had 56 in 148 games.

"Big Hank Greenberg blasted his way to within 2 home runs of equaling Babe Ruth's all-time record today when he smashed homers number 57 and 58," reported the *New York Daily News* about the Tigers' game in Detroit against the Browns on September 26. "Both circuit clouts, which put Hank three games ahead of the Babe's mark for games played, came in the second game of the doubleheader. Detroit won both games, 5–4, 10–2." (The second game was called after seven innings on account of darkness.)

"Both blows were collected off Bill Cox, the St. Louis starting pitcher.

"Greenberg barely cashed in on the first homer. It was a 440-foot drive inside the park, and Hank managed to beat the throw-in by only an eyelash."

◆

Like many star players, I must admit that I got my share of breaks from umpires. In 1938 I was playing against the Browns and my good friend, Bill McGowan, was umpiring behind the plate. I hit a long ball over the center fielder's head and the ball rolled to the wall. I had already hit 56 home runs, so when I came to third base and the ball was still on its way to the relay man, I knew the third-base coach would have to tackle me to keep me from trying for an inside-the-park homer. I slid home in a cloud of dust, but the catcher had me out by a mile. However, McGowan called me safe, for my fifty-seventh home run.

No one could believe it; the Browns' players and manager all jumped up and down and ran out on the field to argue, but, of course, the umpire's call stood. The funny thing is, forty years later I got a letter from Sam Harshaney, who was a reserve catcher for the Browns. The letter said: "Dear Hank: My boys have now grown and have gone off to college. I have been telling them for years that you never hit that home run and that you were out at the plate. Could you get a picture showing that particular incident?"

I wrote back and said, "I'm sorry, I have no picture, but you are absolutely right. I was out by a mile and had no business being called safe. So you can tell your boys that their dad stopped Hank Greenberg from getting home run number 57."

That wasn't the only good call that McGowan ever gave me. I remember one time we were playing the Yankees in Detroit. It was Sunday afternoon in September in the heat of the pennant race. I was at bat with the bases full and two out, and I had two strikes on me. Red Ruffing called for a curveball that fooled me completely. It broke right down the middle of the plate. McGowan paused, then called it a ball. Bill Dickey was beside himself. He called McGowan every name in the book. He said, "What the hell are you doing? This isn't Five-Strike Greenberg. What the hell are you doing?" They argued like hell. Joe McCarthy charged out of the Yankee dugout, kicking dirt and turning red as a beet. Finally the rhubarb subsided and I went back into the batter's box. As I did, McGowan bent down to dust off home plate and, without so much as glancing in my direction, whispered, "For Christ's sake, Hank, swing at those, will ya!" I don't remember if I got a hit or not, but it was the worst call I ever saw. It went in my favor, though, so who was I to complain?

◆

With 58 home runs in 149 games, Greenberg had five games left in which to break the record. Ruth didn't hit his fifty-eighth until the 152nd game of the 1927 season.

"Greenberg," wrote the Associated Press, "is within striking distance."

◆

When I crossed the plate after hitting my fifty-eighth, I suddenly thought, I can do it. We had two games in Detroit and three in Cleveland. I figured I'd get three more easily. I thought that with about twenty at bats to go, and even if the pitchers were extra careful, I'd still get about twenty-five good pitches to swing at.

◆

To add perspective to the American baseball season and Greenberg, Bud Shaver in the *Detroit Times* contrasted it with what was going on in Hitler's Germany: "There is no shuffle of marching feet, no roar of armored tanks down well-paved streets . . . [no] frightening banners of war and all its ghastly consequences. But in Detroit at least the question still is, 'Can he make it?' . . ."

Tom Meany, in the September 28 *New York World-Telegram*, wrote that "the closer Greenberg gets to the record, the more eager Babe Ruth is to admit the chances of it being broken. 'He should break it—in that park,' was Babe's view of the situation yesterday, a statement which would have ended better if Babe had omitted any reference to the Detroit ballpark."

◆

The Browns came into Detroit to play two games against the Tigers. And who would be pitching for the Browns but Bobo Newsom.

I never had much success against Bobo and on this day he was aiming for his twentieth win of the season. Newsom, Mel Harder, Bob Feller, Johnny Allen, Red Ruffing, and, at times, Lefty Gomez were the toughest pitchers in the league for me. Well, Newsom stopped me with only a double.

Incidentally, Bobo was one of the outstanding pitchers in the American League, even though he was playing for a last-place team. He had a fine slider and good control. He kept the ball out over the plate, and it was almost impossible to pull the ball for a home run unless he let one slip. Bobo was particularly careful in pitching to me. He always kept the ball away from me, and I didn't quite have the power to go to right field and hit a home run. I had very little success against Bobo as far as home-run hitting was concerned, and I didn't have any success that day.

The next day, September 28, I faced Howard Mills, a left-hander. He was nervous and he was wild. When the fans booed him for not giving me something to hit, he got more nervous and more wild. He walked me twice. I did get one good swing. I hit a long drive that hit the roof in left field—the first time I ever hit that roof—but it was foul by a couple of feet. That was the closest I came to a homer that day.

We beat St. Louis 12–0, and the Tigers had eleven hits. But none of those hits was by me; that day I walked twice, struck out twice, and hit a pop fly in my five times up. [On one of those strikeouts, Charles Ward of the *Free Press* wrote that Greenberg "swung at a pitch that would have been ball four in order to avoid walking."]

In that game, George McQuinn, the Browns' first baseman, deliberately dropped a foul ball to give me another swing. But, of course, I didn't take advantage of that either.

◆

Billy Sullivan was behind the plate for the Browns during that late-season series with the Tigers. "We were playing in Detroit, a doubleheader," recalled Sullivan, "and it was critical now for Hank to get home runs. I wasn't that close to Hank then, though I would be later, when I went over to Detroit, but here it is I'm calling for a fastball and I get the ball and it's about two feet outside. I went to the mound and I said to the pitcher, 'What are you doing?' He said, 'He's not going to break a record with my name in the paper.' This guy was not one of our top pitchers. I said, 'You're up here to pitch, you're not up here to put somebody on base purposely.' But Hank got walked over and over again. Then there was another pitcher who came in after him named Howard Mills. He was actually trying to get the ball over but he couldn't."

Birdie Tebbetts recalled an incident when there were about six or eight games to go. "The pitcher for the game—I don't remember his name—walked by Greenberg and said, 'Hank, it's not going to hurt me, I'll ease up.' Hank popped up every time with that guy. And the next guy walked up and said, 'You're not going to get any home runs off me you Jew son of a bitch.' And Hank hit two of them. It was in Detroit. It worked both ways."

◆

Sure, there was added pressure being Jewish. How the hell could you get up to home plate every day and have some son of a bitch call you a Jew bastard and a kike and a sheenie and get on your ass without feeling the pressure. If the ballplayers weren't doing it, the fans were. I used to get frustrated as hell. Sometimes I wanted to go up in the stands and beat the shit out of them.

Being Jewish did carry with it a special responsibility. After all, I was representing a couple of million Jews among a hundred million gentiles, and I was always in the spotlight. I was big and I wasn't the greatest player in the world. I made a lot of errors in the field and struck out a lot. Not a lot by today's standards, but it was in those days. I think I struck out 101 times in one year. That wasn't good. Anyway, I felt responsibility. I was there every day, and if I had a bad day, every son of a bitch was calling me names so that I had to make good. I just had to show them that a Jew could play ball.

It was 1938 and I was now making good as a ballplayer. Nobody expected war, least of all the ballplayers. I didn't pay much attention to Hitler at first or any of the political goings-on at the time. I was too stupid to read the front pages, and I just went ahead and played. Of course, as time went by, I came to feel that if I, as a Jew, hit a home run, I was hitting one against Hitler.

◆

"In Europe," wrote Hugh Bradley in the *New York Post*, "they are asking, 'What is Hitler going to do?' I cannot answer that any more than can those experts who are wasting so much space nowadays trying to reach a sane conclusion concerning an insane man. I can only join other civilized humans in hoping as well as in making suggestions which scarcely can be printed here in full view of the tiny tots.

"In America the question is, 'Can Greenberg do it?' There's some sense in that. . . ."

"Don't ask, don't ask," Greenberg told reporters newly arrived at the batting cage. "I've heard that question so much since somebody first thought it up way back in June that I even hear it now in my sleep." He paused and grinned at the interrupter.

On his bruises: "Maybe they were just wild. Or maybe they thought that if they loosened me up a bit I wouldn't be so easy about standing up there and swinging."

There were now four games left, with two homers needed to tie Ruth and one more to break the record.

On September 29, Detroit beat St. Louis again, 6–2, and Greenberg got only one hit, a single to left, and was out on two pop-ups and a fly ball to center field.

"Things are so quiet in the American League these days," wrote Tom Meany, "that it's a headline when Hank Greenberg doesn't hit a home run."

Billy Rogell recalled that with 58 home runs and one week to go in the season, "they'd walk Hank. I guess they just didn't want him to beat Babe Ruth's record." Because he was a Jew? Rogell was asked. "I don't think just because he was Jewish, but that had a lot to do with it," he said. "But the guys on the club were pulling like hell for him every time he walked up there, everybody kept his fingers crossed that he would hit a home run. He was one of us."

There were now three games left in the season, all with the Indians in Cleveland. The second of these was scheduled for Friday, but it rained, and so a doubleheader was scheduled for Sunday, October 2.

◆

Well, Denny Galehouse shut us out 5–0 on Saturday. He pitched the greatest game of his life, and we only got five hits. And he gave me nothing to hit. I went 0–4, with no walks.

[In the ninth inning, Greenberg grounded out to second base and, wrote Ward of the *Free Press*, "was so mad that he kicked bats off the rack in front of the Tiger dugout to relieve his feelings."]

◆

The Sunday games were switched from League Park to the much larger Municipal Stadium in an attempt, said management, to capitalize on Greenberg's home-run record pursuit by getting more fans into the ballpark. In fact, most Sunday and holiday games in Cleveland were switched to Municipal Stadium.

◆

Old League Park was a tough enough park for a right-handed hitter to hit a home run in—it was 374 feet down the left-field line—but Municipal Stadium was almost impossible.

I still had two homers to go to tie the record, and now it was down to two games before the end of the season.

Sunday was cloudy and overcast; seeing the ball was difficult. What compounded the difficulties was that Bob Feller was the pitcher in the first game, and this was when he was really Rapid Robert. Feller was in a class by himself. There's an old expression that describes why hitters were turned back from the Major Leagues, and it goes, "His heart was in his hitting, but his ass was out." And that explains it. You pull back when you see that ball coming at you, but you have to have that instinct to stay in if it's going to break away for a curveball. I suppose it's just an inborn talent; some guys have it and some don't. I guess I stayed up at the plate so many times and watched the ball coming at me so many times that I followed it well, and I was always confident that I could get out of the way of the pitch no matter where it was thrown and when it was thrown. The fear of being hit in the head is always there; it has frightened quite a few ballplayers. You don't mind getting hit in the shoulder or the back or the leg; that's just a temporary bruise and part of the game. That is one of the problems of being a batter—you have to go up there with the thought that maybe the ball will hit you instead of you hitting it. You can't let that worry you. The only pitcher who really ever frightened me and made me think that I wouldn't be able to get out of the way of the pitch if he let one slip by accident was Bob Feller.

Fortunately, Feller was not the kind of pitcher to throw at a batter— he didn't have to be. He didn't try to intimidate you. He had so much stuff on the ball that it wasn't required on his part. Nevertheless, he was wild when he first came up. [Feller, only nineteen years old in 1938, was in his third season in the Major Leagues.] He had a very peculiar delivery, and he liked to blink his eyes when he was pitching. Many times he pitched low and behind you, and that would give you cause to think.

Before the game Feller had said that he was going "to make Greenberg earn any home runs he hit off me."

In that first game on Sunday, Feller really burned them in, and that was the day he set the Major League record for strikeouts in one game: 18. He struck me out twice. It was dark, and I had trouble following the ball. But I did get a double off him, hitting one off the wall in left center. I hit another that might have been a homer, but Roy Weatherly made a running one-handed stab in center field. I was also walked once in that game. That was the best I could do off Feller that day.

◆

The Tigers, however, beat the Indians, 4–1, in the first game of the doubleheader. The winning pitcher for Detroit was Harry Eisenstat, a small left-hander from Brooklyn. "Feller was throwing the ball at about 105 miles an hour, and with a curve at about 95 miles an hour," recalled Birdie Tebbetts, the Detroit catcher in that game. "He just mowed us down. Yet we were able to score off him. Meanwhile, Eisenstat was throwing the ball at about 81 miles an hour, and struck out three guys. And he beat Feller. It was kind of funny."

One game left and Greenberg needed two homers to tie Babe Ruth's record. Not impossible, for he had hit two homers in eleven different games that season.

◆

In the final game of the season Johnny Humphries, a rookie pitcher, was almost as fast as Feller and he seemed even faster because the shadows were starting to come across the field. I hit only one long ball, a 420-footer, but it only went for a single. I had 3-for-3 that game, all singles, and walked once.

It kept getting darker and darker. Remember, there were no lights in those days. The game only lasted seven innings before it was called on account of darkness. It really shouldn't have lasted that long. But the umpire was George Moriarty, my friend. I know that he wanted me to have every possible chance at the Babe's record. After the seventh inning Moriarty said to me, "I'm sorry, Hank. But this is as far as I can go."

I said, "That's all right, George, this is as far as I can go, too." So I missed out on the record.

♦

As for Greenberg's being walked several times in the last week of the season, Eisenstat, a Jewish teammate, said, "Frankly, I think the pitchers were just trying to get him out and they were trying to be too fine. They walked him and he hit a few good balls, but like on that last day, the ball didn't carry. And I don't think they were deliberately walking him."

Feller commented later on the possibility that pitchers didn't pitch to Greenberg in the last week of the 1938 season: "With a very successful hitter, the pitchers were anti-Semitic. That's a joke. The whole thing is ridiculous anyway. We played the Tigers about a week before and Hank got a home run or two in that series."

♦

Naturally I was disappointed in not getting the record after having come so close. But as a matter of fact, my 58 home runs didn't afford me any thrill. I never compared myself to the Babe, and I wasn't that kind of a home-run hitter. I averaged around 35, so this was just a freak season for me. My goal in baseball was always RBIs, to break Gehrig's record of 184 RBIs. I would have loved to do that. I didn't accomplish it, but I came awfully close.

But in 1938 there was no television and no tape recorders that reporters carried around for radio interviews. There were only a relatively few newspapermen following me. There were the wire services, and if I hit a home run, they'd report it around the country, but I was never harassed by the press. As a matter of fact, Ruth broke the record in 1927, and then five years later Foxx hit 58, and then six years later I hit 58. I guess they just assumed that one of these days someone was going to hit over 60 home runs. But from the time I hit 58 in 1938, it was twenty-three years before Roger Maris came up with the record-breaking 61. There was no comparison between the publicity. For one thing, he was breaking the record in New York City, and I was breaking the record in Detroit. The Detroit club never made any fuss about it. They didn't care about it even though I was getting good publicity for the club.

I always felt that Walter Briggs, the owner of the Tigers, was almost pulling for me not to break Ruth's record, because it might mean $5,000 or $10,000 more in salary for me. Today, if a guy had a chance to break the record, they'd be publicizing him and making a folk hero out of him, as they did Pete Rose when he was going after DiMaggio's consecutive-game hitting streak. And, of course, it was a big deal when Reggie Jackson hit 500 home runs; it's sort of a milestone. And Rod Carew got 3,000 base hits. Today owners seek publicity for the teams; that desire is the opposite of the way it was in our time. The owners tried to keep the ballplayers' accomplishments or notoriety under their hats. As a matter of fact, they always said that Branch Rickey would rather finish second than first because then he wouldn't have to pay so much salary to his ballplayers. As long as they finished second, the fans would anticipate a winner next year, and they'd buy their tickets and Branch would figure he came out ahead.

But my 58 homers in 1938—falling two short of the Babe's record—has become so closely associated with my name that by now they usually go together in the same breath: Hank Greenberg—58 home runs. Some people still have it fixed in their minds that the reason I didn't break Ruth's record was because I was Jewish, that the ballplayers did everything they could to stop me. That's pure baloney. The fact is quite the opposite: So far as I could tell, the players were mostly rooting *for* me, aside from the pitchers.

In retrospect it's very peculiar. I'm remembered most for having hit 58 home runs in a season. At the time I didn't consider it a big achievement. I never put myself in Ruth's class as a home-run hitter. He was head and shoulders above any home-run hitter in baseball in my era, and certainly he's in a class by himself for all time. His 714 home runs in a twenty-two-year career—the first four years as a pitcher—were hit in 3,993 fewer times at bat than Hank Aaron, who broke the record and finished with 755 home runs after playing twenty-three years. That's not to take away from Aaron's home-run record, but certainly if the Babe had played in the current baseball climate with the leagues expanded to twenty-six teams and the talent watered down, there's no telling how many home runs he would have hit.

There's no question that the competition was keener in those days. Despite the influx later of great black players, the talent overall then was more concentrated. The reason is, almost all the athletes turned to baseball. There were no other professional athletics to speak of. Football was in its infancy, basketball was nonexistent, tennis was for the newly rich or ne'er-do-wells, and hockey was a Canadian sport that hadn't invaded the United States. Baseball was *the* game, and all the athletes who had any talent at all tried to make a career in professional baseball. That was the kind of competition the Babe was up against.

As for 1938, I always felt lucky just to have had an unusually good home-run season. My batting average was only .315. I drove in 146 runs, which was not outstanding for me at that time, in comparison to the previous year when I had 183. Foxx led the league with 175 RBIs in 1938, so I considered the season not much of a success. History labels you incorrectly. I would have said that I should have been remembered for driving in 183 runs, but instead, I'm remembered for a record that I didn't find particularly satisfying.

There is no doubt that home runs bring publicity and recognition. Having hit 58 home runs and having had so much publicity about my attempt to break the Babe's record, I was now more or less accepted as the new home-run king. Jimmie Foxx was starting to go downhill by this time; in fact, he was nearing the end of his career. I was young and up and coming, and I guess people expected I'd hit 58 home runs the next season as well.

I went home that winter so my brother Joe, a third baseman in the minor leagues, and I could spend a lot of time together. We used to go down to Broadway and play handball and have dinner and go to a show or just browse around. It was a new experience for us, from living in the Bronx and then having all that free time, no more school, money in our pockets. We thought we had the world by the tail.

We were having dinner one night at Toots Shor's when a fellow came in and was introduced by Toots. The fellow's name was David Marx. He asked us if we would like to go to a show and we said, "Of course," so he handed us two tickets. We finished our dinner and hustled off to our first Broadway show. Sitting next to us was another gentleman and his wife. He turned out to be David's older brother, Louis Marx, the toy king. Louis and Dave and I became fast friends over the years. I mention this because Louis Marx was an extraordinary man. He was self-made, self-educated, and he built a tremendous personal empire in the toy business with a very imaginative approach to human nature and world problems and people. I don't know how much business he was doing then, but some years down the line he sold his business to the Quaker Oats Company for $51 million.

What I admired most about him was that he had tremendous physical endurance and ability and, in particular, he required very little sleep. He was

THE STORY OF MY LIFE

the kind of man who could sleep three or four hours a night, and get up with his batteries recharged and ready to go again for another twenty hours at full speed. Of course, being very successful (I guess he was a multimillionaire at that time) he was very generous with his money. Aside from being a natural philosopher, Louis could quote Shakespeare whenever it was apropos. He was much older than I was, about fifteen years older, and the mere fact that he associated with me gave me a certain satisfaction. Over the years he became a very close friend, adviser, and counselor, and I learned a great deal about life from him.

◆

The year 1938 marked the departure from the Tigers of two of Greenberg's favorites in baseball. One was Mickey Cochrane, who was fired as manager in midseason; Greenberg considered him the greatest catcher in the history of the game. The other man to leave the team was Jo-Jo White.

◆

Jo-Jo and I roomed together on the road for about five years, and we had a great relationship. We enjoyed being on the road together and we had a good time. We were coming back from Cleveland at the end of the season. In September it was the custom of most people, not just ballplayers but gentlemen, to buy new fall hats. They would dispose of their summer straw hats and buy felt ones. During the season Jo-Jo had been sitting on the bench having been platooned in center field, and he was very annoyed with Del Baker, our manager. This was now the first week in October and Del had just bought a brand-new felt hat. While we were on the train returning to Detroit, Jo-Jo had a drink or two and decided to attack Del Baker's hat. He did. He messed it up. He got it dirty and pushed the crown and then threw it up on the hat rack and didn't say anything. Of course, when Del came to get his hat he was very unhappy. He knew someone had deliberately ruined his hat. He finally found out it was Jo-Jo, and by next spring Jo-Jo was gone.

◆

Another unusual character in the big leagues in Greenberg's time was Morris (Moe) Berg, the catcher, the linguist, and the lawyer (he received his degree from Columbia Law School while still playing for the White Sox). Berg, who died in 1972, told a story of returning to his undergraduate alma mater, Princeton, and visiting Dr. Albert Einstein at the famous scientist's home there. "Mr. Berg," said Einstein, "you teach me to catch and I'll teach you mathematics." Einstein paused. "But let's forget about it, because I'm sure you'd learn mathematics faster than I'd learn baseball." Einstein smiled, offered Berg a cup of tea, and went on to play the violin for him.

Berg and Greenberg had a great deal in common besides baseball. They were both in the American League, were both born in New York City, both brought a studious approach to their profession, and both were Jewish. There was something else. "Both had style," said Broadway Charlie Wagner. Wagner was a pitcher with the Red Sox in the late 1930s when Berg was a teammate. Berg, then near the end of his career, was a third-string catcher and bullpen coach. "Both Hank and Moe had a good sense of humor, and tact, and each had a great rapport with other players," said Wagner. "I know that Moe admired the way Hank carried himself. He used to say that Hank lent so much class to baseball, and that there should be more class guys like him in the game."

◆

I never saw a less likely ballplayer in my life than Moe Berg. He was an intellectual. He held seven or eight degrees and could speak something like ten languages. He was also one of the few Jews in baseball in the 1930s, and even though you might expect there to be some affinity between us, there was really none. It just happened that we traveled in different circles. Moe was what you would call a special Jew, much better educated than most of the first-generation Jews that I had grown up with in the Bronx. Moe played for the White Sox in the late '20s, then moved to Washington, Cleveland, and Boston when I was breaking in with the Tigers. I'm sure he rooted for me, but we never had occasion to talk much. I never had a conversation with him about being Jewish. He was a good-natured, good-looking guy, and kind of mysterious. In later years we learned that he worked as a spy for the United States just before and during the Second World War.

I remember that Moe used to carry about six different newspapers around with him, and he'd read them out in the bullpen. He couldn't hit much, but he was a pretty good catcher. But we used to tease him. "Moe," we'd say, "you've got seven college degrees, and you still call for the wrong pitch."

Hank Greenberg during his high school basketball days, 1929. *AP/Wide World Photos.*

Hank Greenberg at the age of 19, about to begin his professional baseball career with Hartford's Class A team. A newspaper story accompanying this picture referred to him as "Hyman Greenberg." *National Baseball Library, Cooperstown, New York.*

OVERLEAF: The Washington Avenue Annex settlement house baseball team in 1925, when they were called the Bronx Champions. Hank "Bruggy" Greenberg, age 14, is the second uniformed player from the right in the front row. *The Estate of Henry Greenberg.*

Hank Greenberg with his parents, Sarah and David, at home in the Bronx in November 1939. *UPI/Bettman Newsphotos.*

Hank Greenberg, at left, about five years old. With him are his brother Ben (back), brother Joe (center), and sister, Lillian (right). *The Estate of Henry Greenberg.*

Joe Greenberg, left, and Hank at the Detroit Tigers' spring training camp at Lakeland, Florida, in 1935. Joe, a rookie minor leaguer, had been invited to spend a few weeks in the camp. "At one time," Joe recalled, "some people were writing that the Greenberg brothers might replace the Dean brothers." *AP/Wide World.*

First baseman Greenberg in 1933, his rookie year with the Tigers. *AP/Wide World.*

The stars of the 1937 American League All-Star team pose prior to the game at Griffiths Stadium in Washington, D.C. Left to right: Lou Gehrig, Joe Cronin, Bill Dickey, Joe DiMaggio, Charlie Gehringer, Jimmie Foxx, and Hank Greenberg. *AP/Wide World.*

Hank Greenberg for Wheaties, 1940, Detroit.
Smith Brothers.

Hank Greenberg receives the 19th American
League Most Valuable Player plaque from baseball
commissioner Judge Kenesaw Mountain Landis.
Press Association, Inc.

From left: Hank Greenberg, Joe DiMaggio, and Mel Ott. *Baseball Hall of Fame and Museum, Cooperstown, New York.*

Greenberg, third from left, celebrates a successful hunting trip taken with army comrades in 1944. *Corbis Photos.*

Ted Williams in 1941, when he batted .406. Greenberg said Williams was the greatest hitter of his time. *UPI/Bettman Newsphotos.*

Mickey Cochrane in 1934, when he became player/manager of the Detroit Tigers and led them to the American League pennant. *UPI/Bettman Newsphotos.*

Rudy York, one of Greenberg's favorite teammates, could not adequately play any position other than first base, and thus precipitated Greenberg's move to left field.

CHAPTER 8

"Hank Greenberg is the highest paid player in baseball today and, with the lone exception of Babe Ruth, the highest paid of all time," reported H. G. Salsinger in the *Detroit News* in early 1939.

Salsinger had obtained Internal Revenue records and found that while Greenberg received $25,000 in 1937, Gehringer had received only $20,000. "The income tax returns for 1938 have not been checked and therefore are not available. . . ." Mickey Cochrane had received $45,000, but that represented three salaries: one for playing, one for managing, and the third as vice president of the club.

Ruth had earned $80,000 at his peak in the early 1930s. After the 1938 season Briggs offered Greenberg $35,000, the same salary he received before hitting 58 home runs. Years later, Greenberg told Jim Murray of the *Los Angeles Times*: "I squeezed an extra $5,000 out of them, but it wasn't easy. Back then, if an owner offered you a thousand-dollar raise, you would kiss his hand."

◆

In 1939, when the Tigers were training in Lakeland and the Yankees were at St. Petersburg, we heard rumors about Lou Gehrig not having a good spring, and it seemed as if he wasn't hitting the ball for distance, and his general all-around play was sluggish. Naturally we took it all with a grain of salt; we knew that once the season started Lou would be his old natural self as the backbone of the Yankee ball team. Anyway, it wasn't until early May that the Yankees came out to Detroit for their first series with the Tigers. At that time Gehrig played very poorly through the opening weeks of the season. Then to everyone else's amazement, they announced in Detroit that Lou was terminating his consecutive-game streak, which had reached 2,130 plus games. Of course, this was big news throughout the country because Gehrig was known as the "Iron Horse." He had played in so many consecutive games with all types of injuries. Now in Detroit he was pulling himself out of the lineup and breaking his streak.

It was customary for the visiting team to have twenty minutes to a half hour of batting practice and ten minutes of fielding practice before the game. Usually the pitchers who weren't working that day chased fungoes in the outfield during batting practice. I was very curious about what happened to Gehrig and I noticed that he went out to the outfield with the pitchers to chase fungoes from the right-field foul line to the center-field flagpole, back and forth for half an hour. He had quite a workout; it looked like he was trying to shake himself out of some sort of physical lethargy and get loose. He worked hard. Then when the batting practice period was over, he went to the clubhouse and that's the last we saw of him. Two days later, when the Yankees left town, they went to Chicago and the papers said that Gehrig had gone on to the Mayo Clinic to determine what was wrong with him. After the doctors examined him they discovered that Gehrig had this rare disease [amyotrophic lateral sclerosis, a progressive degenerative fatal disease affecting the spinal cord, usually beginning in middle age, and characterized by increasing and spreading muscle weakness], and it was the kind of disease that could lead to an early death. That was shocking to everyone. Lou Gehrig never wore an overcoat living in New York, never wore a sweater, never wore a hat. He was supposed to be your typical strongman. It was so difficult to associate a deadly disease with this healthy specimen.

When we came into Yankee Stadium a couple of weeks later, in mid-May, there was Lou. His hair had turned white almost overnight and he could barely drag his leg up the steps of the dugout. He was the captain of the team, and he had to come out and present the lineup at home plate. It was pitiful to see what had happened in two weeks' time. Of course, what really had happened was that he was told what was wrong with him, and once he realized he had this incurable disease, the will and desire to carry on left him. He never played another ball game, and passed away two years later. I only mention that because so many times people carry on when they don't know what's wrong with them, but as soon as they find out, the will to fight disappears and they deteriorate very rapidly.

In 1939 the Tigers finished in fifth place. While I didn't have a sensational year, I still led the team in hitting, with a .312 average; had 112 runs batted in, which was fourth in the American League; and hit 33 home runs, which was second in the league only to Jimmie Foxx, who hit 35. So it wasn't a total disaster as far as my personal record was concerned.

But 1940 started with a bang. In January I got a notice from Jack Zeller, who was then the general manager of the Tigers. He wanted to see me in Detroit. So I took the train out to Detroit and went up to the front office. We had a long visit. The sum and substance of the conversation was that Jack wanted me to try the outfield. Rudy York could not cut it in the outfield, nor could he handle the catching job as well as we had thought he would, and they felt his natural position was first base. In order to strengthen the lineup, they decided to move me to the outfield. Of course, this caught me by complete surprise. I had never played any position other than first base, except for that very short period when I was a rookie and was tried at third. I had never worn a finger mitt in a Major League game. The first thing Jack said was that they were going to cut me $5,000 because I hadn't had the kind of year they had expected of me the year before. If I wanted to play first base, I would have to sign a contract for $5,000 less than I had received in 1939. This also took me by surprise, because I had had a decent season.

I went home to think it over, and I came to the conclusion that they were getting ready to trade me. Either they felt my salary was too high or they felt Rudy York could replace me. He was younger and could play first base.

I came back to Jack Zeller a day or two later with my proposition. I figured that if they were going to trade me, I might as well get as big a salary as I possibly could, because then when I went to the new club, that's what my pay would be. I told Zeller I would sign for the same amount of money I received in 1939—$40,000—and I would make an attempt to play outfield. I would go down to spring training and put on a finger mitt and work out in left field and work real hard to try to learn the position. If, at the end of spring training, they were satisfied with my progress and felt I could do the job in left field, then they would have to give me a bonus of $10,000. On the other hand, if they felt that I couldn't play left field, then I would go back to first base and it would be up to them to decide what they wanted to do. Either York could replace me as the first baseman, or I would play first base and they would have to do something with Rudy York.

Well, Jack kicked that thought around and, to my surprise, agreed to it. So we drew it up in my contract and I signed for the same amount as I had received the previous year, with the provision that if I was in the lineup in left field on opening day, I would receive a bonus of $10,000.

That spring the challenge of playing the outfield was great. I really worked my tail off. In fact, Bing Miller, one of our coaches, hit so many fungoes that one day he dropped the bat and said he couldn't hit another one. I was the one who was supposed to be getting the workout, but I was out there prancing around waiting to chase fungoes, and Bing's hands were full of blisters.

I was strong, I was twenty-nine years old and in the prime of my life, and I loved to play. I really could stay out in that outfield all day and shag flies. It got to be quite a challenge and, as a matter of fact, it got to be a pleasure. After a while I started to improve. I learned to judge balls and then it became a matter of learning to play the hitters.

I started in left field for the Tigers on opening day in 1940. And on opening day I went to the club office and got paid the $10,000 that had been agreed upon, and everything was fine.

About a week or so after the season opened we went to Cleveland and played in League Park. I remember distinctly there was a fly ball hit out along the left-field line and there was a question as to whether the third baseman was going to catch it, or the shortstop, or the left fielder. Well, I wasn't about to catch it because the sun was in my eyes and it was equidistant from the shortstop and the third baseman, so I just stood out there and let them fight for it. Of course, it dropped and I think a couple of runs scored. When play was resumed, damned if Pete Fox didn't come out of the Detroit dugout and replace me. I'm standing out there in left field wondering what the hell's going on. Fox came out very sheepishly and said, "Hank, Baker wants me to take your place."

My first reaction was, "Tell Baker to go to hell and go back to the dugout."

But I couldn't afford to embarrass Pete Fox, who was one of the boys I played with in Beaumont, Texas, right on through the Major Leagues.

At the moment he was sitting on the bench as a reserve after having been a regular, and so I didn't want to embarrass him. I gave up my position and came running in. Rather than go to the bench and start a brouhaha, I went into the clubhouse and got dressed. The first thing I did when I got back to the hotel was call Jack Zeller, the general manager who had arranged for me to go to left field.

I said, "Listen, Jack, I don't want to ever be embarrassed again. The season just started. It was a difficult ball out there for anybody. It dropped, and no matter who was playing left field or who was playing shortstop or third, I've seen it happen a hundred times. There was no reason to embarrass me by taking me out of the ball game. If that's going to be the pattern, the hell with it. I'm not going to play the outfield for you. You put me in the outfield, you take your chances that I can play outfield. I'm going to stay out there, even if I get hit on the head with a fly ball. You better tell Del Baker he'd better not pull that trick again because there was no reason to do that. The next time he sends somebody out, I'm not going to get off the field."

It was a high-handed way of responding to Baker's action, but Jack Zeller and I had known each other for years (going back to Beaumont when he was the general manager). In fact, he always teased me when I was in the minor leagues, always spurring me on. We had a great relationship. This was his first year as general manager of the Tigers. Here I was twenty-nine years old and Del Baker was making out like I was Babe Ruth in his forties, putting out a relief outfielder for me, that I was too old to move. I was physically as fit as I would ever be. It was just the manager trying to show his authority by taking me out for defensive purposes. I knew damn well that if that started, there would be a lot of times when, if something went wrong in left field, if I misjudged the ball or threw it to the wrong place, he'd take me out. I didn't want that to happen. I wanted them to know that I'd make my share of errors and mistakes, and if they wanted me to play out there, they would have to bear with me.

Fortunately, it didn't happen again the rest of the season. And as time went by I improved tremendously in the outfield.

◆

Years later Barney McCoskey, the Tiger center fielder then, remembered Greenberg coming to him one day early in the 1940 season: "Hank said, 'I need a little help in the outfield. I never played much of the outfield and I know you're a good center fielder and if I'm going to play alongside of you I'll need your help on where to throw the ball. Could you come out early?' I said, 'Sure, Hank, I'd be glad to.' You know a guy like that had been around and it was only my second year. That was something. So we'd get to the park at about 10:00 or 10:30 in the morning. I would throw balls up against the fence and holler at him, 'Second base!' 'Third base!' You know, where to throw the ball. And we did that for maybe four straight days.

"After we did that for four days, he asked me to meet him downtown in front of a building and I said sure. And we go up to the third floor and walk into a tailor and he tells the tailor to make this young man McCoskey a suit. And that was for helping him. I couldn't believe it. I never had no hundred-dollar suit. I would pay about $38 to $45. And he bought me a tailor-made suit. I didn't know material, but I know it fit good."

Another outfielder Greenberg went to for advice on fielding was Joe DiMaggio. Greenberg, like virtually everyone else, had great respect for DiMaggio's ability in the field. DiMaggio also admired Greenberg. "He was one of the truly great hitters," said DiMaggio, "and when I first saw him bat, he made my eyes pop out. He was so big and he had great power. He was a menacing figure." DiMaggio recalled years later that when Greenberg switched to left field in 1940, it proved that he was a player with "team spirit." "He didn't have to yield his position at first base," said DiMaggio. "When he made the change, he asked me about charging base hits in the outfield. I told him that you can't come in too fast, but you have to try to float in. I also suggested that when he's fielding the ball he put one knee down so that the ball doesn't go through you. Today, with the artificial turf being so lively, that can be dangerous because the ball could bounce over your head. Hank learned to play the outfield well. He was one of the most determined men I've ever known."

◆

Part of my routine was to practice fielding balls in the corner when they came down the left-field line. The balls would hit the corner and carom off the wall. Every park was different and had its own particular angles that would make the balls deflect a little differently. So whenever we'd go to a new park, I'd practice watching them come off the wall. The most famous left-field wall in the league was, of course, Fenway Park in Boston; the bottom part was wood, and the top part was tin. If the ball hit the wood part, it would ricochet off with some pace, but if it hit the tin part, the ball would drop straight down. Knowing how to play the carom meant the difference between a double and a triple. I learned to play off the walls pretty well. Some players never learned that. Pete Fox played in the league thirteen years and never learned. Nowadays you still see players misplay balls off the wall so badly that they end up chasing the ball into the corner, where it hits the angle, and then they have to chase it all the way around toward center field.

I learned to be a better-than-average left fielder. I had a strong throwing arm and a good sense of where to play the hitters. I picked that up very quickly, and playing the outfield was a joy after having played first base. It was easy; there were very few chances in the outfield, and I could concentrate primarily on hitting. That year I batted .340, which was the highest average I ever attained in the Major Leagues. I also hit 41 homers and drove in 150 runs. In fact, I was voted the most valuable player in the league. That was the kind of season I had.

Being voted the most valuable while in left field and having won the honor in 1935 at first base, I believe I'm the only player in the history of the game who has won the Most Valuable Player award playing two different positions. I can't say that I won it in 1940 for my fielding, I'm sure hitting had a great deal to do with it.

◆

Billy Sullivan, who had been traded to Detroit from St. Louis, recalled Greenberg's thoroughness as a player: "He used to really work on me to make me holler and rant at the umpire, saying you're not going to get that call, but you'll get the next one.

"Hank watched everyone, the catcher, the pitchers. In our day pitchers wound up. Now, they practically pitch from the same position we held men on with. Pretty generally, if a fella came up over his cap and was winding up and stopping short of his top button, it was because he was going to throw a curve. The ball was gripped a little differently. If he went back a little farther it was going to be a fastball. You got all kinds of things like that. Then, when they'd hold a man on base, they'd hold the ball up a little higher maybe. There were a million things like that to look for, and Hank was exhaustive."

◆

The Tigers had acquired Bobo Newsom in a trade with the Browns in 1939. And in 1940 he was very important in our drive for the pennant. Before he came to the Tigers Bobo had traveled around the league quite extensively. I believe he played with the Washington Senators on five different occasions; he played with each of the New York franchises—the Dodgers, the Giants, and the Yankees. He made frequent trips to the St. Louis Browns, where he usually wound up because no one else would take him. But Bobo wasn't really a troublemaker. He just liked to brag, and he usually could back up his bragging because he was quite a pitcher. But when he had been playing with a bad ball team, something would always come apart and Bobo never wound up with a good record until the year he came over to us. In 1940 he won twenty-one games and lost only five. During the time that I struggled against him he had a slider, which wasn't used too frequently in the Major Leagues at that time. He'd keep the ball low and outside, and I'd be up there trying to pull the ball. I didn't have much success against Bobo unless he accidentally threw one in the wrong place.

A funny thing happened during the season. Bobo and I were quite friendly and staying at the same hotel in Detroit. This particular evening we were sitting in the lobby and Bobo said to me that he had a date with a young lady and was going to his room and would be down in a few minutes. He went up in the elevator and, as he did, an attractive young lady came into the lobby and looked around. Finally, she came up to me and asked if I had seen Bobo Newsom.

I said, "No, I haven't seen him at all."

She said, "I was supposed to meet him for a date."

I said, "I don't know. Bobo can have two or three dates in the evening, and I haven't seen him."

With that, she got very friendly and said, "Why don't we go out to dinner?"

I said, "Fine."

So I took her to dinner and we came back to the hotel later that night and she said, "Well, as long as I was going to stay with Bobo, I might as well stay with you."

I said, "That's all right with me." After she left the next morning, I went out to the ballpark, and there was Bobo ranting and raving about this girl who stood him up. He had spent the whole evening getting ready for her, and she never made an appearance. To this day I have not told Bobo what had actually happened.

Those escapades were few and far between. I was too interested in baseball to think very much about the ladies. I rarely went out. I had a lot of married friends living in Detroit at the time, and I'd go to their homes for dinner and every once in a while someone would try to fix me up with a young lady, but I was basically wrapped up in the game and I didn't have the inclination to stay out all night and drink and try to romance some girl, knowing that the next day I'd have a big headache and wouldn't be able to do my job at the ballpark.

Over the years, I've seen many a good ballplayer ruin his career by thinking that it would last forever and why not have fun while I'm doing it. They drank too much and smoked too much, and the guys who died earliest were those who smoked and drank beyond their limits. Some of these ballplayers would smoke constantly from the time they got up until they went to bed. They didn't drink like normal human beings. I've seen guys drink Coca-Cola and scotch. The scotch would be out of the bottle and so would the Coca-Cola. They were just young men who came up from the farms and found life in the big leagues very exciting, and they didn't quite know how to handle it. I suppose the same thing goes on today. Human nature being what it is, there are probably plenty of ballplayers today not taking care of themselves and ruining their careers. Probably fifteen or twenty years from now they'll look back and realize what a mistake they've made. We know that's the case today because we see how many ballplayers are involved with drugs.

I was having lunch several years ago with Gary Lavelle, a pitcher and the player representative for the San Francisco Giants. We were talking about the drug problem, and I said, "Gary, I think this is all exaggerated. I think there are very few ballplayers who bother with drugs, maybe 2 or 3 percent, and that puts a black eye on the rest of the players."

He said, "Hank, don't kid yourself. The percentage of ballplayers using drugs is well over 50 percent."

I could hardly believe it, but evidently in the early eighties drugs had taken hold of all the Major League clubs and there was nobody in the front office who was going to bother to do anything about it. They all swept it under the rug until it finally got to be one of the major problems in baseball.

Apropos of the story I told about my experience with Bobo Newsom's date, I want to add that I never considered myself a ladies' man or a bon vivant, but I did socialize.

A few years after I broke into baseball, it seemed that a lot of society people in Detroit began to attend the games. The Briggs family was very prominent in the automotive industry, and they were friendly with the Edsel Fords and the Fisher brothers and all the executives from General Motors. Once they became the visible owners of the team, all their friends had boxes right near the Detroit dugout, and I became one of their favorites. The doctor who attended the players was very well known and very fashionable. He was well up in the jet set in Detroit, and when he invited me to dinner one evening, I accepted.

When I arrived I was ushered into their beautiful home that had a tremendous dining room with a beautiful mahogany table set for twelve or fourteen. The room had parquet floors, shined spotlessly, with a beautiful rug underneath the table. It was an entirely new environment for me. It was way over my head. I remember that when I started cutting away at my chicken one of the bones flew off my plate. It made a tremendous noise as it hit the wood floor and slid over to a corner of the room. I didn't know what to do or what to say. I was terribly embarrassed. None of the other guests made any reference to it, and it sat there all through dinner. I was so self-conscious and so embarrassed. It was the most horrible moment of my life at that time. To show you how I've changed, if this incident had occurred years later, I would have gotten up and gotten the bone and made some joke about it and just carried on with a great deal of self-assurance. But in those days I was just a bumbling, fumbling first baseman; I'll never forget that embarrassing evening.

Nothing interfered with baseball for me, but if there was a second subject, it was usually women, as it was with all the other ballplayers. I was just as interested as anyone else. I had a natural appetite. I just didn't carry it to the extremes that some of the ballplayers did. I'm not going to describe in detail all of my sexual affairs, but I just want to note that I was very normal in that respect.

◆

Billy Sullivan recalled a story Hank told him about living at home during the off-season: "Hank was dating some girl and his mother wasn't too keen about her. Finally a phone call comes for Hank. His mother, who is up on the third floor, answers the phone. Then she hollers down to Hank and Hank gets on the phone but his mother stays on the phone and listens. Hank is trying to dust this girl off and the girl says, 'After all we meant to each other, what am I going to do?' And the mother yells into the phone, 'Go jump in the lake!'"

In June 1940, Greenberg was explaining to sportswriter Jack Miley the difference between playing outfield and playing first base. "On first base I was always arguing with the umpire on close ones," he said. "If the pitcher got into an argument, I helped take his part. At the end of the day's game I would end up sick and tired. I could hardly get to my hotel. And, oh yes, I'd be taking that abuse from the dugout, and I'd try to give it back. . . .

But, Greenberg added, "It still gets awfully lonesome out there where they've got me. It's like a Broadway traffic cop being transferred out to Staten Island."

But he still kept in the ball game in the outfield. He told Bob Considine of the International News Service: "Sometimes I get too worked up over the game. I begin playing the other positions mentally. I'll think Pete Fox isn't playing that right position and I'll wave at him to move over—and he'll get sore. As he has a right to, I guess.

"I saw what was wrong with the batting stance of one of our rookies last year and offered to take him out one morning with me and work at it. He said, 'No. You're hitting .315, Greenberg, and I'm hitting .225. You make thirty grand and I make five. I'm hitting all right. You should be hitting six times as much as me.'" Greenberg chuckled. "I guess that's one of the reasons I'm going to stop worrying about the others and look out for myself this year. I've got a tough job [playing the outfield]. And I still take too many strikes at the plate. I still have a lot of things to learn about baseball."

"Without Greenberg's magnificent hitting the Tigers, the oldest club in the majors, would have finished fifth as they did last year," wrote Stanley Frank in the *New York Post* in late September. "With Greenberg embarked on an incredible streak of long-distance hitting, the Tigers go into the final week the sentimental and actual favorite to win their first pennant since 1935. . . . Since September 3, when the Tigers started their drive from third place, 3½ games behind the Indians, Greenberg has hit in a sustained fashion seldom equaled and never excelled in baseball history.

"In the last 21 games, 15 of which were won by Detroit, Greenberg hit .429. He has belted 14 homers in those 21 games, he has driven in 37 runs, personally scored 33. In only four of those games has he failed to drive in a run and in only one contest has he neglected to drive home a run or score one himself. . . ."

Bill Slocum, in the *New York American* on September 24, said: ". . . If Detroit does win this pennant . . . it will be more for the common sense of Greenberg than even the power he packs in his ringing bat.

"For Hank did something that few ballplayers would do. Something that, to my knowledge, no Major League player has ever done before quite the same way. He gave up a position in which he was an outstanding star, and which he preferred to play, for the good of the Detroit team. . . . 999 ballplayers out of a thousand, I think, would have, in Greenberg's place, gone on playing first base, permitting York and the Detroit management to worry about York.

"First base at Detroit was Hank's. He entered into it by right of conquest and squatter's sovereignty, and had he been any of the sort of guy except the sort of guy he is, the only way they would have gotten him off of it would have been to trade him.

"The majority of us alleged experts were inclined to look on the experiment with a skeptical eye, and to predict that Greenberg would be back on first base by July 4. . . .

"I remember him saying, 'It's the same baseball, Bill, and if I'm a ballplayer I should be able to catch it in the outfield as well as anywhere else. And if I'm not a baseball player, I'm getting old enough to find that out.'"

Joe Williams in the *New York World-Telegram* on September 16: "At the moment Detroit is just about the most amazing city in America. Practically all the big factories are working night and day, most of them geared high for armament production. As a result of the endless shifts of workers, the city never sleeps. Movies, barber shops, and places of entertainment stay open all night.

"This is one of the reasons why Detroit will have night baseball next year. . . ."

Major league baseball had slowly begun to adopt night baseball. There was still opposition to it, with some owners calling it a "circus" atmosphere. The first game under lights was in Cincinnati in 1935, and now more and more teams were putting up lights.

◆

As the 1940 season progressed we wound up battling the Cleveland club for the pennant. It was a very close race. They had a fine ball team headed by some great pitchers like Bob Feller, Mel Harder, and Johnny Allen. They actually had a better ball club than we had, but they had gotten involved in a controversy with their manager, Ossie Vitt. The ensuing publicity reverberated to their disadvantage; the fans around the league, even the local fans, were calling them crybabies for complaining about their manager.

We had to play three games in Cleveland to close out the season. We went down there with a two-game lead and we had to win one out of three. Bob Feller pitched the first game for them and Del Baker, our manager, decided that it would be unwise to use up one of our better pitchers, because Feller, as a rule, could beat not only us, but everybody in the league. He was at the peak of his career and was probably one of the greatest right-handers who ever pitched in the Major Leagues. We had a young rookie pitcher that we had brought up after the minor league season ended, and he had joined the club and hadn't been used. Del Baker, for some unknown reason, decided that he was going to pitch this rookie, Floyd Giebell, against Bob Feller.

Naturally this made a lot of news, a rookie chosen to pitch against Feller in a crucial game. Well, Giebell pitched a strange game. There were men on base every inning, and he managed to get out of jams. I think the Cleveland team hit into three or four double plays, which saved his hide in the early innings, and Rudy York hit a home run with a man on to give us a couple of runs. We finally won the ball game, 4–1, and that clinched the pennant for us.

I think York's bat—he hit .316, had 33 homers and 134 runs batted in—in addition to mine was the key factor in bringing the pennant back to Detroit that year. There was something else aside from the dissension in the Cleveland club that worked against them. We won the pennant partially because of a freak thing in the early days of September. It seemed that Pinky Higgins, our third baseman, had gone out of the lineup with an injury. He and Tommy Bridges, one of our ace pitchers, were hunting friends. At the end of the season they would go hunting in Texas. Tommy had purchased a new rifle with a long-range gauge on it, a sort of telescopic lens. Tommy had pitched the day before so the two of them were sitting in the upper deck of the left-field pavilion during a ball game, and Tommy was pointing the rifle and looking through the telescope, and he looked down at the catcher. Sure enough, he was able to see the catcher's signs to the pitcher and, being a pitcher himself, it wasn't long before he was able to determine what the pitch was going to be. As soon as he assured himself that he could read the pitches, he came down to the dugout and told us that he was able to call the pitches from up in the left-field stands, and that he thought he would be able to relay them to the batter.

The next day we decided to test his ability to read the pitches, and sure enough, he sat up in the stands with Pinky. When the pitch was signaled for a fastball or a curveball, they had arranged a predetermined signal to relay it to the batter. It didn't have to go to the coaches or the bench; it went directly to the batter. Strangely enough, you could look right over the shoulder of the pitcher and look out there in the stands and see the signal. You can just imagine what that did for our ball club. We used the signs for the balance of the season except against the New York club. What we originally did was after Tommy got the signals, he moved from the upper deck where they were sitting alone with no fans around and moved down to the bullpen. A guy was standing out at the center-field bullpen looking in and another player was leaning against the fence and when he pulled his right hand down, that meant it was a curveball, and if he kept his right hand up, that meant it was a fastball.

It was amazing how quickly you could pick it up. Of course, the batter was getting the signal as quickly as the pitcher was. The only club in the league that knew something funny was up was the Yankees. When they came to town McCarthy could sense that the batters were getting the signals. Maybe it was the way we were leaning into the curveballs and were ready for the fastballs. In any case, he sent his squad out to the bullpen and we had to curtail our activities out there. As a result, we moved the spot for calling the signals to the upper deck. We brought one of our minor league managers into Detroit, and he sat up in the upper deck with a pair of binoculars. He'd sit up there all alone and spot the pitchers and if he pulled his right hand down off the binoculars, it was a fastball, and if he left it up there, it was a curveball. The players knew the signs, and even though the center-field bleachers were filled with spectators, we knew exactly where he was sitting. You could look up over the pitcher's head and see him and pick up the sign.

Both Rudy York and I had a field day. Both of us were long-ball hitters who had to get that little extra on the swing to hit the ball out of the park, and it was tremendously helpful to know what the pitch was going to be. Strangely enough, there were some players, like Gerald Walker, who didn't want to take the signs. Charlie Gehringer didn't either, but he could hit without knowing what was coming up; Pinky Higgins would take them. The two players who profited most by it were Rudy York and me. I think the records will bear it out. As I remember it, between the two of us we hit one or two home runs for seventeen consecutive days during the month of September. Either Rudy would hit one, or I would hit one, or sometimes we would each hit two. I think it was picking up those signs that was instrumental in enabling us to win that 1940 pennant. My average from September 4 to 19 was:

AB	1B	2B	3B	HR	R	RBI	Ave.
59	7	5	2	13	30	33	.458

To get a little ahead of the story, we then got into the World Series with the Cincinnati Reds and we picked up the signs against them. We were leading three games to two going into Cincinnati. Unfortunately, we couldn't put our man out in center field in Cincinnati for fear that somebody would pick up on what he was doing and they might lynch him. So we had to do without the signs. However, Ernie Lombardi got hurt, and they put in Jimmy Wilson, a forty-three-year-old catcher. Believe it or not, he was giving his signs so low that we could pick them up from our dugout. So we went into the last game of the World Series, the seventh game, the deciding one, knowing every pitch that was coming up. With all that, Paul Derringer still held us to one run.

Signal stealing is a fascinating aspect of the game. I'm sure it goes on with other ball clubs. I know it went on with the Cleveland Indians in 1948, and in 1959 when I was with the White Sox and we won the pennant in Chicago. We stole the signs from the center-field scoreboard, and I'm sure a lot of other ball clubs do the same. As a matter of fact, it's been rumored that the Yankees were stealing signs from their center-field scoreboard for years. I know that they had a lot of success against Bob Feller. A lot of the hitters who didn't figure to hit Feller had good records against him, and I'm sure they were helped by knowing what was being pitched to them.

Our manager, Del Baker, had a reputation for being one of the best signal stealers in the American League. Del was awfully good at watching how the pitcher gripped the ball. When a lot of pitchers start out in Little League or even American Legion ball, they grip the baseball across the seams for a fastball and with the seams for a curveball. No one told them that they had to disguise their pitches. So they developed that habit and they go on through the minor leagues and even sometimes into the Major Leagues. Because they had formed that habit of pitching the ball in that way, they were very uncomfortable doing it differently. As a result, even when they're pitching in the Major Leagues, the third-base coach can easily call exactly what they're throwing. Even a great pitcher like Rube Walberg, who pitched for the famous Philadelphia Athletics during the years that they won pennants, telegraphed every single pitch that he delivered to the plate. You could read them right from home plate. You could see how he curled his wrist when he threw a curveball, and his wrist would be straight up when he threw a fastball.

I recall many times playing against the St. Louis Browns when they knew we were stealing their signals. The pitcher would wind up with the ball in his glove so nobody could see how he was gripping it until he released it. There were times when the hitter would pick up the signs from the catcher, and the catcher would go and bawl out the pitcher for not covering up his pitches when he himself was giving them away. Many times we picked up the signals from second base. We'd get a man on second who watched the rotation of the fingers going down, and he'd come to the dugout and tell us. As soon as someone got on second base he'd relay the signal to the batter. Taking a step with his right foot toward third base would mean a fastball; if he crossed over with his left foot, that would be a curveball. There were all sorts of tricks that were developed to help the batter in his battle against the pitchers. Hitters always felt that pitchers had a big advantage [from the raised mound to their ability to scuff up the ball] and that anything we did, legal or otherwise, was fair game in trying to defeat the opposing team.

♦

The Tigers were generally favored in the World Series against the Reds, though Detroit was a considerably older team. Charlie Gehringer symbolized for some the oldness of the Tigers even though Gehringer, at age thirty-seven in 1940, had managed to bat .313 in 139 games during the season. "Gehringer is probably being held together with adhesive tape, safety pins and fancy stitching," wrote Joe Williams in the *New York World-Telegram*.

"But," wrote George Kirksey of United Press in analyzing why Detroit should be favored, "there's no antidote for Hank Greenberg's hitting."

Detroit won the first game of the series 7–2 in Cincinnati's Crosley Field, with Greenberg getting a single in his first at bat.

"The contemptuous razzberry was hurled at Greenberg in the fifth when he stood still and watched the third strike spin over the heart of the plate—an old failing with the Detroit slugger," wrote Joe Williams.

Greenberg struck out another time, grounded out and popped out, for 1-for-5.

"The one Tiger who was disappointed over his showing in the first game and determined to do some real celebrating this afternoon was Hank Greenberg. This was the Jewish New Year's day and Henry from the Bronx promised something better than the single he produced against Paul Derringer."

The Reds won Game 2, 5–3, with Bucky Walters outpitching Schoolboy Rowe. "Hank Greenberg was going around before the game moaning that he had lost yesterday's game. 'I hit a bad ball in the first inning and it resulted in a double play. If I had been more patient I might have got hold of one and Walters would have been in deep trouble.'"

In Game 3 Greenberg tripled and scored two runs as the Tigers won in Detroit.

The Reds tied the series in Game 4 by a 5–2 score, with Greenberg going 1-for-4 on a double and one run batted in.

Before Game 5 Bobo Newsom had been unusually quiet in the clubhouse. "The usual boasting and noise were gone," wrote Lou Smith of the *Cincinnati Enquirer*. Newsom's dad had died a few days before, and Newsom had dedicated this game to him. "His sidearm fastball was virtually hurtling down the third-base line at those apprehensive Reds," wrote Bob Considine in the International News Service, "and pounding into Billy Sullivan's catcher mitt with the boom of a bass drum."

Greenberg hit a 3-run homer deep into the left-field stands and had 3 hits in five times at bat overall, driving in 4 runs. Bobo Newsom meanwhile pitched a 3-hit shutout and the Tigers won 8–0.

"Newsom choked up and broke down after reaching the Tiger dressing room," reported the Associated Press. "'It was the hardest game I ever wanted to win,' he said as tears filled his eyes.

"Billy Sullivan, who caught Bobo, wrapped his arm over Newsom's shoulder as they posed for pictures, then said softly, 'Bobo, your dad would have liked this one.'"

With the series back in Crosley Field, the Reds won Game 6, with Walters shutting out the Tigers 4-0. Greenberg went 0-3 with one strikeout. The series now was tied at 3-3.

In the deciding game the next day, Derringer beat Bobo Newsom, working on one day's rest, 2-1. Greenberg could muster just two singles in four times at bat.

◆

What a disappointed lot we were coming back from Cincinnati on that train, losing the final game after a long, hard season. I remember we started drinking on the train, and I think by the time we got back to Detroit, four or five hours later, half of the boys who got off the train had to be helped along. There were thousands of people waiting in the Michigan train depot to welcome the team back and, even though we had been defeated, that made us feel a little better.

◆

A few weeks later Greenberg was named the most valuable player in the league, with Bob Feller in second place and Joe DiMaggio third.

And in November, a social note in a New York newspaper asked this question about Greenberg, and then answered it: "Marriage? Nothing in sight immediately. Hank has been connected up with dozens of local debs and chorus gals and society leaders et al. by the Broadway columnists for years—but they're still wrong and he's still single."

CHAPTER 9

My brother Joe's minor league season* had ended and he had come out to Detroit to see the World Series. He was going to accompany me back to New York. Hitler had marched through the Low Countries and taken France by that time and was on the verge of invading England. The United States had declared that we were going into a draft and everybody had to register. I decided that the smartest thing for me to do to avoid a lot of publicity was to register on our way back from Detroit. So we stopped off en route at Geneva, a town in Upper New York State. We pulled into a school, and he and I both registered. For some unknown reason I gave my address as the Detroit Leland Hotel, Detroit, Michigan. Joe put 663 Crotona Park North, Bronx, which was our home. I don't know what prevailed upon me to list my residence as Detroit. Maybe I thought it would keep me from being drafted so soon. What a mistake that turned out to be! Some 6,000 numbers were drawn out of the fishbowl, and my number was around 5,000, and Joe's was around 2,300. It looked as though I was not going to be drafted immediately but that he, of course, might be. I figured I'd be called, but I thought I'd be able to play out the 1941 season. It didn't work out that way for me.

That winter I took a trip to Hawaii and stayed out there the month of January and part of February. I returned on the *Mariposa*. On the day I docked, February 11, I was met by a battery of photographers and newsmen. It seems my draft number had been picked in Detroit. This was quite a shock to me. It turned

---

* Joe Greenberg would advance as an infielder and play for Baltimore in the International League, the highest level in the minor leagues. But after six years he felt he would go no further, and quit baseball to go into his father's business.

out that the draft number only applied to the area in which you lived. I had registered as a downtown Detroit resident, where mostly transients lived. When the local draft board had to fill their quota, I became available immediately. I learned that I would be drafted in a couple of months.

◆

Greenberg, still "deeply tanned," returned from the West Coast to LaGuardia Field in New York on February 28, and was "besieged by baseball reporters," wrote Arthur E. Patterson in the *New York Herald Tribune*.

"No matter how the question was asked, he emphatically denied he was asking for a deferment.

"'What's all the fuss about?' he demanded. 'You'd think I was the only guy going into the army.

"'I don't know a thing about it, boys. You had better see that draft board; they're making a statement every day.

"'I'm not asking for any kind of deferment. All I'm going to say is that when my number is up I'm going. . . .'

"While the reporters poured questions at Hank he was trying to push his way toward his father's car parked outside the terminal. His father and his brother Joe came to LaGuardia Field to meet him. The surprise of the evening was James (Schnozzola) Durante, who arrived with Hank. It was a grand break for the photographers. Hank was in no mood to pose for anyone after he kissed his father in a posed greeting, but Durante hauled him to an occasional stop. Never let it be said that the Durante nose, even when blue with cold, will avoid the flashlight bulbs.

"After reporters stopped shooting draft questions at Hank and asked him about baseball he was a bit more pleasant.

"'I'm in great shape,' he said, and he looked it. 'Yes, I think the Tigers can do it again. I guess most of the boys are signed up, too. That's swell. I'm leaving next week. No, I'm not signed, but I won't have any trouble signing with them.'"

◆

During spring training in Lakeland the Detroit draft board had me examined. The doctor classified me a 4F. He said that I had supreme flat feet and that I was not acceptable to the army.

That caused some consternation. The newspapers hounded me and reported that I had bribed the doctor to put me in 4F. They made such a big deal about it that I was reminded of how the press had hounded Jack Dempsey in World War I, trying to make a scapegoat out of him because he wasn't in uniform. He had been called a shirker. I thought that this was what they were trying to do with me. I was the perfect patsy for it. Here the country was getting prepared for a world war, and I was trying to duck the draft. This all took place early in 1941, so it was way before the war had started, but it was right down the press's alley. They hounded me until I decided that the best thing I could do was go into the draft and take my chances like everybody else and not worry about whether I was going to be able to play baseball for another year or two.

◆

Upon his return to Detroit before the season, Greenberg was reexamined and declared fit. He was reclassified 1A and was scheduled for induction on May 7.

When *Life* magazine asked Greenberg about the amount of pay he would lose, he said, "It isn't as much of a sacrifice as it appears. After all, the government takes most of that fifty grand." He added, "I never asked for a deferment. I made up my mind to go when I was called. My country comes first."

◆

I was just hoping to go in and get my service done and then come back and resume my career. It was a one-year draft, and war hadn't been declared yet and I thought I'd return for the 1942 season.

Little did I know that it would be four and a half years before I got back into the Major Leagues again.

◆

Greenberg, who played the first three weeks of the season, was then the only star Major League player drafted. Hugh "Losing Pitcher" Mulcahy of the Phillies—a good pitcher, despite his nickname—was drafted, as were three other Major Leaguers, all relatively obscure: Washington pitcher Lou Thurman, Brooklyn outfielder Joe "Muscles" Gallagher, and Pittsburgh pitcher Oad Swigert. Morris Arnovich, a Jewish outfielder with the Giants, volunteered but was not taken because he lacked a pair of occluding molars, which he proved to reporters by removing his false teeth. But when war broke out, Arnovich tried to enlist again, and this time was accepted for military service despite his missing molars.

On his last at bat on May 6, in Detroit, against the Yankees, Greenberg was hoping to hit home run number 250. He wasn't alone. Speaking to Arthur Daley of *The New York Times*, Greenberg would recall: "As I stepped up to bat in the last half of the eighth we had the game won and everyone in the park was pulling for me to finish up with a homer, including myself. Atley Donald was pitching by that time and the bases were full. What a perfect spot it was!

"Donald didn't have a thing. He was wild and threw me three balls. I didn't want to walk. I wanted that homer. Suddenly I hear Bill Dickey whispering where the next pitch will be. I swing from my shoetops and miss. Again he tells me and again I miss. In comes the last pitch . . . and I fanned."

Years later Dickey was asked about that incident. "I don't think Hank believed me," said Dickey. "I just said to him, 'Hank, we're not going to throw you nothin' but fast-balls.'"

What did he say back? "He didn't say a word. He popped it up."

◆

My friends gave me a going-away party on the night after my last game. All of the Detroit players were there, and most of the New York players. They gave me a gold watch with all the Yankee signatures.

I left Detroit right after that game and the following morning I was inducted into the army at Fort Custer, Michigan. I was drafted into an old-line regular army outfit, with men who had been in the army for years and years. It was the Fifth Division, Second Infantry Anti-Tank Company. I don't know why I was drafted into that unit, or why I stayed in Fort Custer, but I didn't go through any basic training. My mind was in turmoil because of all the publicity, so I just went along for the ride and made no effort to direct my own destiny.

◆

On June 10, 1941, an article in *The New York Times* bore this headline: SENATOR PRAISES GREENBERG.

The story related that in Washington, D.C., Senator Joshua Bailey of North Carolina "used Greenberg as an example of young men inducted into the Army who had made a 'real sacrifice.' He reminded the Senate yesterday that Greenberg quit a $40,000-a-year job [it was actually $55,000] to serve his country at $21 a month. 'To my mind he's a bigger hero than when he was knocking home runs,' he said."

◆

It was a rude awakening. I was thirty years old, and I was in with a lot of rough-necks. These were guys who hadn't worked on the outside, who had been in the army for fifteen or twenty years. Some of them were still privates.

I became a PFC after two months. I marched with the Second Infantry down through Cincinnati, where I had played in the World Series the preceding October. People had lined the streets, yelling for me. Guys would come out and offer me a stein of beer as we marched. It was pretty funny.

I still remember my first trip on maneuvers. We went down to Alabama and were supposed to capture the town of Tuscaloosa. We were lying out on one of the street corners all night long, supposedly laying siege to the city of Tuscaloosa. We were sitting in front of the drugstore and could hardly wait for 7:00 A.M. to come, when we presumed the proprietor would open up. Then we'd fill up on a lot of things we hadn't had for a long time. But we got an order to clear out at 5:00 A.M. Back to the woods we went, back to army duty, with all our dreams of ice cream sodas fading rapidly from our minds.

I must say, though, I was never treated badly in the army. I minded my own business and kept to myself a great deal. I did a lot of reading and did my army chores.

Up at Fort Custer one of the chaps who was captain of the army team there was a friend of mine and he would try to persuade me to play baseball at Fort Custer. Well, the only times the team played were on Wednesday and Saturday afternoons—they played two games a week. And, of course, those periods were times when the soldiers were let off from duty. Wednesday afternoon we were free and then on Saturday noon we were free until Monday morning. So I would be giving up my free time to play for an army team and I said, "No way. I've just been inducted into the army, I left a $55,000 contract, $11,000 a month, to sign up for the army for $21 a month and I'm not going to waste it playing baseball."

In any case, I refused to play until one day I got a special request, an unusual request. I was asked by a friend of mine in Detroit named Abe Bernstein to play in a game. Bernstein, I had been told, was head of the Purple Gang. During Prohibition, the Purple Gang used to smuggle cases of liquor from Windsor, Canada, into Detroit across the Detroit River. At some points the river was only about a mile wide and you could almost swim across. Well, it seems that Abe Bernstein's brother, Joe, was convicted of killing someone; he was given a life sentence and sent up to Jackson Prison. And he was spending his off-time training canaries. So Abe asked me, as a special favor, if I would play in an exhibition game between the Fort Custer team and the prison team. He prevailed upon me because he said the warden was a great baseball fan and if I played, he thought I would help his brother. So I consented.

I joined the army team and went to Jackson, Michigan, to the state prison. The uniform the army had brought along for me didn't fit at all and the only uniform I could borrow was a prison uniform. So I thought, "Well, as long as I have a prison uniform, I'll play for the prison team."

Now this occurred some time in June, I had been inducted on May 7, so I hadn't hit a baseball for over a month. They had a nice left-handed pitcher for the army team, and I had no difficulty hitting him. I hit a home run, the longest home run ever hit at the prison. It went clean out of the park—there was no stadium, but a brick wall surrounded the field—the ball sailed over the wall and out of the prison. No one had ever done that before. And of course all the inmates were hollering, "I'll get it! I'll get it!"

The inmates would also ride the umpire, who was a fellow prisoner. They'd holler, "You crook! You thief!"

I also got a double and two singles, so I had a perfect day at bat, and the prison team won. When we got through, the warden took us all up into the auditorium and made me a little presentation. And I got a big hand from the prisoners.

In August, about three months after I went into the service, Congress passed a law stating that men over twenty-eight years of age were not to be drafted. I was thirty years of age and expected that orders would soon come through to release me, but things dragged on until December 5, 1941.

By then I had been in military uniform for eight months. I had advanced from a private to a sergeant, and I had gone through two months of maneuvers in the field and knew a little about army life. I headed back to Detroit, hoping that I could get myself ready for the 1942 season, but that Sunday morning, on December 7, all my plans were changed when the Japanese bombed Pearl Harbor. That changed the lives of everybody in the United States and around the world.

◆

An Associated Press reporter interviewed Greenberg while he was in Philadelphia. "Greenberg said tonight [December 9] he's going back into the Army in a few days and forget baseball as a career," wrote the reporter.

"'I'm going back in,' said Hank, visiting friends here. 'We are in trouble and there is only one thing to do—return to service.

"'I have not been called back. I am going back of my own accord.

"'. . . Baseball is out the window as far as I'm concerned. I don't know if I'll ever return to baseball.'"

He had told another reporter earlier that "when he heard about Pearl Harbor, he said simply, 'That settles it for me, I am reenlisting at once.'"

Greenberg was the first Major Leaguer to enlist in the military after the attack on Pearl Harbor. Greenberg was, of course, the first star player to go in, followed shortly by Bob Feller. Two of the biggest stars in the game at the time, Joe DiMaggio and Ted Williams, played the 1942 season and then enlisted.

◆

I left for New York and in two or three days I went down to Washington and enlisted in the air corps. I had my fill of the infantry and decided that if I was going to serve, at least I would serve in the air force, where I thought I could do just as much for the country and do it in a much more pleasant way.

I went into the air force as a sergeant, which was my rank in the infantry. I reported to MacDill Field in Tampa, Florida, which was just around the corner—about thirty miles—from Lakeland, where the Tigers trained. I spent the spring waiting for an appointment to Officers Candidate School in Miami Beach. Finally, sometime in July, I went to Miami, spent twelve weeks there, and was commissioned a second lieutenant. I was assigned to the Flying Training Command in Fort Worth, Texas, in the Special Services. I spent a year and a half in Fort Worth traveling around the United States on inspection tours for the training program for aviation cadets, bombardiers, and gunners.

When I went into the service, I had loaned a player $1,000. I liked the player very much, and I was willing to make the loan. The 1942 season came and went, and in 1943 I was in the military and this fellow was still playing ball for Detroit and making pretty good money. So I decided to write him a letter and remind him that he owed me $1,000. I never got an answer from him, so I wrote him again. After I didn't get an answer the second time, I wrote to Judge Landis.

In a week I got a copy of the letter that he sent to this player, whose name I don't particularly care to mention. The letter said, "Greenberg states that he loaned you $1,000 and he wants to know why you haven't acknowledged it and when you plan to pay it back."

Another week or two passed, then I got a copy of a second letter, this one addressed to the Detroit baseball club and the player, and it said, "$500 is to be subtracted from the player's contract immediately and next payday another $500 is to be subtracted from his contract. Such $1,000 is to be forwarded to me so I can forward it on to player Greenberg." And that's the way Judge Landis settled that matter.

At the time, in 1943, I was rooming in Fort Worth with a chap by the name of William Holden. Holden was a well-known actor and had just established himself by playing a lead role with Barbara Stanwyck in *Golden Boy*. We shared an apartment and both of us went off on road trips. He was working in the public relations departments and he'd go out and make appearances in training films or for other activities like bond sales. One time I was away on a two-week trip and I returned home to Fort Worth very late at night, about two or three in the morning. I had the key in the door and was trying to open it. Little did I know that Bill Holden was home, sitting up in bed. He had his revolver pulled out and had a bead on the door, thinking that he was being robbed. I burst in the door, and he flashed on the lights and said, "Boy, are you lucky. I thought you were an intruder. I was ready to pull the trigger."

Some time in 1943 I decided I wasn't going to spend the rest of my military career in Fort Worth. I wanted to be assigned overseas and requested a transfer. I was sent to Washington to report for reassignment. I was assigned to the first group of B-29s to go overseas. We spent six months in India getting set up, and then were ferried over Burma into China, and I was assigned to the bases there.

◆

"I'll never forget the first mission our B-29s made from our base to Japan," Greenberg told Arthur Daley, writing in the February 14, 1945, *New York Times*. "I drove out to the field in a jeep with General Blondie Saunders who led the strike, and took my place in the control tower. Those monsters went off, one after the other, with clock-like precision.

"Then we spotted one fellow in trouble. The pilot saw he wasn't going to clear the runway, tried to throttle down, but the plane went over on its nose at the end of the field. Father Stack, our padre, and myself raced over to the burning plane to see if we could help rescue anyone. As we were running, there was a blast when the gas tanks blew and we were only about 30 yards away when the bomb went off. It knocked us right into a drainage ditch alongside the rice paddies while pieces of metal floated down out of the air."

Greenberg said he was stunned and couldn't talk or hear for a couple of days, but otherwise he wasn't hurt. "The miraculous part of it all was that the entire crew escaped," Greenberg continued. "Some of them were pretty well banged up but no one was killed. That also was an occasion, I can assure you, when I didn't wonder whether or not I'd be able to return to baseball. I was quite satisfied just to be alive."

◆

I got recalled from China and came back to New York. It was the middle of 1944: The Italians had been defeated, the German army was being pushed back, and our government didn't want to send me back overseas. I was reassigned to an outfit in New York at 44 Broad Street. My job was to go up to New England and talk to the factory workers, the people who had contributed to the war effort by turning out parachutes and ammunition and planes and gliders and all sorts of military equipment and hardware.

These people had been working in the plants for years, women mostly, some elderly men, and deformed and handicapped people. I would take a group of young officers with me, combat officers who had returned from overseas, and we would spend the afternoon telling stories and complimenting people on their war efforts, which would please them no end. That's how I spent the last few months of my military career until I was finally discharged on June 14, 1945.

I had been in the army from May 7, 1941, to June 14, 1945. It was a long hitch and it was a wonderful experience. I can't say it was enjoyable insofar as we were deprived of our liberties, but considering that so many men had suffered much greater hardships than I had, and quite a few of them had lost their lives, I guess I was just lucky to come back in one piece. While I hadn't played any baseball in all that time—except for that one exhibition game at the prison in Jackson, Michigan—I came back and decided that it was time to get back to work. So I notified the Detroit club that I had been discharged and that I was available to return to active duty on the baseball front.

The Detroit team had lost the 1944 championship race on the last day of the season to the St. Louis Browns—the one and only pennant in the history of that franchise. In 1945 the Tigers were once again pennant contenders. They had two outstanding pitchers in Hal Newhouser and Dizzy Trout; Rudy York had not gone in the service and most of the power came from his bat. They had acquired Doc

Cramer from Boston, who was a good, seasoned ballplayer. They had a lot of older fellows, a lot of them minor leaguers. None of them had been in the service. I was the first Major Leaguer to return after the war, and when I joined the club it was right up there in the pennant race, a game out of first place.

I spent two weeks getting myself in shape. I had so many blisters from batting practice that skin came off my left hand. I took two weeks of batting practice one-handed. The team was on the road, scheduled to return home on July 1.

I was taking batting practice and also trying to get my legs in shape. Strangely enough, my legs gave me the most trouble. I had lost a lot of the bounce and speed. All my leg muscles had tightened up and as Jimmie Dykes subsequently said, "Greenberg looks like a guy who's running on roller skates." I guess I had slowed down, but in any case the competition wasn't so keen as when I had left.

◆

"Nobody has ever attempted to resume baseball operations after so long a lapse," reported *The Sporting News* when Greenberg returned to the Tigers in 1945.

On June 22, Whitney Martin of the Associated Press wrote: "Hank Greenberg is returning to the Detroit Tiger lineup, and no athlete ever had more horseshoes or other good luck tokens draped around his neck than the genial giant from the Bronx.

"There isn't a fan or a rival player who doesn't wish for Big Hank anything but the best of luck.

"The fans wish him well because he always was a gentleman and a credit to the game, and because they admire him for his army record.

"The players are pulling for him because, in addition to being a fine fellow, he is more than just a baseball player trying to resume an interrupted career.

"He will be watched as a symbol of hope to all the other ballplayers in the service who fear their absence from the game might impair their effectiveness and money-earning capacity. He is in the nature of a test case; the answer to the question: Can the Major League stars in the service come back?

"He is the first of the really outstanding stars to try a comeback after a prolonged service during which he and baseball were strangers. Many of the stars have had ample opportunity to at least keep in practice by playing on service teams.

"But Hank had none of these assignments. . . .

"He is 34 years old, an age at which making a sports comeback after a long absence comes under the heading of almost super-human tasks. But he's the fellow [who] could do it if anyone could. . . .

"He has the tenacity of purpose. . . . He showed that in the army in forsaking baseball entirely and concentrating on service duties, and it was that concentration that carried him the hard way from private to captain.

"He showed it in his baseball playing days. . . .

"You can bet he won't let his buddies down by failing to make the grade."

◆

In my first game back, on July 1, I came out in front of 55,000 people, the largest crowd of the year in Briggs Stadium. Everybody was cheering like mad. After four years in the service, the greeting was nice, but it didn't matter all that much to me. I was just glad to be back alive. I just went out there to do my job. I went right back out to left field.

We were playing Philadelphia in a doubleheader and I hit a home run in the eighth inning of the first game.

◆

"Boy, it felt good to hit that one," Greenberg said after the game, in which Detroit won 9–5. Bob Murphy of the *Detroit Times* wrote that Greenberg "smilingly accepted the handshakes and backslapping of his teammates and newspapermen.

"It had been 4 years, 1 month, and 24 days since [Greenberg] had known the thrill of hitting a home run in a Major League ballpark and hearing the roar of the worshipping audience.

"Hank confessed soon after joining the Tigers while serving his country here and in faraway places on the globe that he had many times lain awake at night and dreamed that someday he would return to Briggs Stadium . . . that someday he would park one in the left-field seats and make that majestic trot around the bases. . . ."

The Tigers beat the A's in the second game—Greenberg didn't play—and increased their first-place lead to three and a half games over the Yankees.

Late in August, Greenberg, though hitting over .300, was benched for a series against the Senators. "My legs gave out," he explained. He needed the rest. He mentioned that he and Charlie Keller, a Yankee outfielder who had also returned from military service, "were poor in the outfield compared to our prewar performances. This was a result of lack of conditioning [in spring training]. We were running on our heels instead of our toes. Our legs just never did get enough spring in them."

◆

I played most of the second half of the season and wound up hitting .311 (in 270 at bats in 78 games), which was high for the league though I didn't qualify for the batting championship because I didn't have a sufficient number of at bats. [George Stirnweiss of the Yankees led the American League in hitting in 1945 with a .309 average.]

I did manage to add a dramatic flourish to the final game of the season. We went into St. Louis leading Washington by one game and needing a win in the final two games to clinch the pennant. For three straight days games were rained out. On September 30 a doubleheader was scheduled. The commissioner wanted the games played, otherwise we would win the pennant by default. Of course, he wanted it won or lost on the field.

The Browns were in third place and had been playing well. If we lost both games we'd end up in a tie with the Senators. They had concluded their season and had assembled in their clubhouse, all packed and ready to go, to listen to our ball game on the radio.

Their best pitcher, Dutch Leonard, had been sent to Detroit to rest up for a playoff game in the event we lost to the Browns.

I hated Washington. They had played a lot of dirty tricks on me over the years, like Jake Powell running into me for no reason at all and breaking my wrist, and that catcher telling Jimmie Foxx the pitches so he could tie me for the league home-run title in 1935. And Joe Kuhel, the former White Sox player with whom I once had a fight, was now the Senators' first baseman.

It rained all day the day of the game. The game was delayed for fifty minutes. ["Armies with mops and brooms tried to soak up the water," wrote Lyall Smith of the *Detroit Free Press*.] By the time the game began, there weren't many people at the ballpark.

◆

The crowd at Sportsman's Park for the final game of the 1945 season was 6,613 in a stadium that held 30,808. "Rain continued to fall even as play began," wrote W. I. McGoogan in the *St. Louis Post-Dispatch*. "The baselines were deep in mud and footing was slippery." Early in the game Greenberg was caught off third base to choke off a promising Tiger rally: "I nearly lost the game for us with the most stupid bit of base running that I ever did in my life," Greenberg said afterward, "and then a kind of Providence gave me a chance to finish up a hero instead of a bum."

◆

Rain fell throughout the game. The Browns were beating us 4–3 when we came to the top of the ninth. The afternoon light was now very dim. The umpires didn't want to call the game, though, because the pennant was at stake.

The first man up for us was Hub Walker, pinch-hitting for Hal Newhouser. Hub singled. Then Skeeter Webb bunted him over. The throw went to second base and it hit Walker, putting men on first and second. Then Eddie Mayo laid down another bunt for us, and he was sacrificed at first. Now there were men on second and third. Doc Cramer, a left-handed batter, came to bat and the Browns, who had a right-handed pitcher on the mound, Nelson Potter, decided to walk him.

So the bases were full. That brought me to the plate.

The Browns had loaded the bases to pitch to me because they were hoping that I would hit into a double play. The rain continued to fall. I took the first pitch from Nelson Potter for a ball. As he wound up on the next pitch, I could read his grip on the ball and I could tell he was going to throw a screwball. I swung and hit a line drive toward the corner of the left-field bleachers. I stood at the plate and watched the ball for fear the umpire would call it foul. It landed a few feet inside the foul pole for a grand slam. We won the game, and the pennant, and all the players charged the field when I reached home plate and they pounded me on the back and carried on like I was a hero. There was almost nobody in the stands to pay attention, and there were few newspapermen. Just the ballplayers giving me a hero's welcome.

When we returned to Detroit there were thousands of people in the train station giving me a big hand. But the best part of that home run was hearing later what the Washington players said: "Goddamn that dirty Jew bastard, he beat us again." They were calling me all kinds of names behind my back, and now they had to pack up and go home, while we were going to the World Series.

Greenberg with boxing great Joe Louis. *New York Times Photo.*

Captain Greenberg on his tour of duty in China during World War II. *New York Times Photo.*

Hank Greenberg attends the 58th National Horse Show with his first wife, Caral. Bernard Gimbel, Hank's father-in-law, is sitting behind Mrs. Greenberg. *Corbis Photos.*

At the White House May 9, 1946. President Truman receives an autographed baseball from Hank Greenberg. *AP/Wide World.*

Babe Ruth in his Manhattan apartment signs a photo for his visitor, Hank Greenberg, in January 1947.

Hank Greenberg and George Robert "Birdie" Tebbetts in the dugout before playing in a 1943 war bond baseball game. *Corbis Photos.*

Hank Greenberg, left, and Ralph Kiner with the Pittsburgh Pirates in 1947. *UPI/Bettman Newsphotos.*

Greenberg's Hall of Fame plaque.

HENRY BENJAMIN GREENBERG
DETROIT A.L.1933 TO 1946
PITTSBURGH N.L.1947
ONE OF BASEBALL'S GREATEST RIGHT-HANDED
BATTERS.TIED FOR MOST HOME RUNS BY
RIGHT-HANDED BATTER IN 1938-58. MOST
RUNS-BATTED-IN 1935-37-40-46,AND HOME
RUNS 1938-40-46.WON 1945 PENNANT ON
LAST DAY OF SEASON WITH GRAND SLAM
HOME RUN IN 9TH INNING.PLAYED IN 4
WORLD SERIES,2ALL-STAR GAMES.MOST
VALUABLE A.L.PLAYER TWICE-1935-1940.
LIFETIME BATTING AVERAGE.313.

Greenberg with Bill Veeck, one of his closest friends, whom he once described as a man with nine lives. *New York Times Photo.*

Hank Greenberg with his children in 1954: Glenn at left, Alva on his lap, and Stephen at right. *The Estate of Henry Greenberg.*

Hank Greenberg enjoys a moment with his son Stephen in 1970, when Stephen was captain of the Yale baseball team. *Stephen Greenberg.*

From left: Roger Maris, Hank Greenberg, and Joe DiMaggio, three of baseball's all-time greats. *Baseball Hall of Fame and Museum, Cooperstown, New York.*

Greenberg was very successful as a baseball club owner after his playing days were over.

Mary Jo and Hank Greenberg on their wedding day, November 18, 1966. *The Estate of Henry Greenberg*.

Hank Greenberg and Joe Cronin in 1951, when Greenberg was general manager of the Cleveland Indians and Cronin the general manager of the Boston Red Sox. *Corbis Photos.*

Hank Greenberg at age 70, watching the Israeli tennis team at UCLA.

CHAPTER 10

That ninth-inning home run to win the pennant was really a dramatic conclusion to the year. I had been in the service in India the year before, listening to the World Series over Armed Forces Radio, and now I was preparing to play in the Series.

The 1945 Series was a repeat of 1935. It was again the Tigers vs. the Chicago Cubs. The series was more or less a comedy of errors. The players were mostly minor leaguers, and the caliber of ball wasn't as good, but the competition was the same.

◆

The Cubs, behind Hank Borowy, beat the Tigers and Hal Newhouser 9–0 in the first game, in Detroit, on Wednesday. Greenberg went 0-for-2, striking out once.

In Game 2 Greenberg homered with two on and two outs in the fifth off Hank Wyse to provide the margin of victory for Detroit, 4–1.

In Game 5, with the Series tied at two games each, Greenberg had three hits and three runs batted in to help the Tigers win, 8–4, and take a lead in the Series three games to two.

In Game 6 the Tigers were down 7–3 when they rallied for four runs in the eighth. The run that tied the game at 7–7 was scored on a home run by Greenberg. The game went into extra innings.

◆

A very strange thing happened in the sixth game that I've remembered all through the years. I was responsible in part for an error that was charged to me in the twelfth inning. A ball that was hit out there struck the head of the sprinkling system and bounced over my head, which permitted the man on second base to score the winning run. That tied the Series at three games all. Originally, the official score-keeper marked it as an error even though most of the people could tell by the funny bounce the ball took that it had hit something. The scorekeepers gave me the error, however. Five or six hours later, because of the demand by the major-ity of the sportswriters, the official scorers were forced to reverse their decision and mark it as a hit and run batted in, rather than an error. This was the first time in World Series history that the scorekeepers had ever reversed a decision.

◆

After the Cubs' 8–7 win in Wrigley Field, Red Smith of the *New York Herald Tribune* wrote: "The Tigers were furious and Greenberg was in a towering pet, not because of the scorers' decision but because the ball got away from him.

"'We play to win,' he stormed, 'and I don't even care if they don't spell my name right. But a thing like that, losing that ball, should never happen. I never had a chance at the ball. It was 3 feet over my head.'

"A stranger asked, with uncommon tact, 'What happened to you on that play, Hank?'

"'What happened to me?' Greenberg shouted. 'What happened to you? Did you see the game?' He stalked off to the showers while teammates growled about the scor-ing. All pleasant memories of Greenberg's home run were gone."

Greenberg had injured his right wrist while trying to hit a pitch to right field in the twelfth inning of Game 6, but he told no one except his manager, Steve O'Neill.

'I think for the good of the team I better not play today,' Greenberg said to his manager [according to a report after the World Series by Bob Murphy of the *Detroit Times*]. 'I can't throw. I can't grip the bat properly, and with all that it means to the rest of the players I think I should get out of the lineup.'

"O'Neill had only minutes to make a decision. He wondered what effect Greenberg's last-minute absence from the Tigers' lineup would mean to the morale of the team.

"Greenberg sensed that his manager, looking for his greatest moment out of 36 years of baseball, was in a spot.

"'I'll go in and try it,' Greenberg said to O'Neill. 'If anything goes wrong, get me out of there.' . . .

"Few, if any, noticed that Greenberg had gone to the plate only once in batting practice. Even then he only went through the motions. He did this only to keep the Cubs from detecting that something was wrong.

"In the Tigers' half of the first inning, Greenberg had the perfect setting for his bluff.

"Skeeter Webb had started the inning with a single. Eddie Mayo singled Webb to third. Doc Cramer . . . hit a single to left to score Webb.

"Then came the moment for Greenberg. The crowd didn't know. The Cubs certainly didn't know. And, most assuredly, a lot of the Tigers didn't know about the seriousness of Greenberg's hand.

"The Cub infield fell back. You don't play a slugger like Greenberg up close in a situation like this [with two on and no one out in the first inning]. . . .

"Greenberg did the unexpected. He laid down a bunt that completely befuddled Chicago's infielder. He bunted a sacrifice to the Cub first baseman, Phil Cavarretta. This set up runners on second and third. The next batter, Roy Cullenbine, was intentionally walked to load the bases. Then Paul Richards doubled, driving in 3 runs, for a 5–0 lead. The Tigers went on to win 9–3, taking the World Series.

"'That bunt upset them for the rest of the game,' Steve O'Neill said after the game [as reported by Dan Daniel]. 'Hank had no orders. It was just up to him to do as he pleased.'"

◆

It was an exciting Series and we got $8,000 plus for the winner's share, and that was the highest paycheck for the World Series up to that time. I had a pretty good Series. I guess I was outstanding in two of the games, at least, that we won, and probably would have been picked as the most valuable player if they had had that kind of award back then. [In the Series, he led the Tigers in batting (with a .304 average), in homers (2), and runs batted in (7).]

After coming back from overseas, along about November of 1944, I renewed my close relationship with Louis Marx. He had become acquainted with Bernard Gimbel, who was then president and one of the principal owners of the Gimbel Brothers and Saks Fifth Avenue department stores. When I returned to the States from China, I was stationed in Richmond, Virginia. I took a weekend pass and went up to New York, where Louis Marx invited me to join him for lunch in Greenwich, Connecticut, at the Gimbels' home. I went along, and that's when I met Mr. Gimbel's daughter, Caral, who was about to be divorced from Eddie Lasker.

Mr. Gimbel, Louis Marx, Caral, and I sat down at lunch, and she was giving me the old charm. I thought the air force was going to send me down to Texas, but when I got my orders they sent me back to New York, and that's when Caral and I started going together.

♦

"I met Hank at my family's home in Greenwich, and the grounds were still nice because it was in the spring," recalled Caral Gimbel Lebworth many years later. "Louie Marx was the toy manufacturer for the Gimbel stores. Louie just adored Popsie and thought he was marvelous and they became very good friends and they used to see each other at the races. Louie wasn't very social. He didn't come to luncheons or anything like that. But he had breezed over with Hank one Sunday afternoon and I was out there horseback riding or something and I came in. I just thought Hank was fabulous looking and a giant of a man. He was an old man of thirty-three or thirty-four. And I thought he was the most gorgeous, handsome, virile man I had ever met, and he had a divine sense of humor. He also had this marvelous modesty. I don't remember if he was in uniform or not. Well, he said he was going to be working in New York and he would like to call me some time and I said I'd like that very much.

"I wasn't going to resume my life with Edward, although we're still friends. My father was afraid that I'd marry against his wishes because I had a lot of men friends my father didn't approve of, one in particular that my father was apoplectic about. So I think he was so glad that I fell for Hank. I really fell in love with him."

And he loved you?

"Oh yes. I still remember the first time Hank called and asked me out. I said yes. He said, 'You don't have to feel pinned down to this. If something comes up that you would rather do, then we can switch it. Call me.' And he gave me his number. I had never had anybody ask me to go out to dinner and then say that. It was sort of remarkable, and very modest. I remember it all these years. It was more sort of an insecurity, I think. He felt insecure with me because I was a different type of person than he—he had been with a lot of women—and I was a different type of woman than he was accustomed to being with."

She was asked, Because you were an heiress?

"Yes. My interests and his—opposites attract. It didn't work on a permanent basis because I wanted certain things in life and he wanted different things.

"Hank was going around to defense plants and since I was in the Red Cross—a nurse's aide at Bellevue Hospital—he said, 'Why don't you go with me.' He said, 'You drive the car.' He said, 'You have a car?' I did, and I said I'd love to go to a defense plant. And so I went with him to a defense plant, and that was an experience which I never had before. We were found out and it caused a brouhaha and they gave him hell for taking an unauthorized person, a civilian. I went in my nurse's aide uniform, but he wasn't supposed to do that.

"I had no knowledge of baseball. None. Did I know the rules of the game? No. Absolutely not. Didn't matter at this time. When we went to dinner anyplace, people would come up and ask for autographs and that annoyed him. It amused me. He was so nice to people. But he could be very gruff and say I'm at dinner, don't bother me."

◆

In the winter after the 1945 baseball season, Caral and I decided to get married. It was time to go to spring training, and I said, "Caral, I don't believe in big weddings. Our families don't mesh. Do you want to get married or don't you?" She said yes. [Though the Gimbels were Jews, they were not particularly religious, unlike the Greenbergs, and because of their fortune were in a different social stratum than Greenberg's family.] So we got in the car and headed for Florida. I had asked Caral's attorney, who was also her brother-in-law, David Solinger, what state we could get married in without waiting thirty days. He researched the question and told me Florida.

I realized that we could get married in St. Augustine, the historical village known, of course, for the fountain of youth. It was a beautiful village with an old cannon facing out toward the ocean. I said to Caral, "Let's drive down to St. Augustine. We'll get married there and then drive on to Lakeland." We had lunch in Brunswick, Georgia, en route to Florida, about a hundred miles from St. Augustine.

We got down to St. Augustine around 4:00 P.M. and we inquired at the municipal court where we could get married. We were told then that we couldn't get married in Florida unless we had waited for thirty days and had the blood tests and went through all the formalities. Here we were, expecting to be married in St. Augustine, and concerned because Mr. and Mrs. Gimbel said they would release the announcement of our marriage to *The New York Times* along about 4:00 P.M. So they were announcing it in New York, and we were in Florida, unable to get married.

We were told that the closest place we could be married without any formalities was Georgia, and the closest town was Brunswick, the town where we had had lunch two or three hours before. Anyway, we went back to Brunswick and arrived around 6:00 or 7:00 P.M. We hunted up a justice of the peace, an elderly gentleman who was living on the outskirts of town, and he agreed to marry us. He got his wife as a witness and rattled off the usual marriage vows. We signed the paper, gave him $100, and off we went. It was dark by this time. We searched out the best restaurant in Brunswick and went to dinner. We had a bottle of champagne in the car, all iced, so that we could drink it at the restaurant.

Well, the news had been released in New York and all the newspapermen were trying to find out where we were. While we were having dinner, a young chap from the Brunswick newspaper found me and wanted to get a statement. By this time I was annoyed, and I told him I wasn't going to give him a statement because we didn't even have a place to sleep. He said, "I can get you a hotel. It's very quiet and no one will bother you. I'll do it, if you agree to give me a statement in the morning." I said, "Where is the hotel?" He said it was in Sea Island, Georgia, which was just across the bay from Brunswick, connected by a long causeway. He said it was a summer hotel which was closed, but he knew the owners and could get us a room for the night.

Having no other choice, I accepted his invitation to go to that hotel and would give him a statement the following morning.

The next morning the newspaperman hunted me up and I told him that we were happily married, looking forward to a long marriage and having a large family, and that we were going down to spring training camp. With that, we packed our bags and drove down to Lakeland, arriving some time in the late afternoon. We were greeted by my teammates and the club officials, and that's how the 1946 season got under way.

◆

On February 19, an article in the *New York Daily News* reported:

"Henry (Hank) Greenberg, for years baseball's outstanding bachelor, and Caral Glazier Gimbel, brunette heiress to department store millions, were married at 7 o'clock last night in Brunswick, Ga.

"The ceremony was performed by County Ordinary Edwin W. Dart in the living room of his home. . . . Mrs. Dart was the only witness.

"Mrs. Dart told *The News* by telephone that Caral looked 'awfully pretty' in a dark blue suit, pearl necklace, pearl earrings and orchids. She said Hank looked 'calm' in a pepper and salt business suit. When the ceremony was over Dart merrily told the Greenbergs to 'drive very, very slowly' back to Florida. Caral smiled and said, 'We've got a lifetime to be together so I guess we'll take our time.'

"On the license Hank gave his age as 35; Caral gave hers as 30. . . .

"[Greenberg had] directed the conditioning program of 200 training command installations for a year and a half. Then he went overseas to command the headquarters squadron of the 20th Bomber Command, with bases in India and China.

"He returned last June, an 81-pointer, wearing the Presidential United Citation and Asiatic-Pacific ribbons with four battle stars.

"The former Miss Gimbel, a well-known horsewoman (who had won, among other trophies, the hunt team class at the National Horse Show held at Madison Square Garden), obtained a divorce January 9 in Las Vegas, Nev., from ex-Lieutenant Commander Edward Lasker, son of Albert D. Lasker, chairman of the U.S. Shipping Board in the first world war. . . .

"The Gimbel heiress was educated at Rosemary Hall, Greenwich, and Mlle. Boissier's School in Paris and spent two winters studying painting. Her marriage to Lasker on Feb. 1, 1935, at Chieftains, the Gimbel estate at Port Chester, was one of the season's outstanding social events."

◆

Now I not only had a wife, I had a father-in-law, too. Mr. Gimbel was an unusual man—big, powerful, and athletic with a beautiful face. He was a real man's man and yet a ladies' man, too. He was from Philadelphia and had gone to a private prep school there from which most of the students were accepted at the University of Pennsylvania. Mr. Gimbel graduated and became a big benefactor of Penn after his success as the head of the Gimbel Brothers dynasty. He was a great athletic enthusiast, primarily boxing, and he had told me that he was intercollegiate boxing champion and that he was a great swimmer and loved all sports, particularly horse racing. He liked to bet on athletic events, and he was just an all-around terrific guy, much older than I, but I really enjoyed his company.

Mr. Gimbel was also a close friend of Gene Tunney, the former heavyweight boxing champion. The two of them were almost inseparable, and Mr. Tunney often told me that he thought Bernard Gimbel, had he turned professional, might have someday been the heavyweight champion of the world. I think he was kind of gilding the lily a little bit, because of his friendship with Bernard, but, in any case, they were close friends. I used to meet them almost every afternoon in the wintertime at the Biltmore Baths, which were then located in the Biltmore Hotel. They charged $10 to come in, and it was an unusual place because it had a large swimming pool in the basement of the hotel instead of a steam room. They also had a hot room and dry room, and attendants would give you a massage. The pool was ice cold, because every Friday it was emptied and over the weekend it was refilled with water right out of the Hudson River. Some winter days, when the temperature got below freezing, that water was almost impossible to get into. We used to run out from the steam room and then jump in and out of the water, then sit on lounge chairs around the pool.

It was a very delightful way to spend two or three hours, and I would go there almost every afternoon at three and leave around seven.

Very few people used this place because it was not too well known and because it cost $10 plus the tips. The only people who used it were those with a lot of money. Every day at the Biltmore Baths you'd see Jim Farley, who had been the postmaster general of the United States; Lester Crown, who was one of the wealthy conglomerate owners, out from Chicago; Bob Woodruff, who was then president of the Coca-Cola Company; and other wealthy men, including Mr. Tunney and Mr. Gimbel. I got acquainted with all of them.

◆

"[When I married Hank] I entered the world of baseball," Caral recalled. "It was amazing, because I didn't know a single player. I didn't know how to score or anything.

"The people who were Hank's friends were really pretty civilized people, like Billy Sullivan. I was crazy about Ted Williams. Fantastic man. He used to come to dinner with us and Hank would lecture him and say, 'Ted, you're crazy, you can run like a gazelle, why don't you perfect your fielding?' I just thought Ted had a real independence—nobody influenced him. Fishing and the things he liked were nice. And he's so good looking.

"And DiMaggio. Kind of dull I thought at first. I couldn't understand why Marilyn Monroe married him. Very nice man, but quiet. Someone you could trust, though. Hank always said, 'Just the most gifted ballplayer. He doesn't have to do a stroke of work.' Hank would work all winter and play squash and all that and DiMaggio doesn't have to do anything but show up for spring training. And Bob Feller—I liked Bob. And, of course, Hank told me how hard Bob threw."

◆

Probably the greatest hitter in my time was Ted Williams. He had a fantastic eye at the plate and his record, of course, is outstanding. The only thing about Ted I disapproved of was that he was a little too careful at the plate. He would never be tempted to hit a ball that was a little outside the strike zone, regardless of what the situation was in the ball game. He had trained himself to make them give him his pitch before he'd swing. That's great, but when you're down and fighting for the pennant, and you're the number four hitter or the number three hitter, you're the boy they're all leaning on and looking to carry them to victory. Sometimes you have to hit the ball whether you want to or not. Ted had an inclination to let the ball go and he'd wind up getting a base on balls, which meant that the following hitter [in most cases it was Vein Stephens, a right-handed batter] would have to drive in the runs. I always thought Ted should have taken a little more upon himself, to have been more effective. Aside from that he was just a great natural hitter and loved hitting and loved to discuss it and loved to study it. He understood it well, and nobody worked harder at it.

◆

Years later, Williams, who came into the American League in 1939 with the Red Sox, recalled Greenberg: "Hank was smarter than most players. He was a great guy, a *great* guy, and I wouldn't say that if I didn't mean it. Shit, he was ab-so-lutely terrific.

"There were three or four or five guys when you were coming up that you really looked up to—Jimmie Foxx, Joe DiMaggio, and Hank Greenberg. He was so outgoing with me and when we'd get a chance to talk he'd want to talk about the pitchers, and he was listening with keen ears as to what I had to say, and I know I was listening very close to what he thought was going on.

"And I remember the way he hit, with that bat held high, and he had a nice rhythmic-y cut, not too hard, and he'd hit a ball to left when I was out there and the ball would start coming like you could make a play on it and it would start going up, and up and—Jesus Christ!—it's in the upper deck! He was great."

◆

I must say that I wasn't as enthusiastic about baseball as I had been in prior years. There were two reasons for that. One is that, having been away from the game for four and a half years in the military service, I wasn't physically in the same condition as I had been before I left, plus the fact that I had gotten married, which was a new experience for me. Baseball wasn't that important. I had seen a lot of things happen in the world, and I didn't think that baseball was the only thing in my life. I had a new interest in life. I went to spring training not quite the same man I had been in previous years.

Another change took place. After the 1945 season our shortstop, Skeeter Webb, who was a wartime shortstop really, was cut from the team and we were short a good Major League shortstop. During that period the Detroit management had traded Rudy York to Boston in return for Eddie Lake, an established shortstop. I had to leave left field, which I had grown to like, and return to my old position at first base because we had no other first baseman. I wasn't as agile or quick or nimble. I had to readjust and I wasn't as enthusiastic. As a result, I don't think I played up to my previous performances at first base, and my batting had slumped somewhat, but the season started off right.

◆

"The Tigers opened a new season just like they ended the old one: Hank Greenberg hit a home run off Nelson Potter to defeat the St. Louis Browns, 2–1," wrote Lyall Smith in the April 17 *Detroit Free Press*. "This time Greenberg pounded out his game-winning hit in the fourth inning [with] the score tied 1–1. . . . (His new wife, Caral Gimbel, was in a box seat on the first base side of home plate.)"

"Greenberg," wrote the Associated Press, "provided the throng of 52,118 paid—an opening-game record crowd here [in Detroit]—with its biggest thrill. . . ."

"I had never been to a baseball game before I married Hank," Caral recalled years later. "And I couldn't understand it when he did have good days—he had a lot of bad days, very bad days depressed him—and then the days when he really had a splendid game when he hit a home run or two, he wouldn't rejoice. I don't mean celebrate and have a lot to drink or anything like that, but spiritually he wasn't delighted. He never seemed elated enough. Because I guess he was thinking tomorrow he might go out again and get no hits."

◆

When you're the batter, you learn to despise the pitchers. I never even thought they were athletes. I just thought they were kids who had good arms, and sooner or later they developed into Major League ballplayers. Some were better than others, but I never classified them as athletes. Of course, I was wrong. There were some fine athletes among the pitching staff. On the other hand, there were an awful lot of dumb guys. All they could do was get the ball and fire it to home plate. Some had more stuff on the ball than others, but basically I had to determine in my own mind that pitchers were not intelligent and were inferior. That was part of what I had to convince myself of so that I could hit them. I don't know if every other hitter felt the same way, but I know that's how I felt. I tried to put them down in my mind to enable me to have a little more confidence.

When you talk about great pitching, though, Lefty Grove and Bob Feller were outstanding—they were by far the two best pitchers during my era. Both of them had tremendous fastballs, and Feller had a fantastic curveball that was almost unhittable if you were a right-handed batter; he was also a little wild so you had a little respect for him. As for Grove, he threw left-handed and still he threw so hard and with such ease that even when he went from the Athletics to Boston, probably the worst ballpark for a left-handed pitcher, he was at the end of his pitching career and he had lost most of his fastball, he could still win twenty games with poor Red Sox teams.

But I have no great admiration for Grove, though I respected his pitching. He was kind of a grouchy guy. He tried to intimidate you when he was on the mound. Of course, he was older than I was; he was a veteran when I broke in. He treated every rookie with disdain and tried to intimidate him, and I guess that was his psychological ploy. He was the best left-hander I ever saw. As for a right-handed pitcher, Bob Feller, of course, was in a class by himself.

In July 1946, around the time of the All-Star game, I was hitting only .270, but had 55 RBIs, which put me among the league leaders; my 22 homers were second in the league to Ted Williams, who had 23. Yet I wasn't picked for the All-Star squad and wasn't invited to Boston to play in the game. In 1940, the year I was voted most valuable player, I was picked for the team, but all they did was let me go to bat and pinch-hit with nobody on base to lead off in St. Louis. That was kind of humiliating, too, because in 1940 I was one of the top ballplayers. Gehrig was no longer around, and while Foxx was still great, I was now being accepted as one of the top sluggers in baseball. Then I went into the service in 1941.

This brings up an interesting fact. I was inducted on May 7, 1941, the first outstanding ballplayer to go into the military service. I was stationed up at Camp Custer. The All-Star game was held in Detroit that year, and I didn't even get an invitation to come and watch the games or be an honorary selection to the team since I was in the service. When I came back from the service, just before the All-Star break in 1945, I had no chance to participate in the game. And then in 1946 I was not invited to Boston to play. That was my whole record in the American League. I only played one full game, in 1939. So I often wonder, looking back, why I wasn't selected more often and why I wasn't played more often. Anyway, that's the way it was.

When Bobby Brown appointed me honorary captain of the American League All-Star team in 1983, I was delighted. Bobby was then the president of the American League, and had been a friend of mine since he played with the Yankees. I liked him, and I believe he enjoyed me. We used to play tennis together occasionally, and when he asked me to go to San Francisco for the game, it was really an honor. I felt they were really repaying me for the years I should have gone to the All-Star game and didn't.

◆

"What do you make of these rumors of your retirement in July?" a reporter from the *New York Sun* asked Greenberg.

Greenberg shook his head and said, "I wish they'd ask me. The way I figure it, if I'm so bad I ought to quit, but there are a lot of other guys around in the same category.

"There was one story I read that had me quitting because I wasn't picked for the All-Star game. Isn't that baby stuff? Why should that make me quit? Sure, I felt bad about not making the team. I wanted to get in it and take my wife to Boston. Get a big thrill out of it. And that was my last chance to make it. My wife never did see me in a big game like that. But it would not make me quit."

"What about next year?" the reporter asked.

"I don't know, it all depends on how I feel. But I can tell you this: Baseball is my business and I want to stay in it. All that stuff hooking me up with the department store business is kind of silly. . . . As for [playing ball], I feel I'm on borrowed time anyway, so I don't feel bad. I don't have the old beans anymore out there and I'm not the hitter I used to be [even though he had more extra-base hits than anybody in the majors except Ted Williams]."

◆

The years had taken their toll. The old legs didn't function. Up at bat, the pitchers that I used to be able to handle without difficulty were becoming harder all the time. And then I wasn't prepared to play first base again. My reactions were not as good, I had lost confidence. The ground balls were getting by me, and every day it became more of a struggle. It was a tougher job for me. I accepted it, and naturally everyone knew that I was a high-priced ballplayer, and they expected more than I was able to produce. So along about August I was getting a little weary and making noises like I might retire. The game became drudgery.

◆

Greenberg was also being booed by the fans in Detroit. "They sure are giving it to me this year," he told Joe Williams of the *New York World-Telegram*. "The other day, during infield practice, I let one get by and they gave me a blast that almost carried me out of the ballpark. Still, the booing doesn't really bother me. It's all part of the day's work."

But you could see that the booing bothered Mrs. Greenberg, wrote the reporter. She "winced all over" when the booing was mentioned to her.

On August 22 the *Detroit Times* reported that Greenberg, in a hitting slump, was benched by manager Steve O'Neill. "I'm not benching Hank," said O'Neill. "I'm just giving him a rest."

Referring to Greenberg's "noises," as Hank called them, about retiring, Red Smith wrote in the August 27 *New York Herald Tribune*: "[I]t doesn't seem like Greenberg to quit just because the sledding is a little tough. It doesn't sound like the fellow Al Simmons was talking about when it was announced that Hank, discharged by the Army, was coming back to the Tigers.

"'This is the test,' Al said, 'for all ballplayers past thirty who have been away for more than a year. Hank has more equipment than the rest of 'em, more natural ability. He'll come back in good shape, because he's always kept himself in shape. And he'll be out there working at 8 o'clock in the morning if necessary to get back on his stride.' . . ."

"Simmons's words were recalled the day Greenberg returned to the Tigers' lineup. It was a day that won't be forgotten soon by anyone who was present. There was a doubleheader with the Athletics and Hank's appearance had been advertised, bringing out the crowd that filled big Briggs Stadium.

"Tempestuous applause saluted announcement of his name in the batting order and even more tumultuous cheers welcomed him home on his first trip to the plate. He hit two or three baleful line drives which were caught. Then he got hold of a pitch by a left-hander named Charlie Gassaway and drove it into the left-field seats on a line as flat as old beer.

"What one remembers is not so much the look of him as he loped around the bases nor the unrestrained joy of the crowd. Rather, it was the undisguised pleasure that the other players showed, not only the other Tiger players but the Athletics as well. Detroit had won the game before Hank connected, so the hit didn't affect the outcome. Members of both teams crowed about it for hours, and even Gassaway went around with his chest out as though being on the receiving end of that comeback blow was the biggest thing that ever happened to him.

"This day saw a sample of the respect in which Greenberg has been held by the men of his sport. . . ."

"It's been a tough season for me," said Greenberg, as he lay on the rubbing table for a rubdown in the Tiger clubhouse. This was on August 29, 1946, and he was speaking to John Drohan, a reporter for the *Boston Traveler*. Greenberg had just hit his twenty-eighth homer of the season, to help the Tigers win. "Playing baseball isn't fun anymore. It's hard work. But I have no intention of quitting, despite what's been printed. I'll wait and see what happens over the winter."

◆

Then suddenly at the beginning of September I got into a hitting streak.

◆

By September 16, Greenberg had hit 6 home runs in six days, and had 9 for the month, for a total of 37 for the season.

"So far this season," wrote Lyall Smith in the September 17 *Detroit Free Press*, "Hank has hit more home runs than any player in the Major Leagues except Ted Williams. He is only one behind the slugger who is recognized by everyone as the greatest hitter in modern baseball.

"Greenberg has hit more homers than the entire Chicago White Sox team. He has hit more than the next four Tigers . . . put together. Greenberg has driven in more than twice as many runs as any other Tiger.

"Still some people boo him and some newspapermen keep harping on the tiresome theme that he is over the hill and should hang up his spikes.

"In recent weeks, I have been thinking that Hank Greenberg is a remarkable person, and he is. He is held together with tape and piano wire. He spends most of his time on a rubbing table. He is an old man in the mountains, in a baseball sense. But old as he is and leg-weary as he is and patched up as he is, he's fighting everybody for the leadership in hitting homers and runs batted in."

On September 24, Greenberg hit three homers in a doubleheader against the Browns to raise his total for the season to 41.

He hit three more in the last week of the season.

A photo of Greenberg in the *Detroit News* showed him shaking hands with teammates in the Tiger dugout. The caption read:

"When Hank Greenberg arrived at the Tiger dugout yesterday after hitting his 44th home run, Roy Cullenbine handed him a ball. It is a standing joke among the players that the ball hit by Hank when he homers arrives at the dugout quicker than Greenberg."

It was hardly enough. The Red Sox won the pennant, finishing twelve games ahead of the second-place Tigers.

". . . There was a time [when] no one figured [Greenberg] would make it through the season," wrote Jimmy Cannon in the November 22, 1946, *New York Post*.

"There were guys who said he was a sucker to return to first base. They explained the first baseman is in every play and Greenberg was hounded by the old age that attacks all athletes when they are young men. But the Tigers needed a first baseman and he did the best he could.

"All season long he ached with muscular pains and there were times when he thought he would rack up his cue and try to make a living in cities beyond the outfield fences.

"I know he is a professional athlete playing for money. But pride must have goaded him and the guy lacking courage would have quit when asked to return from the outfield. Out in the meadow an old fellow can rest up between plays and doesn't have to get the year-stiffened legs going every time the ball is hit."

◆

I not only passed Williams in runs batted in but I passed him in home runs, too, and wound up winning the crowns in home runs, with 44, and runs batted in with 127. [Williams had 38 home runs and 123 RBIs.]

◆

Greenberg's home-run total was nearly triple that of his closest teammate in that department, Roy Cullenbine, who had 15, and the RBIs were more than double the next Tiger player in that category, Dick Wakefield, who had 59. Greenberg also played in 144 games, second highest on the club. Greenberg told a reporter: "I played 144 games last season and hit 44 home runs. If I'm washed up, a lot of guys in the majors ought to go back to farming."

"In my opinion Greenberg's surge is one of baseball's greatest achievements," wrote Grantland Rice in the *New York Sun*, "when you consider all the angles involved—the four years away from action, Greenberg's age, the handicap he faced in moving after such a power hitter as Williams has become."

◆

It all added up to my having a pretty good year personally, even though I batted under .300 for the first time in my Major League career—.277. For the team, though, the season was a disappointment because we couldn't catch Boston. We were no longer the American League champions.

◆

After the season O'Neill said that Greenberg would not be at first base the following year, if he planned to play at all. "Hank told me last year that he wouldn't play first base again," declared O'Neill in *The Sporting News*. "I know he means it. He said he was glad to help me out for one season, but that's the end. . . . And he did not look so good on ground balls last year, so a shift is in order."

◆

In 1946 the Tigers seemed to be confused about how much they were actually paying me, and that may have had something to do with what was, for me, a stunning turn of events. One of the reasons, anyway. This is how it came about:

In 1940, when I was voted most valuable player and had moved from first base to the outfield to accommodate Rudy York in the lineup, it all worked out to the advantage of the club, as well as to me. We went on to win the American League championship, though we blew the Series in seven games. I was making $40,000 a year, and automatically Mr. Briggs sent me a contract for $55,000, a $15,000 raise, which I thought was quite generous and didn't necessitate my having to negotiate. I felt that it was more than fair and I signed. In 1941 I was called into the army after three weeks of the season, and my salary naturally was terminated at that time. I didn't come back until July 1, 1945, and my salary was automatically guaranteed by the National Labor Relations Board. They had passed a ruling that all returnees from service were automatically entitled to their jobs and also entitled to the same salary. So my salary of $55,000 was reinstated in 1945. I played half a season, and I hit the pennant-clinching home run in dramatic fashion in the ninth inning in St. Louis. We won the American League pennant and the World Series against the Cubs. So, without my even asking for it, Mr. Briggs sent me a contract for $75,000. I did not hesitate in accepting that salary. It was the highest in baseball; it was the second highest ever paid to a ballplayer, and I was delighted.

However, I asked the new general manager, George Trautman, if instead of taking $75,000, I could resume my $55,000 salary with the $20,000 balance paid to me in a bonus when and if I ever retired or was sold or transferred from the Detroit baseball club. This was money that I was making during the season, except that it was being held aside so that if and when I retired I'd have a little lump sum to tide me over until I found a new occupation. It was as simple as all that, but for some reason I had trouble explaining it to Mr. Trautman. He got all excited about it and finally I guess he went to Mr. Briggs. They finally, agreed to it. I had my attorney, David Solinger, draw up an addendum to my contract and that was that.

During the course of the season I was slowing down. So I had made a few comments about maybe retiring. With that, George Trautman came to me and said, "Well, you know, if you retire, you won't get that $20,000 bonus." I said, "Wait a minute, George, you're not giving me any $20,000 bonus. This is money that I'm earning right along. I had a $75,000 contract, and I'm just taking payment in a different manner. You're not giving me any bonus." He said again that I wouldn't get the money if I retired. I said, "I'm not retiring, I've only got another month left of the season. If I were going to lose the $20,000 I wouldn't retire, even if I wanted to." Anyway, he had difficulty with this. I don't know what he said to Mr. Briggs, or what the conversation was in the front office, but I'm sure it was garbled.

Looking back, I think one of the reasons I wasn't very popular is that I was always figuring out how I could better myself financially. Nothing dishonest; nothing that wasn't permissible under the law, just thinking ahead and coming up with ideas.

The clubs didn't like it; maybe they didn't like Jews coming up with such ideas. They wouldn't go along with them. For example, I thought it was my duty to pay as few taxes as legally possible. Everybody in business was using that deferred compensation deal, but I was the first one in baseball to come up with the idea. You'd think I had dropped a bomb in the Detroit office when I suggested it to George Trautman. He didn't know what I was talking about. He thought this was another one of those ideas that Greenberg had and that they better watch me carefully.

That winter [1946] I had returned to New York where my wife and I had an apartment, and we settled into married life with no problems on our minds. I forgot about the game at the moment and looked forward to the birth of our first child, which we expected in January.

◆

In its January 1, 1947 issue, *The Sporting News* ran an article by Dan Daniel about Greenberg that would prove controversial. Accompanying the story was a photograph of Hank Greenberg in army uniform holding up a New York Yankee uniform with a caption saying he was "admiring Yankee flannels."

The story began: "Your correspondent is in a position to say that Hank Greenberg would like to come to the Yankees, and finish his career at first base—finish it right in the Bronx, where it started at James Monroe High School.

"If Hank had the chance to come to the New York club, there would be no question about his playing in 1947.

"As the situation stands, Greenberg is not going to make up his mind about returning to the Tigers until after the holidays. . . .

"In the meantime, he has to make up his mind if he wants to play baseball another year, and the Tigers have to make up their minds if they want him at the $75,000 rate. . . ."

The Detroit fans and the Detroit management were furious with the story. Sam Greene in the *Detroit News* wrote: "None of the direct quotations in the [Daniel] interview could possibly have offended the Detroit management or the Detroit baseball public. It was the 'indirect quotes' that caused the furor.

"No doubt the readers of *The Sporting News* would wonder how Mr. Daniel was 'in a position' to know all these things if Greenberg or his spokesman never mentioned them, but in none of the three paragraphs did the correspondent directly quote the player. . . ."

◆

Four years earlier, when I was in the army in Fort Worth, I got a telegram from the War Department telling me to report to New York City to participate in a bond game. Larry MacPhail was head of this project, and they were selling $100,000 worth of bonds for the game; it was supposed to be a revolutionary idea. They insisted that I come up and play. Of course, when you get an order from the War Department and you're in military uniform, you don't decline the invitation. Anyway, I went to New York and there was no uniform for me to work out in, and we were at Yankee Stadium. The American League clubs were at the Polo Grounds, and that was where the game was to be played. The Yankees loaned me an outfit to play in, just to work out in. Of course, some enterprising newspaperman took a picture of me in the Yankee uniform, and four years later it ran in *The Sporting News*, and that's the article that Mr. Briggs took exception to. The thing that intrigues me to this day is Mr. Briggs's reaction. Of course, I thought he had a lot of Detroit newspaper people in his hip pocket, and they started to write derogatory columns about me. He got very annoyed with this unappreciative slave who had worked for him and whom he

166

had treated so grandly. His view was that he had given me this $20,000 bonus and I wasn't really entitled to it, and it was just a generous action on his part, which was false.

The third thing that angered him was that I obviously no longer wanted to play in Detroit. I was no longer interested in Detroit. When the question came up about the letter I had written to him asking for consideration as general manager, I went on radio to explain that on a Sunday night. It was pretty odd for a ballplayer who wanted to get away from Detroit to apply for a position as general manager in Detroit. Then, suddenly, Mr. Briggs couldn't find the letter I had sent. They couldn't find it in the office, then he threw the zinger in. Even if he had received the letter he never would have considered Henry Greenberg as general manager material because he didn't have the experience or the know-how, and he thought it was presumptuous of me even to apply for the job.

There were two sides to the story, and press opinion moved back and forth with some newspapers changing their tune and writing in my favor.

The first thing I did was send a telegram to J. G. Taylor Spink, the editor-in-chief of *The Sporting News*, which was then the baseball bible, and questioned him about the picture he used and the article that he ran. He was very indignant and said, "If there's anything you have to say, you can certainly call me up and I'll be glad to print your side of the story." I said, "Listen, Mr. Spink, you've already done the damage. Putting in a repudiation isn't going to do me any good. Why didn't you check out the story before you ran it? Then maybe I'd have a little respect for *The Sporting News*." He didn't like that. He was a tough old coot, and he had been running baseball from his newspaper for some time. He took his position very seriously, and I suppose he had run the article in good faith. But that's typical of the press. They run the story first, and then they look for the facts. That article in *The Sporting News* did a lot of harm, I can assure you. After such an article runs it's always hard to explain what really took place because by that time the original impression has settled in the reader's mind, and he's not interested in getting the true story.

It's strange how baseball has always treated its fading stars so shabbily. In the old days they couldn't wait until one of their favorite ballplayers could no longer perform and they could shunt them aside. Owners almost resented the salaries that they paid them and couldn't wait to almost destroy their dignity. I'm talking about players like Ty Cobb and Babe Ruth and Jimmie Foxx, and so many other star ballplayers. I suppose they were a little difficult to handle, and I guess I was, too. But there's something about being outstanding as a player; that attitude of confidence or arrogance or whatever you call it is what makes you outstanding. Therefore, maybe you are a little more difficult to handle, but that's what puts you out in front of the run-of-the-mill ballplayers; the owners just didn't understand that. They had no sentiment. It was all dollars and cents. Of course, today it's completely different because the players have all the money and they're going to leave baseball with their heads held high. Most of them are even talking about buying the franchise. The players are going to wind up with more money than the people who own the clubs.

I remember poor old Babe Ruth back in the late thirties when he had to take a job as a third-base coach or a first-base coach with the Brooklyn Dodgers. They didn't have much of a team and all they did was use him as a gate attraction, a spectacle, and the guy could hardly stand up. Here was the greatest figure in the history of the game. No one was going to be even close to approaching the man who changed the game and brought millions and millions of people to the ballpark because of his home runs, and they treated him as though he was a stumblebum.

Ruth was terribly bitter when I went to visit him in 1947, when he had cancer and was on his way out. He wouldn't have anything to do with anybody; he wouldn't do any interviews. I was just lucky that he was willing to see me. At that point he was very disappointed by the way he had been treated. It's true that he was a hero for some twenty years, and patted on the back and spoiled and applauded, but that's the way it goes. You're going to get that adulation from a fickle fan, but the owners should have appreciated what he contributed to the game and made an effort to ease him out of baseball with a little more dignity.

Then another twist in the road came about. I heard on the radio one Saturday afternoon as we were driving to Chieftains that I had been sent to the Pittsburgh Pirates in the National League on waivers. I heard later that Briggs was said to have told Billy Evans, who had assumed the general managership of the Detroit club: "We don't deserve that kind of treatment [referring to *The Sporting News* quote] from a player with whom we have been overly generous. This is too much. Get rid of him!"

No trade, Detroit didn't get any players back for me, just the $10,000 waiver price. Naturally I didn't believe it until the telegram was delivered to me. It was laid out in very cold terms by Billy Evans.

◆

The following telegram, dated January 18, 1947, was sent to "Henry Greenberg" at 21 East 66th Street, New York City: THIS IS TO INFORM YOU THAT YOUR CONTRACT HAS BEEN ASSIGNED TO THE PITTSBURGH CLUB OF THE NATIONAL LEAGUE TRUST YOU WILL FIND YOUR NEW CONNECTION A MOST PROFITABLE ONE

    [Signed] BILLY EVANS

◆

After having spent sixteen years in the Detroit organization and having been instrumental in winning the championship for them in 1945 and then leading the league in runs batted in and home runs in 1946, to get that kind of a telegram just left me speechless. At that moment I decided I was through with baseball. It soured me on the game, and since I knew that eventually I had to face a future outside baseball and look for employment, I might just as well do it then.

I left Detroit with a very harsh, bitter taste in my mouth, and I have never really had any feeling for the ball club since that time. I've been back to Detroit only four times in the last forty years.

When I got that telegram from the Tigers my disillusionment with baseball set in. I couldn't believe it, after having served sixteen years, from high school through four years of war and then coming back and helping them win four pennants during my tenure with the club. In every one of the years the Tigers won the pennant, you'll see that I had a fantastic season at bat. Suddenly, out of the blue, they sold me on waivers. This was the most insulting way, waiving out the highest-priced player in baseball from the American League contending team (we had finished second in 1946) to a last-place club in the National League. There had to be something to it. It just took the heart out of me. I became so disillusioned overnight that I made up my mind to quit.

◆

Three days after Greenberg received the telegram informing him of his sale to Pittsburgh, he received a letter from Billy Evans and a check for $16,170. The check covered the $20,000 "bonus" due Greenberg, "less withholding tax of $3,800 and D.A.B. Tax of $30."

"Mr. McKinney, President of the Pittsburgh Club, is a personal friend of mine. I am sure you will enjoy playing under him. Lots of good luck to you.

"Cordially, [signed] Billy Evans."

CHAPTER 11

Walter Briggs "hinted that the sale . . . might have been influenced by national publicity of a week ago suggesting that Greenberg might like to finish his Major League career . . . with the Yankees," according to the *Detroit Times*. In a statement to the press Briggs said: "In light of recent happenings, it was felt that a change of scenery might prove highly beneficial to player Henry Greenberg and the Detroit club. . . ."

Billy Evans, the *Detroit Times* reported, "declared" that "all seven American League clubs declined to claim the big slugger at the $10,000 waiver price. No American League clubs were interested in his contract at that figure, making it possible for us to send him to the National League.

"Several years ago Jack Zeller, the general manager of the Tigers, attempted to sell Greenberg to the Yankees, but the Yanks were reluctant to assume his high salary contract at that time. . . ."

On the following day, January 19, Larry MacPhail, president of the Yankees, refuted Evans's contentions: "We did not claim Greenberg because Detroit would not let us have him on waivers. All we would have accomplished by claiming him was to keep Greenberg on the Detroit club or some other American League club other than New York. . . .

"We approached Detroit last fall, [and twice more] regarding Greenberg. The Detroit club had no intention of letting Greenberg come to New York, except in a player deal which would help them and hurt us.

"When we made up our minds that we couldn't get Greenberg we decided not to claim him and backed a National League deal. We would rather have Greenberg at Pittsburgh than at Detroit. . . ."

Earlier, H. G. Salsinger, a *Detroit News* writer, discussed the rise in attendance at baseball games in Detroit in 1946, for which some had given much credit to Greenberg's presence and bat.

"Detroit drew 1,722,590 customers at home last year, an increase of 442,249 over 1945. The New York Yankees drew 2,265,512 at home, an increase of 1,383,667 over 1945.

"If Greenberg was mainly responsible for an increase of 442,249 in Detroit, who was mainly responsible for an increase of 1,383,667 in New York? Joe DiMaggio, who hit .290? Charlie Keller, who hit .275? Phil Rizzuto, who hit .257? . . . Or the Yankees who were out of the pennant race by the end of May?" Or, as Salsinger did not suggest, was it the great interest in a return to the joys of baseball after the war, and the delight in having the old stars, like DiMaggio, Keller, and Greenberg, back from the war and back in a baseball uniform?

◆

When I came back from the service in 1945, I was disgusted with the game. It had showed me no special interest during my years in the service. So when I came back I decided that there must be other important things in life besides baseball. In the service my horizons were expanded. Then, after the war, I met Caral and I was enthralled by her. Suddenly other places and things seemed to be important to me and my interest in baseball, which had been all-consuming up until then, began to wane. And after my treatment by the Tigers I was totally disillusioned and disgusted.

Roy Hamey, who had assumed the general managership at Pittsburgh, called me and I told him that I decided to drop out of baseball, that I was no longer interested in playing, and that I regretted doing this to him because I knew he was trying to start a new organization with new ownership. Hamey had been a scout with the Yankees and I had become acquainted with him during my playing days. The Pirates had been bought by a consortium of four individuals, headed by Frank McKinney, the banker from Indianapolis, who had been the Democratic national chairman. He had some interest in the Indianapolis baseball club and had gotten three other men together—Tom Johnson, a local resident of Pittsburgh; John Galbreath, who was a prominent citizen of Columbus, Ohio, and a contractor and owner of race horses; and Bing Crosby, who also bought a 25 percent interest in the club. They had gone into this new enterprise with great enthusiasm.

With all the publicity, I think I sold some $300,000 to $400,000 in advance tickets because the new Pirate ownership looked like it was attempting to build a contending team after having finished in seventh place in 1946. [The Pirates had never sold more than $70,000 in advance tickets.] Then suddenly I had to tell them I was no longer interested in playing.

This was a shock to them, too. Even though Mr. McKinney called me repeatedly and Roy Hamey called me, and Bing Crosby wrote me two or three long letters from California. (I had met Bing just before I got married.) He had pleaded with me to play just one more year with Pittsburgh, but I told him my mind was made up. I was no longer interested in playing baseball, and that was final.

Some time near the end of January, Caral gave birth to Glenn, our first child. We were very happy, but I was still concerned about what kind of occupation I would seek since I no longer planned to play baseball. Shortly thereafter I got a telephone call from John Galbreath. He was coming to New York on business and wanted to have lunch with me and get acquainted. He said he had no plans to try to talk me into playing baseball again.

Naturally I couldn't refuse that invitation. During the course of the lunch, he said, "Just out of curiosity, I just wonder why you don't want to play." I said, "Well, Mr. Galbreath, my allegiance has always been to the American League. I've played my whole career there, and I always thought I'd end my career in Detroit, and there's always been bitter rivalry between the two leagues. We never saw much of the teams in the other league except in the World Series and exhibition games. Naturally, in the World Series, the opposing team was your enemy, and there was no love lost between the leagues, especially from the standpoint of the National League. They were always getting whipped in the World Series because the Yankees were dominant in baseball. Going to an alien league and not knowing anybody, and being in a strange city, I'm just not interested in playing. Furthermore, the fans are going to expect a great deal from me since I hit 44 home runs last year and drove in close to 140 runs. Forbes Field is a big ballpark, and I'm not going to be able to hit that many home runs. I don't want to go down there with the pressure of having to duplicate my season in Detroit and know that the fans are going to be disappointed."

He said, "What are the distances in Detroit?"

I told him they were 340 feet to the left-field line, and the fence came straight across.

He said, "Well, we'll do the same thing in Pittsburgh." I asked him what he meant and he said they would build the bullpen out there and start the bullpen in from the wall and make it 340 feet from the home plate and run it straight across, and then I would have the same target in Pittsburgh as I had in Detroit.

I said, "You know, Mr. Galbreath, I just don't want to play. I don't want to travel anymore. I can't travel on the trains. The berths are too small for me. Every time I go on an overnight trip, I wake up with a kink in my neck and I'm stiff and it's just not comfortable for me."

He said, "That's no problem. We'll fly you. You can take a plane from city to city, and you won't have to worry about the trains."

I said, "I don't want any roommates. I'm married now, and I want to be by myself."

He said, "We'll give you a suite. You don't have to have a roommate." Finally I said, "Mr. Galbreath, I'm never going to go through the shock of being traded or sold like a piece of merchandise like what just happened to me with Detroit. If you're willing to give me my outright release at the end of the season, I'll play one season for the Pirates."

He said, "Okay, we'll do that. We'll give you your outright release. We'll agree to it."

I said, "What am I going to get paid?"

He said, "You'll get paid whatever you want."

I said I wanted $100,000, and he said, "You got it."

I agreed to play one more season with the Pittsburgh Pirates. We even worked out a deal for a salary that included more than just a base pay—something other players would do some thirty years later. I told Mr. Galbreath that since I was getting a salary of $75,000 from Detroit, I would like to get a salary of $40,000 from Pittsburgh, and I'd like to buy $74,000 worth of stock in the Pittsburgh club. Then, at the end of the year, I wanted him to buy the stock back for $134,000, so I'd pay a capital gain tax on the $60,000 and income tax on the $40,000. He agreed to that, too.

After lunch I rushed over to the Lone Star Boat Club, where I played squash and handball. I was very enthusiastic, now that I had a lot of pressure off me. I knew now that I was employed for another year and I didn't have to look for a job elsewhere. I guess, in looking back, I was really happy to have decided to play baseball again, even if I wasn't in the condition I had been in four or five years earlier. Baseball was still in my blood and this was a new challenge for me. I was looking forward to it with great anticipation.

That afternoon on the squash court, I played above my ability and hit the ball real hard on the backhand side. I went home that evening feeling in great shape and looking forward to the future.

Early the next morning I got up and my arm was bent so that I could barely straighten it out to comb my hair. At first I thought that I had slept on my arm and it had gotten numb in kind of an awkward position.

I tried to work it out, but couldn't. It turned out that I had developed bone chips playing squash that hard. Naturally, I didn't want to announce that I had arm problems after the Pirates had agreed to all the requests I made, so I suffered with it and went to spring training in Miami Beach and decided I was going to go through with the season, bone chips or no bone chips. The funny thing was that the chips only bothered me when they got lodged in the elbow joint. When the chips floated around and one of them got into the joint, I couldn't straighten my arm and that's when the problem started. When I shook them loose I was fine.

I played with that condition throughout the 1947 season.

◆

Before heading for spring training in 1947, Greenberg made a significant visit to an ailing hero, Babe Ruth.

◆

Babe Ruth had cancer of the throat and wouldn't see anybody; he wouldn't even answer the phone. Bob Considine finagled us in to see the Babe by saying I wanted to stop in and shake hands with him. So Babe was nice enough to invite us to his apartment. Babe showed me all his trophies and he couldn't have been nicer. He gave me a picture of himself that has hung in my house ever since. That's the last time I saw Babe. [Ruth died in August of the following year.]

I've never forgotten that Considine was rummaging around the apartment, swiping snapshots and clippings, and Babe didn't know it. After that visit a picture of Babe and me ran in *Time* magazine. Babe was a sweet man. I never really knew him when he was younger; I'm sure he was a hell-raiser. But he always treated me great. He'd always say, "Hello, kid"—of course, everybody was "kid" to him—and, as a young player in the league, that was enough to make my day.

◆

Bob Considine's piece about that visit appeared in *The Sporting News*:
"America's No. 1 convalescent, Babe Ruth, received his first visitor the other day and told him how to hit a home run. The visitor was Hank Greenberg, who called the visit 'unforgettable'—as indeed it was.

174

"The greatest home-run hitter who ever lived, and the best there is in baseball today, met in Ruth's trophy-littered apartment. I was there to listen.

"Greenberg was like a boy sitting at the feet of the stricken master. He asked for, and got, Babe's autograph.

"'Going to tell you something, Hank,' Babe husked in a voice that is just returning to him after his critical neck operation. 'Hand me that bat. Now I'm going to show you the whole secret of how I hit those home runs. Only fellow I ever told it to was Lou Gehrig, when Lou first came up to the Yanks and Miller Huggins was trying to make a left-field hitter out of him.'

"Ruth wrapped his huge and now gaunt hands around the bat handle, with the little finger of his right hand extending down below the main surface of the handle and butt.

"'Look,' he said, as he sat in his robe and pajamas and lightly swung the bat. 'See how this grip makes your wrists break at the right moment? Throw the whole weight of the bat into the ball. With this grip, you've just got to follow through. Any other grip interferes with your follow-through.

"'I kept it a secret a long, long time,' Babe mused.

"Greenberg has had many misgivings of late about being unceremoniously sold to Pittsburgh by Detroit.

"'I'm glad you finally signed up, Hank,' Babe told him. 'A man's got to keep playing, if he's fit. Keep looking out for yourself. Keep your wind. That's everything.

"'You'll like the National League, especially the ballparks. I got a bum break when I went over there, but that was just accidental. You'll be okay. They'll curveball you a lot, and you'll find that they think a one-run lead is something nice to sit back and rest on. But otherwise it's the same baseball we played.

"'Don't quit until every base is uphill,' the king advised. 'I played just a little too long . . . about a week or so. I should have quit that day in Pittsburgh—I was with the Braves, you know—when I hit three home runs and got gypped out of a fourth one by one of the Waners.

"'That should have been curtains. But I had promised old man Fuchs that I'd hang around for his Memorial Day crowd. Too bad. . . .'"

◆

When I first joined the Pirates they had just traded Bob Elliott, the regular third baseman, to the Boston Braves in exchange for Billy Herman, the veteran second baseman who had also played with the Chicago Cubs and the Brooklyn

Dodgers. He had a reputation for being a very smart baseball player, and the Pirates decided that they were going to hire him as their manager. In exchange, they had to trade Bob Elliott to the Braves. Well, Elliott became the most valuable player in the National League that year. And we, in return, got Billy Herman to play second base for us. I had been moved to first base for the Pirates and I had slowed down considerably, and so had Billy Herman. The right side of the infield was almost like the Grand Canyon; everything went through. Ten days after the season opened Billy decided he was not going to be an active player any longer, that he would be a bench manager. They got a player by the name of Eddie Basinski to play second base. He was known more for his ability to play the violin than second base. They said he was a great double-play man, and one of the reasons for it was that he played very close to second base at all times. Therefore he was in a position to accept a double-play ball before the runner from first base could get down there. What people didn't realize is that he left a wide gap between us, and a lot of balls went through there. That's the way we started off.

We actually had some good ballplayers on that team. Our pitching was suspect, but we had Ralph Kiner, who became my roommate on the road (I became friendly with Ralph and decided not to room alone), and he had led the league in home runs the prior year, and we had Billy Cox, a fine shortstop, who was subsequently traded to the Brooklyn Dodgers. We, in return, got a pitcher by the name of Kirby Higbe and someone else who didn't amount to a heck of a lot.

Kirby Higbe hailed from Greenville, South Carolina. He was friendly and easy-going, a good guy. I always liked him because he had been one of the few guys on the Dodgers who voted for Jackie Robinson to play. Kirby came to the clubhouse and his attitude was that he was going to beat everybody. Of course, he didn't beat too many people in 1947, as his record, 11–17 with the Pirates, would indicate.

We had Frank Gustine, who played third base for us in Bob Elliott's place. We had a pretty good outfield. Jim Russell was in center field, Wally Westlake in right field, and Kiner in left field, so we had a lot of power but we didn't have the pitching. The catching was just adequate. Clyde Kluttz was our catcher.

One of my favorites was Billy Sullivan. We were teammates in Detroit after he had played with Cleveland and Chicago. He graduated from Notre Dame and went right to the big leagues. His father had been a former Chicago White Sox player in the old days, and a good one. When Billy came out of college the

White Sox signed him and put him right in the lineup, and he was a fine hitter and a good receiver. Billy also could have played the outfield or first base or an infield position, and would have if they had made changes in those days. He always made good contact with the ball. He was a dead-pull hitter and he hit .300 in the Major Leagues for a number of years. He was traded to Cleveland, and then from Cleveland he came over to Detroit. I recall, in the 1940 season, our regular catcher was Birdie Tebbetts, but before too long Billy was moving his way into the lineup and since he was a left-handed hitter and Birdie was right-handed, before you knew it, they were alternating. Billy made a big contribution to the 1940 Detroit Tigers championship season.

I lost track of him when I went into the army, and he went into the navy. When I came out in 1945 and finally went to Pittsburgh in 1947, we made contact and I talked him into coming back into baseball because, since he had left, the pension plan had been instituted. I advised him that for $250 he could be a member of the pension plan. All the players had to contribute that amount. He said he didn't know of any team that would want him. When I went to Pittsburgh I told Roy Hamey, who was a good friend of mine and a nice man, that Billy Sullivan would be a credit to the team and could be used as a third-string catcher, and that he ought to be signed. Roy signed him, and Billy joined the Pittsburgh Pirates for the 1947 season. He and Ralph Kiner and I became best friends. Billy dropped out of baseball after the '47 season, but he had become a member of the pension plan. I'm sure to this day he's collecting his pension, and I feel responsible for that.

Anyway, that was the Pirates of 1947, and we started the season with great enthusiasm.

◆

On opening day the *Chicago Daily News* reported: "The Pittsburgh Pirates collected their first dividend on their . . . investment in Hank Greenberg.

"The aging slugger, purchased from Detroit during the winter, celebrated his debut as a National Leaguer by lashing out a line drive double in the sixth inning. The two-bagger scored Billy Cox with the run that gave the Pirates a 1–0 decision over the Cubs before 29,247 fans . . . at Wrigley Field."

The winning pitcher for the Pirates was Rip Sewell, with whom Greenberg had had a fight fourteen years before, when both were with Detroit.

"Greenberg and I got along great in Pittsburgh," Sewell recalled years later. "He paid me one of the greatest compliments that could be paid. He said, 'I admire everything you've done over here in Pittsburgh.' I told him, 'Henry, you know you and I had a fight. You know that you and I have grown up. We've become men instead of kids, so I appreciate your compliment very much.' This is what we said to each other when we first saw each other in training camp that year.

"And when Greenberg won that opening day game for me, I just congratulated him like we all do. That was all I could say to him. We grew up."

Two days later, against the Cubs again, Greenberg hit his first National League home run.

But life in the National League for the 36-year-old Greenberg could be less than pleasant. From *The Sporting News* came this report:

"Hank Greenberg had a tough day with the bat at Crosley Field, April 27. He made seven trips to the plate without a hit in the twin bill, and didn't like it. In the tenth frame of the overtime nightcap, when the Pittsburgh slugger popped out to Ray Mueller, he teed off on the catcher's mask, lying on the ground, and sent it almost to the Pirate dugout. The mask was so bent for Mueller he had to call time while he got another.

"In the twelfth, when Greenberg grounded out, Mueller picked up Hank's bat and beat it in the ground several times until a distinct crack was heard."

◆

Attendance was good, and we won a few ball games. [The Pirates, as Galbreath had promised Greenberg, moved in the left-field fence in Forbes Field from 365 feet to 335 feet, and the area quickly became known as "Greenberg's Gardens."] But when Billy Herman decided to go to the bench, things started to go downhill. Billy had no experience as a manager and, as a result, things got chaotic at times. In fact they were thinking of sending Kiner to the minor leagues because he had got off to a poor start. He hadn't hit any home runs and was not doing much at bat. Roy Hamey and Frank McKinney called me into their office and asked my opinion of sending Kiner to the minor leagues. I told them I couldn't believe they would even contemplate it. I said, "Here you have a guy who hit 23 home runs after he came out of the service and had led the league. He's young, has a beautiful swing, a great stance, and great power. How could you possibly think of sending him to the minor leagues? It's ridiculous."

They said, "Billy Herman thinks he should go down."

I said, "I disagree. Keep Ralph Kiner with the team. I'll take him as a room-mate. He and I will get along great, and I'm sure I can help him; I'm sure he'll put in a good performance." All he did was hit 51 home runs that season to lead the National League. Ralph went on to lead the National League in home-run hitting seven times and would be elected to the Hall of Fame.

Despite Kiner, after Herman quit playing, the team started losing and we sank to last place.

Bing Crosby gave the club a record player, and with it a number of records. One· of the favorite records of this great Pittsburgh team was "Cigarettes and Whiskey and Wild, Wild Women," and after every game everyone would rush into the clubhouse and the clubhouse boy would have this record blaring away, even though we might have got beat 15–2 that day. But that was the attitude of the team.

I wasn't very encouraged by this because I had come from a winning ball team. We'd never been below fourth in the American League, and we had won the pennant four times. Coming to a strange league and a last-place ball club was so demoralizing. I could just imagine what would have happened if Mickey Cochrane had been the manager of the Pittsburgh Pirates. He would not only have broken the record player, he would have torn up the clubhouse. That's the kind of intense, fiery competitor he was. Billy Herman was different. He would go right into the manager's room, which was separate from the players' dressing room, and lock himself in. That was his approach. He didn't want to know what was going on outside, and I can understand that. He was a new manager, just coming out of the player ranks. It was a little different for him, but it was very strange for me to hear the record player going after defeats. There was a deafening silence in Detroit after we lost a ball game.

At one point in the season, one of our players, Vinny Smith, decided to get married, and he held his wedding on the day of a game. It was in the after-noon, and the game was at night. He invited five of the players to the cere-mony, and they all went out there and had a great time. They were sipping champagne or drinking beer and having a ball. They all arrived at the ballpark in time for the game, and Billy Herman had all of them in the lineup. It was hard enough to play with nine players who were sober, much less with six of them slightly inebriated. Needless to say, it was a comedy of errors out there, and the only one not aware of it was Billy Herman. I have never been a man-ager, so I'm not criticizing Billy, because sometimes the manager is the last to know. Players often have little inside jokes of which the manager isn't aware. But we thought it was terribly funny and terribly strange that the inebriated ballplayers were in the lineup on the day that one of them had gotten married. They could no more catch a fly ball than fly to the moon. Of course, we lost.

At one point in the season Branch Rickey of the Brooklyn Dodgers talked our new management, which wasn't too experienced in baseball, into a trade. All we did was give up Billy Cox, our shortstop, and Preacher Roe, our left-handed pitcher, in return for Kirby Higbe, who had been a pretty good pitcher for the Dodgers. But what we didn't know was that he liked to sip out of the bottle and on occasion was not in perfect condition to pitch. Another chap by the name of Dixie Howell, who was a catcher, came along with Kirby to Pittsburgh in return for these two fine players. Preacher Roe won over twenty games one season, and Billy Cox was moved from shortstop to third base and turned out to be one of the great third basemen of the National League. We had gotten skinned by Branch Rickey's smooth-talking, silver-tongued oratory. The amusing thing was that a few years later Branch Rickey sold his interest in the Brooklyn Dodgers and became general manager and president of the Pittsburgh Pirates. It was the last-place team then, and when one of the writers asked Rickey about the players, he said, "There's no way this team is going to improve until we make some changes." One of the writers said to him, "You ought to know, Branch, you sent all these players over here from Brooklyn."

On another occasion Ralph Kiner and I were in St. Louis having our lunch. We were playing the Cardinals that night. We went up to the roof garden of the hotel, where there was tea dancing, and we decided to have our lunch there and listen to the music and watch the people dance. We were joined by Dixie Howell. He asked what we were drinking, and I facetiously said, "Scotch and soda." He said, "Well, I think I'll have one." So he sat down and called the waiter, and he ordered a double scotch and soda. I looked at Ralph because I couldn't believe my eyes. But sure enough, they brought the scotch and soda, and he had one and then another and then started on a third. With that, Ralph and I had finished our sandwiches and decided we'd better leave, which we did. Dixie said, "I'll see you out at the ballpark." Later on, when we got to the ballpark, there was Dixie Howell catching. Well, we knew this was going to be fun, and it was. The first inning there were five or six passed balls, and one ball, a knuckler, hit Dixie square in the chest. The next pitch went through his legs to the screen. The next pitch hit him in the arm and went to the screen. Everybody on the bench almost fell off roaring with laughter, but Billy Herman wasn't aware of what was going on. It really shouldn't have been amusing, since we were blowing the ballgame (which wasn't unusual for us), but it was so funny to watch Dixie Howell trying to catch Kirby Higbe's knuckleball in the condition he was in. How the hell we got through that inning, I'll never know. Dixie finally stopped the balls with his chest protector.

◆

That year, 1947, Jackie Robinson, in his rookie season, was the center of attention around the National League.

Early in the season, Jimmy Powers in the *New York Daily News* quoted Greenberg on Robinson: "The more they ride him the more they will spur him on. It threw me a lot when I first came up. I know how he feels. . . . They will keep needling Jackie, and he will react by forcing himself to play over his head. I'll be awfully surprised if I hear that Robinson fails to hit and hold his job."

Greenberg and Robinson, kindred spirits of a sort, would soon meet.

A short, one-column story in *The New York Times* on May 18 bore the headline: HANK GREENBERG A HERO TO DODGERS' NEGRO STAR.

The story read: "Jackie Robinson, first Negro player in the Major Leagues, has picked a diamond hero—rival first baseman Hank Greenberg of the Pittsburgh Pirates.

"Here's why: Robinson and Greenberg collided in a play at first base during the current Dodger-Pirate series. The next time Jackie came down to the sack, Hank said, 'I forgot to ask you if you were hurt in that play.'

"Assured that Robinson was unharmed, Greenberg said: 'Stick in there. You're doing fine. Keep your chin up.'

"This encouragement from an established star heartened Robinson, who has been the subject of reported anti-racial treatment elsewhere and admits he has undergone 'jockeying—some of it pretty severe.'

"'Class tells. It sticks out all over Mr. Greenberg,' Robinson declared."

◆

Jackie came into Pittsburgh on a Friday afternoon, and the place was jammed. We were in last place and the Dodgers were in first. Our Southern ballplayers, a bunch of bench jockeys, kept yelling at Jackie, "Hey, coal mine, hey coal mine, hey you black coal mine, we're going to get you! You ain't gonna play no baseball!" Jackie paid them no mind. He got on the bases and started dancing. It was beautiful to watch. I couldn't help but admire him. Anyway, we were in last place and these guys were calling a guy on a first-place team names. "We'll get you next time at bat, you dumb black son of a bitch. We're going to get you!"

Jackie turned his head. He was like a prince. He kept his chin up and kept playing as hard as he could. He was something to admire that afternoon.

I got to thinking, here were our guys, a bunch of ignorant, stupid Southerners who couldn't speak properly, who hadn't graduated from school, and all they could do was make jokes about Jackie. They couldn't recognize that they had a special person in front of them, a gem. They just kept ragging him and calling him names.

In a way, it was sad that he was so educated because, had he been just an ordinary bumpkin, it might have been easier for him. But the fact that he was a college man, from UCLA, and a football star, a baseball star, and a basketball star made it difficult for him to accept a role of a subhuman being in a world where he felt he was an equal. In every park that he played that spring he was on exhibition. He was the one the fans came out to see, this first black ballplayer in the Major Leagues.

If it wasn't for Pee Wee Reese, who stood up for him, they would have barred him from the Dodgers. Dixie Walker refused at first to play ball with him. The Dodger team used to stop on the road and everybody would go in and get a sandwich. Jackie would sit in the back of the bus and occasionally some white ballplayer would take pity on him and bring him a sandwich. He never complained.

Finally the season opened and Jackie was leading the Dodgers to the pennant, running the bases like a madman. You couldn't catch him off third base when you got him in a pickle. He was dodging here and dodging there and running like a halfback. It was an unbelievable performance for a ballplayer, never saying a word and taking all that verbal abuse. They called him a nigger, and I don't know how he could stand it, but he stood there and took it and played his game and did exceptionally well.

Jim Bagby was our pitcher in one game against the Dodgers, and he was the worst dumb son of a bitch. Jackie went up to bat and slapped a single off him, and then he'd dance off first to steal second. Bagby didn't know where he was. In an attempt to pick Jackie off, Bagby whirled and threw the ball to second, and quick as a flash, Jackie was standing on third. I'll never forget that.

Jackie had it tough, tougher than any ballplayer who ever lived. I happened to be a Jew, one of the few in baseball, but I was white, and I didn't have horns like some had thought I did. Jo-Jo White had said to me, "I thought all you Jews had horns on your head." But I identified with Jackie Robinson. I had feelings for him because they had treated me the same way. Not as bad, but they made remarks about my being a sheenie and a Jew all the time.

I said to Robinson at first base, "Don't pay any attention to these Southern jockeys. They aren't worth anything as far as you're concerned."

He thanked me and I said, "Would you like to go to dinner?"

He said, "I'd love to go to dinner, but I shouldn't because it'll put you on the spot."

That was our conversation, and we always were friends after that, even though he was in the National League and I went back to the American League as a club executive after that season.

Jim Bagby was a kind of excitable pitcher. Jim, unfortunately, had a harelip, so he spoke strangely. When he played for the Boston Red Sox in the American League, I hit him very well, and he was a clown then. But when he came over to Pittsburgh, I guess things were tough on him. The whole team was inferior and Jim had difficulty holding his own on the mound. I wasn't much help to him, because by this time I was an inadequate first baseman. And at one point we had an altercation, one word leading to another.

◆

"Greenberg was on first and Bagby was pitching," recalled Rip Sewell. "When the batter hit the ball, it was a very easy ball, Bagby ran over to cover first and the ball went through Greenberg's legs. So Bagby right there said, 'Hey you big Jew son of a bitch, you make enough money to catch that kind of a ball.' Greenberg said, 'I'm going to kill you after this game is over.'

"Bagby was taken out of the game, and he went into the locker room and changed his shoes. He put on his tennis shoes. We had just built a new men's room in the clubhouse and it had a tile floor. When the game was over here comes Hank just as fast as he could. Bagby was in the men's room waiting for him."

◆

I forgot to take my spikes off, so when I went to swing at Bagby, my feet flew out from under me and just at that time he punched me in the eye, and I came out of it with a black eye. The players separated us, and that was the end of that, so I guess I lost that one. But considering the long period of time that I played in baseball, there were few incidents where I was involved in fisticuffs. On the whole, I think I managed to keep my sense of purpose, which was to play ball, and not worry about getting into a fight with the players.

◆

"I lived in Pittsburgh that one summer," recalled Caral Gimbel. "Hank had a miserable season and we lived in such a depressing apartment. When I went to the games in Pittsburgh, I always sat in John Galbreath's closed box, completely isolated, which was just as well.

"Hank took a real liking to Ralph Kiner. That summer in Pittsburgh was a disaster, but at least the relationship between Ralph and Hank was meaningful to Hank. He was helping Ralph and advising him and he did extract some pleasure out of the big days that Ralph had."

Years later Ralph Kiner recalled: "Hank was the biggest influence in my life. He was my idol when I was growing up. I was a boy in Los Angeles and I got interested in baseball about 1934, when I was twelve, and the Tigers were my team and Hank was the star. So when he came over to Pittsburgh my whole objective was to get to know this guy.

"We were introduced in spring training in 1947 and the first thing he says to me is, 'Let's stay out here and take some extra batting practice.'

"He would spend hours, literally, at extra batting practice and extra fielding practice. We even did it on the road after games—stay late in the opponent's ballpark and take extra batting practice. I had never heard of anyone doing that. The biggest thing Hank taught me was that hard work is the most important thing. Although I was the kind of guy who would do the best he could, still, it was tough to do on that team. They were all having a good time. I don't know if it was the aftermath of the war, or what. I was young and single and it's a lot easier to go have a good time than to go out to the ballpark early, or stay late, and work. I could have been the same as some of the other guys, if it weren't for Hank's influence.

"As it turned out, he took me in the palm of his hand and we'd go out to dinner after working out. He and Caral and I.

"No one except Hank taught me anything. He said, 'This is what I think you ought to do.' He wanted me to get closer to the plate and pull the ball. Fortunately, I was smart enough to listen to him. We talked for hours about pitchers—he had devoted so much time to the study of what was going on with the pitchers in the National League.

"He did something else that I had had no idea about. I used to get signs for him when I was on base—I usually batted third and he fourth in the batting order, or I batted fourth and he fifth. He loved it when he knew what was coming. That takes a little guts, because if there's a mixup and the pitcher hits you he can kill you.

"Billy Sullivan, a third-string catcher, and Hank were together on the Tigers and they were real close friends. Billy was a very bright guy. Some of the clubs had very tough signs to break down. I memorized the sequence of the way the catcher signaled the pitches with his fingers when I was on base. I'd say, 'Okay, this was the way it was when Hank was up. They gave 2-1-2-1-1 or 2-1-1-1-1, or whatever,' and I gave them to Billy. And Billy would write them down and then they'd try to break the code. If we broke the code and I got on base again I was in a position to relay the signs. And Billy would signal Hank whether it was a fastball or curve that was coming.

"Another thing Hank would do was set pitchers up. He told me he'd go up maybe the first time, and with nobody on base, and purposely look bad on a curveball. Then, later in the game, in a situation where it meant something, he'd look for that pitch and usually get it.

"In the field, he caught almost everything. He was always in the right position. You never caught him napping. And he slid hard into the bases, too, even though he had slowed down a lot by the time he got to Pittsburgh.

"He prided himself on playing hard all the time, and getting an extra base. He was a gambling-type player. He didn't look graceful at all but he got the job done. When he'd hit one down the third-base line, he'd try to make a double out of it. Some might not, especially at the end of a career when they don't give a damn.

"He also helped me on certain matters off the field. I remember in spring training that year, I had met a girl and she invited me to a formal party. I rented a tuxedo but I forgot to get some shoes for them. So I put on the tuxedo and I put on my brown shoes. I was leaving with a player and Hank saw me with the tuxedo and brown shoes. He never let up from then on.

"He had asked to room with me on the road, right from the first, and that was great. And he dressed me. I wasn't that bad, I didn't think, but he took me down to a haberdasher and they tried different clothes on me and Hank said, 'That looks good. That's no good.' He just picked it all out. And when we came into New York he took me to the Copacabana and he knew the owner and they brought out a table and four chairs and put us on the dance floor. That was really my first exposure to New York. And going with Hank, that was big league. He knew how to do it right.

"At the end of the season that year he couldn't wait to get out of Pittsburgh. Not the city but the way the ball club was being run. There was no direction for the players, and we were at the bottom of the standings in the National League."

◆

Many years later, after I had retired, I was up at the Hall of Fame ceremonies in Cooperstown, New York, and I ran into Frankie Gustine, our third baseman that year. We started reminiscing and he reminded me of some of the crazy incidents that brought us down to the end of the season. We had to lose the last game of the year in order to finish in last place, because the Philadelphia Phillies were pushing us for last place. They were in seventh place, a game ahead of us, going into the last day of the season. And the team that finished last would get the first pick in the minor league draft the following year. Billy Herman had handed in his resignation on September 26, with one game remaining in the season, and was temporarily replaced by Bill Burwell, a coach.

We were playing Cincinnati that afternoon and we went out there with the idea in mind that we were going to try to lose the game. Sure enough, we won, 7–0. The other 153 games that we tried to win, most of them we lost. The Phillies split a doubleheader with the Giants, and so we and the Phillies wound up in a tie for last place.

To decide who got the first draft pick, the two clubs had to toss a coin. Needless to say the Pirates lost. So we didn't even get the first draft pick for the year. And that really closed out what I would call a disastrous season, but a very hilarious one.

I didn't have a very good season, at least not by my standards. I hit .249. I had promised John Galbreath that, no matter what, I would hit 25 home runs for the Pirates, which at that time was more than any other player on the Pittsburgh team had ever hit, so he was very happy with the prognostication. I played in 125 games, hit 25 home runs, and drove in 74 runs. I also led the league in bases on balls that year, which is the only outstanding thing I was able to do for the Pirates in 1947.

As I had planned when I signed my contract with the Pirates, I wanted my unconditional release at the end of the season. When I went into the office to say good-bye, Roy Hamey begged me to come back for one more year. He said he would pay me a $75,000 base salary, which was then the highest in either league, by far. I said I had had it with baseball. My legs were aching and I had a bad arm—those bone chips in the elbow had been a problem all season. [Greenberg underwent surgery in December 1947 for removal of the bone chips in his right elbow.] And I couldn't play with a losing team. I couldn't carry a team anymore; I could hardly carry myself. I said, "No, I'm through with active baseball." And with that, I went on to New York with my mind made up to look for another occupation.

◆

The Pirates had their best attendance in history that year. They drew 1,283,531, which broke the record of 869,720, set exactly twenty years before, when they won the National League pennant. "Curiously," said *The New York Times*, "the day when they went over the old mark . . . they were only half a game out of last place. They more than doubled their 1946 figures. . . . And Hank Greenberg's drawing power at the gate [was] a vital factor in compiling those extraordinary statistics." (Kiner's 51 homers also contributed to fan interest in this otherwise drab team.)

About a month after the season ended Greenberg received a letter from John Galbreath. It read in part:

"The season is now over and we can only look at it in retrospect. I want to say, Hank, that you fulfilled every promise you made. No one could have tried any harder or given any more time and effort to try to earnestly carry out every letter of a contract than you did. . . . I could not let the season pass without saying for the record that you did everything that was expected of you—and more. You did something for the Club and for the owners that scarcely anyone could have done and I am proud to have had a part in bringing you to us. The sentiment I have expressed also represents the thinking of the other owners of the Pirates."

CHAPTER 12

Looking back, I guess I was tough to handle. I played hard, I tried my best, I was always trying to overachieve, and I guess a lot of people didn't like that. A lot of ballplayers resented my being out there all the time, never taking a day off. When the other players were playing golf or going to the racetrack, I was at the ballpark taking batting practice. In fact, the ballpark wasn't an unpleasant place for me. I enjoyed being out there. I enjoyed hitting balls. I enjoyed working with my batting stance, judging which way to hit the ball, where to hit the ball, and how to hit the ball. It was no chore for me. But for those players who didn't have as much success as I did, it wasn't as much fun. A lot of them didn't show up at the ballpark. A lot of them were married and had other responsibilities. But as far as I was concerned, I was doing what I thought would be helpful to my career and I think it made a big difference in the results of the few years I played in the Major Leagues.

◆

When Greenberg retired, he had played only nine full seasons in the Major Leagues. He played one game in 1930, when he was brought up at the end of the season from Raleigh; had played twelve games in 1936—the year after he was named most valuable player in the league—before he suffered a broken wrist in a collision with Jake Powell on the base path and was out for the remainder of the season; nineteen games in 1941—the year after he had won his second Most Valuable Player award—when he was drafted into the army; and seventy-eight games in 1945, when he returned to the Tigers after four years of military service.

His lifetime batting average was .313; he had driven in 1,276 runs and had hit 379 doubles and 331 home runs. He hit an average of one home run every 6.4 times at bat, ninth on the all-time list. He is tied for first with Sam Thompson and Lou Gehrig for highest average of runs batted in per game with .925, or nearly one RBI a game for his career. His slugging average, that is, percentage of total bases to career at bats, was .605, fifth all-time.

He also had a .318 average, with 5 homers and 22 RBIs in four World Series.

◆

If I had played twenty years there's no telling what records I would have set during my career. Actually, I shouldn't use the term "my career." I didn't think of it in those terms when I was playing ball. I mean, baseball was my whole life; every day I thought about the ballpark and the ball game. If we had an off day and there was no pressure at all, going to the ballpark was for me almost what going to Disneyland is for twelve- and thirteen-year-olds. I guess the older you get the more inclined you are to think back to your youth, particularly now, when I'm confined to my backyard and have lots of time to think and ponder and ask myself questions.

By the time I closed out my career I had saved $300,000. I only made $447,000, so in all those years I spent $147,000. I remember that every time I got any money I put it into savings bonds. When I came back from overseas I had roughly $300,000 in Treasury bonds. They called them war bonds then. You'd put up $7,500 and at the end of ten years they paid you back $10,000. And it was all taxable income.

I remember having a big argument with the undersecretary of the treasury, Chapman Rose, who was working under George Humphrey at the time. He was a friend of ours and came to dinner frequently. I said to him, "I can't believe it. After all these years I've saved up all this money and now it's all taxable."

He said, "Only a fool would put $300,000 into Treasury bills. These baby bonds were meant for people who save $25 at a time. They'd put up $19.75 and ten years later they'd get back $25. But people who put up real money don't buy baby bonds."

Well, I found that to be true, because many years later when I tried to buy an interest in the Cleveland ball club, I went to the Cleveland Bank & Trust Company and tried to borrow some money on my bonds. They said, "No, we can't take these as collateral." So much for "war bonds."

In 1947 I attended the World Series between the Brooklyn Dodgers and the New York Yankees. I sat in the box along the first-base side where most of the

American Leaguers had their seats, and a young man who was sitting alongside me caught my attention. He had crutches with him: his right leg had been amputated. I recognized him as Bill Veeck, the principal owner and president of the Cleveland Indians. He had come into the league at the tail end of 1946, so I hadn't gotten acquainted with him when I was playing with Detroit. He had been making a lot of people sit up and take notice of the way he ran a ball club. He had been an owner of the Milwaukee Brewers in the American Association back before the war. His leg had been run over by an antitank gun on the kickback and it had to be amputated above the ankle in 1946. Well, after the World Series game, as the crowd was leaving the stadium, I found myself walking alongside him. We walked across the outfield to avoid the rush, because the box seats exited through the right-field stands, and in those days they permitted you to walk across the field after the game. Veeck asked what I was doing for dinner that night and was I going to Toots Shor's Restaurant? I told him yes I was and he asked me to join him. I said I would be delighted.

We had dinner about 7:30 and stayed until the place closed at four in the morning. Bill and I argued a great deal about baseball, but we found ourselves to be very compatible. Evidently he saw something in me, and of course, I was enchanted with him. His exuberance and his enthusiasm and knowledge of the game were extraordinary. Bill's father had at one time been president of the Chicago Cubs, and Bill worked at Wrigley Field as a youngster selling peanuts and scorecards and doing odd jobs around the ballpark. He had learned the executive end of the game from the ground up. Of course, I had no experience in that end. I had been a ballplayer only, so I approached the game from the point of view of an active player. After we had met for the second or third time during the Series, Bill asked if I would come to Cleveland. I told him that I had no intention of resuming my active career and that I was just going to get out of baseball. He insisted that I join the Cleveland Indians and told me that he knew somebody who had a 5 percent interest in the club who was willing to sell it. They sold off pieces of the club when Bill bought the franchise. He told me this chap wanted to get out and he would get me that interest at the same price as the guy had paid for it. Then he said that he would sell me a 5 percent interest of his own stock so I would be owner of close to 10 percent, making me the second largest owner of the Cleveland baseball club. This intrigued me. It was an opportunity to get back into baseball as an executive and also be a part owner. So I agreed, and we planned for me to attend spring training in Tucson, Arizona.

When I got to training camp Bill asked if I would get into uniform and help some of the young Cleveland players. They had one outfielder by the name of Pat Seery, who was a home-run hitter and had batted only about .170 the season before. My primary job was to work with him. My approach to hitting was mental as well as physical—studying the pitcher, studying the catcher, knowing what they're going to throw, when they're going to throw it, and try to hit the ball out of the ballpark. Well, Pat Seery's theory was just to hit the ball. He didn't do any thinking at all. He had a slight hitch in his swing. When the ball was thrown around the letters of the uniform, he would get under it and usually strike out or pop up. I tried to get him to correct that hitch and then I talked to him about the mental part of hitting, of studying the pitcher and all that, and one day he came to me and he said, "I had a nightmare last night thinking about all the things you've been telling me about hitting. I can't hit that way. I can't do it. I just have to go back to my natural style."

He had had some fair years with Cleveland before I got there, but he didn't last very long. When a batter had a hitch or a weakness, the pitchers in the league soon found out what it was and they exploited it. One pitcher would tell it to a pitcher on another club, and it would get around the league. Pretty soon, even with all the power that he had, the only time Seery could hit the ball out of the ballpark was when the pitcher made a glaring mistake and put the ball in the strike zone. If they pitched the ball high inside, there was no way that Pat, who dropped his arm in the hitch, could get under the ball and hit it out of the ballpark or, for that matter, even get base hits. Seery's best day, though, came after we traded him to the White Sox: He hit 4 home runs in one extra-inning game. But overall, in his seven years in the Major Leagues, he batted just .224 and hit 86 home runs.

Well, I worked out with the club in Tucson and Bill kept talking to me about why I didn't want to play again. I hadn't signed any contract with Bill, and I was just out there on his word that I could buy the 10 percent of the club. When spring training ended and we went out to Los Angeles to play some exhibition games, I told Bill that I wasn't going to put on a uniform any more, I didn't want to be a player, spring training was practically over, and I wanted to buy an interest in the club and work as an executive. He had told me originally that he would make me his assistant and teach me the ropes in the front office. So I was prepared for it. As it would happen, the chap who was supposed to sell me his 5 percent interest changed his mind, so I never bought his interest and

I never bought Bill's 5 percent either. And I didn't become a stockholder in the club at that time. However, I told Bill I'd be glad to work as his assistant and I stayed on with the Cleveland Indians in 1948. I was paid a salary of $15,000. I was willing to work for $60,000 less than I would have gotten from the Pirates because I wanted to learn the ropes.

The 1948 season was a great experience for me. It was a change from being an active player to working out of the front office and, of course, it was a delight to be working with Bill Veeck. I had never met a man quite like him. He was a younger version of my old friend Louis Marx; he could stay awake twenty hours a day and was always happy, always smiling. My main role was to accompany Bill on his various speeches around the state of Ohio to help increase attendance at the games. You can see how successful he was in attracting baseball fans. The team was successful, too, because we won the World Series that year. We drew an attendance of 2.6 million plus in 1948, which was a record at the time. It was almost twice as much as any team had ever drawn. Fans flocked down to Municipal Stadium in droves, particularly on the weekends when we had doubleheaders. They came from as far away as Buffalo, New York, and Erie, Pennsylvania, even from Detroit. I called Bill "the Pied Piper." The Indians were the talk of that part of the country, and Bill Veeck was primarily responsible for it.

I used to accompany Bill to luncheons and dinners when the team was out of town, sometimes making two or three speeches a day. I'd sit in the audience and he'd introduce me, but primarily it was his show. I used to listen to him explain what the Indians were doing and tell some of the old baseball stories that everyone enjoyed. It was fun for me, and I spent an awful lot of time with Bill at night. He'd stay up until three or four in the morning, and be back at the ballpark at 8:00 A.M. I frequently had to go home at 1:00 A.M. because I couldn't keep my eyes open.

It was a really tight pennant race, and the Indians hadn't won the pennant since 1920. It was an exciting team, led by Lou Boudreau who was the player/manager. Of course, sitting in the stands, whenever we lost a ball game, it was very easy to second-guess the manager or second-guess the strategies that he employed. Frequently, when Bill got a little annoyed with the result of a game, he turned to me and asked if I would take over as manager of the team. I told him, "No way." Bill was determined to replace Lou and I talked him out of it many times for two reasons. One was that Lou was having a sensational year in the field; and at bat. The other was that he got plenty of advice from

192

his coaches. One was Bill McKechnie, who had managed many National League teams and won the pennant a couple of times, and the World Series when his Cincinnati Reds beat the Detroit Tigers in 1940. Lou was well guided by these older veterans who had seen the game for many years and I'm sure they were giving him the right advice.

It came to the end of the season, and sure enough the Indians wound up in a tie with the Boston Red Sox for first place in the American League. In those days they had a one-game playoff and after the toss of the coin, which Boston won, we had to travel to Beantown for the playoff game. Naturally Bill and I went to Boston with the team. Prior to the game we both went down to the dugout to talk to Lou Boudreau and we asked him if he had any plans or different strategy. To our amazement he did.

He took our regular first baseman, Eddie Robinson, who was a left-handed hitter, out of the lineup, and inserted Allie Clark, an outfielder who had never played first base and was a right-hand hitter, to the position of first base for the final game. On top of that, he was starting a rookie pitcher by the name of Gene Bearden, a knuckleball pitcher who had won nineteen games for the team, but a rookie nonetheless who had no previous experience in pitching in the clutch. That didn't deter Lou Boudreau. Bearden was his choice for pitcher in this crucial game. You can imagine Bill Veeck's shock. I had to agree with him. It was a daring move. It took a lot of guts on Boudreau's part to try to pull it off. And as the results show, he did pull it off, but he did it in an unusual way. He had 4-for-4 with 2 home runs; Kenny Keltner also hit a home run with a few men on base, and that made the difference in the ball game. Red Sox manager Joe McCarthy picked veteran Denny Galehouse to pitch the final game. He was a right-handed pitcher and Clark's playing first base had nothing to do with the game. We won and, of course, there was great celebrating in Ohio.

Bill asked me to arrange a party for the players in the Kenmore Hotel in Boston. It turned out to be one celebration that I'll never forget, because most of the players were veterans and they all rejoiced in having won the pennant. There was plenty of laughing and drinking, and a little fighting as well, before the party ended. On the train back to Cleveland the next day, the party resumed. The players ruined the club car and damages assessed to the team were $6,500.

When we arrived in Cleveland we were overwhelmed by the reception at the train station. It seemed like the whole city had turned out. The next day there was a victory parade through the main streets of Cleveland. It was a holiday for the city and the state, for that matter, and I think well over 100,000 people were in town to salute the players. There was great rejoicing in Cleveland. They didn't win that often in Cleveland, and it was a great treat for them.

The Indians beat the Boston Braves in the World Series in six games, and again it was a great feat for the Cleveland Indians and Lou.

After the Series ended and things had settled down, I went to Bill Veeck and said, "Look, Bill, I really enjoyed my working with you. It's been great to have your company and we had a fantastic season. I really feel I didn't contribute, but I was glad to have been a witness to it. Now I think I'm going to go back to New York and try to find some other employment."

Bill asked what was wrong. I told him nothing was wrong, but I wasn't doing anything. I was just more or less a stooge, and I wanted something to do. He asked me what I wanted to do. I told him I would like to run the farm system.

He said, "You got it."

I said, "What do you mean, I got it?"

He said, "You're the farm director."

I said, "Bill, are you kidding?"

He said, "No, you're the farm director. You can do anything you want. I just want you to stay on."

With this challenge, I decided to stay on with Cleveland. There was no discussion of salary. It wasn't important. I moved my wife and sons, Glenn and Stephen (who was born in September 1948), west, and we spent the year of 1949 in Cleveland. I was the farm director. We had 400 ballplayers under our control.

The first thing I wanted to do was change the way the farm system operated. In prior years it was customary to assign a certain number of ballplayers to each minor league manager and they conducted their own spring training camp wherever their city was located. I wanted to have a combined camp similar to what the Brooklyn Dodgers had at Vero Beach, where I could have all the players under my control and where I could make an appraisal of their talents and also try to instill into the organization a feeling of team spirit—that is, to develop Major League players for the big club and stop worrying about individual glory for the minor league managers or for the little towns they were representing.

I sought out a place called Marianna, Florida. It was an isolated town of 10,000 to 15,000 people, fairly close to Tallahassee in the northwest corner of the state. There was an old, abandoned air force base that had been turned over to the city. We decided to build a training base out there. Four baseball diamonds were built and we used the barracks for sleeping and the mess hall for feeding the players. I brought in all the managers and all the scouts and all the bigwigs from the little towns who represented those teams and explained the novel approach I was going to use.

Instead of assigning any of the players to any of the managers, all the uniforms were to be the same. I designated the players by the color of their socks: brown socks had D contracts; red socks were under C contracts; blue socks had B contracts; and players with the A contracts had green socks. The players under AA and AAA contracts wore the socks of the Major League club, which were striped. And so, when you looked out on the field with all these games going on, four at one time, or watched some of the players working in other areas, catching fungoes and pitching off the sidelines, you could distinguish what classification a player was in by just looking at his socks. In that way, if a player looked pretty good and he was wearing the AAA socks, you might assume he had been playing for four or five years, but that didn't necessarily make him a prospect. But if that same player was wearing brown socks, you knew it was his first year and if he looked that good, he was a fellow we wanted to look over very carefully, because he had Major League potential.

This program didn't go down too well with the managers of the various clubs, who were accustomed to getting their own players and working with them. I tried to explain to them that if a manager was a pitcher, he now had eighteen to twenty players under his control and only eight of them were pitchers. The rest of them were infielders, outfielders, and catchers. I said, "You fellows don't know enough about the other positions; therefore you can't advance these fellows as quickly. You can do well with the players in the positions that you're accustomed to, and that goes for the managers who are outfielders and those who are infielders. Therefore, we're going to put all the pitchers under the control of the pitching managers. All the infielders will be under the control of the infield managers." I said, "In that way, we're going to be able to impart all the knowledge that these fellows have and every player will gain experience and knowledge from the people who are working with him." I also instituted a system whereby all the managers and scouts would come to my quarters after dinner and we'd sit around and talk baseball from about 9:00 to 11:00 P.M.

I had a lot of objections from the managers and scouts and everybody else, and then an unpleasant incident developed. Buzz Wetzel, who had been the previous minor league director, was not notified by Bill that he had been replaced by me, which then led to an awkward situation. I finally had to call Bill in Cleveland and tell him that Buzz Wetzel was still under the impression that he was farm director and that Bill had to straighten it out immediately or else I was going to leave. Well, Bill was a compassionate, kindhearted person who didn't have the heart to fire anybody or let anybody down, and Buzz Wetzel was a kindly old gentleman in his mid-seventies who had been around the Cleveland organization for years and years and years. Bill just didn't know how to go about doing it, but he finally gathered up his courage and called Buzz and informed him that while his title stayed the same, Hank Greenberg was now the actual head of the farm system and was to run it as he saw fit, and he hoped that Buzz would cooperate with me.

Well, Buzz never caused me any trouble. He was perfectly willing to pass the reins to me. I was maybe thirty-five or forty years younger than Buzz, and I had a different approach to developing ballplayers, and he gradually bowed out of the picture. The scouts and managers soon understood that I was running the show and they, too, started to cooperate.

In those days, we had eighteen farm clubs. At the end of the season (there were split seasons in the minor leagues then) I had a record of thirteen teams that finished in the playoffs. That, of course, was an unusual record. I think it was surpassed by the Brooklyn Dodgers, but no other organization was even close. That established my reputation as a farm director. When I was in Cleveland at the end of the season I got congratulations from Bill and everybody else.

When I became farm director Rudy York's wife called me up one day and told me that Rudy was drinking a great deal and he was not taking care of himself, and asked if there was any way I could possibly get him a job. Rudy was always one of my favorites. We were good friends from Detroit. He was a good old country boy, a very decent sort of fellow. I called Rudy and asked how he was getting along, and he told me he was fine. I asked what he was doing, and he said he was just painting fences around his property. He didn't tell me that he was taking a jug of whiskey out there with him, and sometimes he drank so much that he forgot to come home and would sleep out on the ground overnight. I said, "Rudy, I have a job for you. Would you come down to Daytona Beach and help me run this farm system?" Naturally he was delighted, especially since he hadn't been in baseball for a few years. He said, "Sure, Big Pompano"—that was his favorite nickname for me—"I'll be there." Well, when he arrived in Daytona Beach, the site of our new farm system base, I was just amazed. Here was a fellow who, when I had last seen him, had weighed 220 pounds; he was now down to 180. He didn't look like the same person, but he still had that same sweet disposition. I put him to work and said to him, "No drinking around this camp; we've got some 400 ballplayers here and we have to set the example. I know I can trust you." He said, "Don't worry, I'm off the liquor, and I'll give you my best." And he did.

I appointed him manager of a D ball club. It was the only opening we had at that late date, and I got a working agreement going, and I sent him out to that league. Unfortunately they folded in three weeks; I then appointed Rudy as a scout. That really wasn't what he wanted to do, but I asked him if he would go around to the different clubs and make a report on what he saw and what players he liked. About that time, a very fortunate thing happened. The Boston Red Sox called me up and asked if Rudy York was available. They wanted to make him a coach. I told them I needed him but that I would make him available. If he could get back into the Major Leagues he'd make more money and he'd also be subject to the pension plan, and that was something I would never think of denying him.

Rudy stayed on with the Red Sox for a couple of years, but again the money went to his head, and before I knew it, he was drinking again. At least that was the report I got. He had a tendency to light up a cigarette when he went to bed, then he'd drink and he'd forget about the cigarette and it would burn down to his fingers. Rudy burned up a couple of hotel rooms that way. The Red Sox finally got rid of him. Word got around that he was a drinker and not reliable, and so he got out of baseball. When I left baseball for good our paths didn't cross again. Rudy died of lung cancer in 1970.

During the 1949 season the Indians performed well—we finished third—but there was a big letdown on the team, and it was primarily due to Bill Veeck himself. It seems his imminent divorce had gotten him down. Though he had just come off winning the World Series, he had lost enthusiasm for the game, and he wasn't able to instill the same spirit and determination into the entire organization as he had previously. He didn't show up at the ballpark as often or put in as many hours, and while he did a good job, he didn't have the same attitude that he had had in 1948. And it was reflected in the way the team played.

I didn't know it at the time, but it eventually came out that Bill was dickering to sell the ball club. One of our partners, Bob Goldstein, was representing an outside party who had 5 percent of the stock and was determined to buy the ball club. Bill had led the man to believe that (a) the ball club was for sale, and (b) he would be willing to sell it to Goldstein's group. Bob cornered me one day and told me he was dickering for the club and expecting to buy it, and that he wanted me as president and general manager for the new ownership. Naturally I had to keep that confidential, but I was delighted with the opportunity to step up and be in control of the Major League club. Considering that this was 1949 and I had only stopped playing actively in 1947, that was an unheard-of advancement in baseball ranks. However, little did I know that, at the same time, Bill Veeck was negotiating with a group of Clevelanders headed by a chap named Ellis Ryan, that included Nate Dolin, George Medinger, and Don Hornbeck. One day when he was in Chicago, Bill called me and asked if I would meet him at the Blackstone Hotel. He had some news for me. I anticipated that the news was he was selling the club to Bob Goldstein's group, because Bob had tipped me off that he and Bill had practically reached an agreement.

I arrived at Bill's hotel around seven in the morning and went right up to his suite. He used to get up at 4:00 or 4:30 in the morning and get into the bathtub where he would read a paperback while he soaked his bad leg. Then, when he got out of the tub and dried off, he'd put the stump of the leg on the washbasin and, in that position, brush his teeth. The door to his suite was open and he called me in. There he was in the bathroom brushing his teeth.

I said, "Hello," and he said, "I've got news for you. I've just sold the Indians to a group headed by Ellis Ryan."

I didn't know what to do. I said, "I hope you got what you wanted, Bill, and congratulations," but I was definitely chagrined. Little did I know that the Ellis Ryan group would shortly hire me as the general manager.

Having been a ballplayer, all I had thought about was playing the game and what the ballplayers were doing. As general manager I had to take on some of Bill's duties, like going around making speeches. I had a lot of baseball stories to tell, and I could tell them about our prospects and what our hopes were for the future and that we still had a contending team and were drawing well over a million people. All went well for a while, but then the newspaper people started picking on me. It turned out that the sportswriters of the city's three papers were all rivals. Each one wanted a scoop or an exclusive story and I was unable to regularly furnish them with one. I didn't pay nearly as much attention to them as Bill had, so my publicity was unfavorable. I realized that I had to concentrate on getting a pennant-winning team and forget about the press and just take what came. As a result, every time the writers had an opportunity to jab me or the club in the press, they did so. Then, to add insult to injury, after the 1950 season Boudreau told me he was going to be a bench manager and didn't want to play shortstop anymore. I had no great regard for his managerial ability. He was all right, but I didn't think he was anything but a hunch player. I knew I needed to get somebody I could work with. Fortunately, I located a chap by the name of Al Lopez, who had been managing for Indianapolis in the American Association.

Al had been a catcher in the National League for nineteen years and then he had managed in Indianapolis with a great degree of success, but I felt that bringing him to Cleveland was a gamble. I knew it would be very unpopular because the press had already been reporting that Lou Boudreau was going to be re-signed for another year. Those were the headlines on the day I called for a press conference at Municipal Stadium. I had flown Al Lopez into Cleveland secretly, and we were up in the Wigwam, the stadium's dining room for the press and the officials of the club and the employees. Reporters had come from the surrounding cities and out walked Al Lopez from the men's room into the huge dining room. I said, "Gentlemen, here's your next manager of the Cleveland Indians, Mr. Al Lopez." Well, you could have knocked the writers over with a feather. They felt they had been outsmarted even though they had gone out on a limb to announce Boudreau as our manager.

Fortunately for me, Al Lopez had played for the Cleveland team in 1946 and was a veteran ballplayer with a great personality and great disposition. He had been friends with all the writers, and they had enormous respect for him. So while they disliked me for having pulled a fast one on them, they still respected my choice. They heaped great praise on Lopez becoming the new manager but took it out on me for getting rid of a great hero in Lou Boudreau.

I started off my role as the general manager with more or less two strikes against me, so it was fortunate that we had a pretty good team. I had to work with new management people who had no experience in baseball, who, after watching the team from the stands for two or three weeks, thought they knew all about the game. They were second-guessing the manager and second-guessing the players. Whenever you're in contact with new baseball management, that's what you often have to put up with.

I also had about thirty stockholders to contend with. Whenever we'd have a stockholders' meeting there would be some thirty fans who lived in Cleveland and bought a few shares of stock in the club and, of course, they all thought they knew how to run the club better than Lopez or me. In addition to stockholders there were twelve or thirteen directors who had bigger stakes in the club and they felt they had to put their two cents worth in, too.

◆

Greenberg, as a club executive, ran into another problem.

"One winter, after we bought the club," recalled Nate Dolin, who became one of the directors of the Indians after Bill Veeck sold the team in 1949, "we went to Phoenix for the winter meetings. The American League clubs were staying at a big hotel there. We checked in and the fellow said to me, 'Mr. Dolin, I want to tell you something. We have a problem.'

"I said, 'What's the problem?'

"He said, 'Mr. Greenberg can't stay at this hotel.'

"I said, 'Why can't he stay?'

"He said, 'Because he's Jewish.'

"I said, 'Well, we're all Jewish.'

"And he said, 'I didn't know by your name.'

"Well, the National League was staying at the Arizona Biltmore, which was owned by the Wrigleys, and the Cubs got us rooms in that hotel. I called Bill Harridge, who was president of the American League, and I told him under no circumstances were we going to go to any meetings at that first hotel.

"Oh, we had a lot of anti-Semitism from some of those owners. We were just about the first Jewish owners in baseball. But we fought for our rights. You had some of these guys with their fancy clubs and all that stuff. It was just a matter of our not going to any private clubs for meetings. The same thing happened in Cleveland. I refused to have a board of directors meeting at the Union Club because of prejudice in Cleveland. No Jews allowed there.

"Later I told Hank about what had happened in that hotel in Phoenix. He was shocked, and angry. We all were."

◆

In the days when I was a farm director, and even when I was general manager, I used to go down to Daytona Beach and we would have some 450 to 500 ballplayers striving to make good in baseball. I used to have so much fun down there working with the young players and they all looked up to me. I guess I was close to forty years old and they were all in their early twenties. I had the reputation and the record to prove it, so when I talked, most of them listened. The players came from all parts of the United States and they had played in sandlots and on farm teams and high school teams. They may have stood out in their area, but professionally some of them were short of the mark.

I waited until we had four or five who we felt we could no longer keep in camp because they had absolutely no chance of advancing in baseball, and I called them together. I usually did it in a group because it was too tough to do individually. Here they were dreaming of being Major League players and someone was telling them that they weren't even good enough to be in a minor league training camp. I would say to them: "Look, I may be dead wrong and some of my scouts may be dead wrong, but we don't think you have a chance in baseball. My advice to you is, if you think we're wrong, go ahead to some other camp. Every Major League club has a camp, and you can try again. But I don't think there's anything in the minor leagues for you. The salaries are pitiful, the struggle is long and hard, and it appears you don't have the talent to start with. I think the smartest thing you could do is go back home and get a job in some other field and try to make something of yourself, because I don't think you're going to be able to do it in baseball." Believe me, it was a hard message to deliver. While some of the boys took it properly, others resented it and some would break down and cry; it was a miserable scene.

We had to do it because we didn't have enough spaces on the various clubs for all these players. Every player that was sent there was sent by a bird dog or one of the big scouts, so we had to look them over. The sooner we told them, the better we thought it was for them. But that was the toughest chore I had to face; the rest of the spring training was always a happy occasion for me.

After a certain period we had to cut our roster to twenty-five, and there were always extra players. Someone had to tell these players that they were being sent back to AAA or AA and we would see them next year. Well, this wasn't an easy chore either, and Lopez didn't like to face it, so I was the one who had the responsibility of telling the player, "Look, you're not good enough for the Major Leagues at this time. We're going to farm you out and maybe with another year of experience under your belt, you'll come back next year and make the club." Most of the time players realized that they weren't good enough or there was a player in their position who was much better and had a bigger reputation than they had, so they accepted it rather nicely and realized that they had to go down to the farm club and get a little more experience.

In the early fifties a kid from California was sent to Tucson by a scout who said that this boy was unusual, a terrific ballplayer. His name was Rudy Regalado. He was a third baseman. We tried him at third base, and he seemed to be fine in the field. We played him in some exhibition games, and he just murdered the ball. He hit almost .500 in spring training, and we thought we had one of these freak "phenoms" that come along once every twenty years, a guy who didn't need too much minor league experience. When he came up to Cleveland, we played him a few games. As soon as the season got under way, it was obvious he didn't have the talent and, on top of that, he seemed to be half asleep in the field. I learned through the grapevine that he was sitting in the Cleveland nightclubs and dancing with the girls, drinking and staying out late after curfew. He would come to the ballpark practically drunk from lack of sleep.

I called him into my office and told him we were sending him out to San Diego, our AAA farm affiliate. I told him that I had heard that he hadn't been taking care of himself, that he was abusing his body and being unfair to the rest of the club. I told him I was disappointed in him and hoped that he would realize the error of his ways and that when he came back to Cleveland he would perform better. Well, he resented that terribly. He told me that I didn't know anything about ballplayers and that I wasn't a general manager, that I was nothing. He turned out to be not even good enough for San Diego, and he just drifted out of the system before long.

Five or six years later I got a letter from Rudy Regalado, and I was just shocked. He told me how right I had been to send him down to San Diego, that he had made a fool of himself; how sorry he was that he ruined his baseball career, and that he wished that he had had enough good sense to follow my advice when I sent him down. He said he knew he couldn't blame anybody else for his lack of developing as a baseball player, and he just wanted to apologize for the things that he had said to me when I farmed him out.

After Bill Veeck left the Indians he stayed out of baseball for a year or two, then he bought into the St. Louis Browns. That led to a little contest between us. Bill was always trying to get me to trade somebody. He was always offering me players that he wanted to get rid of and no one that I particularly wanted. The St. Louis Browns were in last place; they didn't have many good players that were worth even talking about. We were going for first place in the American League, and we needed players who had established themselves or who could come up and help us. So Bill and I never could get together. (To show the lengths he would go to, in 1952, right after the winter meetings, I went to Europe for a little vacation with my wife. I was sitting in the Hassler Hotel in Rome and suddenly the phone rang and there was Bill on the other end trying to make a trade.) Bill was always on the phone trying to pass off one of his ballplayers. One time it was a first baseman by the name of Henry Arft. The calls went on for days. Bill would call me on the phone or send me a telex. One day as we were leaving the office, it was around 4:30 or 5:00 P.M., during the off-season, I said to my secretary, Bob Gill, "Let's send Bill Veeck a telex and then let's leave the office. Put this on the telex. First of all, ring him, then wait, and let the telex keep marking out x's, as though they were trying to get warmed up. Then type, 'Keep your Arft Arft Arft Arft Arft Arft Arft. Keep your dog in St. Louis,' then hang up." Sure enough, we put this message on the telex, and immediately it rang back. We left the office, laughing, because we knew how frustrated Bill had to be trying to reach me, on the telex and on the phone, and getting nothing but barking.

In 1949 and 1950 we had contending teams. We finished third in 1949 and fourth in 1950. The Yankees had outstanding ball clubs and they were on their way to winning five pennants in a row. They started in '49, and also won in '50, '51, '52, and '53. We should have won the pennant in 1951. We lost two tough ball games in Boston: one game with a 9-run lead with Bob Feller pitching and the next day we had something like a 13-run lead with Bob Lemon pitching and lost that one. We still came into Yankee Stadium after that trip to Boston and lost on a squeeze bunt by Phil Rizzuto scoring Joe DiMaggio from third base, and that beat us 1–0. From then on it was nip and tuck, but the Yankees managed to win out.

In 1952 and 1953 we were contenders but always the bridesmaid. Usually the races went down to the last days, but in 1954 we finally put it all together. We won 111 games, which was a new all-time record, and we went into the World Series against New York. Our pitching was superb. We had Bob Lemon and Early Wynn, who won twenty-three games each. Mike Garcia won nineteen, and Bob Feller contributed a 13–3 record. Feller was past his prime at that stage, but he still was a good spot pitcher. I had made a trade for Art Houtteman, a pitcher from Detroit, who won fifteen games for us that season, but I had to give up a great ballplayer in Ray Boone, who had become our shortstop after Boudreau. We also had a great bullpen in Don Mossi, who was a left-handed pitcher, and Ray Narleski, who was a right-handed pitcher. We could bring them in in the ninth inning or the eighth inning and they would stop the opposing team. Relief pitching didn't have the same importance then as it does now. Nowadays you have to have relief pitching. They expect the starting pitcher to go five or six innings and they expect the bullpen to hold them the rest of the way. But in the fifties it was customary for the starting pitcher to finish his own game. When you have guys like Bob Lemon and Mike Garcia and Early Wynn, you don't need much relief pitching. But on occasion we'd bring in Narleski and Mossi and they'd stop the opponents.

We went into the 1954 Series with great hopes. The Giants didn't seem to be that good a team. They had some good ballplayers, but Willie Mays hadn't quite come into his own yet. We opened the Series in New York. History has shown that Mays made a great catch in center field, robbing Vic Wertz of a triple or a home run with two men on; and Dusty Rhodes, who was a journeyman ballplayer, was sent up to pinch-hit and hit a home run which went about 260 feet down the right-field line. Wertz's hit had gone about 420 feet to deep center field, and it was an out. We lost Game 2 as well, and then we went back to Cleveland for the third, fourth, and fifth games to be played on Friday, Saturday, and Sunday. We lost Game 3. Lopez was criticized for starting Bob Lemon, who was his premier pitcher, for a second time in Game 4 and overlooking Bob Feller, who had not had as good a season. It provided an opportunity for the press to pour more gas on the fire. They wanted something to criticize and they found it. Bob Lemon got beaten, and we lost the Series in four games after having established the record for victories in a season. Naturally it was a great letdown.

In 1955 we had the nucleus of our pennant winners, and so we looked forward to great things in the new season. We felt we had an excellent chance of repeating, and we almost did repeat. During the course of the off-season I had managed to trade for my old friend Ralph Kiner, who was playing out his career with the Cubs. He wasn't having a particularly great season, but I felt he could add a little punch to our lineup. I knew that if we could get him it would enhance our chances of repeating in 1955. Ralph didn't play regularly; Lopez used him only intermittently. He wasn't really happy with the situation: He had been a star in the National League and suddenly he came over to the American League with a pennant-winning team and here he was on the bench part of the time. Near the end of the season we took two out of three games against the Yankees in New York. The Yankees came west and won seven games in a row, and we wound up losing the pennant by three games. That closed out the 1955 season and, believe me, I sat up in the stands biting my nails throughout the whole year. I always thought we were going to win it and then I had to watch as the championship was snatched away from us in the last few days of the season.

In 1956 we didn't win again; the Yankees did. We had a good year, we wound up second, but not as close to the Yankees as the year before. This time we were nine games out. It was a year in which the fans were discouraged, and the press naturally kept the heat on.

At the close of the season the *Cleveland News* came out with blaring headlines on the front page of the papers: BREAK UP THE INDIANS. You'd think we had ended up in last place and needed to refurbish the entire team. That was the kind of press we had. I hate to harp on the press but it was miserable. It followed me throughout my whole time in Cleveland, even though we usually had a first- or second-place team. It was always the same, always looking to find fault with the management, find fault with what the general manager was doing. Under those circumstances it was difficult to have a winning team on the field. Another thing they were wont to do was criticize when we had too many black players. I think at one time we had five black players on the team. One was a right fielder by the name of Harry Simpson, a good ballplayer, and he had to compete against Bob Kennedy, who was more or less a favorite, a nice Catholic boy (I hate to bring religion into this but that's what it amounted to). A black player fighting for a position against an attractive Catholic boy who really wasn't as good a ballplayer as Simpson, but that didn't make any difference to the press. They pulled the same kind of stuff with me when I brought Al Rosen in to play third base to replace Kenny Keltner, but instead of being a black player, Rosen was Jewish, and that caused great controversy. In 1954, the year I brought Art Houtteman and Hal Newhouser over to Cleveland to shore up our pitching staff, we also acquired a catcher by the name of Myron Ginsberg and, of course, that was all the press talked about, adding another Jewish ballplayer to the team.

In May 1957 our leading pitcher, Herb Score, who had been rookie of the year in 1955, was hit in the eye with a line drive off the bat of Gil McDougald of the Yankees. It was the first inning of a night game, and somehow or other Herb lost sight of the ball coming off McDougald's bat and the ball hit him square in the eye. Naturally we stopped the game. I was in the stands and I rushed off with him to the hospital in an ambulance. Fortunately, one of the great eye doctors in the country resided in Cleveland and was a baseball fan, and he took care of Herb Score. Then, to add insult to injury, our star pitcher, Bob Lemon, went off the active list in the middle of the season with a sore shoulder (today they call it rotator cuff). He was operated on, but he was lost to us for the balance of the season. We never did regain his services. So the 1957 season was the first year that the Indians were not a contender. Without that pitching staff, we became a fourth-place ball club. I had been with Cleveland since 1948 and by this time the wolves were howling. The press was on me constantly, and finally the board of directors decided that maybe it would be better to move Hank Greenberg out of the general manager's role than to move the team to another city. I had been pleading with them, because of the constant pressure we had from the press, to move because it was difficult to win in Cleveland.

At the time, Minneapolis/St. Paul was a great baseball town. They had two minor league franchises and they were begging us to come to Minneapolis. I think it would have been a great move, as it turned out to be for the Washington Senators. The fans got behind them. Washington had been a second-rate team because of the lack of fan support, but the Senators won the pennant when they got to Minneapolis and became the Twins. We would have done the same, I think, because all our players needed was some encouragement. It's very difficult for ballplayers to pick up the papers every morning, particularly after losing a ball game, and have the press lecture on what the team's doing wrong. Our management was composed primarily of Clevelanders, and they were afraid to make the move. I was pushing for it, and so were two of my partners, Wing and Andy Baxter. Between us we owned 38 percent of the stock in the ball club, but we had no deciding voice. The management was concerned about the press, so they voted down the move and decided to get rid of me.

I was released at the end of the 1957 season. I had already hired a new manager, Bobby Bragan, because there was pressure on me to get rid of Al Lopez. I did it not because I was unhappy with Lopez but because of the constant criticism against Al and me. I thought I would be doing him a favor if I released him. Fortunately for him, he went right over to the White Sox and was their manager for many years.

When I was fired in 1957 I was out of baseball. I was still a 20 percent owner of the Indians, so I couldn't go to another club. The rules were that you couldn't own stock in one club and work for another. I took 1958 off, and one of the things I remember quite clearly was that, in that whole year, I had only one telephone call from all the people that I had known in baseball. I got a call from my old friend Birdie Tebbetts, who I had made manager at Indianapolis. I had played with Birdie; he was a catcher for us in the late thirties in Detroit. He called me up when he became manager of the Milwaukee Braves, and that winter he asked me if I would like to be batting instructor for the Milwaukee Braves during spring training. That was the only offer I got. I didn't take it, but I appreciated it.

When I was discharged I received notes from so many people in baseball who claimed that they were making a big mistake in Cleveland by letting the best man they ever had go. Three or four Cleveland writers sent me beautiful letters of encouragement. It's just nice to know that when I left Cleveland it was with the knowledge that I had made a good impression on some of the fans and some of the citizens.

When I was a baseball executive we never had a Major League meeting when Del Webb of the Yankees didn't leave the meeting room and go out into the hallway where the reporters were waiting and tell them exactly what was taking place, giving his own version of it, of course, in order to get a little publicity for himself. We never had a meeting that was confidential. Whatever we talked about was leaked to the newspapers before we even got out of the room. All the owners wanted to curry a little favor with the local newspapers, so if you came from Baltimore, you'd whisper a word or two to the Baltimore papers, and they'd be able to run it. And there was no way to control this in the Major League meetings.

I must say the National League owners had a better feeling for each other. They kept the voting and the conversations inside the conference room, so to speak, and very little ever leaked out.

I'll never forget the time we were talking about moving the Philadelphia A's and the St. Louis Browns. Both clubs were not drawing anybody. Connie Mack was then in his nineties and probably senile, and his son, Roy, who was in his seventies, was running the A's. Connie was sitting in that meeting with his head held high, while they put the pressure on Roy. I knew Connie wasn't aware of anything that was going on. He said nothing during the meeting, as the Yankee ball club, represented by Dan Topping and Del Webb, pushed Roy Mack into selling or moving his club from Philadelphia to Kansas City where it would be purchased by their good friend Arnold Johnson, who would become the source of player talent for the Yankees. They traded some forty or fifty ballplayers back and forth between the clubs so the Yankees, instead of losing a ballplayer, would trade him to Kansas City and he'd play there and develop and then come back and play for the Yankees again. This, of course, created unfair competition. On top of that, the Yankees owned the Kansas City athletic field.

We had another meeting at about that time in which we discussed moving the Athletics to Kansas City and Washington to Minneapolis/St. Paul, and then coming up with two new teams, one for the Pacific coast, and I had wanted an expansion team in Washington. At this meeting, which was held at the Commodore Hotel in New York, I was talking about the opportunity to compete against the Dodgers and the Giants as well as the tremendous amount of talent on the West Coast, in which the American League could then share. With that, eighty-year-old Clark Griffith, owner of the Senators, who was sitting with his hat and overcoat on and with a cigar sticking out of his mouth, jumped up and said, "Henry, don't go out there."

I said, "Why not, Mr. Griffith?"

He said, "It's cold and it's damp out there."

I said, "When was the last time you were out there, Mr. Griffith?"

He said, "Well, in 1905 I pitched in Portland, and boy was it cold."

I asked him if he had been out there since then, and he said, "No, I haven't been out there since then." That gives you some idea of the people who were running the American League.

Half of the people who were trying to run their ball clubs had no idea what was going on. The Yankees, of course, did. They were the dominating club. They won practically every year. Cleveland gave them some competition and managed to beat them a couple of times in a ten-year period, but the rest of the clubs were run by imbeciles. As a result, instead of continuing as the dominant league, the American League turned out to be the weaker league. The National League became superior. Its teams started winning World Series games and took complete control of the All-Star games. In my opinion, part of that was due to the fact that the American League was reluctant to hire any black ballplayers. The National League, starting with Branch Rickey, grabbed the great players: Jackie Robinson, Willie Mays, Hank Aaron, Bob Gibson. Meanwhile the American League had only one club with significant black players, and that was Cleveland. St. Louis, when Veeck ran the club, had some black ballplayers, but the other clubs, like the Yankees and Red Sox, were pure white. It wasn't until many years later, when they were forced to take on black players, that they did so.

Larry Doby was a special case. He was the second black player in Major League baseball, the *first* in the American League. He had nothing but talent, but Larry was obsessed with the idea that he wasn't getting the publicity that Jackie Robinson was getting. I tried to explain to him that Jackie was with the Dodgers and he was with Cleveland, and it was like night and day. Playing in Cleveland, Larry could never hope to get the same degree of publicity Jackie received in New York. Larry was very bitter about it throughout his career. But as far as being a ballplayer, he sure could play.

Veeck brought Doby to Cleveland in late 1947, and Bill didn't give a damn what anybody thought about it; he did what he wanted. He had the newspapermen in Cleveland eating out of his hand in those days. Before he brought Doby up the fans and the press in Cleveland were very partial to Bill. After he brought Doby up Veeck caught hell. Larry Doby could be a grouchy person and was not popular with the team, the fans, or the media. Unlike Jackie Robinson, who seemed to take pride in his role as a pioneer in baseball and was extremely popular among the other black players who joined the Dodgers in the late forties and fifties, Doby was as belligerent with his black teammates as he was with everyone else. In fact, I always thought Larry resented the other black players. It was as if Larry felt he was the first black player in the league so he deserved special recognition.

Travel for black players in those days presented problems. In 1955 I went on the Indians' last swing through the east. We were leading the league and it looked like we were going to win the pennant. From Washington we went to Baltimore by bus. When we arrived at the Lord Baltimore Hotel all the players rushed to get off the bus. I waited until all the players had left the bus and then I found myself standing there with five players. They were not going to the hotel because they were black. It hadn't occurred to me that these players would not be admitted into the hotel. I asked them, "What do you guys do?" They said, "We wait for a taxi, and this taxi takes us to different homes, different families in Baltimore, and we stay with them." I thought to myself, This is terrible. Here these fellows are a vital part of the team and contributing greatly to the success of the team, and they have to be segregated and are not permitted into the hotel to spend the night. I said to Spud Goldstein, our traveling secretary, "This is not going on any longer. In 1956 we are going to write every hotel before the season opens and tell them that we will not send our team there unless everyone on the team is accepted and treated as a guest with the same equal rights."

I found that blacks were not permitted into the hotels in St. Louis, Baltimore, and Washington. So the next year Spud wrote to all the hotels and explained that if they wanted the Cleveland Indians team to stay at their hotels they would have to take *all* of our players; it was that or none at all. Surprisingly enough it wasn't that difficult. I guess the hotels were just waiting for someone to put the pressure on them. I hadn't been aware of the problem, and it wasn't until I saw those five players in front of the Baltimore Hotel that I realized how unfair it was. Jackie Robinson had broken into the league in 1947, and eight years later some of the hotels, particularly the Southern hotels, were still not accepting black ballplayers.

In 1949 I had just taken over as general manager in Cleveland and Al Rosen was playing third base for our Triple A club in Oklahoma City. I decided to bring him up. Ken Keltner, our regular third baseman, was getting old; he couldn't play anymore in my opinion. All Keltner could do was drink and smoke with the rest of the boys, like Joe Gordon and Lou Boudreau. He had no discipline whatsoever. But Keltner had been popular in Cleveland and he had hit 31 home runs the year before. The fans got on me for bringing up a Jew against a nice Catholic boy. They rode me terribly, and they rode Al even worse. But Rosen had guts. By the end of the 1950 season he had 37 home runs and 116 runs batted in, and in 1953 he was named most valuable player in the league. Later on Rosen wanted more money than I could afford to pay him, so we got into a beef and he quit. He still blames me, but I can't help that. When he came up I told him not to pay any attention to the bigots, just play to the best of his ability and ignore the bums. Al had a terrible temper; he used to want to go into the stands and murder somebody when they'd taunt him about being a Jew, but he learned to control himself pretty well. On the whole, he did a great job.

◆

"I was aware of Hank Greenberg from the time I was a boy," said Al Rosen. "I had two favorite players, Greenberg and Gehrig. Those two I always watched. But Greenberg particularly because he was chasing Babe Ruth's record in 1938—I was fourteen years old then—and there was a consciousness of his being a Jew. But you're also always rooting for somebody regardless of who it might be if they're after a record—for instance, I was rooting for Hank Aaron to break Ruth's career home-run record. At any rate, I was conscious of Greenberg's try for the record and obsessed by the fact that the newspapers were saying that they were trying to pitch around him, to walk him, things of that nature. I can remember the feeling that he wasn't getting good balls to hit, that sort of thing.

"Maybe they were afraid to pitch to him because he was doing so well, maybe because he was a Jew, maybe because they didn't want him to break Ruth's record. I can think of a combination of those things.

"I can remember that there was very strong anti-Semitic feeling in America about not letting a Jew break the revered Babe Ruth's record. Hank was not a Babe Ruth type, he wasn't a clone of Babe Ruth, it was a whole different kind of deal. And I think it's a combination—they feared Hank, they didn't want him to break Ruth's record, and he was a Jew.

"I grew up in a neighborhood that was a real melting pot, and I was the only Jew in the neighborhood. I had my problems, probably stemming from that, although at that time I wasn't sure. When you're twelve, thirteen, fourteen years old you're not really sure what people mean when they say something. In my neighborhood people referred to the Greeks, and there were the shanty Irish, and the wops. If you go back to Miami in the early days it was a city of about 100,000 people. I lived in what is now the middle of Miami, but in those days it was a long way out if you lived on Tenth Avenue. I can still remember in Miami, no Jews or dogs allowed in apartment buildings. A sign right on the wall.

"In those days people felt that Jews did not like contact sports. If you were going to be in sports, a Jew game was basketball, contact and Jews didn't go hand in hand. I can still remember being in the back of the automobile of an assistant football coach in my sophomore year in high school with about seven or eight kids piled in, and he turned around and looked at me and he said, 'Why are you out for football?' in front of my peers. I was fourteen at the time. Horrible. I said because I love it. And he said to me, 'I didn't know that Jews liked contact sports, I thought you guys only played basketball.' And that was the *coach*. I still remember that. So you can imagine what Hank went through.

211

"I think the experience of that helped to shape Hank's demeanor and outlook later on. I feel it sort of shaped his thinking. You know, Hank lost some of his validity, he didn't carry on his religious background in his marriage to Caral Gimbel. You never got the feeling of Jewishness in their home. I don't recall Hank belonging to a temple in Cleveland; I don't recall him going to a Jewish country club; I don't recall his friends being of the Jewish community—and I'm talking about the majority of his friends. Obviously he had Jewish friends. He left a lot of Jewish friends in Detroit, but I suspect that somewhere along the way the experiences had something to do with molding feelings about Judaism later on.

"Early on he didn't like the fact that people looked at him as a Jewish ballplayer. He just wanted to be a ballplayer. Any minority would say that. You go through difficult times. I can remember saying to somebody at one time that I had considered shortening my name from Rosen to Ross. It's just a passing thing that kids do to make it easier for themselves. Remember, I'm talking about very young men. And later on I really thought, gee, I wish my name were Rosenberg so that there would be no doubt, because there were times people did not identify me as a Jew. I could never imagine why, with a name like Al Rosen. I always felt I looked Jewish, if there is such a thing as looking something.

"I can remember that specifically when I got into the big leagues. At that time there was more acceptance. Remember, Greenberg was to Jewish ballplayers what Jackie Robinson was to blacks. I'm not trying to draw an analogy between the problem the blacks have and the Jews, but there were problems nevertheless. Whenever people don't come to grips with that there can be a real problem. And Greenberg went through a great deal and he paved the way for people like me.

"If you go through the *Baseball Encyclopedia* you see a helluva lot of Jewish names. For very short periods of time. There were some Jewish ballplayers but no one of his kind—don't forget, when you talk about Greenberg you're talking about a man of great stature in the minds of people who never knew anything about baseball. He was a cultured, intelligent, bright, good-looking, massive sort of a man. Today athletes are six foot four—they're all six foot four—but in those days six foot four stood out in a crowd. And he was polished and he was all the things people would aspire to. You feel you're in a vast sea of mediocrity out there and then someone rises above the crowd. Now here comes a Jew who is rising above and going for Babe Ruth's revered record and it's very obvious that more people are going to take shots at him. He was the first big name. The rest of the Jews who came along after that had some problems, but he made it easier.

"I'm sure that even later after I played, there were other Jewish ballplayers—there was Sandy Koufax, one of the greatest pitchers who ever threw, and a Hall of Famer, and I'm sure he had problems. As you get older you shrug those problems off. You're not as quick to react to them.

"I always felt I had to conduct myself—and I'm sure Hank felt that way—in a courtly manner, and I wanted people to think of me in a certain frame of mind, in a certain way. Dignity is the word I am searching for.

"When I joined the Indians, Hank took me to dinner. I remember him ordering a dry martini, and we sat there and talked. I was absolutely in awe, as you can imagine. We talked about what you aspire to in life. I said to him, if I could ever make $10,000 a year, what a huge amount of money that would be. In 1950 I was making $7,500 as a rookie and I led the league in home runs. When he sent me my next contract, I forget whether it was for $12,000 or $15,000—he called me and said something like, 'Well, I'm offering you $15,000 and I still recall the conversation you had with me when you said the greatest thing in your life was to be able to earn $10,000 a year.' So it was sort of tongue-in-cheek because I had had a good year and he knew I wasn't going to sign for fifteen but here he was letting me know that he remembered what I had said. I realized that in my contract negotiations with Hank I was going to have to be wary of anything I said. I signed for $20,000.

"Then, after 1953, when I had my big season, I was supposed to go out barnstorming. I was to get $10,000 to barnstorm for thirty days. I was going to go with Gil Hodges. Hank really didn't want me to go out and play. I said, 'You know, Hank, nobody has a lot of money and while I'm working I have some obligations.' And he said, 'Why don't you come on in and sign a contract and then we can give you an advance.' So I went down to his office. He said, 'Let's see. You just completed your fourth year in the big leagues.' I said, 'Yes, Hank, four years.' And he said, 'Let's see what I did in my fourth year.' And he opened up the top left-hand drawer in his desk and he had a little green book that had all his records in it. I'm not sure that my numbers are right, because I can't remember all the numbers, but he said, 'How many home runs did you hit?' I said, again remembering Hank, 'forty-three.' I think that year he hit more than that. Then he said, 'You knocked in what?' I said, 'a hundred and forty-five.' He said, 'You hit what, .336?' I said, 'Yes, Hank.' Well, he had better numbers than me in every category. When I walked out of there I felt like I had had a bad year. He reduced me to ashes. It was absolutely devastating. At any rate we came to an agreement.

"I wanted much more than I got. I had put together four good years. I thought that I should make about $55,000 or $60,000. I signed for $37,500 with a $5,000 bonus. Which the next year, I might add, they took away from me because I only hit .300. I only hit 24 home runs and I only knocked in 102 or 103 runs. Even though we won the pennant, even though I was off to a great start, even though the club asked me to move from third base to first base, where I sustained an injury which virtually cost me my career, with all of that, they still signed me for $37,500 when I asked for $42,500.

"He said, 'Remember, we gave you the $5,000 bonus.' I said, 'Well, if you're going to talk about bonuses, what about my moving from third to first.' I reminded him that in 1940 he had moved from first to left for $10,000.

"He said, 'Yes, but that was me and this is you.' He could be very tough."

◆

Having been scarred by the treatment I received from Detroit after playing for them for some sixteen years, when I became general manager at Cleveland the first chore I had was to replace Kenny Keltner, an old-time Cleveland Indian third baseman, and I brought in Al Rosen. I let Kenny go as a free agent; I made no attempt to extract a few dollars or a minor league player for him. I gave him an opportunity to go out and see what he could do with any other club. I did the same thing with Bob Feller when he reached the stage where I didn't think he could do himself justice in the Major Leagues. Bob wanted to continue on as an active player and I told him that I thought it was a big mistake. He had always pitched for Cleveland; he was a hero in Cleveland. It would be foolish for him to try to hook on with another team that would only use him for a few months or maybe one season and then discard him. From the time he was a boy, playing baseball was his entire life, but he finally realized that the advice I was giving him was the proper advice, and he took it. Even today he's still associated with the Cleveland club. He'll always be known as Bob Feller of the Cleveland Indians.

Then again, I traded away a few ballplayers I really was fond of, and I did it for their own good, not for any gain for the Cleveland club or for myself. I let Ray Boone go. He was a good ballplayer, but unfortunately he came up at a time when he was required to take Lou Boudreau's position at shortstop. Here he was replacing one of the most popular ballplayers in the history of the Cleveland Indians, and he put a lot of pressure on himself. He wasn't quite that good a fielder, but he could have been if they gave him time. The fans started to get on him, and he didn't play up to his capabilities, so finally I traded him to Detroit. I knew he would do well there because it was a short left-field fence with a good background, and Ray was a natural hitter. I wanted to trade him either to Boston or Detroit, since both of them were good parks for him to hit in. I had nothing but respect and admiration for him, and I realized that he had suffered a great deal of the unfavorable publicity because of my actions in releasing Boudreau. I let him go to Detroit and he played third base for them and had five marvelous seasons.

I did the same thing for another favorite of mine, Jim Lemon, who was a big, tall outfielder. He didn't fit into our Cleveland club. Al Lopez was not in favor of a long-ball hitter unless he could hit .330, and Al was geared to a team with speed and stealing bases; I guess that was the way they played in the National League. He played for some poor teams in the National League that didn't have the players. The American League was known as the long-ball league, with Babe Ruth and company leading the way. They didn't give Jim a real opportunity to break into the Cleveland lineup, so I traded him to Washington. It was a tougher ballpark for him, but at least it gave him an opportunity to play every day. He subsequently did play every day and became a pretty good outfielder and a good hitter. He wound up managing the Washington Senators, so I like to feel I did him a favor when I let him go.

One of my favorite ballplayers was Rocky Colavito. He joined us in Daytona Beach when he was sixteen years old, and I must admit that he was the only kid who stayed in the batting cage longer than I did when I first broke in. He couldn't get enough hitting, and he tried so hard. He had the strongest throwing arm in baseball at the time; he had a good, powerful swing with a slight hitch in it, but he wasn't a fast runner. He had the determination and desire to make good, and no one worked any harder to achieve that goal than Rocky, and anyone who worked hard became a favorite of mine because it was my style to give everything I had to baseball and not let a lot of outside influences interfere with my primary goal. Rocky, of course, was a chip off the old block. I was very happy that he finally made the grade. I had the misfortune of having to send him to the minor leagues a few times when he didn't want to go, but, in my judgment, he wasn't ready yet for the big leagues. I always promised that I'd bring him back. I finally did, but by the time he was ready to play Major League baseball I had lost my job at Cleveland. Still, I had the pleasure of watching him progress, and he wound up with close to 400 home runs.

The only owner I ever knew who gave a damn about his players was Bill Veeck. Bill genuinely cared about them, and he always worried about them individually. It was almost like hero worship for Bill. The ballplayers were first in his book, and he would do anything to help their families, or ease the way if they got into trouble. None of the other owners were that concerned about their playing talent. They all felt that they were overpaying them and not getting enough back in return.

Talking about owners and clubs, it recently occurred to me that I never made a trade with the New York Yankees or the Boston Red Sox, no matter how much talking I did and how much I tried to make a trade of some mutual interest and help.

I never could understand the attitude of the Red Sox management. We were beating them year after year, and so were the Yankees. They didn't resent the Yankees winning because it seemed that they respected teams they considered in their own class, whereas Cleveland was a scavenger outfit and really had no business finishing ahead of the Red Sox. It's interesting that the Red Sox were bought by Tom Yawkey in 1933, and his widow still owns the team. In all those years they only won the pennant twice,* and they lost in the World Series both times. The club just wasn't run right. With all that money and all the fan support they have throughout New England you would think they'd have a better record than just two pennants in all those years.

Neither the Yankees nor the Red Sox would deal with me. I was like an outcast. The only clubs I could possibly deal with were the clubs in the second division who had very little to offer, and in my desperation to make trades, I often gave them the best of it. They couldn't hurt us anyway.

Some odd incidents occurred while I was general manager at Cleveland and one of the strangest happened in New York. Our team was playing in Yankee Stadium and I flew in to watch the weekend games. On a Saturday, right behind the Cleveland dugout, was a fan who kept riding our ballplayers when they came up. He was calling them all kinds of names and getting on them all the time. He was very loud and he just never stopped. Whenever the players would go out to their positions, he would yell at them. This guy came from Philadelphia, and the Yankees had paid his way up to Yankee Stadium to harass our ballplay-

---

* The Red Sox won a third pennant, in 1986, a month after Greenberg died.

ers. He was a professional jerk, and they paid him to come up and heckle our players. I learned that he worked for Gimbel Brothers in Philadelphia during the week, and he always came out to the ballparks to yell at the players. He was just one of those guys who likes to attract attention. He didn't realize what an ass he was making of himself. People would yell at him to sit down and shut up, and he would feel important. On Sunday, when he came out to the ball-park and started to get on the Cleveland players, I walked up to him and said to him, "I understand you work for Gimbel Brothers." He said, "That's right." I said, "Well, you won't be working for them anymore. I'm Hank Greenberg and I married into the Gimbel family. If you don't stop this nonsense right now, you won't be working there anymore." He realized then that he was putting his job against the few bucks the Yankees paid him, so from then on we never heard from him. It was just a strange coincidence that I had learned he worked for Gimbel's.

In 1949, when I was appointed farm director for the Cleveland Indians, my wife sold her apartment in New York and we bought a house in Shaker Heights. We had two acres of ground and a tennis court and a swimming pool, so it was an ideal place for the children to grow up. My wife loved riding horses; she had been at many horse shows in the east and won a great many blue ribbons. Out in Cleveland, in Gates Mills and Mentor and Kirkland County, there were a lot of people interested in horses, and they had quite a few local horse shows, so that was ideal for Caral. Aside from raising three children—our two boys and our daughter, Alva, born in 1952—she had an opportunity to pursue her own interests. While she liked baseball, she wasn't the type of wife who came to every game and followed every box score. She had other interests, and some-times our two worlds seemed to grow farther apart.

Once again, after I had been fired as general manager in 1957, I felt this was it. I had had it with baseball. I was having a little difficulty with my marriage. My wife had become disenchanted with Cleveland and with me, and she wanted a divorce. So I had a lot of problems, domestic and otherwise, and I had just about made up my mind that I wasn't going back into baseball. I sat around the 1958 season. I stayed in Cleveland. The boys were in grade school. I didn't know what I was going to do. In 1958, toward the end of the year, Caral decided to file for divorce, so I was faced with the problem of what to do and where to move. Bill Veeck came along and told me that he had an opportunity to buy the Chicago White Sox. At first I didn't believe him. I knew that the White Sox had been in the Comiskey family for seventy-five years or so, and the stock was then in the hands of the two Comiskey children, Chuck and Grace. For some reason the mother had turned over 54 percent of the stock to her daughter when she died and only 46 percent to her son. I guess she didn't trust Chuck. He was running the ball club but he was a wild kid. He drank a lot and wasn't too responsible, and she didn't feel that he should have control of the franchise, so she put the control in the hands of her daughter. That created a problem between the two of them, and by this time the daughter was married to a former White Sox pitcher by the name of John Rigney. John and Chuck had had a couple of verbal disagreements, and he threw up his hands in disgust with Chuck, and so Grace decided to sell the ball club. It was at that time that Bill contacted her, and she said she would sell the club to him.

In 1958, after I was discharged by the Cleveland management, I couldn't be employed by any other Major League club, since I still owned part of the team. So now I was anxious to sell my stock and debentures any way I could to anyone I could.

I eventually sold my stock, worth some $350,000 at the time, and bought an interest in the Chicago White Sox. Bill Veeck and I formed a company called C.A.C. and bought out Grace Comiskey's stock, thereby becoming owners of 54 percent of the franchise. The Major League meetings were being held in Columbus, Ohio, that year and Bill asked me to report to Columbus and announce to the commissioner that we had purchased Grace Comiskey's stock and that we were taking over and I was being appointed vice president of the club representing the new management.

To add to my problem, I had gained custody of my three children and my job was now going to be in Chicago. Caral had gone back to New York after the divorce, so I decided to rent an apartment in New York so the children could be near their mother, and I would commute between the two cities. I'd fly into Chicago on Monday morning and stay until Friday, and then I'd come back to New York and spend the weekend with the kids, who were taken care of during the week by a housekeeper. So I was involved in running a ball club in Chicago and a family in New York. It was quite an adjustment.

CHAPTER 13

"The qualities that especially attracted me to Hank were his gentleness, and his wonderful sense of humor," Caral Gimbel Lebworth remembered. "And also I felt I was bringing a whole life to him that he had never seen or perceived. My world. But this caused a lot of friction. Instead of bringing us closer together, it forced us apart. Most of our married life was spent in Cleveland. I had season tickets to the symphony and I was invited to join the junior council of the Museum of Art in Cleveland. William Milliken, the director of the museum then, and Sherman Lee, the head of the Oriental department, both became instant friends. They'd come over and play tennis and have dinner. I made a lot of friends and it was a great place.

"I had show horses, but Hank wasn't too interested in them. He was very frightened on a horse. I put him up on some of my Thoroughbreds a few times. He was very uncomfortable about it.

"We had a full life, with three children in five years, a life in baseball, entertaining sportswriters and Bob Feller and his wife and Ralph Kiner—you name it. But I also had my own friends, who hunted and showed horses and were involved in art and music. And there were a lot of activities on weekends. I went out all the time. Hank was always at the ballpark on weekends.

"I thought he was always finding something to pick on. He would say, 'Nobody else, none of the other baseball players, have wives who sleep as late as you do'—Hank would get up a couple of hours before me. I said, 'Is there something you want me to do in the morning? I'll get up and do it.' I said, 'I'm not going to get into a competition with other ballplayers' wives. Why didn't you marry one of those?' I could get very angry.

"Well, when I eventually told him I wanted a divorce he was terribly upset. He adored Glenn, our firstborn. He said, 'I've got to get to know Stephen. I don't feel I really know him.'

"He tried to keep me from going through with the divorce because he wanted custody. It was a long battle and very, very painful for me. And then we finally signed for joint custody and he insisted that the children live with him, which made it difficult on the children because they lived with him in his apartment in New York during the school year when he was with Bill Veeck in Chicago. I'd go to his apartment on Park Avenue to see the children.

"In Cleveland we had very few Jewish friends. None of the people we saw in my world were Jewish. In Hank's world many were Jewish. We weren't members of a Jewish country club because there was no reason to be. I liked horses, so I was delighted that I could join the hunt club.

"Hank never went to synagogue. He never read the Bible or a prayer book. During Yom Kippur he didn't play, but I think that was just to keep the image, because he really didn't have a sound feeling toward religion. I know people who do. I wish I did. I never did, toward any religion. I never did observe.

"But I don't ever remember talking to Hank about religion or about whether the children should have some religious training. Hank didn't give them any feeling of Jewishness at all."

◆

Caral and I had three children. Glenn was the oldest. He was a high-strung, high-spirited young man. My second son, Stephen, was more docile and mild-mannered. Fortunately the two of them got along beautifully. I'm very happy to report that they're in their mid-thirties, and they still have a great rapport and great respect for each other. They were both good athletes. Glenn was a football player because of his physique; he was a rugged, tough young man, about six feet tall and about 180 or 190 pounds by the time he was thirteen. Stephen, on the other hand, was built more like me. He's tall and rangy, about six foot two, and didn't weigh as much as Glenn, but he had a lot of natural athletic talent. When they were kids they played ball constantly. Our daughter, Alva, is five years younger than Stephen. She was too young to play with the boys, but she tried and they were very sweet with her. The boys were totally involved with athletics, and Alva didn't always fit into their program, and we'd have a few squabbles around the house.

Glenn graduated from Andover, played on the football team there for four years, graduated with high honors, and went on to Yale. He played three years of varsity football at Yale as a defensive tackle. Glenn played with one of the championship teams, an undefeated team, so he had the pleasure of playing with a winner. After he graduated from Yale, he decided to take a postgraduate course at NYU, then went on to Columbia University to get a degree in business administration. At the end of all that time he was ready to go to work. He got himself a job at Morgan Guaranty Bank. He now co-operates a fund called Chieftain Capital Management. They have roughly $150 million worth of stock under their control, and I'm happy to report that they're doing exceedingly well.

Stephen was always interested in baseball. He always thought that he would follow in my footsteps, and there was nothing I could do to talk him out of it. He pitched for the baseball team at the Hotchkiss School in Connecticut, then went on to Yale two years behind his brother and played four years of varsity baseball at Yale. He was also the goalie on the soccer team, and was a pretty good one. The coach, a professional from Europe, wanted to take Stephen to Europe after his graduation and make a professional soccer player out of him. But Stephen had his mind and heart set on being a baseball player, so he pursued that course.

He was signed by the Washington Senators as a draft pick. His first assignment was Geneva, New York, where my brother Joe and I had signed up for the military draft many years earlier. I went up there to watch Stephen play. He was a great defensive player and a good hitter, but unfortunately everybody was expecting him to be my clone. They were looking for the long ball and, while he contributed his share of long hits, he wasn't really a home-run hitter. For some reason or other the management didn't think as much of him because they were always comparing him to his father. Stephen went on from there to North Carolina for one season, then he played three years in Triple A ball. He played one year at Denver and a couple of years at Spokane in the Pacific Coast League. He had a good record there; his team won the pennant both years he was there. He was known as a good clutch hitter and a standout first baseman. His manager, Del Wilber, who had been a catcher in the Major Leagues, told me that Stephen was as good a first baseman as he'd ever seen. By then Washington had moved to Texas and become the Texas Rangers. Just about that time the team changed ownership and a friend of mine, Bobby Brown, who is currently president of the American League, was appointed president of the ball club. Bobby called me up one day and said, "Hank, we have two first basemen that the organization considers ahead of your son. I tried to do Stephen a favor and send him to some other club and maybe he'll have a chance to break into the

Major Leagues, but at the current time his chances of breaking in with the Texas Rangers are practically nil."

That was a very nice gesture on the part of Bobby Brown, and I thanked him. Shortly thereafter Stephen was sold conditionally to the Chicago White Sox. That winter he talked to Roland Hemond, who was then general manager of the White Sox, and asked him what he thought his chances were of making the big team. Hemond told him that his chances of making the White Sox were less than fifty-fifty. So Stephen wisely decided that he was going to give up the game, and he moved out to California with his wife, Myrna, and went to law school at UCLA.

UCLA had a very difficult law course, but Stephen had no trouble getting through it. He passed the bar exam on his first try and was immediately offered a job with a law firm. Stephen had played ball with Bill Madlock in their first year of pro ball at Geneva, and they became good friends. When Bill made good in the Major Leagues, he asked Stephen to represent him as an agent. So Stephen started right in representing ballplayers, his clients coming, at first, through Bill Madlock's contacts and reputation (Bill went on to win batting championships in the National League four times). They've remained good friends, and Stephen has represented Bill Madlock along the way. He's developed quite a clientele, and at the moment he's representing some thirty-five ballplayers. My boys have, to my pleasure, developed very well. I've never had a bit of trouble with either one of them.

My little girl came to me one day at about age ten and said that the children at school couldn't understand why she was living with her father. I asked her if she wanted to live with her mother, who only lived four or five blocks away. She said, "Yes, I do, Dad." I said, "Fine, from now on you're living with your mother. But just remember one thing. Don't come back to me when you have an argument with your mother and say, 'No, Dad, I'm living with you.' It's not that I don't want you to live with me, but you're not going to use your parents, play one against the other, and every time you get in a little tiff with your mother, you're going to run back to me, and then run back to your mother again. Let's get it straight. Make up your mind. If you want to go live with your mother, I'm perfectly happy with that. You're always welcome to come here any time. You can spend the weekends whenever you want, but from now on, your mother is in complete charge of your activities." Well, she agreed to that, so she moved over to her mother, and her mother took good care of her. She sent her to a good private school. Alva went on to Kenyon College in Ohio, and met a young chap by the name of Fritz Gahagan, and they became very friendly. After she graduated she moved up to Connecticut, close to where Fritz lived. She took it upon herself to buy a piece of a local newspaper. She was a 51 percent partner in this newspaper, and part of her job was to handle the advertising. She even made the deliveries and would often write articles. This took me by surprise, because I always envisioned my daughter as a little five-year-old, and here she was, graduated from college and a businesswoman. She made a success of it, and it was a great experience for her.

Eventually she and Fritz got married. They still live in Connecticut, in a big, rambling, old house with lots of acreage. They have two boys of their own, and last year they adopted a little Korean girl. Fritz is working at a law firm in New London, Connecticut, which is about a twenty-five-minute drive from their home. They're living a very happy life.

I have no complaints about my children. They've all been great examples of how all children should develop. They never had a drug problem, I never had a school problem with the kids, and they all managed to get by on their own. I used to think it was my example that was responsible for the way they developed, but I realize now that I was just plain lucky and my children had a little something on the ball of their own that kept them on the straight and narrow. As I look back I realize now that I'm very fortunate. I'd say we're batting 1.000.

◆

Glenn Greenberg remembered:

"When I was growing up in Cleveland, it was impressive that my father was the owner of the team. I loved it and I was proud of it. His owning the team was a bigger deal to me than his having been a great baseball player.

"We lived in a nice house with a lot of space around it and I can remember when my brother and I were seven or eight years old and Dad would hit a tennis ball into the air with a tennis racket. He'd give my brother a dime or a quarter—or even a dollar—if we could catch it. We'd circle under it and often it would bounce away. Once, he hit one very high and said, 'I'll give you a hundred dollars if you catch it!' I caught it, but I never got the hundred dollars. But it was fun, anyway.

"I remember some of the stories he told, about how when the other guys were out chasing girls, he was out chasing fly balls. He told me about how the pitchers were ahead of the hitters early in the season, but then in July when they started getting tired, and when all the other players were getting tired, that's when he felt he had an advantage because he always kept himself in such good shape. That's when he said he would dig in deeper, grip the bat tighter, and concentrate harder.

"He had two other advantages as well. You don't hear much about them. One was his size; he was a really big guy, bigger than many of the other players. And second, I think he was a much more talented athlete than a lot of people gave him credit for. He was a great all-around athlete. I remember he came to a grade-school soccer game that Steve was playing in. The ball bounced over to the sideline and Dad kicked it back. I mean kicked it! I had never seen anyone kick a soccer ball that far.

"Beyond all that, maybe the single most striking factor about my father was his drive. He drove himself hard and thus drove people around him hard. I guess he expected as much from us as he did from himself.

"He could be very complimentary to complete strangers, but he'd rarely say anything like that to us. He was also very critical of himself. You couldn't underestimate his drive, or his will to win. That's how he succeeded in almost everything he did. He instilled that in us. I think all of us still play tennis, for example, not with joy but with a fierce determination to win. He would do anything to win. There were always arguments and little points of calling a ball out when it was really in. My mother says he was even a sore loser at poker, that he was impossible to play with.

"He was competitive with us kids, too. For example, when Steve and I would come back from college during a vacation, we'd get into a discussion and we might use a high-flown word or phrase we had learned in class. Or we'd take a particular side of an argument that he disagreed with. My father would say, 'What the hell do you know? You go to school and now you think you're such a big deal. Now you're an expert.' I thought he resented our getting this education, even though he was sending us to the best schools. He seemed to resent his own lack of formal education and was defensive about it. Maybe there was a rivalry, but it was also a part of his deep, deep sense of competitiveness.

"It turned out that I was never much of a baseball player. I played football in college and at one point in later years I was the fourth-ranked amateur squash player in the country. But baseball wasn't my game, and this never bothered Dad. He never put any pressure on me to play baseball. And I appreciated that. Maybe he felt that there was enough pressure on me just being Hank Greenberg's son. I don't know.

"When I went to Yale I didn't go out for the baseball team, but I did make the football team. And an interesting thing happened one day. A newspaper reporter came to do a story on me because I was the son of Hank Greenberg and I was playing on the varsity football team. The reporter had checked my biographical file in the athletic department and had seen that under 'Religious preference' I had listed, 'Congregationalist.'

"The reporter said to me, 'Gee, there must be some mistake here. You're Hank Greenberg's son. You're Jewish, aren't you?'

"I said, 'I don't know.'

"When I was in prep school at Andover, we were required to attend chapel services and we read the New Testament. The school was Congregationalist.

"But when I was growing up, my family never practiced any formal religion at all. I know my father had gone through substantial abuse as a ballplayer for being a Jew, and maybe in some way he was trying to shield us.

"The fact is, he never told his own children that we were Jewish. Dad never told me I was a Jew. The closest he came to that was when I reached thirteen years of age and he gave me a ring. He said, 'This is the ring my father gave me when I was thirteen. In the Jewish religion when you turn thirteen you are said to be a man. And now I pass this ring on to you.' That was it. The ring was a symbol, but I really wasn't sure what it was a symbol of. He didn't explain another thing about it. I really had no idea what the history was behind this tradition.

"No one in our family ever went to synagogue, no one ever celebrated or observed any Jewish holidays. We did have Christmas, but I never gave that a second thought. After all, didn't everybody celebrate Christmas?

"We also had very little to do with my father's parents. My grandmother died before I could remember her, and my grandfather was an old man and I guess growing senile. I think my father was a little embarrassed by him. Whatever, he certainly didn't follow their religion.

"I discovered in my later years, though, that my father did have a strong feeling for Jewishness. I remember one time—it was about 1971—when he and I and my first wife, Judy, were having dinner in a restaurant in Manhattan. Judy was pro-Arab, though she wasn't anti-Israel. She and Dad got into an argument about the Mideast in which I felt he was abusive to her.

"I said, 'Dad, I think you should apologize to my wife.'

"He said he would not.

"So Judy and I got up and left the restaurant.

225

"He and I didn't speak to each other for five years. It was only after Stephen worked pretty hard to patch it up that we finally began speaking to each other again."

Alva Greenberg Gahagan remembered:

"My father was a hero to a lot of people because of his sports accomplishments, because he was the first Jew to make an impact in baseball, but there was something else. He was known for being approachable, for treating everybody like a human being. Not, well, I'm the great Hank Greenberg. Look at how he treated the new guy on the block, Jackie Robinson. That's the way Dad was. Walking down the street in New York, coming back from a restaurant around eleven at night, he'd say hello to the man selling newspapers on the corner of Lexington Avenue and 68th Street. 'Hi, Harry, how are you tonight?' 'I'm fine, Mr. Greenberg.' He never walked by a wino without giving him $5. He'd say, 'Go buy yourself a bottle.' He had no illusions about it. He said, 'What, am I going to pretend that he's not going to use the money for what he wants?' He was very generous. I'll never forget one time I had a friend over and I had wanted a skateboard. He said to my friend, 'Do you have a skateboard?' She said no. He said to me, 'Here's $20, buy two skateboards.' That's the way he was.

"But Dad was not an easy father. He wanted us to do the right thing. Once he caught me smoking and said, 'I'll tan you within an inch of your life if I catch you doing that again.' He set very high standards for his children. He was not full of praise, which was a little easier for me I think than it was for the boys because I don't think he expected as much.

"Still I grew up with a desire to top my brothers. To do something that was better than them.

"It was embarrassing to me when I realized that my father was a Jewish hero and I didn't even know what anything meant. Why, for example, he didn't play on Yom Kippur. He said, 'Jesus Christ, here I grew up and I had to go through this stuff and I hated it, and I thought I'd spare my kids, and now they are all coming back to me and saying, 'Why didn't you send us for Jewish education?'

"He also said that his experiences during the war soured him. He said that when he served in the Second World War he saw all these people, all these different religions, killing each other. He said what was the point? As a rabbi had said of him: If there had been a disorganized religion, he would have joined.

"Dad did have strong Jewish feelings, though. It was just that as far as he was concerned, organized religion is not the answer.

"On his seventieth birthday, my brothers and I bought him a round-trip ticket to Israel. He often talked about going to Israel but he was never able to make the trip. There was a division for him between his heritage and his religion. He certainly felt himself to be a Jew, though, there's no question about that.

"I think he drew away from his family to an extent because he felt that he was at times being exploited by them, that whenever he came home there were always pictures of him to sign. He told me the story of his father standing outside the ballpark—it may have been the World Series—and he didn't even care how the game had gone, Granddad just wanted Dad to sign some more photos.

"Dad was a double-edged father. The end result is I loved him a lot and I miss him a lot."

Stephen Greenberg remembered:

"My father encouraged me when I played baseball in boarding school at Hotchkiss, he always came up to a game once a season. He was encouraging but never coached me. When I started playing in the Cape Cod League, which was a summer league with good college players, he came up for a couple of games my last summer there. First of all he knew I was going to graduate from college. When I was a sophomore in college I certainly wasn't thinking about a pro career, and he always stressed that getting an education was first and foremost. But by junior year he began to get feedback from scouts that I was a pretty good player. I had made the USA team to play in the Pan Am games and seemed to be doing pretty well vis-a-vis the competition. So he started to coach me a little bit and talked way over my head. I remember he would talk about the psychology of hitting, the one-on-one competition between the batter and the pitcher. And the little things you do to intimidate the pitcher. I was a college kid just trying to swing the bat and hit the ball.

"First of all, in college you're not facing the same pitchers over and over again the way you do in pro ball. You play one game against Holy Cross and that's the last time you see that pitcher.

"So you don't have the opportunity to do things on an ongoing basis. Dad always stressed digging in to the plate. He used to tell me to put my left hand up and motion to the pitcher to stop while I dug in. He said he would dig a hole—I bet it pissed a lot of pitchers off.

"He told me twenty times: The turning point in his career was 1934, after his rookie season when he hit around .300. He had a pretty good year. I think he may have driven in 100 runs but was still very much a rookie. He said he had talked to Ty Cobb and Cobb used to say that his whole psychology of hitting was that when you go up to the plate, you say, Look at that poor son-of-a-bitch pitcher out there, he's got to pitch to the great Ty Cobb with the bases full. Rather than worrying about, Gee, am I going to strike out with the bases loaded.

"And Dad said that that spring, after his rookie season, he got more introspective and thoughtful about how he approached things. I could really see him kneeling in the on-deck circle during an exhibition game literally looking at each individual player on the field. He looked at all the players and realized he was better than any of them—bigger, stronger, more dedicated. Dad said that from that point on his whole philosophy changed. He psyched himself up much like Ty Cobb had done. He began swinging three bats in the on-deck circle and probably began with the digging-in nonsense. Psyching himself to the point where that poor bastard has to pitch to Hank Greenberg. He can't get me out. Now admittedly, when you're facing Bob Feller, it doesn't work, because you can't convince yourself of that, and you're never going to convince Feller of that. But he said that from that point on he used to stare at the pitcher's eyes. When he'd come up to the plate he'd look at them and stare them down, they'd look down and turn around and he knew they may get him out or he may get him out, but he had that guy.

"He told me another story. There was one mediocre pitcher that everybody else used to hit pretty good, but for the first five or six years in the league he could not hit this guy. In those days the visiting team would get to the visitors' dugout by coming up through the home dugout. They didn't have a separate tunnel. The Tigers were on the first-base side, and one day, Dad was in the dugout. This guy was pitching. The pitcher came up through the tunnel, up the dugout steps to walk over to the visitors' dugout and Dad said to him, 'Hey, you're in trouble today because I figured out how you've been getting me out, and you're not going to get me out anymore, I figured out the secret. You watch the difference.'

"Dad hadn't figured anything out. Absolutely nothing. He just said that to him. The first time up he hit a home run off him on a fastball. Next time up he said the guy's going to throw me a curveball. He got a curveball and hit another home run. The guy got Dad out sometimes, but now he was hitting .300 or .350 against him. Dad was convinced it was just because he said he figured it out.

"How strongly did he feel about being a Jew? I think he felt pretty strongly about it, but I think he had very mixed feelings. My perception is that here's a guy who grew up in a traditional, Orthodox Jewish household and he's suddenly thrust into prominence in a world which is virtually devoid of Jews. And the few that were Jews often changed their names. He was only twenty-three in 1934 when the Tigers won the World Series. He had a big year in '34 and suddenly he's a big star. A twenty-three-year-old kid and the only Jewish kid around. I think there was a tremendous amount of pressure on him to conform, or at least not to stick out like a sore thumb. I think he liked a lot about what was happening to him in his life. He liked the fact that he was becoming a big star, and getting the notoriety, getting real good money. Was there an element of embarrassment about the old neighborhood or whatever? I don't know. I don't think he was embarrassed because he'd go home in the off-season and spend the winter there.

"My grandfather had a fit when my father wanted to be a professional baseball player. The next thing you know my grandfather is signing his autograph in Hebrew outside the clubhouse. I guess my dad came out after a game one time in Yankee Stadium and there was my grandfather autographing baseballs. Dad noticed that the kids were looking at the ball kind of strangely; he went over and said, 'What are you doing?' He said, 'I'm Hank Greenberg's father and they wanted my autograph so I'm signing.' The kids were looking at this ball and they didn't know what was on it. That's the kind of thing that would drive Dad nuts, I think.

"The bottom line, I suppose, is that he could not escape even if he wanted to. He had a very strong sense of being a Jew. Maybe he didn't always view it as 100 percent positive during those days, but as he got older he clearly became a kind of militant good Jew. Certainly very adamant about Jewish history.

"I know Glenn said that he grew up with no sense of being a Jew, no sense at all. I'm sure Dad would remember it differently. Dad would say, 'How could you not?'

"But Dad never took us inside a temple. He was very down on religion. In Dad's mind there was a distinction between being a Jew and being a religious person. He felt that all religion was a con game. All organized religion had ever done over the centuries was to promote wars, dissension, and hatred among people. That was his view of organized religion regardless. He certainly felt that Christianity and Judaism were ways to draw people apart.

"He became very sensitive to which issues were critical for Israel politically. Which presidents were friendly toward Israel and which ones weren't. Which issues he should support based on how they affected Israel and therefore the Jews as a people. Domestically he was always aware of the undercurrent of anti-Semitism, whether it was a club that didn't allow Jews in or an industry, and I think he realized that a lot of the hard battles he had to fight as an owner related to the fact that a substantial group of owners resented him and tried to make life difficult for him because he was a Jew.

"One of my favorite stories about my dad reveals everything about him that I love. I must have been living in New York, Dad and my mother were divorced. I was eleven, my brother was thirteen. Glenn should have just had his bar mitzvah but he'd never been in a temple. It was the fall of 1959. It was early October. It may have been right after or right before the World Series. We got up to go to school. My dad said, 'You're not going to school today.' We said why not. He said, 'I'm taking you someplace.' 'Why, Dad?' 'Well, this is Yom Kippur.' 'What's Yom Kippur?' 'This is the holiest day in the year—it's the day of atonement for the Jews. You're not going to school today.' Terrific.

"My brother and I got dressed. We went to the Hayden Planetarium. I had never been there. We spent two or three hours there. Traditionally, on Yom Kippur, Jews fast, but we didn't. Jews ask for forgiveness for all their sins of the past year, the slate is wiped clean, and they start a new year making vows to be better the next year. And to reinforce that, you don't eat. I came home and I distinctly remember that I felt real good. It was a great day. But it was several years before I realized that Yom Kippur was not a day that Jews went to the planetarium. What else would I think? He's not going to take us to temple, because he doesn't believe in that. He took us someplace that was obviously special. Someplace that maybe represented the vast unknown; someplace he hadn't been to for a long, long time. It was for him a reaching out halfway or three quarters of the way back to something, but he couldn't go all the way. He couldn't call up his brother Joe and say, 'I know you're going to the synagogue on Yom Kippur, could you take me and the boys along with you?' He couldn't go that far, but he wanted to do something. And that's what he came up with.

"It was going someplace peaceful and thinking about what you've done in the last year, how you might do it differently or better next year, and without the supposed trappings of religion.

"My mother, even though she was Jewish, wasn't involved in the Jewish community in Cleveland, where I grew up. She was used to traveling in different circles. Part of the paradox, part of the dilemma my dad might have faced throughout his life was that despite being a Jew, he had access to circles traditionally closed to Jews—but only because of who he was. Very presentable on one level, a good-looking, dashing bachelor for all those years. He could go anywhere. If a club was going to let in a token Jew, it would want that person to be Hank Greenberg. Because he had access to all these places, he probably had a very distorted view of how society treated Jews. And yet he probably noticed they still don't treat him quite the same. I'm sure that was very difficult for him. I'm sure there was a certain allure to hanging around with that level of society, especially when he was younger.

"One Passover when we were living in New York, out of the blue Dad decides we're going to have a seder at the house. So my grandfather comes and I think my aunt Lil came and maybe Donald, her son, and my uncle Joe might have been there, too. There were ten or twelve around the table. My grandfather conducted the ceremony, mostly in Hebrew, and no one knew what he was talking about. But it was wonderful.

"Many years later, Dad gave me a picture of himself with this inscription, 'Kipling said it all for me.' The only Kipling quote that I could think of was 'You're a better man than I am, Gunga Din,' or something like that. I thought why would he say that? Sheepishly I asked him what the inscription meant. He loved that. He did one of his famous double takes; he was in total disbelief. He said, 'A Yale graduate, an English major doesn't know? His father doesn't have a college education.' He said, 'Don't you know that poem called "When"? "When you can walk with kings . . ."' I went to the library and looked it up and the poem was entitled 'If.' 'If you can walk with kings . . .' I Xeroxed the poem and put it up on the wall next to the picture so when people like me look at it and say I wonder what the hell he meant by this, it's there. The picture even said, 'Affectionately, Dad,' yet he never told me he loved me. He probably said it to my sister because she was a girl, but I'm not sure Glenn could remember him ever saying he loved him. He's signing this inscription, not 'With love,' but 'Affectionately.' He had a hard time with that with us.

"Dad wrote me a letter years later, right before he went into surgery. Typical of him. He wrote it and told me he was mailing it so I would get it after the surgery. He said in the letter that he loved me. It was a wonderful letter. Basically, he said all the things I knew, and I never doubted how he felt. And I knew he loved me and he appreciated the things I did with him and for him and he was proud of me and all of that, so I never felt the need to have him prove it. I came to understand that one of his quirks was that he couldn't say it. So he wrote it in a letter just before going into surgery, which he might not have come out of.

"Sometimes it annoyed me if he praised other people to the heavens and wouldn't praise me. But I knew he felt it. Glenn, probably because he was the firstborn and had all the traditional pressures being the older son, really needed to hear it from Dad. But he never did.

"Dad was always, and this is part of the paradox, sensitive to the other Jews who were trying to make it in baseball. I know that he felt that he went out of his way to make things easier for Al Rosen. At the same time he wanted Al to make him look good for having done it. And he wanted Al to succeed for his own sake. I'm sure Rosen always felt the extra pressure Dad was putting on him.

"Dad also followed Koufax. In those days, in the 1960s, we were living in New York. Dad was out of baseball and we didn't talk a lot about it. I think he still used to get a ballot every year to vote for some baseball-related award. He'd go to an occasional game—he didn't go to a lot of them. But he used to talk about Koufax all the time. He compared him to Feller. Koufax was the first pitcher he had seen since Feller who had both an intimidating fastball and a great curveball. And the combination made him unhittable.

"Did Dad follow Koufax's career because he was Jewish? I'm sure it must have been a factor.*

"In his own mind Dad was in competition with Gehrig. It was Gehrig's record he really wanted to break. Ralph Kiner, in particular, cut out little things like all-time baseball statistics from the paper and sent them to Dad until the day he died. No matter what Dad did, Gehrig was always one notch ahead of him. There would be a list of ten people and the one thing Dad would pick out on the list was, 'Son of a bitch, I was fourth but Gehrig was third.' RBIs per times at bat or whatever it happened to be. Gehrig was ahead of my dad in a lot of things. Gehrig was the standard Dad compared himself to. He never in his wildest dreams ever thought he could replace Babe Ruth. But Lou Gehrig, yes. From the time he broke into the big leagues, if you were going to be the best first baseman in baseball in the American League then you had to be better than Lou Gehrig. And clearly his drive was to be the best first baseman in the American League."

---

* Greenberg and Koufax, the only two Jewish players elected to the Baseball Hall of Fame, met a few times when both were living in California. "We talked only briefly," recalled Koufax. "What I remember about Hank was that he was a terribly nice man. As for his being an influence on me, he really wasn't. When I was growing up in Brooklyn, I wanted to be a basketball player. My hero was Max Zaslofsky."

CHAPTER 14

When I went to Chicago in 1959, Bill Veeck said to me, "Now you run the farm system," as I had done in Cleveland. I immediately said to him, "I'm not running the farm system. I'm not going to work for five years developing players to have you decide one day to sell the ball club; all that work will go down the drain. It's beneficial to somebody else, but not to us." He said, "Well, what do you want to do?" I told him I wanted to be treasurer. I invested every cent I owned and bought more stock and debentures in the White Sox. I just felt that I wanted to be close to the financial picture rather than down in the farm system trying to develop ballplayers for the White Sox. I didn't think Bill was going to stay with the team very long, and so this was the best thing for me to do.

It turned out to be a hell of a year. In 1959 we took control of the team over Chuck Comiskey's objections, and he immediately sued us. It was the most ridiculous lawsuit I'd ever heard of. He sued his sister and us for taking over the Comiskey dynasty. He said that the White Sox belonged to the Comiskey family and had been in the family for seventy-five years, and therefore no interloper had a right to buy the stock and control the Comiskey franchise. That lawsuit went on for most of the summer. I tried desperately to get Chuck to cooperate with us, but he wouldn't. Every time I got him to the point where he thought maybe I was making sense, he brought his father-in-law in to represent his interests, but the two of them were outranked by Arthur Allyn, a Chicago businessman and Bill Veeck's partner, Bill Veeck, and me. We had three votes to two, and we could run the ball club as we saw fit. But Chuck never got over his pique at losing the club to outsiders—"raiders," as he called us.

The team got off to a great start that year and suddenly we found ourselves in first place. The White Sox had not won a pennant in forty years, since the

Black Sox scandal. Needless to say, Bill Veeck still had that magic touch, and the team stayed in contention.

We drew 1.7 million people—the best attendance record the team had ever had. We won the American League pennant and were very popular in Chicago. The Cubs had their usual bad team, and so most of the baseball interest was for the White Sox. It was a great season for all of us.

In the World Series we faced the Los Angeles Dodgers, who had won the pennant in a playoff against the Milwaukee Braves. We opened in Chicago, and we split the first two games. Then we went to Los Angeles, and two very interesting things happened. One was that we played in the Coliseum, which was a football and track stadium. The Dodgers had been in Los Angeles for two years and their new stadium in Chavez Ravine wasn't completed. The Coliseum was an unusual baseball field. It was about 250 feet down the left-field line and about 450 to right. But it did have seating capacity for about 93,000. When we played our three games in Los Angeles, we sold out every game. That was an all-time record for a three-game series.

Aside from the fact that we lost two out of three and were losing three games to two when we came back to Chicago, the most important thing that happened to me came when a friend of mine, Jerry Orbach, called and asked if I had a ticket for the World Series. I said, "Sure, Jerry, are you coming?" He said, "No, I don't follow it, but my wife is a fan and she'd like to go to the game." I said I'd be delighted to have her sit with me. He called back about twenty minutes later and said, "Now I need two tickets because Marjorie wants to bring a friend." I told him that was fine. Marjie brought her friend, Mary Jo DeCicco, and that's how I met my future wife. But more on that good fortune later.

We came back to Chicago for Game 6, but unfortunately we were never in it. The Dodgers scored eight runs early, and it was over by the fourth inning. They eventually beat us 9–3, so we lost the World Series four games to two. Still, it was a great season for Bill and a great season for the Chicago fans.

After the season I was still commuting between Chicago and New York, where my children lived. I spent a lot of time that winter going back and forth until spring training of 1960 started. We had basically the same team, but Bill pulled a big trade that we thought might assure us of another pennant. He traded for Roy Seivers, who was playing for the Washington Senators. We gave up a pretty good catcher, Earl Battey, in return, but we were counting on the same players who had won the championship for us in 1959. In retrospect that was a mistake, because some of them were older players. We expected Sherm Lollar, our regular catcher, who was in his late thirties, to do well again, but he didn't have as good a year. Some of the pitchers were not as good either. While we drew over a million people again and had some exciting games, we didn't repeat as pennant winners, and the bloom was off the rose.

Along about the close of the 1960 season, Bill Veeck got sick. He smoked packs and packs of cigarettes every day, and he developed a bad cough. Sometimes he'd cough so much that his face would turn blue. Bill finally decided that he had to do something about it. His doctor advised him to go to the Mayo Clinic. They were concerned that he might have a brain tumor. This changed the entire baseball situation for us, because Bill had been running the team. I was always there in my role as treasurer. Most of my job was confined to trying to get Chuck Comiskey to join us, which he never did. His father-in-law also became a pain in the neck because he, too, was always wanting to know why we weren't doing things differently, and he was checking the books all the time. Since I was the treasurer, he would always come to me. They both despised Bill Veeck. Bill gave them no time at all, so they came to me with all their problems. I was the one who had to try to keep peace in the family. I managed, but great animosity always smoldered between Chuck and his father-in-law and Bill.

My other problem was that I was being sued by Chuck Comiskey. We had to testify in court that we had bought the 56 percent from Grace Comiskey without any coercion. It was a straight business deal. She wanted to sell; we wanted to buy. We didn't know what Chuck was talking about, but we had to go to court on it. In the end the court ruled that it was perfectly legal for us to buy Grace Comiskey's stock, and Chuck lost the case.

As the winter progressed, Bill decided that since he was ill he'd sell the team. He had a large family and he wanted to leave them in good financial condition; he didn't want all his money tied up in a ball club run by somebody else. I decided to go along with Bill. I had never seen our purchase as a long-term investment; I knew that one day Bill would get tired of it just as he did in Cleveland.

We sold the team to Arthur Allyn, Jr. When I presented my stock certificates to him, he gave me a check for around $1.1 million in return. I looked at it and said, "Wait a minute. This isn't a certified check." He looked at me very angrily, as though an ordinary check should be sufficient. I said, "I'm not accepting this, and I'm not turning my stock over to you until I get a certified check." He said,

"Okay, you sit there and I'll get a certified check for you." He sent one of his employees to the bank, and about twenty minutes later the man returned with a certified check. I waited in his office while he continued working at his desk, ignoring me completely. We had had some conflicts before about the sale of the team, but I didn't give a damn about it; I was only concerned with getting the right amount for my stock. As far as I was concerned, I was finished with the White Sox and finished with Arthur Allyn, Jr.

Just before he presented me with the check, he drew it back and said, "Wait a minute. There's one more thing that you have to promise me." I asked, "What's that, Arthur?" And he said, "You have to stay on with the White Sox and be general manager." I told him that I would be very happy to try; I was commuting from New York, but I said that I would run the team to the best of my ability and do the trading and keep abreast of the financial events of the club. He said that was exactly what he wanted me to do because he had no intention of spending all his time in the baseball business, and besides, he didn't know how to run the club. With that we parted on a friendly basis. Things had changed abruptly.

I proceeded to run the club for the balance of the 1961 season. I made a big trade with Kansas City, four players from our club for four from their club. Two of the players we got were Andy Carey, a third baseman, who had once played with the Yankees, and a pitcher, Ray Herbert. We got off on a winning streak; I think we won six or seven straight games. It looked for a while like I was going to be a genius. Al Lopez was the field manager, and we had a very close relationship. We eventually sank to fourth place, but we had a pretty good year with attendance of over a million.

At the end of the season I told Arthur Allyn that he required a full-time general manager. He needed a man on the scene constantly, and there was no way I could run the club commuting from New York. I would stay on as an adviser if he wished, but I felt I couldn't run the club on a day-to-day basis because I had children in New York and I planned to live there permanently. So we parted on very friendly terms. I decided I had to look around for something else to do, but at that moment I had a considerable amount of money in my bank account.

For me it was the end of the road for baseball. I had lost interest in the game. I was completely dissatisfied with the commissioner and with the other owners. I found that their word wasn't worth their bond. Many times they had promised one thing, then turned around in the meeting and voted against me. They always offered to have a secret ballot; but nobody could check up on whether they kept their word.

For example, in 1952, when I was general manager at Cleveland, I proposed interleague play. I canvassed the American League first. I argued vociferously that we should have interleague play because it would increase attendance. We had three or four clubs in the American League that were in one-team cities. My thought was that we could develop a rivalry between Cincinnati and Cleveland or Pittsburgh and Detroit, and certainly the two St. Louis clubs. It would be fun for the residents of St. Louis to see the Browns play the Cardinals.

I managed to get six of the American League clubs to agree to it, so it passed there, but I knew there were objections in the National League. We finally went to the joint meeting that year where Commissioner Ford Frick asked the American League how they voted on interleague play, and the American League said they had voted for it. Then he asked the National League how they voted, and the league owners said they were against it. Normally the commissioner would cast the deciding vote when the two leagues were at odds. Commissioner Frick, who was a typical middle-of-the-roader, said, "It's a league matter, so I'm going to call for a vote among all the clubs." Believe it or not, he started off with the American League and six clubs voted against it and two clubs voted for it, the White Sox being one of the clubs and St. Louis the other.

That was only one instance among many in which an owner promised to vote one way and voted the other way. There was no integrity at all among the owners. They were egotistical as far as their other businesses were concerned. Most of them owned their own businesses and came into baseball as more or less of a lark, like Tom Yawkey. He was very wealthy and bought the Red Sox and you couldn't talk to him. He just felt that his judgment, because of the millions of dollars that he controlled, was much better than that of someone who didn't have his wealth.

When Mr. Briggs sent me over to the Pittsburgh club in 1947, I thought that I had the worst break in the world, yet it turned out to be the luckiest thing that had ever happened to me. From there I went on to the Cleveland organization and wound up a 20 percent owner of the club—the second largest stockholder—serving there for close to ten years and getting to know Bill Veeck. Then came the second shock of my professional life when the board of directors and stockholders suddenly fired me in 1957. I lost my enthusiasm for the game. Then, out of the blue, Bill Veeck gained control of the White Sox and asked me to join him. And at the end of the 1961 season we sold the White Sox for a tremendous profit. It was enough money for me to retire on and not think about baseball again, and so what appeared to be my second bad break, getting fired in Cleveland, turned out to be a good break after all. Looking back on these events I realize that sometimes life's bad breaks can turn into good breaks, though you may not recognize that at the time.

By the time we sold the White Sox in 1961 I didn't have to be beholden to anyone; I didn't have to go to winter meetings and stand around the lobby the way a lot of ex-ballplayers do, begging someone to give them a job even though they are no longer able to play. It was always embarrassing to see these men who I had played against, good ballplayers, standing around the lobby for three or four days waiting for someone to approach them. I knew how much pride they had to swallow to stand around like that. Everyone knew why they were there, and people were passing them by.

In 1961 I left baseball. I did so with a lot of pride. I didn't do it like Babe Ruth, who was put out on the coaching line to try to entice a few fans to come to the ballpark. It was pitiful the way they treated the Babe and guys like Jimmie Foxx and other great ballplayers. Baseball was a cold, cruel business. There was no sport in it when you could no longer produce. The public looked upon it as the great American sport, but the owners had a different feeling about the game.

Much of the beauty of the game, though, can be felt at the Hall of Fame. I remember going to Cooperstown for a baseball game in 1939. They didn't have a Hall of Fame game then, but they picked all-star teams from both leagues to play an exhibition at Abner Doubleday Field. That was the year the original five members entered the Hall of Fame. They had been elected in 1936, but weren't inducted until the Hall of Fame had been built. By then, a number of other players had also been elected to the Hall.

I was fortunate enough to be selected as the first baseman for the American League in that 1939 game. It was awe-inspiring to see the greatest players of the game there in person, such as Honus Wagner, Tris Speaker, Walter Johnson, Ty Cobb, Babe Ruth, Cy Young, Connie Mack, and George Sisler. I said to myself then what a thrill it must be to be elected to the Hall of Fame.

◆

Sixteen years later, on January 25, 1956, Greenberg, then general manager of the Indians, was elected to the Baseball Hall of Fame.

A total of 193 ballots from eligible baseball writers was received in the election process, and Greenberg got 164 votes, substantially more than the three quarters (or 145 votes) needed for election. Joe Cronin was the other player voted in at that time.

"In all my years of being on the playing field I never dreamed that this would be the final result," Greenberg told the press in Cleveland. "I can't possibly express how I feel. It's just too wonderful for words. I'm deeply grateful and humble for this honor.

"I'm also glad that Joe Cronin was named, too," Greenberg added. "He was one of the greatest ballplayers and toughest competitors I ever saw."

From his home in Newton Center, Massachusetts, Cronin said he was "thrilled" and added congratulations to Greenberg. "Hank is the greatest right-handed hitter I ever saw," Cronin said.

At the induction ceremonies on July 23, 1956, Greenberg stood on the flag-bedecked dais, while his wife, Caral, his two sons and daughter, his brothers, Joe and Ben, and sister, Lillian, looked on.

"I have had many thrills in baseball," said Greenberg. "This, though, is the greatest. Today I have the same butterflies in my stomach that I used to have when I came to the plate with the bases full with Grove or Gomez or Ruffing pitching."

◆

I've never been asked by any member of the Hall of Fame for any of my memorabilia to be included in a display. I have no idea, even to this day, what articles they have portraying my baseball career. They tell me that they have a Ted Williams room and a Joe DiMaggio room and a Willie Mays room, so I guess my plaque will just be up on the wall. They can't take that down, and that's good enough for me.

During my last visit to the Hall of Fame, the year I went up to attend Ralph Kiner's induction, 1975, we were at the commissioner's dinner. Everybody was sitting around after the main course and the commissioner called on different players to get up and say a few words. I remember distinctly when they called on Satchel Paige, who had been inducted four years earlier. I guess Satch had had a few drinks by then. He got up and started talking about how pleased he was to be there and that it was fairly new to have a black Hall of Famer. Then he went on about why it took so long, and he started to get a little bitter about the fact that the black players had been denied an opportunity to play Major League baseball while so many of them were so talented and now were being overlooked for admittance to the Hall. I recall distinctly that Chub Feeney, who was then National League president, got up and said, "Look, Satchel, this is a fun dinner and we don't want to get into any controversial subjects, and I think you're off base in bringing up your unhappiness with the fact that black players were not recognized until recently." Satch sat down and I thought to myself that the day would come when Satch won't have to talk about the black players because most of the guys sitting around the table will be black. Sure enough, ten or fifteen years later, it's the truth. Every time they induct new players it's the black players. And rightfully so, because they're the ones who, in recent years, have established the records.

During the 1950s I was invited to a black all-star game at Comiskey Park by my friend Abe Saperstein. He had a box down near the dugout. There were some 55,000 fans on hand, but I think only about four or five of them were white. Abe, of course, knew a lot of the owners of the Negro League and was treated with great respect. They considered him one of their saviors because he ran the Harlem Globetrotters. Anyway, when I saw they had a left-handed shortstop I wanted to laugh, because how could anybody play left-handed shortstop. And then they had a catcher whipping the ball down to second base underhanded like a softball pitcher. In the outfield they had guys clowning around. I thought that these blacks couldn't play Major League baseball, that they were all just a bunch of clowns, so I looked at the game with prejudiced eyes.

As time went on, I realized how wrong I was about them. There were many good ballplayers on that field who would have been capable of playing Major League ball with a year or two of minor league training. Some of them might have been able to step right in there. But it didn't occur to me that these fellows were future Major League ballplayers. Of course, you're talking about early on when only Jackie Robinson and a few others were playing Major League ball, and black players were not accepted by all the clubs. Even though Cleveland was one of the foremost clubs to accept black players, I realize now that I had been brainwashed. I sat in that ballpark amused by it all instead of taking those players seriously and looking for those who might be capable of playing Major League ball—and all of them were available.

You could buy most of them for a few thousand dollars. Most of the club owners in the Negro League recognized that the handwriting was on the wall for black baseball because the stars were going into the Major Leagues, and they would be eager to sell a player for a few thousand dollars.

Unfortunately, many black ballplayers back then didn't have much formal education, so they had to develop on sheer natural talent. It took them a while, even after they proved they had the talent. Then they had to assimilate into the outside world, which was mostly white, and to learn to control their temper and to associate with the white players in a white world. It's much more difficult. They had more things to overcome than the average white ballplayer.

To give some idea of how talented these players were, Abe Saperstein called me one day and said, "I'm sending a player over. I want you to give him a tryout." I said, "Well, Abe, do you think he has a chance to make it?" He said, "You judge for yourself. This fellow has never played baseball, but he's a great athlete and he's played some softball. I think you'll be surprised when you see him."

The player came in and he was mammoth. He was about six foot seven and must have weighed about 220 or 230. We couldn't get a bat that was thick enough at the handle for him to grab because his fingers were so long. His name was Sweetwater Clifton. We let him take a turn at bat. The next thing I knew, he was hitting balls into the upper deck in Municipal Stadium in Cleveland, and we were throwing old balls out there! Even though he was inexperienced, he had tremendous power. We thought we could certainly develop it. We sent him down to Wilkes-Barre, Pennsylvania, which was our A club, and he played a whole season down there and hit around .325. When the season was over he went back to playing basketball, and that's the last we ever saw of him. During the winter he made $25,000 a year playing basketball for the New York Knickerbockers. That gives you an idea how talented some of those black athletes were. Had some of those early black players had the proper training and seasoning, they might have become the greatest players the game ever produced.

CHAPTER 15

I had to look for a new pursuit after I left the White Sox in 1961. When I got back to New York, where I planned to live permanently, I continued my association with my two good friends Louis Marx and his brother, David. While both brothers were in the toy business together, Louis was the leader and David was supposed to be the follower. David was the younger of the two and he was smart enough to let Louis have his head because Louis was a dominant type and wouldn't brook any interference. So David stayed in the background.

David was interested in the stock market, which Louis wasn't, and he spent a lot of his time and money investing in stocks. I had become very interested in the stock market as well. David had great contacts in New York. (He used to have dinner every night at the "21" Club, where he'd meet some of the top executives in America.)

David and I decided to form a partnership. We each put up $100,000 and opened an office at 580 Fifth Avenue. We rented a ticker-tape machine and hired an interior decorator, who designed the office like a living room. We had a large table in front of the ticker-tape machine and a couple of telephones and one big lounge chair in bright orange and other lounge chairs in gray. It was very striking, but the orange got very wearing on you after a while, particularly on a day when the Dow Jones tumbled.

We started this little partnership in 1962, and, as luck would have it, things started to move up. We got a few tips on airline stocks. I think the first tip was Northwest Orient, then we went into Braniff, TWA, and National Airlines. We got started at the right time because the airline industry had just changed from prop planes to jets, which saved a lot on fuel.

I had my $100,000 in the partnership, but I also invested the money that I had gotten from the sale of my stock in the White Sox. At that time the margin requirements were very minor and you could hypothecate your portfolio two or three times. At one time we had $600,000 worth of stock while we only had $200,000 in cash invested. It turned out that we had one of our real bull markets from 1962 to 1968.

In the meantime, many things were taking place in my personal life.

I bought a house on 70th Street, between Park and Lexington avenues. It was a beautiful five-story town house, beautiful architecture, and it suited my needs perfectly. The ground floor had been a doctor's office previously and had a private entrance; my housekeeper, Gertrude Garland, stayed there. Gertrude had come with me and the children when I moved from Cleveland to New York and took care of them when I was away. When my daughter moved over to her mother's and the boys went off to boarding school, I had this big house all to myself. I also engaged a cook, so I was living high on the hog.

I was having lunch at the "21" Club with David Marx one day and while I was standing at the bar waiting for him who comes up to me but Marjie Orbach. We had last seen each other at the World Series and she said to me, "Mary Jo DeCicco is coming to town tomorrow and she's getting a divorce. Would you like to have lunch with us?"

I said, "Well, if she's available, I certainly would. I enjoyed meeting her and she's very attractive."

The next day I arranged to meet Marjie and Mary Jo and a friend of mine by the name of Norton Mailman at the Little Club—the owner, Billy Reed, was a friend of mine.

The luncheon turned out to be a very friendly one, and Mary Jo and I became infatuated with each other.

◆

Mary Jo DeCicco, tall and blond, was, as Dr. Rex Kennamer, the widely known physician in Los Angeles, recalled, "one of the well-known beauties in this city, where physical beauty, because of the movie industry, of course, is usually a topic of conversation. I think most people agreed that Mary Jo was special. She was breathtakingly beautiful."

She had been a movie actress only briefly, having made three films, and those almost by accident. When she was seventeen years old she had left her hometown of Portland, Oregon, to visit her mother, Mildred Tarola, who was in Tucson, Arizona. Her mother suffered from arthritis, and the dry Arizona air had been recommended to possibly improve her condition.

One evening Mary Jo was sitting alone in the hotel lobby when a man approached her and said, "You oughta be in movies." "Or," recalled Mary Jo, "words pretty much to that effect. I got frightened and ran upstairs to my mother."

It turned out that the man, who would apologize profusely for scaring the girl, was a talent scout for Howard Hughes, the eccentric millionaire who owned RKO Studios.

The talent scout would shortly arrange for Mary Jo—who had never acted before, had never had any interest in acting, but now was excited by the idea—and her mother to fly in Hughes's private plane to meet the famous man in Hollywood.

"Even then," said Mary Jo, "Howard Hughes had a questionable reputation regarding women. This was after he had produced *The Outlaw* with Jane Russell and had a slew of famous girlfriends, including Jean Harlow. Anyway, my father got wind of this—my parents were divorced—and he got word to Howard Hughes that if he laid a hand on me, he'd shoot him."

Hughes assured the Tarolas that there were "no strings attached," and, Mary Jo says, "He never did lay a hand on me.

"I took screen tests, and even though I had never had an acting lesson in my life, Hughes wanted me to work as an actress for RKO. But my father wanted me to finish high school, and so I went back to Portland and completed my senior year.

"But after that I returned to Hollywood, and actually became friendly with Hughes. At the time he was crazy about Janet Leigh. He was quite eccentric, but attractive—like a dark Gary Cooper—and he'd call me up at ten at night and ask me to meet him on a corner in Beverly Hills. Then he'd come by in his beat-up Chevy and drive me out to the beach, and we'd sit there and talk about Janet Leigh, who was then seeing Arthur Loew, Jr. Hughes needed consoling, and there I was, eighteen years old, sitting on a beach in the middle of the night consoling Howard Hughes."

Mary Jo made three movies. Two were westerns with Tim Holt, *Trail Guide* and *Target*, in which, given the stage name Linda Douglas, she played the typical ingenue in the western plains. Then she made an "A" feature, *An Affair with a Stranger*, in which she was the third lead, behind Victor Mature and Jean Simmons.

At this point she met Pat DeCicco, "the glamour boy of Hollywood," she said. DeCicco had been married to the actress Thelma Todd as well as to the heiress Gloria Vanderbilt.

DeCicco, recalled Rex Kennamer, was "a two-fisted, hell-raising playboy." DeCicco was also known for a terrible temper, and flew into blind rages. Mary Jo and DeCicco were married in 1953. Her life was a fast one, and the marriage was difficult. She became a part of the jet set, socializing with the Vanderbilts and Whitneys and Henry Ford and Aly Khan.

"I believe it was Joe Schenk, a friend, who said, 'I don't want to be a millionaire, I just want to live like Pat DeCicco,'" recalled Mary Jo Greenberg. "Pat had many business ventures going, including 'DeCicco's Bon Bons.' We lived a grand life-style. But most of all, Pat was charming, charming, charming—when he wanted to be."

In a few years, though, the charm wore off. And Mary Jo had had "enough jetsetting." The couple was divorced in 1960.

After marrying DeCicco, Mary Jo gave up her acting career. "I was never really interested in it," she said. "And I was never comfortable with it. I was satisfied with my life and had no desire for a career. Hank saw my films and he said I was a fool to quit. He thought I had a lot of talent, and all I'd have had to do was work at it. He said, 'You're a natural.' But it simply wasn't for me."

Mary Jo Greenberg continued:

"I'll never forget the first time that I met Hank. Pat and I had gone to New York for the Brooklyn Dodgers–New York Yankees World Series in 1955. We were the guests of Dan Topping, then the co-owner of the Yankees. He and Pat were very close friends— Dan was Pat's best man at our wedding. As we were getting into our limousines in front of the Park Lane Hotel, Pat took me aside to introduce me to Hank Greenberg. He was also staying at the hotel, in town from Cleveland to attend the Series. Hank had that gentle, sloping bend of his upper body as he spoke to you. It almost made you feel like royalty.

"We each got into our own limos, then, and headed for Yankee Stadium. With Pat and me were Topping; George Weiss, the Yankees' general manager; and Del Webb, the other Yankee co-owner; they were discussing Hank with great respect, but as I sat there listening I remember them making joking references to Jews, and it was my first experience with anti-Semitism. It left an impression. Meanwhile, this was my first World Series, and I was quite excited. Having grown up with two older brothers who loved sports, I was a bit of a tomboy, and had a pretty good knowledge of the game. But I didn't have good social knowledge. I sat there in Dan Topping's private box cheering madly for the Dodgers, and particularly Jackie Robinson. You can imagine how that went over. They weren't terribly crazy about Jews, so you know how they felt about Jackie. DeCicco wanted to kill me, and when we returned to the hotel he told me in no uncertain terms how he felt about my behavior. The point of the story is that years later, when Hank and I became involved, we shared a common dislike for the Yankees.

"My second meeting with Hank was three years later, in 1958. Buddy Adler, who was then a movie producer at 20th Century-Fox, had just produced a very important movie, *Love Is a Many Splendored Thing*, with Jennifer Jones and William Holden.

"A private screening was held at the studio followed by a black-tie party at Romanoff's. I never particularly enjoyed those affairs. I was very shy and lacked confidence, and suddenly I'm in a room with the likes of Gary Cooper, Humphrey Bogart, and David Niven. It was a lot for a girl from Portland, Oregon, who, until my marriage to Pat, had been quite sheltered. In fact, these insecurities would later become a thorn in my relationship with Hank, who was always comfortable in those surroundings. I don't think he ever understood my feelings. He used to say, 'I don't understand you. You're the best-looking woman in the room and you have no self-confidence.'

"Well, during the cocktail hour of that party the music was playing and people were dancing and suddenly there was Hank standing at the bar. He reintroduced himself to me and we chatted. He was out for the winter baseball meetings and, being a friend of Buddy Adler, had been invited to the party, too. He asked me to dance. I always felt very awkward dancing but I quickly accepted. I thought I'd never make it to the dance floor. Hank was terribly graceful and I remember wishing that I could just stand on his feet and have him glide me around the floor.

"For the second time, he made quite an impression on me. I knew then he was someone special. And he would say that he felt the same about me, and even remembered what I wore that night—a white evening gown. Then I saw him at the ball game in Los Angeles, and when Marjorie Orbach arranged the luncheon at Billy Reed's Little Club, I was more than looking forward to it.

"Six years had passed since our first meeting. Hank was divorced and I was in the process of getting mine.

"I was in New York at that time at Pat's request. He was renting a beautiful house in the Bahamas and had asked me to come to New York to visit and perhaps go to the Bahamas with him.

"I agreed to fly in from California to see him—with one stipulation: that I would have my own accommodations in the Waldorf Towers, where he was staying. He agreed. (For some strange reason Pat liked being married, although his success rate was not too good—he had been married three times.)

"While I was in New York, I had lunch with Hank and Norton and Marjorie. After lunch, Hank and I were alone, and we wandered back to the Waldorf. Hank suggested that we stop at Peacock Alley off the lobby for a drink. There was very definitely something happening between us, but Hank was gun-shy about getting involved again, and I was still reeling from my own marriage fiasco.

"Finally, about 7:30, Hank walked me to the elevator to say good-bye. The elevator door opened and there stood DeCicco, looking daggers at me. He quickly got hold of himself, greeted Hank warmly, and off he went.

"Hank stood there looking very uncomfortable. In my infatuation with Hank, I had totally forgotten about DeCicco. It was the beginning of my relationship with Hank, and the end of DeCicco."

◆

David Marx and I had struck it rich in the investing business, and I did most of the work. When I went out to California the office was practically closed because David had to be at the toy company. Then I'd return after two or three weeks from visiting Mary Jo, and I'd get interested in picking out stocks. I didn't really know what I was doing. I traded by the seat of my pants; fortunately we were in a bull market and almost anything you bought went up. We really got to thinking we were very smart. When our lease was up at 580 Fifth Avenue our landlord refused to renew it; he wanted to move us to other quarters. I decided that since I was doing most of the work I might just as well do it for myself rather than move to another office and continue my partnership with David. So we split up, each taking half the stock. We repaid each other the $100,000 that was our original investment, and we divided another $1.6 million, and we remained good friends.

Mary Jo and I didn't get married right away because she was living in California and I was in New York raising my three kids. I would fly out to California at least three or four times a year, and she would come to New York once a year. We kept this up until we finally got married in 1966.

My kids were at school and spending more time with their mother, and I was newly married. We were living luxuriously in New York, and we'd usually go out to California every summer. In the winter we'd go to Palm Springs for a holiday. Life was just a bowl of cherries.

After numerous trips to California, Mary Jo asked if I would someday like to move there. She didn't have too many friends in New York, and she felt she would be happier in California. Finally I decided to sell the town house and make the move.

My daughter was now in boarding school in McLean, Virginia, outside of Washington, D.C., and she was living permanently with her mother. Stephen had gotten married the day after he graduated from Yale, and Glenn married subsequently. There was no reason for me to stay in New York.

In 1974 we bought a house in Beverly Hills, about half a mile up from Sunset Boulevard, just enough above the smog to get a little blue sky. We really enjoyed living up there. It wasn't a very big house, but it had almost an acre of grounds with a lot of trees. It was very private, and I think we got one of the best lots in Beverly Hills. I continued to invest in the stock market and I was doing pretty well. After the 1974 semicrash the market turned up again. I had no financial problems. I joined the Beverly Hills Tennis Club and spent most of my time playing tennis, and made a new circle of friends.

I also played regularly in the Dewars Celebrity Tennis Tournament. It was started back in 1971 when I was living in New York. The original tournament was held at the Concord Hotel in the Catskill Mountains and later was played in Las Vegas. They invited some thirty athletes from different sports—mostly active players—and I was invited to play as well. It was a singles tournament the first year and I won the title. As the years went by the tournament became more popular and a great many athletes were delighted to participate. Unfortunately it was held in June, which precluded any active baseball players from being invited. Primarily there were football players, basketball players, track and swimming stars. I became acquainted with seven or eight of the NFL football quarterbacks including Roger Staubach, Jim Plunkett, Jim Hart, and Kenny Anderson. There were basketball players like Earl Monroe, Rick Barry, and Julius Erving, who loved to play tennis.

I also played a lot of tennis with Bobby Riggs over the years, on his side and against him. He was always a winner. No matter what happened, he always managed to come out on top. He has lots of personality and used to play a beautiful game of tennis. He could make a tennis ball talk.

I was able to clip Bobby only once. I played him with two benches on his side of the court. He originally proposed to play me with two chairs in his court. If I hit a chair with the ball it was my point, and, of course, Bobby would have to run around the chairs to get the ball. I told him I wouldn't go for the chairs, but I would play him for $100 if he put two *benches* in his court. Bobby was so much better than I that he couldn't resist the bet. But I insisted on placing the benches myself. Well, the benches finally got to him, and he lost. But he was always a good sport and never complained on those rare occasions when he did lose.

I admire him greatly for his talent. He was one of the most talented tennis players in the world, but he was also one of the greatest con artists who ever lived. With his brains he could have made a living at anything, but he preferred to hustle and make a quick buck and give you a big smile.

For example, Bobby was a great basketball player in his day, with terrific touch. One of his "hustles" was to bet some unsuspecting sucker $20 that he could sink more free throws *blindfolded* than the other guy could with his eyes open. Bobby would regularly sink eight or nine out of ten while blindfolded and clipped many a person with that ploy. What those suckers didn't realize was that Bobby would practice shooting hundreds of free throws blindfolded. He was always looking for the edge.

He always made you feel like he was doing you a favor, even when he was taking your money.

◆

Mary Jo Greenberg remembered: "Hank went down to play in the Carl Reiner tennis tournament in La Costa. I think Hank donated $2,500 to be part of that. Charity. Exceptionally handicapped children. We were getting ready to drive back when Hank said let's go watch for a while. So we sat down and Hank pulled out a Chesterfield cigarette. And this big guy sitting next to him said, 'I wish you'd put the cigarette out.' And Hank said, 'It's a free country and we're outdoors.' So then the guy made some remark about it—we did not know he was a marine then—about who the hell do you think you are and just sitting anywhere you want. You're supposed to pay $5 for these seats. He did not know who Hank was or that Hank had donated $2,500 and could sit anywhere he wanted. He looked around forty-five. Hank was sixty-eight. I said to myself, Oh Christ. Well, one word led to another. The guy stood up and Hank stood up and Hank belted him in the stomach. The guy did not flinch. Then he knocked Hank back. Then everyone came over, including the security guards. Finally Hank and the guy shook hands. The guy went away. Hank had on a wonderful sports coat and, when he hit the guy in the stomach, he split his jacket. As we were driving home later I noticed that his hand had started to swell up. When Hank told the story later he said he punched the guy as hard as he could and broke his hand. Hank loved to tell that story.

"Hank went to some of these old-timers' baseball games. I think Bill Dickey said Hank was the worst-looking old-timer he'd ever seen. Williams would get a hit, Musial would get a hit, Hank would not get a hit. The last one we went to, at Dodger Stadium, he met me afterward in the press room. I had just seen him two hours before, and now he could barely walk. He said he'd never play in another old-timers' game. He said, 'I'm not going to make a fool of myself.' So that did it."

◆

When Roger Maris died, a number of writers called to ask what I remembered about him. They started out by asking what was the pressure like when I was going for the home-run record in 1938. They were trying to compare it to what it was like when Maris hit his 61 home runs. Of course, there was no comparison because of the change and growth of the national media.

Maris, coincidentally, was signed by Cleveland, and I was responsible for this. He came into Cleveland on the recommendation of one of our scouts. Roger had a scholarship to play football with one of the Midwest universities. He was a great athlete, a good football player. I worked him out in the field, and it was obvious then that here was somebody who could develop into a Major League ballplayer. He had a great, level swing; he was stocky; he could run fast; he had a good arm; he was a good fielder. I knew that this was the kind of talent that we were looking for to send to the minor leagues and hopefully come back in a year or so and play for the Indians. Sure enough, Maris did just that, and I had talked him into doing it. I had told his father that he'd be wasting time in college, that he wanted to be an athlete. If it was a choice between football and baseball, he'd be better off in baseball. At that time that was the case. They weren't paying big money in football yet. In any case, when he came up with Cleveland he was developing into quite a ballplayer. He was very aggressive on the base paths and always played hard. He was a very introverted, quiet kind of guy. He was just the kind of ballplayer you'd like to have eight of on a club.

When I left Cleveland, at the end of the 1957 season, Frank Lane came in. Lane had a reputation as a trader. He tried to trade everybody. Prior to that time Lee MacPhail, who was with the Yankees, asked me if I had any interest in letting Maris go to the Yankees. You'd have to be stupid not to see that Maris, who was a dead-pull hitter, would be perfect at Yankee Stadium. Nobody dreamed that he would hit 61 home runs, but still you knew that he would be a pretty dangerous hitter in Yankee Stadium. Everything he hit went right down the right-field line, and it was a short distance in the stadium. I said, "No, we aren't interested in trading him." But Lane came along and sent Maris to Kansas City. Kansas City was a virtual farm club for the Yankees, and it wasn't long before Roger went to New York.

Nineteen sixty-one was one of those freak years, similar to the year I hit my 58. Roger had a little encouragement with Mickey Mantle on the team. Mantle was right up there with him until the last couple of weeks of the season.

Everybody expected Mantle to break the record but, instead, Roger got off on a home-run-hitting spree at the right time and did it. I think the newspapermen were chagrined. They would rather have seen Mantle break the record. He had more personality. But that was too bad for the New York writers. I also believe it was wrong for Ford Frick, the commissioner, to even consider putting an asterisk next to the record. It should have been 61 home runs for Maris and that was it, regardless of whether Maris played a 162-game schedule and Babe Ruth a 154-game schedule.

I remember meeting Roger in a restaurant shortly after he broke the record. He had received a lot of notoriety and publicity and tried to avoid the press. He had had a real tough month, or maybe three weeks. From the time he was ahead of Mantle in the home-run derby, all the publicity centered on him. He wasn't accustomed to it and didn't know how to handle it. The press didn't help him. They were very belligerent. If you didn't cooperate the way they wanted you to, they got very hostile. Roger was the kind of guy who would put his head down and go the other way. I said, "Roger, try to loosen up a little bit and relax. Take advantage of the publicity. It can't do any harm. It's a bore and a pain in the neck, but it might mean something to you later on." I don't think Roger was able to do it at that time. I think later in life he was more relaxed and more mature, but at that time he was bullheaded, determined that nobody was going to tell him what to do. As a result I think he got a lot of unfavorable publicity after breaking Ruth's record—and I think he was glad to get out of New York. He had two more good seasons with St. Louis. Later he decided he had had enough of baseball and went into business and was extremely successful.

In looking back, I believe I have a lot to be proud of regarding my contributions to baseball besides my record on the field. I was responsible for revolutionizing the shape of the glove, not only the first baseman's glove—which I had enlarged and which some people ridiculed as a "fisherman's net"—but other gloves as well, and also the decision to take the equipment off the field rather than leave it on between innings. And I had a small part in changing the scoreboards, making them mechanical, and interesting, too, because they used to be dull, drab with no advertising, nothing except the numerals on the board. Today everybody is fighting to invent a different and more spectacular scoreboard. But more important than anything else is my contribution of a pension plan. I'm sure a pension plan would have come into existence whether I was there or not, but the fact remains that I was responsible for getting the players and the owners together—I represented the owners—and working out a pension plan. I came up with the 65–35 division of the spoils, 65 percent going to the owners and 35 percent going to the players. The split's been changed since then, but the players are still getting a fair percentage of the television and radio receipts from the World Series and the All-Star game, and that's what has made the pension plan not only successful but profitable as well.

I often think of how much the game has changed since I broke into baseball. Of course, the big change came about with the Messersmith case, which broke open free agency. Andy Messersmith was a pitcher for the Los Angeles Dodgers and he was holding out for more money. The Dodgers weren't going to pay him any more, so he went to a lawyer. The lawyer's interpretation of the contract was that if Messersmith did not sign the contract and went on to play for whatever the club paid him, he could, at the end of the season, ask for his unconditional release. This was revolutionary because the reserve clause had been a part of professional baseball almost from the beginning. And in 1922 the Supreme Court ruled that baseball was not a business but a sport and therefore owners had a right to retain their players because of the uniqueness of the game and how much it contributed to the national morale. They also permitted the clubs to retain possession of a player from year to year until such time as they decided to get rid of him.

Messersmith took the advice of Marvin Miller, executive director of the Players Union, and didn't sign a contract and continued to pitch for the Los Angeles Dodgers. At the end of the season he automatically claimed he was a free agent. It was taken to an arbitration board and Peter Seitz, the arbitrator, ruled in favor of the player. That opened up a whole new can of worms: It was the first time a player had been awarded his free agency and was not required to abide by the reserve clause.

A few years before that, in the 1960s, there was an outfielder by the name of Curt Flood who belonged to the St. Louis Cardinals. Curt played for St. Louis for thirteen years and one day in October of 1969 he got the kind of notice that I got years earlier, that his contract had been assigned to another club, the Philadelphia Phillies. This didn't sit too well with Curt, so he sued for his free agency. His case was handled by former Supreme Court Justice Arthur Goldberg. I was living in New York at the time, and I was contacted and asked if I would testify on Flood's behalf, and I agreed. Bill Veeck also agreed to testify for Flood.

I maintained that in my judgment the reserve clause was unfair. I had been a ballplayer, a club farm director, and a general manager as well as a club owner. I could understand Curt Flood's point of view—serving thirteen years with a club and then the management not having the decency to ask him what club he would like to go to or whether he would like to be a free agent, but automatically sending him to another club in the National League. I felt baseball should have got together at that point, and I suggested as much. The union was just under way, and Marvin Miller had been appointed to represent the players. He was new at the job and he wasn't looking for any trouble. He was certainly willing to negotiate a reasonable deal between the owners and the players. But the owners fought it in court, and won. The Court said it was up to Congress to change the 1922 Supreme Court ruling. But a few years later, when Seitz ruled for Messersmith, every player was eligible for free agency.

That created turmoil in the ranks, and the owners argued that baseball couldn't survive if every player could ask to be a free agent; they would be shifting around and it would destroy the game. The players, of course, were eager to continue playing, so they came up with a new formula. A player had to be in the Major Leagues for six years and be with a club a certain length of time before he could ask for his free agency. In recent years you can see how many great players have shifted from one club to another so that today there is no real player loyalty in baseball as there was when I played. When I joined the Tigers, that was my team. Every other club was an alien club and an enemy. I couldn't conceive of playing for any other team in the American League, much less going to the National League.

Now, of course, players automatically declare themselves free agents. Then the clubs with money bid for them, and that's how George Steinbrenner got players like Catfish Hunter and Reggie Jackson. He didn't develop them on his own in his farm system, he just plucked them off the other teams' rosters by offering them more money. That opened the floodgates, and the salaries became outrageous compared to what we were paid. Today, some of the players are getting $2 million a year and others are getting lifetime contracts. Not only that, but now the agent who represents the players comes in with all sorts of proposals in order to earn his fee. Agents demanded a no-trade clause, or you could pick the club you want to be traded to, and you were entitled to a car and an apartment in the city you were going to play in. The owners were forced to give in to their demands. We've had two players' strikes in recent years and, in both instances, the owners weakened and gave in, and the players stuck together as a union and refused to compromise their position. They came away with the bulk of their requests, and so today the shoe is on the other foot. The players are telling the owners what to do, and the owners are screaming bloody murder. They're still making money, but not as much as they would like to.

I was considered the highest-paid ballplayer from 1938 to 1947. Prior to that Babe Ruth received something like $80,000 a year back in the thirties. When I added up all my earnings as a ballplayer, from 1930 to 1947, it amazed me that my total salaries for my years in the Major Leagues were $447,000. That included bonuses that I had earned, but basically that's what I was paid for my seventeen years of service. Of course, I spent four of those years in the army.

Having participated in four World Series, two on the winning side and two on the losing side, I came up with $24,600 in World Series shares. I remember 1935 particularly. When we beat the Cubs in the Series we got a winning share of a little over $8,000, and at that time it was a record for World Series payouts. The year prior to that we finished second to the Cardinals and we got $3,300 for our losing share. That was big money in those days and we found no fault with it. So adding in my World Series shares, my total income from my baseball activities—salaries, bonuses, and World Series shares—was $447,950. At the time it seemed a princely sum, and I managed to save something like $300,000.

I am certain that there weren't too many ballplayers who could retire on their baseball earnings; even those who went back to little farm towns probably saved $40,000 or less over their careers. Back then it wasn't easy to get by on even that amount if you didn't find some new line of work. That's the reason so many ballplayers died broke. They didn't make enough to save any money, and they mistakenly figured that baseball would go on forever.

They spent their money as freely as they earned it and when they got through playing baseball, they were penniless. Unfortunately that was the case with a fantastic number of greats. I remember when Joe Cronin and I went into the Hall of Fame in 1956, all we were given as a token for having earned that great honor was a photograph of the bust they put up in Cooperstown. I couldn't understand why we didn't get a replica of the bust, and the president of the Hall of Fame told me, "We can't do that. If we gave out these replica busts, some of them would wind up in pawn shops or a barber shop, having been sold because the recipients were broke and needed the money."

CHAPTER 16

People have asked me many times how anti-Semitism affected me during my career. They all assumed that it was a terrific burden. I answered honestly that I found it to be a big help. Many times during a long 154-game season, especially in the dog days of August, you had an inclination to kind of drag a little bit. Whenever I was having a bad day, even in Detroit, somebody would yell out from the stands, "Come on, you big Jew, can't you do better than that?" Or something to that effect. It would always hit me like a cold shower. It would make me angry, but it would also put me on my toes again. Just *anticipating* a barb from the stands did the same thing.

I got a call recently from an acquaintance in Detroit. He had been after me to come to Detroit because they were having a Jewish Hall of Fame dinner and they wanted to honor me. I've been elected to the Baseball Hall of Fame. I've been elected to the State of Michigan Hall of Fame. I've been elected to the Texas Hall of Fame. I've been elected to the Jewish Hall of Fame, and now they want to have a Detroit Jewish Hall of Fame. I've always thought it was peculiar that they insist on having a Jewish Hall of Fame. I'm not aware of a Dutch Hall of Fame or an Italian Hall of Fame or a Polish Hall of Fame. Usually a ballplayer is in the Hall of Fame for the state or city he represents. I guess there are so few Jewish athletes that people are particularly proud of the ones there are. I was always called a Jewish ballplayer and a Jewish hitter and Jewish this and that, not just a ballplayer like everybody else. The other ballplayers weren't segregated by their religion. I could never fully understand this tenaciousness of the Jewish fans who followed my career in the thirties. Their standard comment was that they followed the game only because my name was Hank Greenberg and I was Jewish.

My parents came over from Romania as kids, and their religious training was important to them. They read Hebrew fluently. The trouble was that their kids didn't understand Hebrew. Jewish kids always spoke Yiddish. When it came to Hebrew, we couldn't write it or understand when it was spoken. Whenever we went to the synagogue for the high holy days, the rabbi spoke in Hebrew. We sat there like dummies. We were young, and they were up there talking and we didn't understand one word they were saying. Nobody explained it to us, so we came away not knowing what the service was all about.

When we were thirteen and were bar mitzvahed, there was a ceremony we had to perform.

Since we didn't know Hebrew, the synagogue had to have a rabbi teach us the words. The rabbi didn't speak English well, so he could teach us the words in Hebrew but could not explain anything. There we were, parroting words without any knowledge of what we were saying and what the occasion meant. When I finished my bar mitzvah, I didn't know any more about the Jewish religion than before. As a result, when I got older, I asked myself what it all meant. The old-timers were talking in Hebrew, and my father spoke and wrote Hebrew, but he never bothered to explain any of it. He picked up enough English to cope with his daily life, and he was busy working every day, taking care of four kids and keeping the house in order. Looking back now as an old man I can't understand how they could expect the young people to follow the Jewish religion when they couldn't speak the language.

Out in the world we were the minority; only when you were in the Bronx, where everybody else was Jewish, were you in your own environment. When I was eighteen and started to play ball, there were very few Jewish ballplayers. And I was really the only prominent one. I got to thinking about what it meant, and how to explain it, if there was any way to explain it. The older I got, the more I realized I didn't have much contact with the Jewish religion except that I was Jewish. I had begun drawing away from it even as a boy. Now they have reform temples where they say the prayers in English, so at least the kids can understand the words. I've looked at a lot of prayer books, and even after you understand the words, you don't know what they're talking about. It's a big thing now to be proud of your religion. I've read all about history, how religion has created hatred and animosity between people, and has caused death and wars, yet so many people believe in something. I don't know whether it's the fear of the unknown or what. Meanwhile people are fighting wars and killing each other. Today you don't need a reason; it's enough that you don't speak the same language. Yet even people from the same country are annihilating each other. We're seeing it now in so many parts of the world—Nicaragua, the Philippines, Afghanistan. You can understand the Depression, when people didn't have enough food for their families. They were out on the streets and there were protest marches and things like that. That grew out of a desire for some kind of standard of living. Too many people still don't have what they want, and the only way they think they can get what they want is through crime—stealing, selling drugs.

It befuddles me, this religion matter. Instead of bringing people together and teaching them how to love and understand each other, religion seems to have had just the opposite effect. It has torn people apart and created nothing but death and destruction.

After I came back from the war and worked as a general manager and was known among the owners and the more successful businessmen in the Cleveland community, I came in contact with anti-Semitism. In many situations I had the feeling that had I not been Jewish I would have been accepted, but instead the door was shut to me.

I've been invited to many athletic clubs that are restricted. They let in a token Jew or two, and then think they are very liberal. I realized that I would be "passing" in that environment, and I never joined any of those clubs. Surprisingly enough, when I joined predominantly Jewish clubs, I found them just as prejudiced against other religions as other people are against the Jews. It's hard for me to understand. Here are people claiming that they are being discriminated against and segregated and they are just as prejudiced and just as anti as the other religions.

If there really was a true religion, it should bring people together, or at least that's what I've always thought. God loves everybody and we're all the children of God. As a matter of fact, at an early age I took the Ten Commandments as my code of living. I'm satisfied that I've tried to live up to the Ten Commandments, and I have no guilty conscience in any respect. I realize that I've had a very fortunate life and never had any money problems and, for the most part, few health problems, all of which made it easy to abide by the Commandments, whereas other people might have been tempted to overlook one or two.

I might add that even though I don't attend synagogue very often, I contribute most of my money to Jewish causes, and I just assume that the Catholics help their causes, and the Protestants theirs, and therefore the Jews should make an attempt to help their own people.

The man with nine lives, my friend Bill Veeck, died on January 2, 1986. He had been operated on over thirty times and the incredible thing about him was his spirit. He never complained, he was never down, he was always cheerful and optimistic and friendly. He wouldn't permit his handicap to dampen his spirit and enthusiasm for living. He never exploited it. In fact, he turned it around and tried to make it an asset. Instead of feeling sorry for him, people were always applauding him for his courage.

There are so many things to be said about Bill Veeck besides his having been the head of three Major League teams (Chicago twice, Cleveland once, and the St. Louis Browns), and that he set attendance records in all three cities, records that stood for many years. Or that he brought in a midget to bat. It's not just that he was the one who revolutionized scoreboards by introducing the exploding scoreboard in Chicago in 1959, and invented bat night and ball night and cap night and glove night. It isn't just that he introduced fan appreciation night so that the fans who came to the park would be honored instead of vice versa. It isn't just that he was the first one to put names on the back of the uniforms so the fans who didn't buy scorecards could still identify the players on the field. Nor that he broke the color line in the American League by bringing in Larry Doby. None of those things made Bill Veeck outstanding to me—it was all the other things about him that people who didn't know him couldn't appreciate.

I've always thought that someday I would have the honor of extolling Bill's virtues at Cooperstown when he was inducted into the Hall of Fame. I was planning on it; I was preparing for it. I was so eager to tell, not only the baseball world but the world in general, what an unusual man he was.

When I first met him back in 1947 he was talking to me about the Indians. I thought he was talking about the ball club, but no, he was talking about the American Indians who were treated so badly by the U.S. government. He was very concerned about them and what a shabby deal they had gotten. He loved them. He collected Indian artifacts long before anybody thought about collecting things the Indians made.

Funny thing about Bill, he could watch television, read a book, and carry on a conversation on the phone all at the same time. He had that kind of concentration and he had terrific peripheral vision. He read five or six books a week; he marched to the beat of a different drummer. He was an athlete in school in his younger days. He was a great swimmer and played tennis; he was an author and book reviewer; he was a horticulturist and had his own hothouse and grew his own flowers. He would go out and buy old furniture and refinish it. He knew all about swimming and about fish. He was a dog fancier and a horse lover. I don't know anything he *wasn't*. He was a radio and television performer. Once

THE STORY OF MY LIFE

in Cleveland he starred on the stage in *The Man Who Came to Dinner*. And he was good for an amateur. He didn't get a Tony, but he lasted out the week. It was a one-week performance and he did a good job. He was the only man I knew who could drink a case of sparkling burgundy and still look as if he hadn't taken a drink. He could work for twenty hours a day, sleep for four hours, and his generator would be recharged, his eyes would be bright; his eyes were never bloodshot, he was always ready to go. I never saw a man with that kind of energy.

They tell me that he had a record for attending prep schools and never graduating, so I guess he was Peck's Bad Boy before I knew him. But when I knew him he was a tax expert, he was a lawyer, he was a politician. He could charm anybody. The only person he could not charm was Chuck Comiskey. He could charm every bartender, every taxicab driver, every fan on the street, but he wouldn't try with Comiskey. When he bought the team in 1975 for the second time, he was able to raise $8 million from his hotel room. He never showed a balance sheet, and he didn't have a .300 hitter on the team. But he had friends and people had confidence in him. People enjoyed being around him. Bill called everyone by their proper names. He insisted that his first name was Bill. He hadn't worn a tie in the last thirty years that I knew him. (As a matter of fact, he was the only man I knew who didn't go to the Kennedy inaugural when he was invited because he didn't want to wear a tie.) He had the good fortune and good judgment to marry Mary Frances, who was the perfect wife and perfect mother. She understood him, and they had a romantic, loving relationship.

I haven't talked about Bill Veeck the romantic, and he was a romantic in many ways. Years ago, when he was single, he was enamored of a young dancer. At one point she was traveling from New York to Los Angeles on the train, the 20th-Century Limited, and the train made frequent stops. (In fact, you had to change in Chicago and spend the night.) Anyway, Bill had a florist meet the train at every stop and deliver a basket of roses to this young lady. When she finally arrived at the California station, it looked like she came with a flower shop. But that was Bill's idea of charming a lady.

259

CHAPTER 17

All through my life I have been in fairly decent shape and in relatively good health. I had one operation on my elbow back in 1947, but since then I had been exercising regularly and eating well and sleeping well and hadn't had any problems physically. Suddenly, in October 1984, I came up with a disease that they could name but couldn't cure. My doctor sent me to Dr. Ronald Andiman at Cedars-Sinai. I had been having increasingly severe back and leg spasms and my doctors were hard pressed to diagnose the problem and treat it. Dr. Andiman put me through one of those tests where they put a needle into your muscles and it registers on a machine and it tells you how much response you have. Then he put a shock apparatus on various parts of my legs to see what the responses were. After he got through, he said, "I think you have peripheral neuropathy." I said, "Well, what do I do about it?" He said, "One thing you can do is to go to a specialist and they'll take a piece out of your leg or cut a little piece of the nerve. It wouldn't be too painful or harmful." I said, "Then what happens after they take part of the nerve out of my leg?" His comment was, "Well, then they'd find out if you really have peripheral neuropathy." I asked him what they could do about it, and he said that they couldn't do anything about it, but they'd know for sure that that was what I had.

So you can see what kind of a dilemma I was in. My other doctors had told me they thought I had arthritis and stenosis, and that they could operate on me and cure it to a certain extent. They would not guarantee anything. In fact, Dr. Charles Carton was very hesitant about the operation. I went back to see him three or four times, and he never said, "Yes, I can operate and cure you and take care of your peripheral neuropathy." So that left me in a quandary. I figured that as long as I was going to undergo an operation, I might as well see

Dr. Edgar Dawson, who performed surgery at UCLA, and he recommended that I have the operation.

But a strange thing happened just before we left Dr. Dawson's office. I told Dr. Dawson that I had had this pain in my groin for about three weeks. I said, "It's just like a groin pull. I've had groin pulls frequently in the past, but usually they go away in three or four days. This is severe pain, and it bothers me whenever I twist my leg or try to walk. It's very annoying." He said, "You know, I once had a patient who had a pain in his leg and we operated on his back. After the operation was performed, he still complained of pain. We decided to do a bone scan and we found out what his real problem was." So he suggested that I go back to Cedars-Sinai and get a bone scan. During this period I had been going through all kinds of tests. Everything seemed to come out okay, except that I was feeling terrible. They took the bone scan, and sure enough it showed that I had two little spots in my right leg. All the other tests were okay, so they couldn't find any reason for me to be having pain except that I had had a severe attack of gout prior to this incident. However, they recommended that I go back and have more X-rays. The urologist, Dr. Norman Nemoy, put me through a different set of tests. He examined my kidneys, and found a tumor in one of them.

The two spots in my right leg had come from that tumor. I was told it was cancer. An immediate operation was recommended. By this time I was feeling miserable and confused. I had been deciding for almost a year whether or not to have a back operation that would cure my problems, and now I was a victim of cancer. No one in my family had ever had cancer. My dad had lived to the ripe old age of eighty-five, and my mother died of a heart attack during an operation for her gallstones. My brothers and sister had never had any trace of cancer, but here I was, supposedly the most athletic and best conditioned in the family, and I had this dreaded disease.

♦

Stephen Greenberg recalled:

"My wife and I had gone to Europe on vacation in August 1985; while there we received a phone call from Mary Jo. She said that they had found a tumor on Dad's kidney; it was malignant and they were going to operate. We flew right home.

"I went up to his house the day after we got back. The surgery was scheduled for the following week. Mary Jo left the house; she sensed that Dad wanted to be alone with me. It was the first time I ever remember seeing him cry. Boy, did that shake me. He just started crying. He told me he wanted to get things in order and some-one had to revise the will, and then he just started to cry. He said, 'I can't believe this is happening, I never thought this would happen to me. I just can't believe it.'

"He was seventy-five years old, after all, and he had a couple of minor scares. He had always made light of any physical problems. He had a heart arrhythmia that he was taking medication for, and until Mary Jo really came down on him he would skip his medication periodically. He felt he didn't need it. And if you asked him, when he was seventy-two or seventy-three, 'Hank, how do you think you're going to die, and when?' I'm sure he would have told you, 'Maybe when I'm eighty-five. I suppose I'll go to sleep one night and not wake up. Die of old age.' He still saw himself as a power hitter.

"After the diagnosis and after the surgery when they removed his whole kidney and the tumor he was still confident, I think. He used to lie there after his surgery and do exercises for his upper body. When he got sick he (a) couldn't believe it, (b) felt betrayed by that part of him that had always been his strength, (c) was embar-rassed by the illness, and (d) thought he was going to beat it. I think it was a com-bination of those things that made him so secretive. I think a part of him was really looking forward to the day a year later, or whenever the doctors said he had an absolutely clean bill of health. You can go out and play tennis. You still have a bad back, but you're healthy. It would have been as if he'd never had this thing. At that point I think he was relishing being able to say to people, This is what I've just been through, no big deal."

On the morning of August 21, 1985, the day Greenberg was scheduled to go into the hospital to have his kidney removed, he sat at his desk in the office of his home and wrote a few letters. One was to Mary Jo and one to Stephen.

He handed Mary Jo the letter. "For you," he said. She sensed that it was some-thing very personal, and felt that she simply couldn't open it and read the contents. Not now. When she drove Hank to make some transactions before going to the hos-pital, she went to her bank vault and placed the letter in it. She left it there, with-out opening it, for more than a year.

Stephen Greenberg continued:

"I think there was that part of my dad that really felt he was invincible. I can remember now how, when I was a little kid, he used to talk to me about the impor-tance of physical exercise, building up your body, playing different sports.

"I'm sure he felt that during his playing days there was no one bigger, stronger than he was. And part of it was a con job. He admitted that when he took three bats to the on-deck circle—most players would take only two—and twirled them around as he walked up to home plate and then threw two away, a part of that was to psych the pitcher. But part of that was to psych himself—what an ox I am! I guarantee you that of the 331 home runs he hit, probably 70 percent of them were against pitchers who would be looking and noticing the swinging of those three bats. But he really came to feel that his body—and by that I mean physical strength, his physical prowess—was what carried him to the Hall of Fame and beyond. To a great extent the success he had on the ball field was a sort of springboard for him psychologically and in a lot of other ways. So when he was faced with cancer he couldn't believe it. He couldn't believe that his body had let him down.

"Before the surgery he could barely move. He had a nauseated, burning sensation in his stomach every time he tried to eat. It permeated his chest to the point where he would gag if he ate. When they took the tumor out, I think it alleviated that immediate sensation of nausea so he just felt a lot better. He lost weight in the hospital after the surgery, which is natural. And then he started eating better and he sensed he was the athlete again. He was training for his next big event, which was recuperating from cancer. And he was determined in the way he approached his meals. You could tell that a lot of times he wasn't really hungry, but he would make himself eat.

"Every week he would go to the doctor for that weigh-in like a football player. He didn't want to cheat, so he would always take his belt off and his shoes and he wore the same outfit every time because he wanted a consistent weigh-in on the same scale with the same pants. He had the ugliest double-knit pants, but he used to wear them, I think because they were comfortable. His weight started creeping up and we all felt he was improving. He gained a lot of weight. He was about 190 right after the surgery and then he got up to 215.

"During that period of time I think he was confident he would beat it. After one of the visits to the doctor following the surgery he started to leave, and he passed another examining room and the door was open. Another patient, a black gentleman about sixty-five or seventy years of age, was sitting on the table waiting for the doctor. Just then the doctor came running out and said, 'Hank, wait a minute.' He took us aside. 'It just occurred to me, did you see that gentleman in the next office waiting to be examined when you walked by?' Dad said yes. 'I just wanted to let you know that he had a kidney tumor removed eight years ago. I just wanted to let you know that.' Dad's reaction was not, Gee, that's great, he's still around and looks like he was doing pretty well eight years later. His reaction was, 'You mean it's eight years and you haven't cured him yet?'

"Four months later he felt pretty good, he was going out, really getting back into the swing of things. On New Year's Eve he was with Mary Jo and friends and they were up till two in the morning. I think he was feeling pretty confident."

Mary Jo Greenberg:

"Over the years, New Year's Eve had become very special for Hank and me and a few close friends. We celebrated two things, the start of the New Year and Hank's birthday. As New Year's Eve 1985 approached, I knew our friends were waiting for the invitation, and the mounds of laughter, good food, and champagne. I kept them at bay by saying Hank's back was acting up terribly. I was trying to decide if Hank could last through the evening. If he excused himself around ten o'clock, his charade would have been over. And I was concerned about myself. Could I handle it emotionally? I was reaching physical and mental exhaustion. I knew in my heart this was to be our last celebration, although I was fighting it fiercely. When midnight came and 'Auld Lang Syne' and all the kisses, would I fall apart? I didn't.

"The guests arrived at nine, and Hank, with that inner strength and determination, dressed himself up and looked like a million bucks. One of my last memories of the evening was Hank holding court at two in the morning, and one by one everyone was nodding off. They all left our home thinking that there was not much wrong with Hank, just his bothersome back."

Stephen Greenberg:

"He was adamant that no one know about his illness. And so we all had to concoct ridiculous stories for where he was and when and why. I'm sure a lot of people out there suspected something. Glenn came for the surgery, so he knew from the beginning. And my sister knew from the beginning. We were tight-lipped people so word didn't get around. And in retrospect, Dad being such a private person especially regarding his health, it may have been for the best. I think he would have been devastated early on if he had picked up the paper one day and saw that he was in the news for having experimental cancer treatment, as was the case with Roger Maris. It turned out that people from the lab in Tennessee where Maris was being treated were trying the same antibody procedure for Dad. Dad read the paper when he was feeling reasonably good and didn't want to read—and the whole world to read—about his cancer treatment.

"The countervailing argument is that he was a person who loved to have atten-tion lavished on him for positive things he'd done. I think part of him would have been much happier if everybody had known and been able to express to him during those months when he did feel pretty good, just how special they thought he was. There were people that he would have liked to have seen on his own terms. But he didn't want sympathy.

"Dad happened to be feeling healthier at the time Maris died. He commented about the memorial for Roger, and was impressed that so many people showed up. And he commented on how Steinbrenner had orchestrated the memorial. He thought that it was nice for Roger but it was typical of Steinbrenner to be the guy at the center of the action."

◆

When you get married you never really know what's going to happen to your marriage. You try your best and hope that it will strengthen as the years go by. I'm the luckiest man in the world to have Mary Jo as my wife. I've never found anyone so devoted and so caring and so willing to put up with me. She's been a jewel, cooking me three meals a day, every day, nothing but encouragement and smiles from her. Meanwhile it breaks my heart to see her as worried as she is, losing a lot of sleep over my condition, using up her energy in the hopes of doing something for me. It's been a twenty-four-hour-a-day job for her. It's brought tears to my eyes many times to see her and know what she's going through. They say it's not only the patient but the people close to them who have to share the grief and the pain. Since I've come out of the hospital we've never told anybody. I've been staying home ever since I was released from the hospital [on August 29]. I haven't gone out except to visit the doctor. The people at the tennis club have been calling, wondering what's happened to me. Before the operation I used to play tennis almost every day. You can imagine how many calls I've had and how many times I was invited out to dinner and par-ties and different things. We've had to cancel all our social obligations, and my wife is the one who had to bear the brunt of that. She's had to tell friends in from New York that I went to Carmel to visit and she told people at the club that I went to New York; it's been a real charade. Naturally, we're not eager to have the press get hold of the news, because then I would be deluged with phone calls.

◆

At this point Greenberg, who had been dictating random parts of his life story into a tape recorder while sitting by the pool at his home in Beverly Hills, began to relate this new crisis that absorbed his days.

◆

Yesterday, December 17, I went to have my second bone scan since the operation. The last one I had was taken on October 2, which was about six weeks after my operation, and they asked me to wait about ten weeks before the next one. Yesterday, I had the second bone scan and was delightfully surprised when the doctor called me and told me that the results were exceptionally good. He thought that the tumors were shrinking a little; at least they weren't spreading. He was very enthusiastic about the results of the bone scan. So that gives me something to be thankful for at this moment.

February 10. I went again to see Dr. Larry Heifetz, a cancer specialist. He seems to feel that I'm showing improvement in my overall condition. I tend to agree with him. I'm getting stronger and gaining weight. I couldn't weigh myself yesterday, but I just feel generally stronger. I still have the pain in the hip, whether it's coming from the tumor or whether it's coming from my back condition, I don't really know. My stomach seems to have improved considerably. I still have one little knot on the side where the operation was performed, but overall I'm being well fed. I think I'm back up to 204 or 205, considering I got down to about 190. I'm starting to use dumbbells and working out with them. My chest is filling out. I still have a long way to go. If I ever get back my full strength, then I still have to face the fact that my back pain will not go away, and I'll have to decide about the back operation.

I do have spells of nausea from time to time and I still have that pain in my hip—it's no fun living with constant pain. I'm going to give it my best shot, not only for myself but for Mary Jo, who's been my nurse twenty-four hours a day, always encouraging and willing to do anything to please me. That in itself has been a great reward, even though I've been going through this terrible ordeal.

A strange thing happened on Saturday, May 30. I woke up in the middle of the night and I felt so good that I stretched my legs really hard, just like you might do after a hard day on the tennis court and all the muscles are kind of tight. When I woke up in the morning I had pulled the groin muscles in my right leg. I could hardly stand even with the crutches. My whole leg was knotted up and cramped, and the bone in my hip was painful. I went up to see Dr. Heifetz, and he suggested that I go for another bone scan, which I did on Friday, June 5.

They took a bone scan of my entire body, which takes about an hour. First they inject some kind of dye into the bloodstream which collects wherever there is a sign of disease. You have to wait two hours and drink a lot of water. Finally, you come back and they put you on the table and X-ray you. I had to lie on my back for damn near an hour and the bone in my back ached so terribly I could hardly stand it. My right leg was numb; I couldn't feel anything in either leg for that matter. Dr. Waxman came in after the X rays were taken; he took me into his office and said that there wasn't much change in my condition. He verified that the tumor was showing a little sign of scarring, but not enough to render me painless in the back. I was a terrible mess on Friday. I took some pain pills and came home and tried to get comfortable and let the pain in the bone subside. I put the heating pad on my back and somehow or other I finally got to sleep.

Today [Saturday] I feel a lot better. At least I'm not aching. I'm not going to do anything; I'm just going to sit outside and relax and try to get the pressure off that bone. I'd be happy if I could walk from the car to the restaurant and sit down and have dinner and not feel too uncomfortable. Those are big privileges now. I don't take too many things for granted anymore. If I can get back to doing that, it will be very helpful because it will give me a change of pace rather than sitting here all day long. The strange thing is that last Saturday, the same day that I pulled my leg muscles, I got up in the morning and said to Mary Jo, "I can't see out of my right eye." My eye had been bothering me a little bit, and I thought I had an eyelash or something in it. I washed my eye out, but it seemed to be getting worse. Turns out I have a cataract. Now I have to start seeing an eye doctor. When the machinery starts to fall apart, everything seems to disintegrate at the same time.

June 12: I went back to Cedars-Sinai and had a brain scan. For some reason I thought I would be lying on my stomach, but I was lying on my back for about an hour. Naturally, lying on that hard table irritated my back, and I was in terrible shape when I came home. The good news was that the brain scan was okay. I was going to tell them that I was like Dizzy Dean back in 1934 when we played in the World Series. They put Dean in to run for somebody, and when a ground ball was hit and the shortstop touched the base and threw the ball, Dean didn't slide, and the ball hit him right in the head. They took him to the hospital and gave him an X ray. The next morning the headline in the paper said, DEAN'S HEAD X-RAYED; SHOWED NOTHING. I guess that's like me, the X ray showed nothing.

Monday, June 16: The doctor suggested a booster radiation treatment. I have my fingers crossed that this might be the solution to my problem because they're concentrating on the tumor. Maybe this time they'll find a solution to the problems I've been having.

◆

Greenberg struggled on, suffering excruciating pain, still seeing doctors, hobbling on crutches, and hoping, *expecting* to return to health. Mary Jo drove him wherever he needed to go, waited on him, cooked for him, filled his huge coffee cup (he liked big things, except for small onions in his martini), and encouraged him to try to stay strong. Greenberg spoke with his children, and Stephen came over, and Rex Kennamer, and Hank would sit and chat.

Hank's condition worsened. By August of 1986 he was living on medication, confined to his bed, and had nurses, as Mary Jo recalled, "around the clock."

His life was slipping away. At 8:50 on Thursday morning, September 4, 1986, Henry Benjamin Greenberg, at age 75, died in his sleep.

When news of Greenberg's death was made public, the response from around the country was remarkable.

In a press box in Fenway Park, while broadcasting a Mets–Red Sox exhibition game, Ralph Kiner was handed a brief news release. He turned to Tim McCarver, his broadcasting partner, and said into the microphone, "This is the worst day of my life. My dearest friend, and the man who was like a father to me, Hank Greenberg, has died."

Joe Altobelli, then a coach with the Yankees and a former manager of the Baltimore Orioles and most recently a coach with the Chicago Cubs, had grown up in Detroit. He recalled to a friend that Hank "was an awful lot of ballplayer, a hero of incredible dimension in Detroit." Joe's father, who worked for the bus company, had cut out a large picture of Greenberg from a newspaper, framed it, and hung it, recalled Altobelli, "over the door of our main room—the kitchen. It was in the place of honor in our home."

Greenberg's death was reported on the network television news.

In the *Detroit News* several pages were devoted to the death of Greenberg. And it printed letters from fans in "A Tribute."

One letter was from Lorna Dodd of Ypsilanti, Michigan. She wrote:

"Jimmy K. was a fifth grader in my Sunday school class in Presbyterian church years ago. Like most boys of that age, he would rather tease girls, make faces, giggle and generally be obnoxious than listen to the lesson. One morning, though, he heard me say something about Jesus being a Jew. He blurted out, 'You mean like Hank Greenberg?' 'Yes,' I said. 'Oh, wow!' he replied.

"After that, Jimmy was more interested in the Sunday school lessons. I had an easier time teaching because Hank Greenberg was a Jew. . . ."

Another was from Ben Rose of Southfield:

"The fondest memory that I have of Hank Greenberg was the time the Tigers paid for the United Hebrew Schools to see a game. It must have been about 1940. In about the seventh inning Hank came lumbering out to left field as usual and my friend, Joe, as a joke, yelled to him in Yiddish that he was hungry. Hank turned around and called to the peanut vendor and told him to give us a box of peanuts and charge it to him."

Peggy Rossiter of Royal Oak remembered Greenberg at the "packed" Eastwood Gardens in Detroit, "on a summer night in 1937 or '38" when her date and she "were dancing under the stars to the music of Tommy Dorsey." Her date noticed that Hank Greenberg was there and suggested she go over and ask for his autograph. She did, and he signed his name, saying to her, "Hey, you look just like Claudette Colbert." She would recall, "It was a lovely compliment, and I have to smile whenever I think of him."

And Jack Poole of Warren recalled that "the bigots came to taunt him because he was a Jew," and Greenberg "silenced the boos" with "mighty blows."

On November 16, 1986, at 5:00 P.M. on a gentle Los Angeles evening, a quiet memorial service was held for Greenberg at the Wadsworth Theater. About three hundred people attended, including friends, family, a scattering of fans who wished to pay last respects, and some old ballplayer associates, like Bob Lemon, who lived nearby.

The small program included a postcard from the National Baseball Hall of Fame & Museum depicting Greenberg's Hall of Fame plaque, and the program included Edgar A. Guest's poem from 1934, "Speaking of Greenberg," about the Yom Kippur game that he sat out, and which concluded with the now ironic lines:

We shall miss him on the infield and shall miss him at the bat,

But he's true to his religion—and I honor him for that!

The program also listed the five speakers: Ralph Kiner, Walter Matthau, Dr. Rexford Kennamer, Anne Taylor Fleming, and Stephen Greenberg.

Ralph Kiner spoke first:

"Hank was the type of person that would give his time freely, who would help anybody. In those days of baseball the stars never talked to anyone, and if you were a rookie you never got a chance to get in the batting cage unless one of the regulars invited you in. But Hank was the type of person who would invite anybody else in. And from that time on we became very close. . . . If you knew Hank, and if he liked you, he would really needle you. He was one of the great needlers of all time.

"We roomed together many times and he was constantly trying to help me along. He taught me more about how to live, how to live the right way. There has never been anyone with his class and there never will be anyone with his class in baseball. He was a great owner. He fought for the ballplayers after he became an owner . . . and, with me and with Allie Reynolds, who were the National League and American League representatives, we set up the pension plan. Hank was so honest and so great. I can't tell you how many people he has helped where no one ever knew about it. He was the biggest contributor to the baseball fund for old-time ballplayers that are not in the pension plan. He did all these things but wanted no praise for it. He was the man who in 1938 hit 58 home runs, more than any right-handed batter, which is more of an accomplishment than the 61 Roger Maris had or the 60 that Babe Ruth had because they had much shorter fences in right field to hit at. But Hank did all this in the tough parks, hitting into left field. He never complained about that. He also hit 183 RBIs one season, one short of the all-time record held by Lou Gehrig. And for a right-handed batter that's a feat that no one will ever touch. All these things were there but they're not the important things, because Hank Greenberg was a man that, if you were fortunate enough to be around, you never forgot him. He was a great leader and a great example for all of us. I want to thank the Lord that He gave me a chance to be with Hank."

Walter Matthau:

"There is a story that James Mason was walking around Dublin a couple of years before he died and some lady came over to him and said, 'Excuse me, would you be James Mason in his later years?' Hank Greenberg wanted me to play him as he was in his later years. He said, 'You can't play me as a ballplayer. You don't walk right. You got a funny walk.'

"When I was growing up on the Lower East Side of Manhattan in New York City, my idol was Hank Greenberg. Greenberg for me put a stop to the perpetuation of the myth at the time that all Jews wound up as cutters or pants pressers. Or, if they were lucky, salesmen in the garment center. Well, I identify very strongly with Hank. He was six foot four, Jewish, and an athlete. I was six foot three, Jewish, and I wanted to be an athlete. I thought, now there's Hank Greenberg amongst all those ferocious, skilled, tough, tobacco-chewing, cursing, and spitting ballplayers who were the best in the world. Other professional sports did not hold the same esteemed niche that baseball did for the kids in the ghettos and the farms of America. The sports pages were full of stories about Hank. And how could I forget that famous picture of the four infielders kneeling on their bats? Billy Rogell, Marv Owen, Charlie Gehringer, and Hank. Of course, Hank kneeling still looked like a giant. That was the infield, by the way, that batted in 463 runs. I think that record still stands. He looked like a giant kneeling on his bat and this image was reinforced when he came down to a settlement house I used to attend on the Lower East Side of New York called the Emanuel Brotherhood. He came down to play some basketball for a fund-raiser. They had a dance and a basketball game. I used to describe Hank's arms as looking like steel cables on a bridge. Well, that's how they looked to me. When you're running around in the jungle of the ghetto on the Lower East Side you couldn't help but be exhilarated by the sight of one of our guys looking like a Colossus. He eliminated for me all those jokes which start out: Did you hear the one about the little Jewish gentleman?

"For thirty years I told a story which I read in the newspapers, about Hank Greenberg at a port of embarkation during World War II. The story had it that there was a soldier who had had a little too much to drink, and he was weaving around all the soldiers sitting there. He was quite a big fella. And he said in a very loud voice, 'Anybody here named Goldberg or Ginsburg? I'll kick the livin' daylights out of him.' Or words to that effect. Hank had been sitting on his helmet, and he stood up and said, 'My name is Greenberg, soldier.' The soldier looked at him from head to foot and said, 'Well, I said nothin' about Greenberg, I said Goldberg or Ginsburg.' I told this to Hank when I met him at the club. He said it never happened. I told him I didn't care to hear that. I was going to continue to tell that story because I liked it. He said, 'Okay, whatever you say, Walter.'

"I'm a member of the Beverly Hills Tennis Club, which is where I met Hank. I don't play tennis, I just have lunch there. The only reason I joined the club—and it costs a fortune—was because Hank Greenberg was a member. I told him that once, he didn't believe me. He scoffed. I knew my chances of seeing him around were good. I was right. He was there a lot and I got to talk to him a great deal. He generally spoke about three subjects: sports—with me anyway—movies, and Jews. Three fascinating subjects. I asked him a lot of stupid questions and he always replied with great patience and courtesy, even though his equanimity must have been rattled on more than one occasion.

"I saw him get very angry once and later, when I spoke to him about it, he smiled sheepishly and implied that his anger may have been less than genuine. The incident happened a few years ago when I brought a fella to the club by the name of Mark Fidrych. We have the same agent. He used to pitch for the Detroit Tigers. Fidrych, that is, not my agent. Fidrych was known as The Bird, or flaky one. He talked to himself on the mound. He strutted around like a peacock. I introduced him to Hank. Hank, of course, knew all about him, but he had never heard of Hank Greenberg. I don't think this sat too well with Hank. I asked Hank, kidding of course, if he ever made the Hall of Fame. He gave me a four-minute Jack Benny look and then he just said, 'Yes, yes, I did make it.' Anyway, after a while Hank got up from the table and went to play tennis on the center court. Fidrych began to heckle him: 'Serve it to his right!' 'Serve it to his left!' 'He can't hit it down the middle!' He kept this up for a while until Hank, red in the face, his veins popping on his neck, dropped his racquet, came over to the fence, and said, 'I can hit anything you pitch—down the middle, outside, inside, curveball, slider, screwball!' Fidrych was stunned. Never said a word. Later I asked Hank why he got so angry. He said, 'You gotta intimidate pitchers.' He was still a competitor.

"Hank got into a fistfight at seventy-two or thereabouts with a 250-pound wise guy about half his age. I said, 'Hank, you can't go around getting into a fistfight at seventy-two.' He said, 'I know that, but I got mad at him, and I forgot how old I was.'

One time I asked Hank how he felt about being famous. Pretty dumb question I admit, but I would ask anything just to hear him talk. Hank said he liked being well known, or at least most of the time he liked it. He thought it was better than anonymity. He told me about some rude shocks that went along with a recognizable face. He was on vacation in Hawaii for three days, and there was a couple who kept staring at him and smiling. Finally the man came over and said, 'My wife and I are long-time fans and we want to tell you that you are a credit to your profession. You have given us countless hours of enjoyment and happiness at times when we may have been down in the dumps. Mr. Youngman . . . thank you.' 'Can you imagine?' Hank said to me. 'He thought I was Henny Youngman.' Then, after a few quiet moments, he said, 'I'm better looking than Henny Youngman, don't you think, Walter?' I said, 'Of course.'

"As I said, I was always asking him ridiculous questions. Like if the batted ball hit the pitcher's mound on the fly and then went foul, what was it? He'd look at me with very quiet exasperation, shake his head, and say, 'It's a foul ball, of course, Walter.' Sometimes he'd make a mistake on one of those gimmick technical questions. And I'd say, 'No, that's not right, Hank. Here's the answer, it's right here in *The New York Times.*' Hank would say, 'Well, the paper's wrong. Who are you going to believe, Walter? Me or the paper?' I said, 'You, Hank.' As I said, I went to the tennis club so I could talk to Hank because I don't play tennis. Now I call my brother Henry, whom everybody calls Hank. He lives in New York, and he's an old athlete, too. He still plays handball. I call him and at least I get to say, 'How ya doin', Hank?' So I don't feel so bad."

Dr. Rex Kennamer:

"I'm proud of the opportunity to participate in a tribute to an American hero, but I found it a demanding assignment because of the necessity to explore the intricacies of a wonderful friendship. I also had a doctor-patient relationship with Hank that was put to the ultimate test of a fatal illness. That combination evoked complex emotions. I had and have strong feelings for this man. I enjoyed him, I admired him, I miss him. It seems appropriate to share my memories because I do so rounding out the picture of the total man. You see, I do not know Hank Greenberg the baseball legend. I know no baseball statistics. I hardly understand the game and I never had a conversation about baseball with Hank. I speak because Hank provided me with that happiest of assets, an undemanding friendship. It is one of the treasures of my life, and I'm sure he provided many of you with a similar friendship. Think of it. An undemanding friendship. That is an extraordinary gift, and Hank was extraordinarily generous.

"As I noted, I was Hank's doctor and that allowed me a unique perspective into his personal strengths. Although we're here to share memories about Hank and not to bring tears to family and friends, I would tell you that the last year was a long and cruel ordeal. Cruel for Hank, cruel for Mary Jo, and cruel for his children. Yet in typical Hank fashion he did not impose the turmoil of that year on his friends, or even some members of his family. Though he had a stoic attitude his well-known competitive spirit made him fight the good battle. He was no fainthearted man who went gently into the night. Hank was a man aware and appreciative of the good life he had earned. Friends, fame, wealth, successful children, and a wife whose devotion was almost biblical in magnitude. Many deaths are meaningless, but the death of a superior man is a lesson for all of us. For one thing, it inspires us to follow their example and emulate their spirit. The memories I share with you are of the spirit of the man. They do not include any specific events. I have no anecdotes to tell.

"I could readily picture in my mind the physical man. He is indelibly imprinted. Hank was an imposing figure of a man. He had a lumbering grace that I suppose was the result of years of athletic prowess. His personality was so compelling that there was a physical quality to it. One actually felt the warmth of his personality. His boyish charm was always evident. Certainly he had charisma. At the forefront of my memories are those that had to do with the quality and character of the inner man. I will not add anything new to what you already know. Hank wasn't the kind of man who spoke and acted one way to one person and another way to someone else. Hank was strong-willed and firm but not intractable. He was gentle but not weak. He was powerful but never cruel. Hank was proud but never haughty. He was disciplined but never rigid. I remember a man who was enthusiastic, adventurous; he was witty; he was fun to be with. In our society, where everyone seems filled with complexities and inner turmoil, Hank was remarkably uncomplicated, unsophisticated and without guile. If he had inner devils he was a private man and kept them to himself.

"Hank was a pillar of strength and was always willing to be helpful. I can attest to the fact that if you had a problem he was willing to involve himself. He did not equivocate or hedge on advice. He could empathize with you. Hank did not shrink from the responsibilities of friendship.

Whenever the name Hank Greenberg is mentioned I will remember stimulating conversations. That is when his superior intellect was apparent. That was when I discovered that he was a voracious reader, that he was a man on a lifetime course of learning. He displayed a shrewd understanding of his fellow-man. He was astute at analyzing a situation. His conversations were not of past glories. Hank did not talk of his achievements. I always found him shy and modest about his accomplishments. It was in conversation when one discovered that this was a man with a keen perception of the intricacies of the financial world, that he had a remarkable knowledge of and interest in history, that he enjoyed a good argument about politics. This liberal man gave a good conservative like me a tough time on many occasions. It was in one-on-one conversations that one learned about his humanitarian attitude toward the unfortunate, his contempt for people who had no charity in their hearts, and how much he hated bigotry and intolerance. Thus, the legendary American hero had become a man for all seasons.

"A Roman philosopher wrote: 'Life is a play, 'tis not its length but its performance that counts.' Hank's was a full-length play, and we all know the performance was unforgettable."

Anne Taylor Fleming, writer and radio and television commentator:

"I am honored to have been asked to speak, especially since there are no doubt many of you here whose memories of Hank Greenberg predate my own. I think I first met Hank a decade ago, more or less. When Mary Jo asked me to speak I tried to remember the first time we met, but I don't. So quickly did Hank become so much a part of my life and my joy that it seems that he had always been a part of it and always would be.

"There was a strange, magical connection which took place between us, so magical to me because it made so little sense. We came from worlds and years apart. If anyone had told me while I was growing up that later on I would be enchanted by, taken up by, a big-time Bronx-born baseball hero, I would have told them they were crazy. In fact, in the beginning I really didn't know who Hank was. That will probably shock some of you out there, but I didn't. I knew he played baseball, but I didn't know that he was such a hero. A lot of that, of course, was in the way that Hank Greenberg carried himself. I'd never seen anybody stand so little on the ceremony of his past glory and yet at the same time retain such an afterglow from it. It was such a winning combination. He'd done what he had to do and he'd done it as well as he could and had no need to tell you about it or flaunt it. More than anybody I know who had that kind of early fame, Hank lived the joy of the present. He didn't live off old memories even if he told wonderful stories about the old days, about this pitcher or that outfielder, but they were never self-serving stories.

"Later I would hear or read about those. About Hank's refusing to play on Yom Kippur, for example, about Hank's saying encouraging words to Jackie Robinson about not letting people razz him, about Hank's re-upping in the army at the height of his career. But I never heard any of that from Hank himself. He always downplayed everything with wonderful self-amusement. I remember once he sent my husband, Karl, and me to his favorite restaurant in New York, telling us to go in and tell the bartender that Hank Greenberg had sent us. So we dutifully went off to this restaurant, called Gino's, on Lexington and 61st. Went in, and told the bartender that Hank Greenberg had sent us. And the bartender said, 'Hank who?' So we didn't bother to sit down. We asked for the telephone and promptly called Hank across the country and said, 'Hank, this bartender doesn't know you. Nobody in the restaurant knows you.' Hank loved the story. He told it for years afterward.

"Hank made light of his fame even as he was quietly proud of it. Just as he was very proud, I think, of his Jewishness, which he also did not make light of. There were things that mattered deeply to him, but he never made a big demonstrative deal about it. Yet you'd never be mistaken about where his heart lay. With the underdog, always. He was fond of calling a certain politician, who shall be nameless, 'That bum.' 'Did you see what that bum did now?' he'd say to me on the telephone. Or 'Did you see that bum didn't give anything to charity once again this year?' And it was always clear that beneath it he cared deeply. He was always very encouraging to me about speaking out and speaking up, also encouraging me to speak more slowly whenever I was on the radio or television. And he'd often call me afterward and say, 'Gee, you were terrific.' I always felt as if he dropped out of the sky into my life to goad me in my own small search for fulfillment at a time when his own search was in some ways done. Maybe he did that for a lot of people, if not directly, at least by example. But what he mostly did was goad me toward joy. So many little fragments float up. Meals we shared, cigars we smoked. Hank became my chief cigar supplier when he found to his delight that I loved them.

"And then there were all the games. The games we played and the games we watched. I have never in my life seen anyone so competitive. Hank Greenberg wanted to win in ways that I couldn't even imagine. Again, that's no revelation to most of you, I'm sure, but it was to me. Whenever we watched the World Series together, which we did every year, he always managed to sucker me into these dumb bets. Was the pitcher going to throw a slider or a knuckleball? Was the batter going to loop one into right field or left? I didn't know, but I bet. I fell for it every single year. I suspect I still owe Hank Greenberg a couple thousand dollars at least in uncollected bets. And then there was the tennis. It was much easier to play against him than with him. Because although he was a formidable foe, he was a much more formidable partner. Hank would be serving behind me and I would be cowering at the net praying to God that nobody hit the ball to me. Praying to God I wouldn't miss it if they did. I'd feel these little darts coming from Hank zinging me in the back and I'd miss it.

And it was the only time in all the time I knew Hank Greenberg that he was slightly bereft of his customary humanity and laughter.

"That's what I miss more than anything. The sound of his laughter. Sometimes it seemed to echo through my small house where he and I and Mary Jo and Karl spent so many happy nights. I see him all crumpled up, that great big bulk of him, in one of our much-less-than-comfortable tiny chairs. His big knotty fingers slashing the air in the way he always had and laughing, always laughing, sometimes so he couldn't even talk. Laughing when he was already in pain and we didn't know it. And he did everything to keep us from knowing it. False bravery? I don't think so. Just as I don't think there was any false pride in the way Hank Greenberg chose to die. Like most of you, my husband and I didn't know that Hank was dying until the end. He had just a few weeks left when we found out. At first I hated it, that it had been kept a secret, and I felt cheated. But then I realized that Hank had always been there, never held back, that we said what we wanted to say, that we shared what we needed to say, and that his love to me was so freely given that there was no need for death-bed confessions or good-byes even. No need, and I'm sure Hank felt this keenly for those of us who loved him and saw him gaunt with pain. So, in fact, after feeling cheated I've come to admire the way he chose to die as much as the way he chose to live. And I miss him."

Stephen Greenberg:

"It's somewhat ironic, I guess, that the feats for which Dad will be remembered by the public are not at all what I remember him for. I was born in September 1948, one year after he hit his last home run, so I learned about his baseball exploits solely by hearsay. To me the legend of Hank Greenberg was a story of a man I'd never met. Over the years I heard so many stories about Dad that I came to develop a vivid image of an almost mythical person. The great Lefty Gomez used to tell about the time he announced to one New York sportswriter, 'I've come up with a foolproof way to get Hank Greenberg out.' When questioned further Lefty revealed his secret. If there is a man on second base, said Lefty, all you have to do is get two quick strikes on Hank. Then you call the catcher out to the mound for a conference. You chat a little bit. You send him back behind the plate and the catcher stands up and signals to the infield for an intentional walk. You throw ball one, ball two, ball three, and as you're about to throw ball four, the catcher jumps back down behind home plate and you zip a fastball by him when he's not looking. 'How did it work?' asked the writer. Lefty said, 'I don't know, I never got two strikes on him.' That story epitomized my early images of Dad as an invincible slugger who struck terror into the hearts of every pitcher in the American League.

"Then there were the stories about how he used to round up peanut vendors and neighborhood kids to throw extra batting practice and shag balls for him on off days and in the morning before day games. That's how I learned that Dad was not a man to whom anything was handed on a platter. He had to work long and hard to achieve success.

"I recall the highlight film of the 1945 World Series against the Cubs when Dad broke his wrist sliding home in the second game. Dad knew he couldn't play the next day, but he didn't tell anyone except his manager. And he agreed to be put into the starting lineup knowing that he couldn't hit. In the first inning he came to bat with two men on base, and, unable to swing, he bunted, moving the runners over to second and third. Dad then left the game, but the Tigers went on to score that inning and they won that game and the Series. Obviously Dad was first and foremost a team player.

"While others may have focused simply on his heroics, I came to see my dad as a man who embodied many paradoxes. A future Hall of Famer who thought of himself as awkward and toiled long and hard to achieve his prominence. A prolific slugger who helped his team win the World Series by bunting. This sense of paradox, the contradiction between the public persona and the private man, was very much evident in my relationship with him. He set demandingly high standards for his own children and encouraged us always to aspire to excellence, and yet he was exceedingly tolerant and understanding of other young people despite their shortcomings. He dropped out of college after one year to pursue his baseball career and yet preferred debating history or talking about the last book he'd read to rehashing yesterday's box scores. He had a strong sense of pride in his accomplishments and yet among friends he was the first to poke fun at himself and laugh at his idiosyncrasies.

"For many years Mary Jo, Myrna, and I urged him to write his autobiography. But he used to tell me, in all seriousness, 'I don't want to write my story yet because I keep thinking that one day I'm going to do something really great, and I want to wait until that time to write my book.' I'll never know nor can I imagine what it was that this man who rose to the very top of his profession and then went on to successes in the front office and on Wall Street could possibly have thought he would accomplish that would be greater than what he had already done. . . .

"He was my mentor, my best friend, and, yes, my favorite doubles partner. He taught me many lessons that I will carry with me forever. But, most of all, he taught me that you don't have to break every record to achieve greatness, you don't have to be invincible to be strong, and you don't have to be perfect to be loved."

On November 18, two months after Hank Greenberg's death, Mary Jo Greenberg went to her bank and withdrew from her safe-deposit box the sealed letter that Greenberg had written to her more than a year before. She now felt she could emotionally handle the contents, something she had previously sensed she could not.

In his then still-firm hand Greenberg had written:

> *My dear loved one. There is no way in which I could repay you for the love, devotion and affection you have showered on me during the past 25 years.*
>
> *No man has been more fortunate in having a mate who has devoted herself to making her husband happy. I hope the future will reward you with peace of mind, contentment and someone you can share your love with, as you have so much of it to give.*
>
> *Remember, I said, "shed no tear for me." I've had a wonderful life, filled with personal success and blessed with very good health. Plus, wonderful children who have never caused me a moment's concern. They have brought only joy and pride in their accomplishments.*
>
> *Most importantly I shared the last 25 years with you, and that's more than any man is entitled to.*
>
> *Most men never have the opportunity to express the above in writing. So, again I'm lucky.*
>
> *If perchance I should get a reprieve, I'll try to make up for any anguish I have caused you in the past.*
>
> *And so my love, we will meet again somewhere, sometime.*
>
> *Your husband*
> *and sweetheart*
> *xxxx*
> *Hank*

HENRY BENJAMIN (HANK) GREENBERG'S CAREER STATISTICS

Born January 1, 1911, at New York, N.Y. Height, 6'3½". Weight, 215. Threw and batted right-handed.

Tied Major and American League record for most home runs (58) by right-handed batsman, season, 1938. Set Major League record for most times two or more home runs, game, season–11 (1938–May 25, June 24, July 9-26-27-29, August 10, September 11-17-23-27).

World Series record–co-holder, most hits in game (4), October 6, 1934. Named by Baseball Writers' Association of America as first baseman for *The Sporting News* All-Star Major League Team, 1935, and left fielder, 1940. Selected as Most Valuable Player, American League, 1935 and 1940.

General manager, Cleveland Indians, 1948–57; vice-president, Chicago White Sox, 1959–63.

Year Club	League	Pos.	G.	AB.	R.	H.	2B.	3B.	HR.	RBI.	B.A.	PO.	A.	E.	F.A.
1930—Hartford	East.	1B	17	56	10	12	1	2	2	6	.214	157	13	2	.988
1930—Raleigh.	Pied.	1B	122	452	88	142	26	14	19	93	.314	1052	*78	23	.980
1930—Detroit	Amer.	1B	1	1	0	0	0	0	0	0	.000	0	0	0	.000
1931—Evansville	I.I.I.	1B	126	487	88	155	*41	10	15	85	.318	*1248	*84	*25	.982
1931—Beaumont	Texas	PH	3	2	0	0	0	0	0	0	.000	0	0	0	.000
1932—Beaumont	Texas	1B	154	600	*123	174	31	11	*39	131	.290	1437	103	17	.989
1933—Detroit	Amer.	1B	117	449	59	135	33	3	12	87	.301	1133	63	14	.988
1934—Detroit	Amer.	1B	153	593	118	201	*63	7	26	139	.339	1454	84	16	.990
1935—Detroit	Amer.	1B	152	619	121	203	46	16	36	*170	.328	1437	*99	13	.992
1936—Detroit	Amer.	1B	12	46	10	16	6	2	1	16	.348	119	9	1	.992
1937—Detroit	Amer.	1B	154	594	137	200	49	14	40	*183	.337	*1477	102	13	.992
1938—Detroit	Amer.	1B	155	556	*144	175	23	4	*58	146	.315	*1484	*120	14	.991
1939—Detroit	Amer.	1B	138	500	112	156	42	7	33	112	.312	1205	75	9	.993
1940—Detroit	Amer.	OF	148	573	129	195	*50	8	*41	*150	.340	298	14	*15	.954
1941—Detroit	Amer.	OF	19	67	12	18	5	1	2	12	.269	32	0	3	.914
1942-43–44—Detroit . .	Amer.	(In Military Service)													
1945—Detroit	Amer.	OF	78	270	47	84	20	2	13	60	.311	129	3	0	1.000
1946—Detroit (a)	Amer.	LB	142	523	91	145	29	5	*44	*127	.277	1272	93	*15	.989
1947—Pittsburgh (b) . .	Nat.	1B	125	402	71	100	13	2	25	74	.249	983	79	9	.992
American League Totals			1269	4791	980	1528	366	69	306	1202	.319	10040	662	113	.990
National League Totals			125	402	71	100	13	2	25	74	.249	983	79	9	.992
Major League Totals.			1394	5193	1051	1628	379	71	331	1276	.313	11023	741	122	.990

* Led the league

(a) Sold to Pittsburgh Pirates for undisclosed sum, January 8, 1947.

(b) Released unconditionally by Pittsburgh Pirates, September 29, 1947, and joined Cleveland Indians' front office, March 27, 1948.

WORLD SERIES RECORD

Year Club	League	Pos.	G.	AB.	R.	H.	2B.	3B.	HR.	RBI.	B.A.	PO.	A.	E.	F.A.
1934—Detroit	Amer.	1B	7	28	4	9	2	1	1	7	.321	60	4	1	.985
1935—Detroit	Amer.	1B	2	6	1	1	0	0	1	2	.167	17	2	3	.864
1940—Detroit	Amer.	OF	7	28	5	10	2	1	1	6	.357	12	0	0	1.000
1945—Detroit	Amer.	OF	7	23	7	7	3	0	2	7	.304	8	1	0	1.000
World Series Total			23	85	17	27	7	2	5	22	.318	97	7	4	.963